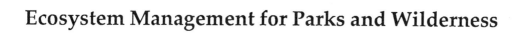

Ecosystem Management for Parks and Wilderness

ECOSYSTEM MANAGEMENT

for Parks and Wilderness

Edited by *JAMES K. AGEE*
and DARRYLL R. JOHNSON

University of Washington Press
SEATTLE AND LONDON

Library of Congress Cataloging-in-Publication Data

Ecosystem management for parks and wilderness.

  (Institute of Forest Resources contribution ; no. 65)
  Contains papers presented at the Ecosystem Management Workshop, held Apr. 6-10, 1987, at the University of Washington's Pack Forest.
  Includes bibliographies.
  1. Wilderness areas—Management—Congresses. 2. National parks and reserves—Management—Congresses. 3. Biotic communities—Management—Congresses. I. Agee, James K. II. Johnson, Darryll R. III. Ecosystem Management Workshop (1987 : University of Washington) IV. Series: Contribution (University of Washington. Institute of Forest Resources) ; no. 65
  SD12.W33 no.65 634.9 s [333.78′15] 88-27673 [QH75.A1]

Institute of Forest Resources Contribution No. 65

Contents

Preface

A group of thirty-three managers, scientists, and planners met in April 1987 to discuss and develop an improved conceptual management approach for park and wilderness ecosystems. The focus of this approach was cooperative ecosystem management, which recognizes that most ecological problems, whether biological, social, or both, are often unconstrained by political boundaries.

In recent years, managers at all levels, biological and social scientists, and conservation groups have recognized the need to redefine our vision of park and wilderness management if such areas are to successfully meet the challenges of the future. Early versions of park and wilderness management drew lines around protected areas, with the intent that undeveloped, essentially unmanaged areas within the boundary would be adequately protected. Later paradigms, including the classic Leopold Report, recognized the need for active management within park and wilderness boundaries. We now recognize the need not only for active management inside these boundaries but for refined goals and implementation of cooperative management with neighboring landowners.

The purpose of this book is to indicate why a new vision is necessary for park and wilderness management and to discuss strategies for cooperative management. It is not intended to define precisely what those goals should be. The workshop participants represented too narrow a group to set those goals even in a preliminary way, a fact recognized early in the workshop. However, this group was able to define a framework for future management (see Chapter 1) to serve as a forum for park and wilderness ecosystem management.

There will never be a single blueprint, a cookbook approach that will fit every park and wilderness situation. Unique legal, biological, and social situations guarantee that individualistic solutions be defined, and that those solutions remain flexible to incorporate new information and values within the intent of Congress.

These themes comprise the common thread of the chapters to follow. The first and last chapters synthesize the workshop discussions. The intervening chapters are organized in a disciplinary fashion discussing legal issues, vegetation, wildlife, effects on terrestrial and aquatic resources from long-range air transport, perspectives on economics and human ecology, and finally three management perspectives. Each recognizes the problems of managing these park and wilderness ecosystems through past, outmoded paradigms, and the dangers of defining a rigid set of new paradigms. As a whole, the book provides a comprehensive view of our current problems and future opportunities for ecosystem management in parks and wilderness.

Acknowledgments

This book is published in partial fulfillment of the requirements of National Park Service, Pacific Northwest Region Cooperative Agreement CA-9000-3-0004, Subagreement 9, Ecosystem Management Workshop. Additional support for the workshop and the book was provided by the USDA Forest Service, Pacific Northwest Research Station, Portland, Oregon, and the University of Washington, College of Forest Resources (Long Fund).

We would like to acknowledge the assistance of the following individuals and organizations who contributed to the workshop: Dr. Richard Briceland, National Park Service, Washington, D.C., and Dean David Thorud of the College of Forest Resources, who cooperatively initiated the concept of the workshop; National Park Service, Pacific Northwest Regional Director Charles Odegaard and Regional Chief Scientist James Larson for supporting publication of this book; Diana Perl of the College of Forest Resources Continuing Education Office, for organizing the myriad details related to the week of the workshop; Laury Istvan, Craig Shinn, and Rob Schachter, who acted as facilitators for discussion sessions; the Battelle Institute for advice on workshop structure; Associate Professor Gordon Bradley of the College of Forest Resources for helpful comments on early drafts of the report; and members of the steering committee from the College of Forest Resources: Associate Dean Dale Cole, Professor Robert Lee, and Affiliate Professors Russell Dickenson and Russell Cahill. We would also like to acknowledge the production and editing assistance provided by Beverly Anderson, Nancy Jorgensen, and Leila Charbonneau, and the University of Washington Press.

Ecosystem Management
for Parks and Wilderness

1

Introduction to Ecosystem Management

DARRYLL R. JOHNSON and JAMES K. AGEE

Park and wilderness managers face significant challenges and opportunities in the stewardship of park and wilderness resources for present and future generations. Serious problems have emerged that require management approaches incorporating cooperation between many institutional sectors of society. Populations of "heroic species," such as grizzly bears and wolves, have disappeared or nearly disappeared from many landscapes. Other animals that range across park and wilderness boundaries are increasingly affected by a wider diversity of uses. Natural disturbances, such as fire, have been disrupted. Air pollution may be having a variety of effects on park and wilderness ecosystems. Development is encroaching on park and forest boundaries. Resource allocation choices are far more costly economically and politically than in the past. At the same time, communication barriers exist between managers of park and wilderness areas, adjacent landowners, and various user groups.

Basic information about plant, fish and wildlife, and human populations in and around park and wilderness areas is frequently lacking. Even though managers care deeply about the resources they manage, they must often function in a reactive mode, knowing that the tasks at hand are at best overwhelming, at worst hopeless.

To develop an improved conceptual approach to managing change in park and wilderness areas, the University of Washington College of Forest Resources, the National Park Service, and the USDA Forest Service convened an Ecosystem Management Workshop, April 6-10, 1987. Thirty-three scientists, planners, and managers gathered for a week at the University of Washington's Pack Forest to discuss these issues in a retreat environment. Their names and affiliations are included in the List of Participants at the back of the book. Even though the perspectives at this workshop were diverse, they did not totally reflect the diversity of interests found in park and wilderness management. Participants were selected for their disciplinary expertise, or for their orientation toward certain aspects of natural resource management.

The workshop focused on cooperative approaches to park and wilderness ecosystem management. It served as an interdisciplinary forum for the expression of ideas and was not intended as a vehicle to arrive at a consensus on issues of park and wilderness management. Subjects discussed included ecosystem management problems and issues, the increased insularity of natural areas, impacts of expanding use of natural areas, opportunities for mitigation via cooperative ventures, planning approaches to deal with ecosystem management questions, legal tools that help or constrain ecosystem management, and summary recommendations designed to guide management thinking about ecosystem management issues in parks and wilderness areas.

Three perceptions repeatedly surfaced at the workshop and are worthy of introductory mention. First, the term "ecosystem management" means different things to different people: it is a buzzword for park expansion, a way to manage only natural areas (e.g., Chase 1987), and a process by which all multiple wildland uses can be coordinated. Discussion revealed erroneous perceptions that the term "ecosystem" applies only to lands managed for park or wilderness values.

Second, participants with biological expertise tended to underappreciate the role that people play in defining both the problems and solutions for park and wilderness issues: people are both managers and components of park and wilderness ecosystems. The biocentric orientation dissipated as the week progressed.

Third, some participants were suspicious of the motives behind the workshop, wondering if one agency (National Park Service) might attempt to use this process to control what goes on in another (Forest Service). Given the competitive relationship of the two agencies, and the fact that many national parks are contiguous with wilderness managed by the Forest Service, such perceptions are well grounded historically. But the workshop objectives were just the opposite: to foster cooperation between agencies managing similar resources, often for similar objectives (in this case, park and wilderness management). While the "land grabbing" perception was not dispelled during the week, it faded from the discussions and hopefully will continue to decline as these agencies embrace the ecosystem management concept.

SYSTEMS, ECOSYSTEMS, AND ECOSYSTEM MANAGEMENT

The workshop began with considerable ambiguity surrounding the meaning of the concepts "ecosystem" and "ecosystem management." These concepts have been used across the country and in other parts of the world, in both formal and informal ways, for decades. But they suffer from the same semantic difficulties as "diversity," "carrying capacity," "stability," and other resource-related terms: they mean different things to different people. For the reader who may not be familiar with these concepts, a brief background discussion of systems and systems analysis, as these terms are applied to wildlands, is appropriate.

The study of nature and man is a study of systems (Odum 1971). A system can be defined as an organized or connected group or set of objects, principles, or ideas related by some common function or belief (Dickey and Watts 1978). There are generally natural or social elements in the system and physical and behavioral connections between the elements. When the system contains living organisms, it is frequently called an "ecosystem." Ecosystems have boundaries, but the boundaries are defined arbitrarily.

The concept of "system" provides the basis for a conceptual model that can be used in decision making related to park and wilderness management. Systems analysis emphasizes the relation of system components to each other and to the rest of the system. Implicit in this approach is a search by logical process for alternatives to achieve clearly defined system objectives.

Several definitions were initially proposed at the workshop for the term "ecosystem." Many others are available in environmental and ecological textbooks. A working definition was agreed upon: an ecosystem is any part of the universe chosen as an area of interest, with the line around that area being the ecosystem boundary and anything cross-ing the line being input or output. This definition encompasses more specific areas having geologic, biologic, legal, and social components.

For parks and wilderness areas, an adaptation of a graphic device used in set theory and known as a Venn diagram is useful to illustrate the relation of park and wilderness ecosystems to neighboring landscapes (Figure 1-1). Several implications of our working definition of "ecosystem" for park and wilderness management follow.

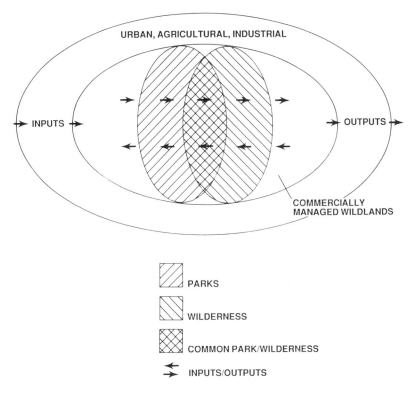

Figure 1-1. Relation of park and wilderness ecosystems to neighboring landscapes.

Ecosystems are spatially variable. A vegetation management problem in one park or wilderness area may have different spatial boundaries than the same problem in another park or wilderness.

Ecosystems are temporally variable. A given problem may have one set of spatial boundaries now and quite another a decade from now. The form of the problem and the solution may change over time.

Different ecosystem components may have different boundaries, implying a set of overlapping and interacting systems. For example, some vegetation management problems could potentially be confined within a park or wilderness area. A wildlife management problem may influence and be influenced by adjacent land uses and social values; the boundaries of the ecosystem for that issue would encompass those adjacent lands. Visitor use of an area may be strongly affected by the regional social system.

Politically defined boundaries frequently do not contain all the ingredients (resources, people, etc.) necessary to resolve resource management issues. There will be inputs and outputs for any ecosystem, and any lines drawn around park and wilderness ecosystems will have flows across them: people, animals, air, and so forth. Political boundaries can be seen as "permeable membranes" through which continuous flows of energy, organisms, and ideas pass. External (or exogenous) factors may influence or be influenced by the ecosystem.

The ecosystem concept may be applied to all lands, not just those managed for natural values. Lands managed for timber production, quarried for minerals, and so forth, are also ecosystems with similar components and interactions. Recognizing the connections between the parts of the system will be important in every use, but not every action will affect adjacent lands or require significant interagency coordination.

These implications can be placed in a management context by summarizing four biological and social system properties that underlie successful environmental assessment (Holling 1978).

1. *Ecological systems are continually changing.* Such dynamic variability determines part of the structural and functional aspects of ecosystems. Low intensity, frequent burning in a mixed conifer forest, for example, has had a significant controlling influence in historically open, pine-dominated forests (Parsons 1981, van Wagtendonk 1985). Continually changing social systems are intuitively apparent and reinforce the concept of reciprocal influence that components of a social system have on each other.

2. *There may be substantial spatial heterogeneity in impacts from a particular action.* Impacts may not be gradually diluted over space, like the ripples of a wave from a rock thrown into a pond. Some affected people are near at hand; others are quite distant. Ecological consequences may occur nearby or at distant points. The presence of automobile exhaust along the Interstate 5 corridor near Seattle creates a soup of hydrocarbons that become photochemically active downwind and show up as increased ozone levels near Mount Rainier; the ozone levels near the source are much lower (R. Edmonds and T. Basabe, University of Washington, pers. comm.).

3. *Systems may exhibit several levels of stable behavior.* With disturbances of either human or nonhuman origin, ecosystems may evolve into systems different from any that existed before, and may stabilize at one of several levels. When goats were removed from Hawaiian parks, alien grasses and trees increased, while native trees were not able to reinvade the previously grazed areas (Mueller-Dombois and Spatz 1975). Similarly, a decline in a major economic institution may not signal a return to earlier social conditions but an evolution of a unique social system with a new set of structural characteristics.

4. *There is an organized connection between parts, but everything is not connected to everything else.* For example, each species in a biological system has a limited set of connections to other species. The moose-wolf interactions at Isle Royale in Michigan, while complex and not yet fully understood, have been effectively studied without total knowledge of every species or energy linkage in the Isle Royale ecosystem (Peterson, this volume). Similarly, agencies have extensive political constituencies that are directly and indirectly influenced by each other. However, many social groups are not affected by park or wilderness decisions and are not interested in them. It is not necessary to know all the linkages to move ahead, although the important ones should be understood in advance.

In summary, the ecosystem concept, with its biological and social components, can be applied to any geographical area. The manager can be administering a grazing allotment, a commercial forest, or a park or wilderness. It is a flexible concept recognizing variability in time and space. Given that management actions will occur in changing environments, the important linkages between components must be known in order to be able to predict effects. Past effects, although a good guide, may not always be a road map to future effects.

Ecosystem management involves regulating internal ecosystem structure and function, plus inputs and outputs, to achieve socially desirable conditions. It includes, within a chosen and not always static geographic setting, the usual array of planning and management activities but conceptualized in a systems framework: identification of issues through research, public involvement, and political analysis; goal setting; plan development; use allocation; activity development (resources management, interpretation); monitoring; and evaluation. Interagency coordination is often a key element of successful ecosystem management, but is not an end in itself. Success in ecosystem management is ultimately measured by the goals achieved, not by the amount of coordination.

GOAL DEFINITION FOR PARK AND WILDERNESS ECOSYSTEMS

Park and Wilderness System Dynamics

Considerable confusion has resulted from a widespread misconception of the dynamics of ecosystems. Such systems are envisioned as having a natural balance or static equilibrium that in fact does not exist. Although periods of stability may exist, and multiple levels of stability can be defined (Holling 1978), park and wilderness ecosystems are non-equilibrium systems. A "balance of nature" occurs only over short and constrained periods: the constant in these systems is change. This fact is fundamental to establishing realistic goals for park and wilderness management.

Components of these ecosystems cannot be defined at a particular level that will unequivocally be perceived as "natural." The word "natural" evokes diverse value judgments that are difficult to reconcile. Plant species have reacted individually to climatic changes for millennia, so that the communities seen today on the landscape are in part a result of past climatic shifts (Figure 1-2) and the differential colonization rates associated with each species (Brubaker, this volume). They represent the state of the vegetation of the ecosystem today, but are not necessarily representative of some past equilibrium vegetation mosaic.

Knowledge of sustainable yields of herbivores and the relationships between predator and prey populations (Figure 1-3) suggests that equilibrium levels of animals may be maintained infrequently (Peterson, this volume). Similarly, visitor uses of wildland areas have changed over time, and are not always directly related to population growth (Figure 1-4). Even standards of appropriate behavior change; it was once considered quite appropriate to feed bears and kill carnivores in national parks. Park and wilderness management, therefore, is the management of change where the basic values and knowledge underlying management may change.

Complex ecosystem models that incorporate either human culture or nonhuman biological components accurately are not likely to emerge in the near future, if ever. In plant ecology, the evolution of theory has moved away from the grand unifying theory proposed by Clements to more diverse views (Christensen, this volume). Some of the

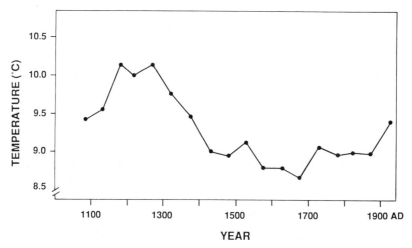

Figure 1-2. Climate over time (average temperature) as an indicator of a nonequilibrium system. Source: Brubaker, this volume.

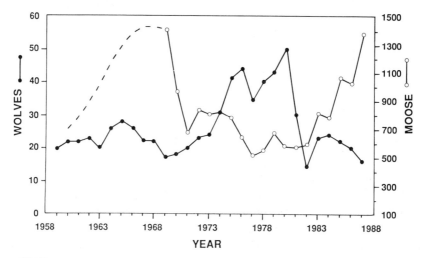

Figure 1-3. Wildlife relationship (predator-prey populations) as an indicator of a nonequilibrium system. Number of wolves in relation to number of moose in the Isle Royale ecosystem, 1959-87. Source: Peterson, this volume.

newer models, particularly in the area of conservation biology—such as managing for minimum population size (Salwasser, this volume)—or in landscape ecology (Forman and Godron 1986), are in embryonic stages or are still untested theory. Methods to measure intrinsic (existence) values of parks and wilderness do not exist (Irland, this volume). Therefore, while system models offer no panacea for predicting precise effects of park and wilderness management, they can provide frameworks for assessing the importance of data gaps, identify interrelationships between components, and assist in defining monitoring plans to measure effectiveness of management actions.

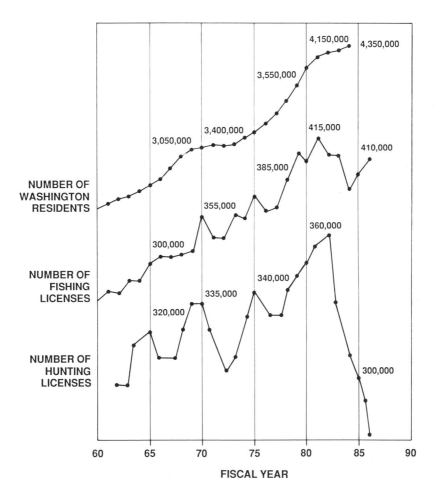

Figure 1-4. Wildland visitor uses, in relation to population growth in the state of Washington, as an indicator of a nonequilibrium system.

Ecosystem Goals in Parks and Wilderness

The National Park Service Organic Act of 1916 states that the mission of the Service is to conserve "the natural and historic objects and the wildlife therein . . . for the enjoyment of present and future generations." The legislation is very object oriented, and several papers have reviewed the evolution of process-oriented management (e.g., allowing lightning fires to burn; Agee 1974, Graber 1985). The Wilderness Act (1964) projects a similar mission. Wilderness land is to be "protected and managed so as to preserve its natural conditions." It is to be "administered for the use and enjoyment of the American people . . . unimpaired for future use and enjoyment." Analyses have also been done on the intent of this legislation (Hendee et al. 1978, Crandell 1987). At a minimum, the conservation-preservation mandate in the two statutes imposes a legal obligation on park and wilderness managers to manage these lands to maintain "natural" conditions, and to protect them from adverse external impacts (Keiter, this volume).

A major shift in National Park Service policy occurred in the mid-1960s with the Leopold Report on wildlife management in parks (Leopold et al. 1963). This landmark report recommended a primary goal of management to restore national parks to "the conditions which prevailed when the area was first visited by the white man": a "vignette of primitive America." The report suggested that a pre-Columbian vegetation mosaic could be restored by reinstituting natural disturbance processes, particularly fire, to park landscapes. Since that time, reintroduction of fire has occurred in many parks. The report provided a stimulus for a positive shift in park, and later wilderness, policy by emphasizing the need for active management.

Despite the widespread influence of the Leopold Report, the creation of a static "vignette of primitive America" is probably not a desirable or feasible goal for future park and wilderness management. To use any narrow window of time as the basis for establishing management goals is inappropriate for systems characterized by nonequilibrium conditions. In fact, the four centuries preceding the voyage of Columbus to America had anomalously warm weather, which has not since recurred (Brubaker, this volume). Vegetation conditions, wildlife populations, and disturbance processes were different then. Similarly, an attempt to reconstruct the scene of 1870 is an inappropriate goal, because it imposes static conditions on systems that are inherently dynamic. Although Leopold and other committee members are reported to have later stated that they wished the "vignette" language had not been used, this issue has never been formally resolved.

Recent discussions have attempted to shift away from the goal of recreating a "vignette of primitive America" to one of restoring and maintaining "natural processes" (Parsons et al. 1986). The vignette might now be termed a "moving picture" (Christensen et al. 1987), although national policy does not formally recognize this perspective. The "moving picture" scene implies that a dynamic, continually changing landscape, primarily in response to nonhuman processes and disturbance factors, is more realistic than an implied static landscape.

The word "natural" remains difficult to define because it incorporates value judgments that cannot be scientifically resolved. If natural process management is assumed to mean evolution free of human influence, implementation of natural process management as a sole goal for park and wilderness management will be difficult to accomplish. Disturbance patterns did not stop at park and wilderness boundaries in primeval times; such boundaries were nonexistent. Disturbances, such as lightning fires, that once entered these areas from adjacent lands may not now, because of different land uses outside parks or wilderness. Some previous disturbances had a human origin (Indian fires) and are not present now.

Most of the wildlife species near the top of the food chain have large territories, and cross park and wilderness boundaries regularly or seasonally. Some, such as the grizzly bear, wolf, and cougar, are already missing from their recent natural ranges in parks and wilderness areas. Factors outside the boundary such as hunting or habitat manipulation (or in the case of Forest Service wilderness, hunting inside the boundary or livestock grazing), and fishing (except for some "catch and release" programs) inside most parks and wilderness, are evidence that management without significant human influence is not a realistic goal for many ecosystem components.

Areas outside the park or wilderness will usually be managed for other than park and wilderness values. Extinctions of wildlife in parks or wilderness may occur because of loss of essential habitat outside the area. Preservation of such species has received considerable attention by federal land managers.

Colonizations of park and wilderness areas by species native to the surrounding region may be difficult to categorize as "natural" range extensions or alien intrusions. The native flora and fauna at the time of park or wilderness establishment are most often viewed as static lists, with further colonizations or extirpations considered a deviation from "natural" conditions. Recognition that plant and animal ranges are not static will be important in determining alien or native plant and animal range extensions and contractions.

Despite its utility, natural process management can create a number of external problems for park and wilderness managers. Since ecosystem components may range beyond park and wilderness borders, it follows that deleterious effects (from the perspectives of neighbors), natural as they may be, can be exported to surrounding areas. Disturbances such as fire have potential exogenous effects: smoke can create air pollution, fires can cross park or wilderness boundaries, and the habitat of rare or endangered species may be affected. Wildlife may carry native diseases to livestock outside the boundary; large carnivores may prey on livestock or endanger human lives.

Laws for social purposes other than park and wilderness preservation (e.g., the Clean Air Act, the Clean Water Act, and the Endangered Species Act) constrain management options and effectively preclude a natural process policy inside parks and wilderness for reasons discussed above. They can, however, be used to protect the areas from external influences. Air pollutants—primarily acid rain in the eastern United States (Schofield, this volume) and photochemical oxidants in the western United States (Grigal, this volume)—are predicted to affect both aquatic and terrestrial components of park and wilderness ecosystems. Air quality legislation can be used to impose significant legal constraints on adjacent landowners or managers (Keiter, this volume) to protect parks and wilderness.

In summary, the concept of natural systems remains viable, but only in a dynamic and flexible context. Change, and sometimes unpredictable change, is essential to the natural systems concept. The application of this concept will continue to be experimental, just as all management approaches in natural systems are (Walters 1986). An easy systems "fix" to predicting effects of management actions is not on the horizon.

Managing Uncertainty

Social and biological information will probably improve over time but will never allow precise prediction. Given the political boundaries of park and wilderness ecosystems and unavoidable and uncertain human influence, change will occur in those systems. If managers take no action, that decision is itself a decision for a particular type of change.

Alternatively, a four-step approach can be used as a process to meet park and wilderness ecosystem goals: (1) define goals and measurable targets for ecosystem condition, (2) define the ecosystem boundaries for the primary components, (3) develop management strategies to achieve goals that transcend political boundaries, and (4) establish a program to assess the effectiveness of the management strategies in achieving the identified goals. Adequate definition of ecosystem-level problems and solutions may not occur if political boundaries are used as ecosystem boundaries.

Define the Goals. Goals should be phrased in terms of ecosystem condition and represent desired conditions for primary components. Workshop participants felt that they were not the appropriate group to define these goals, although some broad statements fostered consensus. Most important, the goals should preserve options for the future.

This point means maintaining the indigenous diversity of these areas in the largest context, to ensure not just species richness (number of species) but structural and successional diversity across the landscape. The scale of the landscape is larger than any traditionally dealt with in natural resources management.

Although our ability to quantify appropriate geographic scales and desired levels of diversity is relatively weak, there is agreement that maintaining diversity over a large area is different from maximizing diversity on every site. Maximum species richness of sites may occur in early successional periods for many ecosystems. For example, losing old-growth stages of those systems may result in loss of species richness over the whole area as well as significant losses in structural and functional diversity. A possible diversity goal might be to maintain viable populations of all native vertebrates within the region that encompasses the park or wilderness. Each park or wilderness would contribute those habitats and degrees of protection from human activities that best complement conditions on adjoining lands. This would be an application of "total area," or gamma, diversity (Whittaker 1972, Salwasser et al. 1984). This broad-scale diversity as a management goal has been largely ignored, yet may be quite relevant to the purposes of park and wilderness management (Samson and Knopf 1982).

Workshop participants also agreed that thresholds for minimum acceptable ecosystem conditions should be set. But these thresholds should be flexible enough to accommodate visitor preference, conflicting legislation, and other detractions from unattainable, ultimately pristine conditions (Mealey, this volume).

Define Ecosystem Boundaries for Primary Components. Each component, whether it be populations of grizzly bears or giant sequoias, will most likely have a different ecosystem boundary. These boundaries may range beyond political (park and wilderness area) boundaries. Some may involve other federal land; others, state or private lands. Interest groups may also be defined as components, either because they are the focus of management (e.g., backcountry visitors) or because they may have positive or negative influences on management strategies designed for other components of the system.

Adopt a Management Strategy to Achieve Component Goals. Ecosystems generally are too complex to manage as unified wholes. One approach to ecosystem management, therefore, focuses on components but recognizes the linkages between various parts of the system. The strategy for one component may be more complex than the strategy for another, and may possibly conflict with management of another component.

Management strategies should also take into account the defined ecosystem boundaries. Regional or national strategies may need to be developed. Examples of regional strategies are grizzly bear recovery areas in the northern Rockies and Cascades, spotted owl population areas in the Pacific Northwest, and red-cockaded woodpecker population areas in the South and Southwest. An example of national initiatives may be the efforts to deal with air pollution, although the scope of these problems varies by region. Air pollution issues have been and remain a federal legislative concern.

Monitor Effectiveness of Management Strategies. Ecosystem condition goals create needs for information on ecosystem components, natural disturbance processes, and rates of change. This information is used to monitor progress toward the chosen goal. It is only within well-defined system management objectives that needs for information is only within well-defined system management objectives that needs for information can be defined: obtaining and using information to track an ecosystem component or process that is unrelated to management is wasted effort.

Natural resources management, including park and wilderness management, is an experiment (Macnab 1983, Walters 1986). We simply do not know precisely the outcome of most management strategies. Many of our goals will therefore be achieved through hypotheses that are continually tested and refined. Two common themes emerge through these strategies. The first is that people are a part of the management solution. This is true of visitor preference as well as external costs (predator effects on livestock) and benefits (economic returns to local communities). The second theme is that because "naturalness" is subjectively defined, park and wilderness preservation goals will have to be stated in more precise system-component terms depending on the values represented by the individual area. These themes comprise the core of the chapters to follow.

LITERATURE CITED

Agee, J. K. 1974. Fire management in the national parks. Western Wildlands 1:27-33.

Chase, A. 1987. How to save our national parks. Atlantic Monthly, July 1987, pp. 35-37, 40-43.

Christensen, N. L., L. Cotton, H. T. Harvey, R. E. Martin, J. R. McBride, P. W. Rundel, and R. H. Wakimoto. 1987. Review of fire management program for sequoia-mixed conifer forests of Yosemite, Sequoia, and Kings Canyon National Parks. Report to Regional Director, NPS Western Region, San Francisco. 37 p.

Crandell, H. 1987. Congressional perspectives on the origin of the Wilderness Act and its meaning today. In R. C. Lucas (comp.) Proceedings, National Wilderness Research Conference: Issues, state-of-knowledge, future directions, pp. 9-14. USDA For. Serv. Gen. Tech. Rep. INT-220.

Dickey, J. W., and T. M. Watts. 1978. Analytic techniques in urban and regional planning. McGraw-Hill, New York.

Forman, R. T. T., and M. Godron. 1986. Landscape ecology. John Wiley and Sons, New York.

Graber, D. M. 1985. Managing for uncertainty: National parks as ecological reserves. George Wright Forum 4(3):4-7.

Hendee, J. C., G. H. Stankey, and R. C. Lucas. 1978. Wilderness management. USDA For. Serv. Misc. Pub. 1365.

Holling, C. S. (ed.) 1978. Adaptive environmental assessment and management. John Wiley and Sons, London.

Leopold, A. S., S. A. Cain, C. M. Cottam, I. N. Gabrielson, and T. L. Kimball. 1963. Wildlife management in the national parks. Transactions, North American Wildlife and Natural Resources Conference 28:28-45.

Macnab, J. 1983. Wildlife management as scientific experimentation. Wildl. Soc. Bull. 11:397-401.

Mueller-Dombois, D., and G. Spatz. 1975. The influence of feral goats on the lowland vegetation in Hawaii Volcanoes National Park. Phytocoenologia 3(1):1-29.

Odum, H. T. 1971. Environment, power, and society. Wiley-Interscience, New York.

Parsons, D. J. 1981. The role of fire management in maintaining natural ecosystems. In H. A. Mooney, T. M. Bonnicksen, N. L. Christensen, J. E. Lotan, and W. A. Reiners (eds.) Fire regimes and ecosystem properties, pp. 469-488. USDA For. Serv. Gen. Tech. Rep. WO-26.

Parsons, D. J., D. M. Graber, J. K. Agee, and J. W. van Wagtendonk. 1986. Natural fire management in national parks. Environ. Manage. 10:21-24.

Salwasser, H., J. W. Thomas, and F. Samson. 1984. Applying the diversity concept to national forest management. In J. L. Cooley and J. H. Cooley (eds.) Natural diversity in forest ecosystems, pp. 59-69. Institute of Ecology, University of Georgia, Athens.

Samson, F. B., and F. L. Knopf. 1982. In search of a diversity ethic for wildlife management. Transactions, North American Wildlife and Natural Resources Conference 47:421-431.

van Wagtendonk, J. W. 1985. Fire suppression effects on fuels and succession in short-fire-interval wilderness ecosystems. *In* J. E. Lotan, B. M. Kilgore, W. C. Fischer, and R. W. Mutch (eds.) Proceedings, Symposium and Workshop on Wilderness Fire, pp. 119-126. USDA For. Serv. Gen. Tech. Rep. INT-182.

Walters, C. 1986. Adaptive management of renewable natural resources. Macmillan, New York.

Whittaker, R. 1972. Evolution and measurement of species diversity. Taxon 21:213-251.

2

Natural Ecosystem Management in Park and Wilderness Areas: Looking at the Law

ROBERT B. KEITER

ABSTRACT Natural ecosystem management means maintaining the natural integrity and pristine character of "preserved" park and wilderness lands. But most large national parks and wilderness areas are bordered by other public lands, which may be open to consumptive development activities, or by virtually unregulated private lands. And the laws governing the public lands define legal responsibility and authority in terms of human boundaries—boundaries that usually reflect political judgments, not ecosystem realities. This can present serious legal problems for the Park Service, because it has no clear jurisdictional authority beyond its borders, though it has a legal duty to protect park resources from damage. On the other hand, the Forest Service does not lack jurisdictional authority over its lands bordering designated wilderness areas; its primary problem is in reconciling its multiple-use and wilderness management responsibilities. Both agencies are constrained by their organic mandates, and they must comply with environmental laws. They also may invoke these same laws against neighbors whose activities threaten the integrity of park and wilderness ecosystems. Since federal law reflects a significant national commitment to environmental protection, it affords park and wilderness managers an opportunity to promote natural ecosystem management beyond their borders.

Should the Forest Service lease its property to oil companies to drill exploratory wells on still primitive forest lands abutting a national park and several wilderness areas? This is the question facing Lewis and Clark National Forest officials in the Badger-Two Medicine region of northwestern Montana.[1] Thus far they have answered the question in the affirmative by authorizing a well on Hall Creek, less than two miles from Glacier National Park in the wildlife corridor connecting the park to the Bob Marshall Wilderness complex. They are also currently reviewing an application for drilling near Goat Mountain in the heart of this region. And the recently completed Forest Plan sanctions further leasing for oil and gas exploratory activity throughout the area.

The drilling proposals and the Forest Plan have not been well received by other federal and state agencies,[2] and they have met stiff resistance from local and national environmental groups. Opponents have charged the Forest Service with overlooking the environmental consequences drilling and development could have on the largely undeveloped Badger-Two Medicine area, which affords important habitat for wildlife such as the grizzly bear, elk, and gray wolf. They would like to see the region designated as wilderness, thus adding a "critical missing link" to the Glacier and Bob Marshall ecosystem complex. But the Forest Service has rejected this proposal, citing objections from the Blackfeet tribe, which claims treaty access rights to the lands (Act of June 10, 1896, 29 Stat. 353, 354). Moreover, according to forest officials, there is no reason why environmental values cannot be adequately protected if proper mitigation measures are used in developing the area's oil and gas potential. And, of course, the oil companies claim a property right to explore for mineral resources once a lease is granted.

The Hall Creek case illustrates the issues public land managers face today as they confront ever-mounting conflicts between development and preservation interests on multiple-use lands bordering park and wilderness areas. And it raises the broader issue of whether federal land management agencies—principally the Park Service, the Forest Service, and the Bureau of Land Management (BLM)—should or must take account of the regional impact of development activity, including its potential effect on adjacent lands set aside for their natural values. Natural ecosystem management may make good sense scientifically, but does the law necessarily require it? Even national park and wilderness legislation, though mandating preservation, specifically provides for human presence and use. Yet the law is also firmly committed to environmental protection as a primary value, particularly where the public lands are concerned.

The concept of a natural ecosystem begs further definition. For purposes of this paper, I will use the term to refer to an ecosystem where the natural processes (interacting parts of the physical and biological environments) are intact and the integrity of the system has not been significantly altered by human development. The concept of natural ecosystem management, therefore, means the administration of public lands to ensure that their natural integrity is not impaired, by maintaining existing ecological systems and perhaps restoring missing ecosystem components. In other words, natural ecosystem management envisions preserving a pristine area in its original undisturbed character (i.e., a state comparable to that contemplated by the Wilderness Act). This sort of management can be distinguished from multiple-use management, which although concerned with ecosystem dynamics and cross-boundary environmental impacts, tolerates human disturbance that can reach major proportions so long as the basic components of the ecosystem are not destroyed and mitigation measures are available to palliate the impact of the activities. Multiple-use management sanctions a range of consumptive use activities, such as timber harvesting and mining, that would be unacceptable under a natural ecosystem management regime. For example, while permitting the Hall Creek drilling proposal might not violate multiple-use management principles, it raises serious questions under natural ecosystem management principles.

This paper will examine the relationship between public land law and the concept of natural ecosystem management, using national park and forest wilderness lands as the focus.[3] After defining the legal issues confronting park and forest managers responsible for preserving the natural character of their lands, the paper will review the law establishing their fundamental obligations and limiting their management authority.[4] The paper will then discuss management of these "preserved" lands, an issue that does not ordinarily present difficult legal problems, since park and wilderness managers have authority over most matters occurring on their own lands. Finally, the paper will address the complex question of how the law might be invoked to promote ecosystem planning on lands adjacent to natural areas, or to challenge activities threatening the ecological integrity of these preserved lands. Because adjacent lands are either not under the direct control of park and wilderness managers or are subject to different management standards, this issue presents difficult legal problems, particularly since our legal system traditionally adheres to boundary lines as the means of defining ownership and management responsibility.

THE ISSUES

Beginning in 1872 with the creation of Yellowstone National Park, Congress has followed a consistent national policy of setting aside unique natural areas as national parks to preserve their scenery and natural features. Acting under the mandate of the Organic Act of 1916, the Park Service is responsible for managing the nation's parks to ensure that they are preserved for the benefit of future generations while providing for public enjoyment (see 16 U.S.C. §1). Under this organic mandate, the Park Service has the authority to regulate most activities occurring within the parks to limit environmental damage. Hence it has the legal opportunity to manage the national parks according to natural ecological principles, at least to the extent that the parks themselves represent independent ecosystems.

But the problem is that park boundaries reflect the art of political compromise, not the science of ecology. As our knowledge about the complexity of ecosystem dynamics becomes more sophisticated, it is evident that our established boundaries rarely correspond with the natural systems influencing evolutionary processes within the parks. Moreover, the modern phenomena of industrial development and rapid population growth have changed and intensified the impact of human activities on the environment, and the parks now find themselves facing environmentally harmful effects arising from activities occurring well beyond their borders. Thus, notwithstanding the Park Service's ability to control internal activities, external influences pose a serious threat to the ecological integrity of many parks. And as we shall see, the Park Service has only limited authority to do anything about it.

Although the ecological problems confronting the Forest Service are similar to those facing the Park Service, the Forest Service wilderness managers are in a somewhat different legal position. Wilderness gained its present status as a legal entity in 1964 when Congress adopted the Wilderness Act, providing that designated tracts of undisturbed federal lands should be preserved in their primitive state (see 16 U.S.C. §§ 1131-1136). Although Congress retained the sole authority to create these areas, it vested management responsibility with the agency originally charged with overseeing them. Thus the Forest Service now finds itself responsible for over half of the nation's wilderness areas, usually carved out of other lands that it still manages under its original organic mandate. (Other agencies responsible for managing federal wilderness lands include the Park Service, the Bureau of Land Management, and the Fish and Wildlife Service.)

From the perspective of the Park Service, the designation of park lands as wilderness does not appreciably alter its management philosophy; nor does it alleviate the difficulty it faces responding to environmental harms originating outside park boundaries. In the case of the Forest Service, however, the situation is different. Once Congress has designated a segment of its land as wilderness, it must adjust its management philosophy by disregarding its otherwise governing multiple-use mandate and limiting development activity within the designated area. In most cases this is not difficult: by definition the land must already be undeveloped to qualify as wilderness, and even before the Wilderness Act, the Forest Service had set aside and was managing some of its land as primitive areas. But since the Forest Service is usually responsible for the lands surrounding designated wilderness areas, it has the apparent authority to control most activities that may threaten its own wilderness. For the Forest Service then, unlike the Park Service, the problem is not one of legal authority; it is one of reconciling conflicting legal responsibilities.

In a related but different respect, the Park Service also confronts the problem of reconciling conflicting mandates. When establishing certain parks or designating National Recreation Areas or historical areas, Congress sometimes sanctions activities or uses inconsistent with the Organic Act, thus leaving park managers to establish an appropriate balance between these legislative mandates. See the section on the Park Service under the heading "Managing the Preserved Lands" below.

THE LEGAL FRAMEWORK

The public land management agencies are today governed by a complex array of federal laws. Understandably, the Park Service and the Forest Service primarily define their legal mission in terms of the initial organic legislation establishing them, as amended throughout the years. But in the case of the Forest Service, recent legislation mandating that it undertake comprehensive land and resource planning efforts—evaluating environmental values as well as consumptive use benefits—has at least subtly shifted its traditional multiple-use agenda.[5] Moreover, the Wilderness Act imposes severe restrictions on the Forest Service's management options, at least with respect to those lands classified as wilderness. Finally, general environmental protection laws, such as the National Environmental Policy Act of 1969 (NEPA), the Clean Water Act, and the Endangered Species Act, impose procedural and substantive restraints on both agencies, limiting their discretionary authority. But these environmental laws also provide the agencies with some extrajurisdictional leverage and enable them to respond to external activities threatening the ecological integrity of their lands.

The Park Service

The Organic Act of 1916 established the National Park Service and provided that the fundamental purpose of the national parks is to conserve scenery, natural and historic objects, and wildlife, and to provide for public enjoyment while leaving the parks "unimpaired for the enjoyment of future generations" (16 U.S.C. §1). Since its inception the Park Service has faced numerous difficulties reconciling its preservation and public access responsibilities, but it now appears firmly committed to a policy of ensuring that park resources are protected in the event of a conflict between preservation and use. See, for example, W. Mott, Twelve Point Management Plan (1985); Yellowstone National Park Master Plan (1973). This position is certainly defensible. The act's public enjoyment provision is modified by strong preservation language, specifically providing that access must not impair the lands for the use of future generations. See Lemons and Stout (1984). Moreover, the courts have consistently sustained Park Service regulations limiting public access or even closing areas when resources were threatened. See *Organized Fishermen of Florida v. Watt*, 590 F. Supp. 805 (S.D. Fla. 1984), aff'd 775 F. 2d 1544 (11th Cir. 1985); *Eiseman v. Andrus*, 433 F. Supp. 1103 (D. Ariz. 1977), aff'd 608 F. 2d 1250 (9th Cir. 1979). See also *Conservation Law Foundation v. Clark*, 590 F. Supp. 1467 (D. Mass. 1984); 36 C.F.R. §1.5 (1986).

Any question about the Park Service's primary responsibility for resource preservation was clarified by Congress in 1978 when it amended the Organic Act in response to the Redwood National Park crisis and the litigation it spawned. In *Sierra Club v. Department of the Interior*, 398 F. Supp. 284 (N.D. Cal. 1974), a federal district court found that the Park Service had violated its statutory and common law trust responsibilities by failing to protect Redwood National Park from harmful adjacent logging activities.[6] Congress responded to this ruling in 1978 by enlarging the Redwood Park boundaries (Public Law 95-250, 92 Stat. 163), and clarifying the Park Service's organic mandate, decreeing that "the protection, management and administration of those areas [national parks] shall be conducted in light of the National Park System and shall not be exercised in derogation of the values and purposes for which these various areas have been established . . ." (16 U.S.C. §1a-1).

The courts have interpreted §1a-1 as imposing an absolute legal duty on park officials to protect park resources from threatening activities, regardless of the source of the threat or the nature of competing user claims. See *Sierra Club v. Andrus*, 487 F. Supp. 443 (D.D.C. 1980); *National Rifle Ass'n. v. Potter*, 628 F. Supp. 903 (D.D.C. 1985). The courts have reviewed the Park Service's management actions under an abuse of discretion standard, according park officials considerable leeway—but not unlimited discretion—in deciding how to meet their responsibilities. So long as they respond reasonably to a resource threat, a court is not likely to find them in violation of their Organic Act duties.[7] Of course, the reasonableness of their actions depends on the scope of their legal authority, as well as the legal tools and strategies they might realistically rely on—issues that are deferred until later in this paper.

The Forest Service

Unlike the Park Service, the Forest Service does not operate under a preservationist philosophy. It is governed by organic legislation establishing a multiple-use management policy; it must balance competing uses and resource values in order to maximize public benefits. Only when Congress has classified particular forest lands as wilderness is it constrained by a narrower preservationist mandate.

The Forest Service's multiple-use mandate has evolved over the years. It originally appeared in the Organic Administration Act of 1897, which provided that the forests were reserved for the purposes of supplying timber and protecting watersheds (16 U.S.C. §475). In 1960, Congress passed the Multiple Use-Sustained Yield Act (16 U.S.C. §528 et seq.), substantially broadening the agency's mandate by requiring it to administer the forests for "outdoor recreation, range, timber, watershed, and wildlife and fish purposes" (*id.* at §528). With the passage of the Wilderness Act in 1964, Congress formalized wilderness as a Forest Service management responsibility. And when Congress passed the Resources Planning Act of 1974 and the National Forest Management Act of 1976 (NFMA), it further clarified the Forest Service's multiple-use responsibilities (16 U.S.C. §§1600-1687). Under the NFMA the Forest Service is required to undertake forestwide planning efforts, considering "the economic and environmental aspects of various systems of renewable resource managements, including the related systems of silviculture and protection of forest resources, to provide for outdoor recreation (including wilderness), range, timber, watershed, wildlife, and fish"; see 16 U.S.C. §1604(g)(3)(A). See, generally, Wilkinson and Anderson (1985:15-46) for a concise history of the evolution of Forest Service management and planning policies.

The NFMA commits the Forest Service to forest planning as its principal means of setting its management agenda. While the NFMA reinforces the Forest Service's multiple-use philosophy, it also injects distinct environmental values into the calculus. Indeed, Congress adopted the statute in response to the controversy that erupted over the agency's clearcutting practices, and it accordingly imposes substantive limits on timber harvesting practices within the national forests; see 16 U.S.C. §1611, §1604(g)(3)(E),(F).[8] The act mandates a "systematic interdisciplinary approach [to forest planning] to achieve integrated consideration of physical, biological, economic, and other sciences"; *id.* at §1604(b). Under the act, forest planners must weigh both "economic and *environmental* aspects" in striking a multiple-use balance; *id.* at §1604(g)(3)(A). They also must provide for plant and animal species diversity; *id.* at §1604 (g)(3)(A). And they must follow NEPA procedures, a significant requirement ensuring public involvement and interagency review; *id.* at §1604(g)(1), §1604(d). Significantly, the regulations promulgated under the NFMA endorse the concept of ecosystem management—see 36 C.F.R. §219.1(3) (1986)—and reflect a serious commitment to ecological principles in forest management. See, for example, 36 C.F.R. §219.27(5) (plant and animal species diversity); §219.19 (fish and wildlife habitat). As we shall see, the NFMA planning process has become a crucially important dimension of the Forest Service's wilderness management responsibilities, determining not only the wilderness potential of roadless forest lands but also the management direction for lands adjacent to designated wilderness areas.[9]

The Wilderness Act

The Wilderness Act (16 U.S.C. §§1131-1136) provides Congress with authority to set aside wilderness lands to be "administered for the use and enjoyment of the American people in such manner as will leave them unimpaired for future use and enjoyment as wilderness"; 16 U.S.C. §1131(a). Under the act, "wilderness" is defined as "an area where the earth and its community of life are untrammeled by man, where man himself is a visitor who does not remain." It is an area "retaining its primeval character and influence, without permanent improvements or human habitation"; *id.* at §1131(c).[10] Federal lands reflecting these characteristics are eligible for wilderness classification, and they are to be managed by the agency originally responsible for them; *id.* at §1131(b). The act requires the agency to protect and manage its wilderness land "so as to preserve its natural conditions"; *id.* at §1131(c). It specifically provides that "each agency administering any [wilderness] area . . . shall be responsible for preserving the wilderness character of the area and shall so administer such area for such other purposes for which it may have been established as also to preserve its wilderness character"; *id.* at §1133(b). Although the statute contemplates human presence in wilderness areas, its clear message is that the wilderness management agencies have a legal duty to preserve designated wilderness lands in their natural state. See *Sierra Club v. Block*, 622 F. Supp. 842, 864 (D. Colo. 1985).

Despite the predominant preservationist tenor of the Wilderness Act, it also sanctions incompatible human activities within wilderness areas. Grazing and mining are specifically permitted, as well as the use of aircraft and motorboats, where these uses were preexisting; 16 U.S.C. §1133(d). In addition, the act authorizes the responsible agency to control fire, insects, and disease—a management prerogative, if exercised, that could disrupt the natural processes in any wilderness area. Such provisions are plainly incompatible with the notion of natural ecosystem management. Thus, although the responsible agency may aspire to manage its wilderness lands by prohibiting intrusive human activities and permitting natural processes to evolve unchecked, it may not consistently be able to pursue such a management philosophy. Yet even when it is compelled to allow other activities, it has a statutory responsibility to see that the activities are conducted in the least intrusive manner to preserve the area's wilderness character. See 16 U.S.C. §1133(b); *Cabinet Mountains Wilderness v. Peterson*, 685 F. 2d 678 (D.C. Cir. 1982).

The Wilderness Act imposes no specific constraints on the use or management of lands adjacent to designated wilderness areas. Nor does it explicitly provide agency officials responsible for wilderness management with any authority to regulate adjacent lands, even contiguous public lands that they may otherwise manage under multiple-use principles. But the courts have held that the act limits the authority of public land managers to develop adjacent roadless lands without evaluating fully their potential as wilderness additions. See 16 U.S.C. §1132(b); *Parker v. United States*, 448 F. 2d 793 (10th Cir. 1971), cert. denied 405 U.S. 989 (1972). And the courts have read a protection responsibility into the act, obligating agency officials to protect wilderness resources against degradation from outside influences. See 16 U.S.C. §1131(c); *Sierra Club v. Block*, 622 F. Supp. 842, 866 (D. Colo. 1985). Moreover, statutes such as the NFMA, FLPMA, and NEPA suggest that the multiple-use agencies must take account of existing wilderness areas when reviewing development proposals for adjacent public lands.

Federal Environmental Laws

The public land management agencies not only face clear environmental protection obligations under their respective organic statutes but also must comply with the multiple environmental protection laws Congress has enacted over the past twenty-five years. The National Environmental Policy Act imposes procedural constraints on land managers, effectively limiting their discretionary authority by requiring public participation in agency decision making and interagency consultation on matters within the jurisdictional expertise of sister agencies. Other statutes such as the Endangered Species Act, the Clean Water Act, and the Clean Air Act establish substantive environmental quality standards that the agencies must meet, irrespective of their organic mandate. Collectively, these statutes impose significant restraints on consumptive use activities and afford some protection to major components (water, air, and wildlife) of park and wilderness ecosystems. Moreover, these laws are not boundary limited; they apply regardless of which agency manages the land.

The NEPA (42 U.S.C. §§4321-4370) is perhaps the single most important federal law governing environmental quality. It requires federal agencies contemplating actions "significantly affecting the quality of the human environment" to prepare an environmental impact statement (EIS) evaluating the environmental effects of the proposal and alternatives to the action; 42 U.S.C. §4332(c). The act provides for public review and comment on the EIS, including participation by other interested agencies. See *id.*; 40 C.F.R. §1503, §1506.6 (1986). But NEPA does not mandate any particular result or decision, only that the proposing agency reach a reasonable decision in view of identified environmental concerns. See *Strycker's Bay Neighborhood Council v. Karlen*, 444 U.S. 223 (1980). Nevertheless, under NEPA the courts take a "hard look" at agency decisions to ensure that they reflect a thorough environmental review fully complying with statutory procedural requirements. See *Kleppe v. Sierra Club*, 427 U.S. 390, 410 n. 21 (1976); *California v. Block*, 690 F. 2d 753, 761 (9th Cir. 1982).

For the public land management agencies, NEPA means that their internal management and planning decisions must meet minimum procedural requirements and reflect a comprehensive evaluation of the expected environmental consequences of proposed projects. And NEPA also means that the agencies will have an opportunity to evaluate and respond to other agencies' development proposals when they might affect park or wilderness lands. The NEPA regulations indicate that one factor to be considered in the environmental review process is whether the proposed project is likely to affect nearby park lands, historic or cultural resources, or ecologically critical areas; 40 C.F.R. §1508.27(b)(3) (1986). This provides park and wilderness managers with a key opportunity to ensure that their ecosystem management objectives have been considered in the NEPA review process.

The NEPA regulations establish a procedure for resolving interagency conflicts through referral to the Council on Environmental Quality for its recommendation; 40 C.F.R. §1504 (1986). But the federal agencies have only infrequently resorted to this referral procedure: they are reluctant to air their disputes publicly, and they are even more reluctant to allow authority to slip from their hands, even if only for a recommendation. Instead, owing to the NEPA participation and consultation requirements, most interagency disputes are likely to be negotiated to resolution, generally at the local level and presumably against the backdrop of other federal environmental laws.

The NEPA has spawned a vast amount of litigation, attaching considerable judicial gloss to its seemingly simple statutory language. It is impossible to undertake a comprehensive review of the decisions here, but it is useful to note some recurring issues likely to influence agency actions involving park and wilderness lands. The threshold decision whether or not to prepare an EIS is often critical. An agency determination to forgo an EIS, relying instead on a less thorough environmental assessment, is subject to judicial reversal if a court finds that the proposal could significantly affect the environment. For example, in *Sierra Club v. Peterson*, 717 F. 2d 1409 (D.C. Cir. 1983), the court ruled that the Forest Service could not issue oil and gas leases without "no surface occupancy" clauses on nonwilderness forest lands on the basis of an environmental assessment; NEPA obligated the agency to undertake a full EIS evaluation of the environmental consequences of leasing. See also *Foundation for North American Wild Sheep v. U.S. Dept. of Agriculture*, 681 F. 2d 1172 (9th Cir. 1982); *Conner v. Burford*, 605 F. Supp. 107 (D. Mont. 1985), aff'd in part 836 F. 2d 1521 (9th Cir. 1988). Under NEPA, the courts have held that agencies must consider the cumulative impacts accompanying development proposals; they cannot segment the environmental analysis process and review each proposal in isolation. In *Thomas v. Peterson*, 753 F. 2d 754 (9th Cir. 1985), for instance, the court held that the Forest Service must prepare an EIS analyzing the total effect its road building decision would have on an existing roadless area, particularly since timber sales were contemplated once the road was completed. See 40 C.F.R. §1508.25(a)(2)(1986); see also *National Wildlife Federation v. U.S. Forest Service*, 592 F. Supp. 931, 942-44 (D. Ore. 1984). Hence, while the courts are generally deferential to agency decisions respecting whether to proceed with a proposed project, they do interpret NEPA's procedural requirements strictly, insisting on a careful environmental evaluation at the outset. And as we shall see, the courts have been especially rigorous in their review of agency proposals affecting undeveloped areas potentially suitable for wilderness classification.

The Endangered Species Act (16 U.S.C. §§1531-1543) has also proven to be a powerful law, imposing substantive and procedural constraints on the discretionary authority of public land managers. The act requires any federal agency contemplating a project that "may affect" listed species to consult with the U.S. Fish and Wildlife Service (FWS) to ensure that its actions are "not likely to jeopardize the continued existence of any endangered species or result in the destruction or adverse modification of (critical) habitat of such species"; *id.* at §1536(a)(2). Ordinarily, the consultation occurs as part of the NEPA environmental review process, and a failure to follow the act's procedural requirements provides a basis for a court to enjoin the project. *Thomas v. Peterson*, 753 F. 2d 754 (9th Cir. 1985). Unless the FWS is convinced that the proposal will not adversely affect protected species, it is obligated to issue a "jeopardy" opinion, which effectively blocks the project.[11] The initiating agency may then either redesign the project, mitigating identified adverse impacts, or forgo it. Other agencies should have the opportunity throughout this process to advise FWS officials of their concerns and to share scientific data about the potential impact the proposal may have on listed species found on their lands.

When a listed species is present, the Endangered Species Act requirements are a primary consideration in agency planning processes. It has been suggested that the act can virtually dictate public land management policy, severely limiting the options available to the agencies when their lands provide critical habitat for a listed species.[12] When this involves multiple-use lands, it often means that existing natural conditions must be preserved intact to protect the species. This certainly appears to be the case with the grizzly bear: an interagency committee charged with overseeing bear policies has developed extensive land management guidelines that limit development activity on multiple-use public lands. Therefore, the Endangered Species Act can be viewed not only as a means for protecting listed species but also as a means for protecting roadless and other lands from development. Indeed, the impact of this law is not constrained by the geographic boundaries of a wilderness area or federal landownership.

Since many parks and wilderness areas provide critical habitat for endangered or threatened species, the FWS frequently holds the balance of power in disputes concerning development proposals that might alter either these lands or, more likely, multiple-use lands adjacent to them. For example, in the Hall Creek exploratory drilling proposal noted at the outset, the FWS initially blocked the project after concluding that unrestricted road access into the Badger-Two Medicine country would jeopardize the grizzly bear. The project was eventually redesigned to minimize the extent of human intrusion into the area, thus limiting potential harm to the bear and damage to the wildernesslike character of the region. But this does not necessarily end the matter. Since the Endangered Species Act can be enforced by citizen suit, even if the FWS acquiesces in a project like the Hall Creek well, its decision may be challenged in court by environmental groups unhappy with its "no jeopardy" assessment. In this event, the courts will examine the agency's decision to determine whether it was arbitrary or capricious. See *Cabinet Mountains Wilderness v. Peterson*, 685 F. 2d 678, 685 (D.C. Cir. 1982).

The Clean Air Act (42 U.S.C. §§7401-7626) and the Clean Water Act (33 U.S.C. §§1251-1376) provide the national parks and wilderness areas with some protection against air and water pollution. Under the Clean Air Act, park and wilderness areas established by 1977 are generally afforded the highest degree of protection against pollution from either public or private sources. Similarly, under the Clean Water Act, rivers or other waterways traversing parks or wilderness areas usually receive the highest protection against deterioration in water quality.[13] For the management agencies this means two things: they must conduct themselves in a manner consistent with the statutory mandates, and they may rely on the statutes to respond to certain pollution problems originating from sources beyond their borders. Because both laws figure prominently in the NEPA environmental review process, agency planners must thoroughly evaluate the impact their proposals will have on air and water quality. See *Northwest Indian Protective Ass'n v. Peterson*, 795 F. 2d 688, 696-97 (9th Cir. 1986), rev'd on other grounds, 108 S. Ct. 1319 (1988). However, there are notable shortcomings in both statutes, leaving some pollutants uncovered (e.g., acid rain) and others inadequately regulated (e.g., nonpoint source water pollution). See, for example, *United States v. ARCO*, 478 F. Supp. 1215 (D. Mont. 1979) (utilizing common law nuisance doctrine to address fluoride pollution problems). See also U.S. Congress, House Committee on Interior and Insular Affairs (1985).

Other preservation-oriented laws also may influence public land management decisions. The Wild and Scenic Rivers Act (16 U.S.C. §§1271-1287) imposes severe restraints on management options once a river has been designated under the act, by generally limiting development activity in the river corridor. See, for example, *Town of Summersville, W. Va. v. F.E.R.C.*, 780 F. 2d 1034 (D.C. Cir. 1986) (sustaining denial of hydroelectric project permit pending wild and scenic river designation decision); see also Gray (1988). Thus park or wilderness areas containing or bounding a designated river derive an additional degree of protection against adverse multiple-use activities. The National Historic Preservation Act (16 U.S.C. §§470-470t) protects registered historic properties by constraining agency decisions that might adversely affect listed properties, but it does not absolutely forbid activities potentially affecting the structure or surrounding lands. Furthermore, various federal resource management statutes, such as the Surface Mining Control and Reclamation Act (30 U.S.C. §§1201-1328), impose both substantive and procedural requirements governing development activities involving the covered resources. See *Utah International, Inc. v. Dept. of the Interior*, 553 F. Supp. 872 (D. Utah 1982) (upholding the secretary of the interior's decision designating certain multiple-use federal lands adjacent to a national park as unsuitable for surface coal mining).

Since these laws are not boundary limited, public land managers are affected by them in several different respects: they may find their management prerogatives constrained by these statutory requirements; they may rely on the statutes to limit private activities on their own lands; or they may utilize them to challenge threatening activities occurring on adjacent lands. In total, the statutes reflect a significant—albeit somewhat incomplete—congressional commitment to protecting ecosystem components and to preserving the environmental integrity of natural areas.

MANAGING THE PRESERVED LANDS

The property clause in the Constitution grants Congress broad power to regulate the public lands (U.S. Const., art. IV, §3, cl. 2). In *Kleppe v. New Mexico*, 426 U.S. 529 (1976), the Supreme Court concluded that "the general [federal] Government doubtless has a power over its own property analogous to the police power of the several States, and the extent to which it may go in the exercise of such power is measured by the exigencies of the particular case"; *id.* at 540, quoting *Camfield v. United States*, 167 U.S. 518, 525 (1897). When enacting the organic legislation creating the national park and forest systems, Congress has relied on the property power to delegate considerable regulatory authority to the federal agencies responsible for managing these lands. Over the years they have used this power to fulfill their management obligations, regularly limiting activities on their own lands and occasionally even seeking to control threatening activities arising on adjacent, nonfederal lands. And, as we shall see, the courts have generally not intervened to limit their authority.

The Park Service

The Organic Act provides the secretary of the interior, acting on behalf of the Park Service, with authority to regulate activities occurring on park lands (16 U.S.C. §3). The courts have consistently sustained Park Service regulations limiting activities, such as commercial rafting and fishing, that threatened to alter the natural character of the area or deplete important natural resources. See *Eiseman v. Andrus*, 433 F. Supp. 1103 (D. Ariz. 1977), aff'd 608 F. 2d 1250 (9th Cir. 1979); *Organized Fishermen of Florida v. Hodel*, 775 F. 2d 1544 (11th Cir. 1985). Indeed, the courts have concluded that the Organic Act conveys sufficient authority for the Park Service to regulate activities on state or private property located within park boundaries. See *Free Enterprise Canoe Renters Ass'n. v. Watt*, 711 F. 2d 852 (8th Cir. 1983); *United States v. Brown*, 552 F. 2d 817 (8th Cir. 1977), cert. denied, 431 U.S. 949 (1977). The Supreme Court's recent decision in *Clark v. Community for Creative Non Violence*, 104 S.Ct. 3065 (1984), essentially confirms these rulings. In *Clark* the Court held that the secretary of the interior enjoys such broad regulatory power over the national parks that the courts generally should not second-guess his decisions, even in the face of First Amendment claims (*id*. at 3072). Thus the Park Service has the inherent authority to protect the park ecosystem from incompatible activities occurring within the parks. As long as it does not abuse its discretion, its actions are not likely to be overturned by the courts.

Internal park management is governed principally by the Organic Act, which requires park officials to conserve and protect park resources (16 U.S.C. §1). But the Organic Act does not contemplate an entirely "laissez-faire" management approach; it provides that the Park Service may harvest timber and destroy wildlife within the parks, if *necessary* to preserve other park resources (16 U.S.C. §3). The Organic Act even sanctions livestock grazing within the national parks, if consistent with the park's purpose. Moreover, the separate organic statutes creating each national park unit establish important management principles that may limit the discretion available to park officials and effectively preclude them from implementing an entirely natural management regime. Depending on the particular establishing legislation, activities inconsistent with the Organic Act's strictures may be permitted within one park but not permitted within others (16 U.S.C. §1c). For example, Congress has authorized hunting and trapping within some parks. See, for example, 16 U.S.C. §460n-4 (Lake Mead); §230(d) (Jean Lafitte). Yet the Park Service retains the authority to regulate these activities, and the courts have sustained stringent regulatory limitations. See 36 C.F.R. §2.2, §9.1, et seq. (1986); *National Rifle Ass'n. v. Potter*, 628 F. Supp. 908 (D.D.C. 1985). Thus, while Park Service officials generally have the authority to implement a natural ecosystem-oriented management philosophy, they occasionally may find this option foreclosed.

Park management goals are set through general management plans which afford park officials an opportunity to systematically assess ecological conditions and to formulate strategies for protecting resources against degradation (16 U.S.C. §1a-7). When implementing management policies or undertaking projects that could affect park resources, park officials must comply with applicable environmental protection laws, such as NEPA and the Endangered Species Act. For example, when deciding whether to remove the Fishing Bridge campground complex located in important grizzly bear habitat, Yellowstone National Park officials were obligated to consult with the Fish and Wildlife Service, and to meet NEPA requirements. This should ensure a thorough environmental review of such proposals, including any effects on the existing ecological balance, and provide an opportunity to consider alternative courses of action and mitigation measures. It also enables other agencies and persons interested in the matter to participate in the decision-making process—a fact, in itself, that reinforces the inevitable cross-boundary impact of natural resource decisions such as this.

The Wilderness Act addresses the question of how park officials should approach conflicts between their organic mandate and their wilderness preservation responsibilities when park lands have been designated as wilderness areas. As a practical matter, of course, such conflicts are not likely to arise frequently: the strong preservation philosophy reflected in the Organic Act virtually mirrors the definition of "wilderness" set forth in the Wilderness Act. But since Congress has designated some park lands as wilderness—see, for example, 92 Stat. 3490 (Everglades National Park); 86 Stat. 918 (Lassen Volcanic National Park)—a conflict involving management of these lands, particularly the degree to which they are improved or maintained to accommodate visitors, is possible.[14] In this event, the Wilderness Act provides that the conflict must be resolved to maintain the natural wilderness character of the lands; see 16 U.S.C. §1133(b). Alternatively, if wilderness classification of park lands permits more intrusive management than the Park Service has traditionally practiced, it is obligated to continue administering the lands as it did originally; see 16 U.S.C. §1133(a).

One other matter bears noting. Natural ecosystem management ordinarily implies a management strategy that permits nature to take its course, with instances of human intervention severely limited. Adopting that approach raises the question whether the Park Service could face legal liability if its failure to intervene causes human injury or damage to adjacent property. The Park Service is generally under no duty to protect visitors from natural hazards, though it may have a duty to warn them of hazards that would not be apparent. See *Mandel v. United States*, 793 F. 2d 964 (8th Cir. 1986). On the other hand, a Park Service decision allowing a forest fire to burn when it could have been controlled on park lands might open the Park Service to liability if the fire spills over the park boundary onto adjacent private lands. See *Rayonier, Inc. v. United States*, 352 U.S. 315 (1957); *Coe v. United States*, 502 F. Supp. 881 (D. Ore. 1980). These same legal principles, which have evolved from the Federal Tort Claims Act, 28 U.S.C. §§1346(b), 2671, et seq., should govern questions of liability in the case of the Forest Service or other federal land management agencies responsible for managing wilderness lands.

The Forest Service

Under the Organic Act of 1897, the secretary of agriculture was granted authority to issue regulations governing the use and preservation of the forest reserves, and this authority continues unabated under present law (16 U.S.C. 551). In *United States v. Grimaud*, 220 U.S. 506 (1911), the Supreme Court construed the statute to afford the secretary broad discretion in regulating activities within the national forests. This interpretation has withstood the test of time; the courts have consistently sustained Forest Service regulations implementing its statutory responsibilities. For example, in *McMichael v. United States*, 355 F. 2d 283 (9th Cir. 1965), the court held that the Multiple Use-Sustained Yield Act provided sufficient justification for a Forest Service regulation prohibiting motorized vehicles within national forest primitive areas. Other cases have affirmed the secretary's authority to regulate activities on nonfederal lands within national forests. See *United States v. Lindsey*, 595 F. 2d 5 (9th Cir. 1979); *United States v. Arbo*, 691 F. 2d 863 (9th Cir. 1982). Although the NFMA has not yet received much judicial attention, the courts can be expected to continue taking an expansive view of the secretary's authority under this statute, and deferring to his regulatory judgments.

The Forest Service's wilderness management responsibilities are defined by the Wilderness Act, which requires the agency to preserve the primitive character of the designated areas, permitting natural processes to prevail; see 16 U.S.C. §1131(c). The Forest Service is therefore effectively under a mandate to engage in natural ecosystem management for its wilderness areas, and its current regulations reflect a primary commitment to such an approach. The regulations explicitly endorse the principle of ecosystem management, and provide for limiting human use if it threatens the natural character of the land; 36 C.F.R. §293.2, §219.18(a) (NFMA carrying capacity regulations). With the broad judicial construction the courts have given the Forest Service's general administrative authority, there should be no question about the validity of these regulations. Furthermore, although the Wilderness Act provides that the states retain jurisdiction over wildlife, which could undermine or frustrate Forest Service wildlife management efforts, 16 U.S.C. §1133(d)(7), the secretary of agriculture has the authority to displace state wildlife laws if he perceives this is necessary to reduce pressure on wilderness lands. See *Hunt v. United States*, 278 U.S. 96 (1928); see also *Hughes v. Oklahoma*, 441 U.S. 322 (1979) (rejecting the state ownership of wildlife principle).

As we have noted, however, the Wilderness Act does not establish an entirely "pure" wilderness system. The act permits established activities and uses to continue within designated areas, most notably grazing and mining; see 16 U.S.C. §1133(d). It also provides for controlling fire, insects, and disease. Moreover, the specific establishing legislation for particular wilderness areas may contain provisions authorizing activities inconsistent with the concept of wilderness. See, for example, Wyoming Wilderness Act of 1984, §201(c), 98 Stat. 2809 (exception for water project). See also 16 U.S.C. §1133(d) (granting the President authority to permit water projects in wilderness areas). Thus, although the Forest Service is obligated to pursue a dominant management strategy of non-interference with natural processes within its wilderness areas, it is in effect legally compelled to deviate from this in some instances.

Nevertheless, Forest Service regulations promulgated under the amended Organic Act of 1897, as well as the Wilderness Act and the NFMA, impose significant environmental restrictions on multiple-use activities within forest wilderness areas. See, for example, 36 C.F.R. §219.20 (1986) (NFMA grazing regulations); 36 C.F.R. §228.15 (1986) (wilderness mining regulations). See also *Perkins v. Bergland*, 608 F. 2d 803 (9th Cir. 1979) (sustaining a Forest Service decision reducing grazing allotments due to environmental damage). Moreover, the Forest Service must comply with other environmental laws when implementing its wilderness management plans, particularly when multiple-use activities are sanctioned within wilderness areas. In *Cabinet Mountains Wilderness v. Peterson*, 685 F. 2d 678 (D.C. Cir. 1982), for example, the court held that the Forest Service must comply with NEPA and the Endangered Species Act when reviewing an exploratory drilling proposal within a wilderness area, ruling that its analysis was adequate because propr⌐ d mitigation measures would sufficiently protect the grizzly bear. However, in *Sⁱ ₁ub v. Block*, 614 F. Supp. 488 (D.D.C. 1985), the court enjoined a Forest Service decision to cut pine beetle infested trees in several southern wilderness areas because it had not undertaken an adequate NEPA review. But see *Sierra Club v. Block*, 614 F. Supp. 134 (E.D. Tex. 1985). Therefore, when multiple-use activities or management strategies threatening natural ecological processes are permitted within wilderness areas, the Forest Service still has a legal responsibility to minimize environmental harm accruing from these activities.

RESPONDING TO EXTERNAL INFLUENCES

While park and wilderness managers have a similar obligation to protect the integrity of their preserved lands, they face distinctly different legal problems implementing a natural ecosystem management strategy that effectively addresses threats arising from activities beyond their borders. For the Park Service, the primary problem is one of jurisdiction. Lands adjacent to the national parks are ordinarily either managed by another agency or owned privately, and may therefore be beyond the Park Service's regulatory authority. Consequently, park managers must look to general environmental laws as a means of influencing their neighbors' decisions.[15] On the other hand, jurisdictional authority is generally not a problem for the Forest Service, since it is usually responsible for the public lands located adjacent to its wilderness areas. Its problem involves reconciling its multiple-use philosophy with its wilderness management responsibilities—a dilemma that the law does not fully address.

The Park Service
The Organic Act. As previously noted, the amended Organic Act imposes an unmistakable legal duty on park officials to protect park resources, regardless of the source of the threatened harm (16 U.S.C. §1a-1). But the amendment also limits the Park Service's responsibilities. It contains an "exceptions clause" relieving the Park Service of any obligation to protect park resources when Congress has "directly or specifically" authorized the threatening activity. The question this raises is whether the Park Service's §1a-1 responsibility applies when Congress has adopted a general policy promoting or sanctioning development on public lands bordering the national parks. In other words, does a broad statute like the FLPMA, which contains a general multiple-use mandate, override the Organic Act's preservation mandate, leaving the parks without any statutory protection under the Organic Act and the Park Service without any legal responsibilities should the BLM authorize mineral development activity on its multiple-use lands adjacent to a park?

For several reasons the answer appears to be no, although the matter has not been definitively resolved by the courts. The language and legislative history of the §1a-1 amendment indicate that Congress intended the "exceptions clause" to be construed narrowly, and only invoked to relieve the Park Service of its protection responsibilities when Congress has specifically authorized a particular project or activity on adjacent lands.[16] Recent court decisions lend support to this interpretation of the provision. See *Sierra Club v. Watt*, 566 F. Supp. 380 (D. Utah 1983); *National Rifle Ass'n. v. Potter* (see above). Unless Congress has specifically mandated mineral development on the particular BLM lands in question, the Park Service should derive legal protection from its organic legislation, and it is probably under a legal obligation to respond if park resources are threatened. Hence a general multiple-use statute like the FLPMA should not trump the Park Service's organic mandate or its preservation responsibilities. Of course, the "exceptions" clause will not ordinarily have any application to development projects involving state or private lands adjacent to a national park; park officials are thus under a clear §1a-1 duty to respond to these threatening activities.

But the amended Organic Act does not provide the secretary of the interior with any explicit authority to regulate activities occurring on either public or private lands outside the parks. Whether the secretary enjoys this authority has not been conclusively resolved by the courts. A strong argument can be made, however, that since the Organic Act imposes protection responsibilities on the secretary, it also implicitly grants him the authority to regulate activities on lands adjacent to the parks. The courts have sustained Park Service regulations governing activities on state and private property within the parks. See *Free Enterprise Canoe Renters Ass'n. v. Watt*, 711 F. 2d 852 (8th Cir. 1983); *United States v. Brown*, 552 F. 2d 817 (8th Cir. 1977), cert. denied, 431 U.S. 949 (1977). And in *Kleppe v. New Mexico*, 426 U.S. 529 (1976), the Supreme Court sustained a federal statute regulating activity on nonfederal lands to protect federal property, noting that Congress's power over the federal lands "is broad enough to reach beyond territorial limits." The same reasoning would support Park Service regulations limiting activity on adjacent federal, state and private lands. See "Protecting National Parks . . ." (1984).

The secretary of the interior is unlikely, however, to intrude this directly into the management prerogatives of a sister land management agency, and he is probably even less likely to intervene in state or local land-use planning matters. Direct confrontation in this manner is not the Park Service's style (see Sax and Keiter 1987:207), particularly when the precise scope of its regulatory power is largely untested. Since the secretary is accorded considerable deference in deciding how to meet his park protection responsibilities, he is under no apparent legal duty to promulgate such regulations. As a practical matter, therefore, the Park Service must look elsewhere to establish a legal basis for promoting its cross-boundary resource management goals.

Other Legal Alternatives. The Park Service can rely on general federal environmental laws to encourage interagency ecosystem management cooperation or to challenge threatening activities. Since federal agencies do not typically sue each other, these statutes are primarily useful as a basis for negotiating with sister agencies. However, should inaction by the Park Service put park resources at risk, the agency may expose itself to a citizen's suit for violating its Organic Act responsibilities. If it was established that the Park Service acted unreasonably (i.e., abused its discretion), a court could order it to take appropriate action to protect park resources. See *Sierra Club v. Dept. of the Interior*, 398 F. Supp. 284, 293 (N.D. Cal. 1975); *Sierra Club v. Andrus*, 487 F. Supp. 443, 449-50 (D.D.C. 1980). Among other things, appropriate action may include invoking environmental protections readily available under existing laws.

How might the Park Service utilize federal environmental laws to either promote cross-jurisdictional planning or protect park resources? NEPA, as well as the NFMA and FLPMA statutes, afford park officials an opportunity to participate in the planning and decision-making processes of neighboring federal agencies. NEPA regulations indicate that one factor to be considered in the environmental review process is the project's proximity to park lands or ecologically critical areas. See 40 C.F.R. §1508.27(b)(3). Thus the Park Service should be consulted by any federal agency contemplating a project in the vicinity of a national park with potential environmental consequences, and have the chance to express its concerns, as well as suggest alternatives and mitigation measures. See 40 C.F.R. §1500.5(b). The NFMA and FLPMA laws require the Forest Service and the BLM to coordinate their planning efforts with other federal agencies. See 16 U.S.C. §1604(a); 36 C.F.R. §219.7 (1986); 43 U.S.C. §1712(c)(9). Because both statutes reflect a strong congressional commitment to coordinated land-use planning that takes account of environmental values, Park Service concerns about the ecological implications of development activities on nearby lands should carry some persuasive weight with neighboring agency planners. Furthermore, the Park Service's comments could strengthen the arguments of others opposed to the plan who are willing to litigate.[17]

Federal resource protection laws, such as the Clean Air Act, the Clean Water Act, and the Endangered Species Act, are specifically designed to protect against degradation of important ecosystem components: air, water, and wildlife. Since certain park air and water resources are afforded the highest degree of statutory protection, neighboring land management agencies (and even adjacent private landowners) undertaking projects threatening air or water quality must comply with specific pollution control requirements, or else they may be denied an operating permit or subjected to enforcement proceedings. Similarly, because the U.S. Fish and Wildlife Service has authority under the Endangered Species Act to "veto" projects threatening protected species, parks with wildlife populations containing "listed" species that have habitat requirements extending onto adjacent public lands should derive some protection from this act. In the Hall Creek case, for example, Glacier National Park has plainly benefited from the Fish and Wildlife Service's decision requiring forest officials to redesign the drilling project. Quite obviously, however, parks lacking listed species among their wildlife populations cannot draw upon the act for protection; they will most likely find it advantageous to ally themselves with state game and fish officials as a means of influencing adjacent development activities.

Effective enforcement of these statutes ultimately depends on reliable scientific information establishing baseline environmental conditions, and monitoring data documenting changes linked to development activities. The Park Service can therefore play a critical role in the enforcement of these statutes by developing high quality research and monitoring programs, and sharing its information with enforcement officials. Or alternatively, when negotiating with other land management officials, the Park Service may be able to use its information to influence their decisions if it can scientifically demonstrate environmental harm and hence a potential legal violation.

Preservation-oriented statutes, such as the Wilderness Act and the Wild and Scenic Rivers Act, also afford the Park Service a prime opportunity to promote natural ecosystem management goals. Whenever public lands adjacent to the national parks are designated as wilderness areas or wild and scenic river corridors, this guarantees that they will remain largely undeveloped, providing a natural buffer for the parks. Park Service participation in the statutory review and classification process therefore represents an important park protection strategy—one that could not only protect the park itself but also preserve intact those ecosystems straddling park and forest boundaries. Although the Forest Service's NFMA planning process afforded the Park Service an opportunity to involve itself in the wilderness review process, it apparently did not participate actively, perhaps perceiving that its involvement would unduly impinge on the prerogatives of a sister land management agency. Such "turf" sensitivity is not unusual within the federal bureaucracy, especially among public land management agencies accustomed to a largely discretionary management style. In addition, an interesting opportunity for interagency cooperation exists under the Wild and Scenic Rivers Act. Congress has occasionally provided for joint management of designated rivers bordering both park and forest lands, thereby creating an arrangement that can ultimately lead to broader interagency cooperative endeavors. For example, the North Fork of the Flathead River, which separates Glacier National Park from the Flathead National Forest, is jointly managed under the Wild and Scenic Rivers Act. Park and forest officials have built upon this management relationship to address other cross-boundary land and resource management problems in the North Fork region. See Sax and Keiter (1987:235-236).

Even when no federal environmental statute applies, however, park officials still might rely on common law principles to confront threatening activities on adjacent lands. Common law nuisance doctrine allows a landowner to challenge adjoining property uses unreasonably interfering with the use and enjoyment of his own property. See Rogers (1977, 1984 Supp.), §2.2. Although *federal* common law nuisance doctrine can provide effective injunctive relief against damaging activities—*Illinois v. City of Milwaukee*, 406 U.S. 91 (1972)—it is likely to apply only in those cases where there is virtually no preexisting congressional legislation. See *Illinois v. City of Milwaukee*, 451 U.S. 304 (1981); *Middlesex Cty. Sewerage Authority v. National Sea Clammers Ass'n.*, 452 U.S. 1 (1981). In the case of the national parks, this may mean that federal nuisance doctrine will apply only in instances of aesthetic or noise intrusions, which, depending on how the concept of an ecosystem is defined, may not qualify as appropriate ecological concerns.[18] Otherwise *state* common law nuisance doctrine applies; and because judicial remedies may be severely limited under state law, this may not adequately protect park interests. See *International Paper Company v. Ouellette*, 107 S. Ct. 805 (1987); see also *United States v. ARCO*, 478 F. Supp. 1215 (D. Mont. 1979) (sustaining a common law trespass action). In addition, park officials might cite a common law public trust responsibility as a basis for challenging threatening adjacent activities. See *Sierra Club v. Dept. of Interior*, 376 F. Supp. 90 (N.D. Cal. 1974). But a more recent court decision suggests that the amended Organic Act has effectively displaced any common law trust responsibility park officials may have. See *Sierra Club v. Andrus*, 487 F. Supp. 443 (D.D.C. 1980); see also Sax (1970) and Wilkinson (1980).

Since the Park Service is unlikely to initiate litigation against another federal agency, these common law remedies are probably useful to it only in cases involving adjacent state or private landowners. (Of course, citizen suits are also available as a means of enforcing these common law doctrines against recalcitrant landowners whose activities threaten park ecological resources). But in this case, the Park Service has the alternative of relying on state environmental and land-use planning laws to encourage ecologically sound land management practices or to challenge harmful activities. Of course, this option would apply only where the state has adopted such legislation, something that many states have not done. However, some states, such as Montana, have adopted state NEPA statutes, while Michigan and others have adopted more rigorous environmental rights statutes. See, for example, Mont. Code Ann. §75-1-101 et seq. (1983); Mich. Comp. Laws Ann. §691.1201 et seq. (West 1983); Minn. Stat. Ann. §116B.01 (1977). Several states have also adopted air and water pollution control legislation setting more stringent standards than the federal statutes. Moreover, some state land-use planning statutes require planning officials to provide specially for "areas of critical concern," often defined as environmentally sensitive lands, which should include ecologically important lands located adjacent to a national park. See, for example, Wyo. Stat. Ann. §9-8-202 (1985). But even in the absence of specific state legislation such as that described here, the Park Service can still participate in local zoning and planning matters. This process affords park officials an opportunity to advance their resource protection concerns, and to demonstrate a connection between the health of the ecosystem and the long-term health of the local economy.

The Forest Service

The Forest Service's multiple-use philosophy creates an inherent tension between its management goals for multiple-use forest lands and its preservation responsibilities for adjacent wilderness areas. For the most part, Congress has not addressed the problem, leaving the agency to reconcile the conflicts on a case-by-case basis. One approach that the Forest Service could adopt to insulate wilderness ecosystems from threatening activities is to recommend that undeveloped surrounding public lands be included in the wilderness preservation system. The NFMA planning process provides a ready opportunity for careful review of the wilderness potential of such lands. Alternatively, the Forest Service might manage its adjacent lands to protect wilderness ecosystems by limiting potentially harmful multiple-use activities. The NFMA plainly affords the Forest Service wide discretion in determining how to manage its lands, and it likewise enjoys broad regulatory authority over activities on its lands. Of course, should the Forest Service open such lands to commodity development, it must still comply with NEPA and other relevant environmental requirements.

Wilderness Classification. Under the NFMA, the Forest Service's wilderness review process has become fragmented. Congress has recently enacted several state wilderness bills designating roadless forest lands as wilderness, and "releasing" the remaining undesignated lands from further wilderness review until the next forest planning phase. In these states, using wilderness classification as a device to promote ecosystem management or to protect already designated wilderness is not an available legal option. But in other states, such as Montana and Idaho, Congress has not yet enacted state wilderness legislation, and the Forest Service is under a NFMA-imposed legal obligation to evaluate all roadless lands for their wilderness potential. See 16 U.S.C. §1604(e)(1); *California v. Block*, 690 F. 2d 753 (9th Cir. 1982). In these states, therefore, the wilderness review process provides an opportunity for forest planners to consider ecosystem characteristics in determining whether roadless lands adjacent to existing wilderness areas should be recommended for preservation or opened to commodity development activities.[19]

Under the NFMA regulations, forest planners are required to evaluate the wilderness potential of all qualifying roadless areas contiguous to existing wilderness or other undeveloped areas. See 36 C.F.R. §219.17(a)(1); see also 16 U.S.C. §1132(b). The regulations also provide that wilderness potential is to be reviewed in terms of the area's wilderness values, proximity to other wilderness areas, plant and animal species diversity, and the effects wilderness management may have on adjacent multiple-use lands; *id.* at §219.17(a)(2)(i)-(v). While these standards certainly suggest that ecological considerations are an important dimension of the wilderness review process, it would infer too much to construe them as mandating evaluation based solely on this criteria. Nonetheless, one court has ruled that the Forest Service must consider the wilderness potential of an area as a whole; it cannot subdivide its lands just because an old jeep road still bisects the area. See *Northwest Indian Protective Ass'n v. Peterson*, 565 F. Supp. 586, 603 (N.D. Cal. 1983), aff'd on other grounds, 795 F. 2d 688 (9th Cir. 1986), rev'd on other grounds, 108 S. Ct. 1319 (1988).

The courts have carefully policed the Forest Service wilderness review process. They have consistently concluded that the Forest Service is obligated under the Wilderness Act and NEPA to maintain the wilderness suitability of its roadless lands until it has finally determined whether to recommend them for wilderness classification. See 16 U.S.C. §1132(b); *Parker v. United States*, 448 F. 2d 793 (10th Cir. 1971); *Northwest Indian Protective Ass'n v. Peterson*, 565 F. Supp. 586 (N.D. Cal. 1983), aff'd 795 F. 2d 688 (9th Cir. 1986), rev'd on other grounds, 108 S. Ct. 1319 (1988); *Getty Oil Co. v. Clark*, 614 F. Supp. 904, 919 (D. Wyo. 1985). Moreover, the courts have indicated that under NEPA, before foreclosing the wilderness option for roadless lands, forest planners must prepare a detailed site-specific analysis of the environmental consequences of nonwilderness management and consider shifting development activities from undeveloped to already developed portions of the forest. See *California v. Block*, 690 F. 2d 753, 764-65 (9th Cir. 1982); *Earth First v. Block*, 569 F. Supp. 415 (D. Ore. 1983). One knowledgeable commentator has noted that the courts have regularly resolved cases challenging the Forest Service's wilderness evaluation and management policies against it, indicating that the courts have assumed an active interventionist posture when wilderness values are at stake (Wilkinson and Anderson 1985:334).

Multiple-Use Management. Once the state wilderness classification review process is completed, the Forest Service is under no clear legal obligation to continue managing roadless multiple-use lands—even those adjacent to existing wilderness—to preserve their wilderness characteristics. Unfortunately, neither the Wilderness Act nor the NFMA answers the question of precisely how the Forest Service should reconcile its existing wilderness management responsibilities with its general multiple-use mandate, particularly when commodity development activities might have an undesirable impact on the natural character of its nearby preserved lands. Indeed, these laws create an apparent quandary for forest managers. Although the Wilderness Act imposes no specific constraints on the use or management of public lands adjacent to designated wilderness areas, it does expressly require the Forest Service to protect its wilderness lands; see 16 U.S.C. §1131(c). The NFMA clearly adopts an environmental perspective toward forest planning, and the Forest Service's implementing regulations specifically endorse the principle of ecosystem planning; see 36 C.F.R. §219.1(b)(3) (1986). However, several recent state wilderness bills use "release" language providing that any lands not included within the designated wilderness areas are to be treated as available for multiple-use purposes. See Wyoming Wilderness Act of 1984, §401(b)(3), 98 Stat. 2812. Moreover, some of these state wilderness acts explicitly preclude the use of buffer zones adjacent to wilderness areas, as does general Forest Service policy. See *id.* at §504, 98 Stat. 2813; *Park County Resource Council v. BLM*, 638 F. Supp. 842, 845 (D. Wyo. 1986); *Forest Service Manual* 2320.3-2 (4186, Amend. 97). Given these evidently conflicting statutory policies, only one conclusion makes much sense: while such lands are available for multiple-use management, the Forest Service is not compelled to open them to intrusive commodity development activities.

Initial Forest Service decisions respecting management of roadless lands adjacent to wilderness areas will be reached in the NFMA forest planning process. The decisions will mostly be reached at a local level, inasmuch as the NFMA envisions forest planning as primarily a local responsibility, consistent with the Forest Service's tradition of decentralized management. As noted earlier, the NFMA imposes certain standards that must be followed. Forest planners must factor both environmental and economic benefits into their determinations, and they must adhere to NEPA requirements, as well as other environmental laws. Moreover, the act imposes substantive constraints on Forest Service timber management practices, which accordingly reduces the agency's discretion. But since the courts have not been called on to interpret the NFMA, it is difficult to know just how much discretion the Forest Service will ultimately enjoy.

A few tentative observations are nevertheless in order. Under NEPA and other environmental laws, such as the Endangered Species Act and the Clean Water Act, the courts have taken a "hard look" at the adequacy of the Forest Service's environmental review of development projects disturbing undeveloped forest lands, not hesitating to overturn agency decisions when its analysis was incomplete. See the cases cited in the preceding section ("Wilderness Classification"). Although most of these cases also involved the wilderness suitability maintenance issue (which is rendered moot once the lands have been "released"), the decision in *Thomas v. Peterson*, 753 F. 2d 754 (9th Cir. 1985), is still relevant. In *Thomas* the Court of Appeals found NEPA and Endangered Species Act violations in the Forest Service's environmental review of a road construction project on "released" multiple-use forest lands adjacent to designated wilderness areas. See also *Wyoming Outdoor Council v. Butz*, 484 F. 2d 1244 (10th Cir. 1973). Because the NFMA itself envisions an integrated forest planning process accounting for all resources, including wilderness, and the NFMA regulations endorse the concept of ecosystem planning, the courts will most likely take a "hard look" at any forest planning decisions demonstrably jeopardizing the environmental integrity of designated wilderness lands. Indeed, recent decisions involving the BLM's FLPMA planning responsibilities indicate that the courts are quite sensitive to environmental considerations when reviewing agency planning decisions. See *American Motorcyclist Ass'n v. Watt*, 534 F. Supp. 923 (C.D. Cal. 1981), aff'd 714 F. 2d 962 (9th Cir. 1983); *American Motorcyclist Ass'n v. Watt*, 543 F. Supp. 789 (C.D. Cal. 1982). But as long as the Forest Service meets its procedural obligations during the environmental review process and is otherwise in compliance with relevant environmental laws, its decision to open an area for commodity development is likely to withstand judicial scrutiny. See *Park County Resource Council v. U.S. Dept. of Agriculture*, 613 F. Supp. 1182 (D. Wyo. 1985); *Park County Resource Council v. BLM*, 638 F. Supp. 842 (D. Wyo. 1986).

One particular issue that has surfaced is the extent to which the Forest Service is obligated in its NFMA planning process to analyze the environmental impact of development activity on roadless lands that have been "released" for multiple-use activities. Apparently some forests have adopted the view that extensive environmental analysis (including discussion of specific development plans, relationship to other forest resources, and cumulative impacts) is called for under the NFMA regulations, while other forests have concluded that no detailed analysis is required, leaving unclear the effect their forest plans will have on these areas. Although Congress has concluded the wilderness review process in several states, the released roadless lands should still receive careful attention in the forest planning process, including consideration of the effect development activities might have on nearby wilderness areas. The "release" language in most state wilderness bills (which is generally identical), as well as the legislative history accompanying the "release" concept, indicates that Congress did not intend to relieve forest planners from complying with NEPA and analyzing the future use of these forest lands, even though they are no longer actively being considered for wilderness designation. Furthermore, the Ninth Circuit's decision in *City of Tenakee Springs v. Block*, 778 F. 2d 1402 (9th Cir. 1985), strongly suggests that congressional "release" language in state wilderness bills should not be construed broadly to relieve the Forest Service of its NEPA responsibilities, including consideration of a "no action" alternative, when contemplating development of roadless forest lands; *id.* at 1406. See "The National Forest Management Act of 1976" (1987). Thus the congressional "release" decision should not be construed as obviating the Forest Service's responsibility to consider the ecological implications multiple-use development could have on adjacent or nearby wilderness areas.

While the NFMA planning process is now establishing the standards (actually the "law") governing resource use in the national forests for the next ten to fifteen years, the Forest Service must still comply with federal environmental laws when it considers specific development projects. As has been the case, NEPA will almost certainly continue setting the procedural requisites for Forest Service decision making, generally requiring site-specific analysis of proposals involving roadless forest lands. See, for example, *Thomas v. Peterson*, 753 F. 2d 754 (9th Cir. 1985); *Park County Resource Council v. BLM*, 638 F. Supp. 842 (D. Wyo. 1986). Critical issues will most likely involve whether or not to prepare an EIS, whether the forest plan EIS has substantially modified the agency's subsequent NEPA review obligations, whether relevant statutory environmental constraints have been sufficiently considered and met, and whether cumulative impacts likely to result from the project have been adequately addressed. See the section "Federal Environmental Laws" above. State law may also impose environmental constraints that must be met before development proceeds. See *California Coastal Comm'n. v. Granite Rock Company*, 107 S. Ct. 1419 (1987).

Once a project is authorized, it is still subject to substantive requirements imposed by applicable environmental protection statutes. Forest Service monitoring programs, as well as the threat of administrative or judicial enforcement proceedings initiated by the responsible agency or citizen suit, ensure a reasonable degree of compliance with laws like the Clean Water Act or the Endangered Species Act. Hence, even after the forest plan has set the general direction for management of specific roadless lands, the Forest Service still has an opportunity to undertake further, more detailed environmental review of specific proposals and to implement appropriate monitoring programs. Needless to say, the Forest Service can also always rely on its general regulatory authority to control multiple-use activities threatening forest resources. See the section on the Forest Service under the heading "Managing the Preserved Lands" above. In addition, the FLPMA granted the Forest Service authority to control access to the forest lands, and it specifically mentions environmental concerns as a primary consideration in road construction decisions; see 43 U.S.C. §§1763, 1765.

Other Adjacent Lands. Whenever Forest Service wilderness areas face ecological damage from activities occurring on adjacent lands owned or managed by someone else, the Forest Service is in virtually the same legal position as the Park Service when it seeks to address external threat problems. Under the language of the Wilderness Act, the Forest Service's wilderness protection responsibility appears comparable to the Park Service's §1a-1 responsibility under the amended Organic Act. Therefore, whether and how the

Forest Service responds to development activities threatening its wilderness lands is potentially subject to judicial review under an abuse of discretion standard. See *Sierra Club v. Andrus*, 487 F. Supp. 443, 449-50 (D.D.C. 1980) (reviewing Park Service actions under the abuse of discretion standard). The Forest Service can rely on the same legal tools and opportunities available to the Park Service as a means of influencing adjacent federal, state, or private landowners to protect wilderness areas, or of encouraging joint ecosystem management efforts. As a practical matter, therefore, its strategic options include participating in land-use planning activities or environmental review proceedings, negotiating with its neighbors to mitigate harmful impacts, or even litigating in extreme cases. How effective the Forest Service is in using these options will, of course, depend on the above-noted federal and state environmental or land use planning laws, as well as its own resolve in overcoming political obstacles and bureaucratic inertia.

CONCLUSION

Public land law only generally addresses the notion of ecosystem management, a concept that does not fit neatly our traditional, boundary-oriented system of public land management. Few of our "preserved" lands are defined in terms of their ecological characteristics, and they are not infrequently bordered by multiple-use lands open to commodity development activities. This means that the organic laws governing our national park and wilderness systems are inevitably in tension with the organic laws governing management of these adjacent public lands. Consequently, decisions like the original Hall Creek leasing decision tend to be reviewed in isolation, without regard to the larger ecological ramifications such a proposal could have on nearby park and wilderness resources.

Some change is evident, however. The recent NFMA and FLPMA statutes have revised multiple-use management policies, requiring an integrated planning process coordinated with adjacent land management agencies. Both statutes commit the public land management agencies to environmental protection as a primary responsibility, and the implementing regulations endorse the concept of ecosystem management. However, neither statute purports to resolve the underlying preservation-development conflict, leaving public land managers with apparent discretion to resolve the issue on a case-by-case basis.

But agency officials do not enjoy unlimited discretion. General federal environmental protection laws impose some significant constraints on public land managers, representing a clear national commitment to environmental protection on the multiple-use public lands. NEPA establishes a rigorous procedural framework for agency decision making, obligating officials to review the environmental impact of major federal projects. Other laws (such as the Clean Water Act, the Clean Air Act, and the Endangered Species Act) establish specific environmental standards that agency officials must observe, hence ensuring a certain degree of protection for key elements of any ecosystem. Moreover, the courts have intervened in public land management controversies to ensure compliance with these statutory mandates. While consistently endorsing the notion of managerial discretion, the courts have nevertheless overturned agency decisions not reflecting sufficient sensitivity to environmental considerations, particularly when wilderness values have been threatened.

Although the law does not completely protect the ecological integrity of designated park and wilderness lands, it does support ecosystem planning as a legitimate management prerogative, especially when the recent NFMA and FLPMA legislation is read collectively with the environmental protection laws. Thus public land managers have the apparent authority to implement the concept of natural ecosystem management on multiple-use lands surrounding park and wilderness areas. Viewed from this perspective, then, the Hall Creek case might have been approached quite differently.

NOTES

1. Technically, the Bureau of Land Management has final responsibility for mineral leasing on the public lands; but when the proposal involves Forest Service lands, the BLM regularly defers to the Forest Service's recommendations. Memorandum of Understanding, Bureau of Land Management and Forest Service 3 (1980). See Wilkinson and Anderson (1985:262). Congress has, however, recently given the Forest Service authority over mineral leasing decisions on its own lands: 100-203, Sec. 5102(h); 101 Stat. 1330-258 (1987).

2. The National Park Service, the U.S. Fish and Wildlife Service, and the Montana Department of Fish and Game have all expressed reservations about various features of the proposals, agreeing generally that development is likely to have an adverse impact on the wilderness character of the region and wildlife habitat.

3. Although the BLM is also a principal federal land management agency responsible for wilderness acreage, as well as vast multiple-use lands, this paper will not address the BLM's legal responsibilities as a wilderness manager. Its wilderness management experience is limited, and its wilderness responsibilities under the Federal Land Policy and Management Act of 1976 (FLPMA), 43 U.S.C. §§1701-1784, are just being established. Moreover, since the BLM is a multiple-use agency like the Forest Service, the laws governing the Forest Service generally also apply to the BLM, except when the FLPMA dictates otherwise. I will, however, note similarities and differences between the legal missions and responsibilities of the two agencies when appropriate.

4. The paper does not address specific legal issues arising under the Alaska National Interest Lands Conservation Act (ANILCA), 16 U.S.C. §3101 et seq., which governs management of park and wilderness lands in Alaska. Two points are worth noting, however. First, the ANILCA legislation is specifically intended to preserve and protect the ecological resources and scenic values associated with these lands—*id.* at §3101(b)—while also compatibly integrating traditional human uses (i.e., subsistence hunting and fishing) into the park and wilderness concept; *id.* at §3101(c). Second, the legal requirements and standards established by environmental statutes like the NEPA, the Endangered Species Act, and the Clean Water Act, as outlined in this paper, also apply to public land managers in Alaska, and therefore limit their discretionary authority.

5. The same is true of the BLM with the passage of the FLPMA, which parallels the National Forest Management Act of 1976 (NFMA) multiple-use philosophy. Both statutes specifically endorse wilderness as a legitimate multiple use and establish a wilderness review process. See notes 9 and 19 below for a more detailed comparison of the FLPMA and NFMA.

6. The *Redwood* litigation consists of a trilogy of court decisions. In *Redwood I* the district court held that the secretary of the interior had a legal duty to protect park resources from adjacent logging activities. See 376 F. Supp. 90 N.D. Cal. 1974). *Redwood II* found that the secretary had breached this legal duty, and ordered him to take steps to protect the park. See 398 F. Supp. 284 (N.D. Cal. 1975). Finally, in *Redwood III* the court dismissed the suit, finding that effective relief required congressional action—something the court had no authority to order. See 424 F. Supp 172 (N.D. Cal. 1976). Also see, generally, Hudson (1978).

7. Moreover, in *Sierra Club v. Andrus*, 487 F. Supp. 443, 449 (D.D.C. 1980), the court rejected the argument that the Park Service has a common law public trust duty to protect the parks from environmental damage, ruling that §1a-1 had displaced any such doctrine. The case is generally regarded as having effectively undermined the *Redwood I* common law trust duty holding.

8. During 1976 when it adopted the NFMA, Congress also amended the Resources Planning Act, obligating forest officials to provide in their planning for "the fundamental need to protect, and where appropriate, improve the quality of soil, water, and air resources"; see 16 U.S.C. §1602(5)(c). The obligation to protect these resources is not boundary limited.

9. Similar observations may be made respecting the FLPMA, which now serves as the BLM's organic legislation. As with the NFMA, the FLPMA contemplates multiple-use management based on a comprehensive planning process requiring consideration of multiple factors, several of which reflect environmental concerns; see 43 U.S.C. §1732(a). The concept of "multiple use" is defined to include "recreation, range, timber, minerals, watershed, wildlife and fish, and natural scenic, scientific, and historical values"; *id.* at §1702(c). The statute prohibits multiple-use activities that might permanently impair "the productivity of the land and the quality of the environment," and it specifically instructs against management based on the "greatest economic return." Moreover, the FLPMA requires the BLM to give priority to the designation and protection of areas requiring special protection to preserve "important historic, cultural, or scenic values, fish and wildlife resources or other natural systems or processes"; *id.* at §1712(c)(3), §1702(a). And finally, the FLPMA establishes a wilderness review process similar to the one implemented by the Forest Service; *id.* at §1782. See note 19 below.

10. The act also refers to "wilderness" as an area "which (1) generally appears to have been affected primarily by the forces of nature, with the imprint of man's work substantially unnoticeable; (2) has outstanding opportunities for solitude or a primitive and unconfined type of recreation; (3) has at least five thousand acres of land or is of sufficient size as to make practicable its preservation and use in an unimpaired condition; and (4) may also contain ecological, geological, or other features of scientific, educational, scenic, or historical value"; 16 U.S.C. §1131(c).

11. The courts have not construed the Endangered Species Act to require the Fish and Wildlife Service to base its opinion on irrefutable, "iron-clad" data. Some uncertainty respecting the impact of a project will not open the biological opinion to challenge. See *North Slope Borough v. Andrus*, 642 F. 2d 589, 610 n. 131 (D.C. Cir. 1982).

12. See also 16 U.S.C. §1539(a) (providing for habitat conservation plans as another means of regulating the impact of development on "listed" species found on either public or private lands); *Friends of Endangered Species v. Jantzen*, 760 F. 2d 976 (9th Cir. 1985). See, generally, "Habitat Conservation Plans . . ." (1987).

13. Other laws also provide some additional protection to park and wilderness water resources. The NFMA contains substantive provisions designed to protect water quality within the national forests from adverse consequences associated with timber harvesting. See 16 U.S.C. §1604(g)(3)(E)(i)(iii); 36 C.F.R. §219.27(e), §219.19 (1986). In addition, a federal district court, relying on the Wilderness Act, has ruled that federal reserved water rights must be recognized for wilderness areas, meaning that such areas are legally entitled to receive a sufficient water flow to maintain their natural integrity. See *Sierra Club v. Block*, 622 F. Supp. 842 (D. Col. 1985). Moreover, if no statutory provisions cover a pollution problem, it may still be possible to maintain a legal challenge based on common law nuisance principles. See the section "Other Legal Alternatives" below.

14. This problem may arise because wilderness managers are confronted with two fundamentally conflicting philosophical approaches to wilderness management issues. They may adopt an anthropocentric view, and manage wilderness to facilitate human use of it; or they may opt for a

biocentric view, managing wilderness to maintain natural systems, regardless of the impact on human access or use. See, generally, Hendee et al. (1978).

15. A good deal of scholarly attention has been devoted recently to the topic of how the Park Service might legally deal with its "external threats" problem. See Sax (1976), Keiter (1985), and "Protecting National Parks . . . " (1984).

16. See Keiter (1985:369-375) and Lemons and Stout (1984:42). But see also U.S. General Accounting Office (1987), concluding that the §1a-1 language and legislative history are ambiguous, and setting forth the contrary arguments.

17. The Hall Creek case provides a good illustration of how Park Service comments on environmental review documents can prove important if the matter is litigated. Glacier officials did not clearly express opposition to the Forest Service decision authorizing the well just beyond the park boundary. Consequently, when environmental groups appealed the decision to the Interior Board of Land Appeals, the board rejected their NEPA claim that the Forest Service had not adequately considered the project's proximity to the park, noting that the Park Service had not objected. See *Glacier-Two Medicine Alliance et al.*, 88 IBLA 133, 141-43 (1985).

18. But see 16 U.S.C. §1604(g)(3)(F)(iii); 36 C.F.R. §§219.12(g)(i), 219.21(f) (legitimating forest visual resources as a factor in the NFMA forest planning process); 43 U.S.C. §1702(c) (including scenic values as a multiple use under FLPMA).

19. The FLPMA has established a BLM wilderness review process similar to the one established in the NFMA for the Forest Service. The BLM lands are to be evaluated for wilderness on the basis of the criteria set forth in the Wilderness Act, and once designated as wilderness are to be managed accordingly; see 43 U.S.C. §1782(b). During the review process, the secretary of the interior is required to continue managing BLM roadless lands to preserve their suitability for inclusion in the wilderness system; *id.* at §1782(c). The FLPMA, like the NFMA, provides no definitive guidance respecting management of multiple-use lands adjacent to wilderness lands. The act does, however, provide for "coordinated management" taking account of environmental factors, and it also requires special attention to "areas of critical environmental concern," which includes protecting "scenic values" and "natural systems or processes"; *id.* at §1702(a), (c). Thus Congress plainly intends for the BLM to preserve and protect unique roadless lands as wilderness; and it has given the BLM sufficient discretion under the FLPMA so that it can integrate ecosystem-based management principles into its planning process, and protect its wilderness (or roadless) lands against incompatible development activities occurring on adjacent public lands. But Congress's continued commitment to the multiple-use management principle also suggests that the BLM is under no legal obligation to rely exclusively on environmental concerns in setting its agenda.

LITERATURE CITED

Gray, B. E. 1988. No holier temples: Protecting the national parks through wild and scenic river designation. University of Colorado Law Review 58(3):551-598.

Habitat conservation plans under the Endangered Species Act. 1987. San Diego Law Review 24(1):243-271 (Comments section).

Hendee, J. C., G. H. Stankey, and R. C. Lucas. 1978. Wilderness management. USDA For. Serv. Misc. Pub. 1365.

Hiscock, J. W. 1986. Protecting National Park System buffer zones: Existing, proposed, and suggested authority. Journal of Energy Law and Policy 7(1):35-93.

Hudson, D. A. 1978. *Sierra Club v. Department of Interior:* The fight to preserve Redwood National Park. Ecology Law Quarterly 7(3):781-859.

Keiter, R. B. 1985. On protecting the national parks from the external threats dilemma. Land and Water Law Review 20(2):355-420.

Lemons, J., and D. Stout. 1984. A reinterpretation of national park legislation. Environmental Law 15(1):41-65.

Mott, W. 1985. Twelve point management plan. USDI National Park Service.

Protecting national parks from developments beyond their borders. 1984. University of Pennsylvania Law Review 132(5):1189-1216 (Comments section).

Rogers, W. 1977, 1984 Supp. Environmental Law. West Publ. Co., St. Paul.

Sax, J. L. 1970. The public trust doctrine in natural resource law: Effective judicial intervention. Michigan Law Review 68:471-566.

———. 1976. Helpless giants: The national parks and the regulation of private lands. Michigan Law Review 75:239-274.

Sax, J., and R. Keiter. 1987. Glacier National Park and its neighbors: A case study of federal interagency relations. Ecology Law Quarterly 14:206-263.

The National Forest Management Act of 1976: A critical look at two trees in the NFMA forest. 1987. Land and Water Law Review 22:413-431.

U.S. Congress, House Committee on Interior and Insular Affairs. 1985. Impact of air pollution on national park units. In Hearings before Subcommittee on National Parks and Recreation. 99th Cong., 1st sess., pp. 371-401 (U.S. Dept. of the Interior Solicitor's Office Legal Memorandum dated Sept. 10, 1985).

U.S. General Accounting Office. 1987. Limited progress made in documenting and mitigating threats to the parks. In Report to the Chairman, Subcommittee on National Parks and Recreation, Committee on Interior and Insular Affairs, U.S. House of Representatives, pp. 51-57.

Wilkinson, C. F. 1980. The public trust doctrine in public land law. U.C. Davis Law Review 14(2):269-316.

Wilkinson, C. F., and H. M. Anderson. 1985. Land and resource planning in the national forests. Oregon Law Review 64(1&2):1-373.

Yellowstone National Park Master Plan. 1973. USDI National Park Service.

3

Vegetation History and Anticipating Future Vegetation Change

LINDA B. BRUBAKER

ABSTRACT Over the past two decades numerous paleoecological records have become available for describing past plant communities. They show that vegetation has changed on almost all temporal and spatial scales in response to natural environmental variation. Because species have responded individualistically to climatic variations, plant communities have been transient assemblages, seldom persisting more than 2,000 to 5,000 years in the fossil record. Plant communities of the last ice age typically do not have counterparts on the modern landscape, and plant species dominating present-day vegetation were exceedingly rare during the last ice age. Because glacial periods are much longer than interglacials, these records suggest that modern species were selected under much different conditions than exist today. Most of the tree species dominating North America today became common 8,000 to 10,000 years ago, when they expanded rapidly from ice-age refugia. Most species spread at different rates and in different directions, reaching their current range limits and populations only about 3,000 to 5,000 years ago. Thus present-day North American forests are relatively recent assemblages and should not be considered stable over evolutionary time scales. Although vegetation change in recent centuries is less extreme than over longer periods, numerous studies at major vegetation ecotones show significant changes in recruitment and survival in the recent past. The response of species to climatic variations over decades and centuries depends primarily on the direction and magnitude of the climatic change, life history of the species, and effects of disturbances. The most important implication of paleoecological records to managers of national parks and wilderness areas is that these areas are dynamic systems that continuously change even in the absence of human activity. It may be unrealistic, therefore, to assume that a given area should be maintained in a condition similar to a particular time in the past. It is also probably unrealistic to think that future vegetation changes can be precisely anticipated from observation of present vegetation.

Concern over increasing concentrations of carbon dioxide and other trace atmospheric gases has heightened interest in global climatic change. Although the effect of rising carbon dioxide on twentieth-century climate is debated, most investigators agree that climatic change in the twenty-first century is inevitable if carbon dioxide concentrations increase at projected rates (MacCracken and Luther 1985). This realization has prompted speculation about vegetation responses to future climates. Many possible vegetation responses to CO_2-induced climatic change have been suggested, ranging from modest shifts in the productivity of intact communities (Kaupp and Posch 1985) to large-scale alterations in species ranges (Leverenz and Lev 1988). The realization that the environment of future centuries may be different from the present one also has important policy implications for managing national parks and wilderness areas.

Paleoecological data broaden the data base for anticipating vegetation responses to future change by revealing community and species responses to climatic variations over longer periods than are recorded by human documents. Records of the past cannot provide precise descriptions of vegetation responses to given climatic scenarios, because information on past environments and vegetations is imprecise. Nevertheless, they provide invaluable data for understanding how vegetation responds to climatic change (e.g., rates of population growth and decline, dynamics of range boundaries, integrity of species associations).

Knowledge of North American vegetation history has increased dramatically during the past two decades, and several recent review volumes provide excellent summaries (Porter 1983, Wright 1983, Bryant and Halloway 1985). The composition of ice-age communities is known in many parts of North America, and in some areas information is sufficiently detailed to map the rate and direction of species movements following deglaciation (Davis 1981, Webb 1981, Ritchie and McDonald 1986, Anderson et al., in review). Besides revealing the origin of modern forest associations, such information provides an important data base for assessing the temporal and spatial characteristics of vegetation responses to climate.

Of particular interest to managers of national parks and wilderness areas, the paleoecological record reveals that ecotones between major biomes are most sensitive to climatic change. National parks and wilderness areas include representatives of most of the important ecotones in North America: for example, forest-prairie, Yellowstone National Park, Theodore Roosevelt National Park; forest-alpine tundra, North Cascades National Park/Wilderness, Olympic National Park; forest-arctic tundra, Denali National Park, Gates of the Arctic National Park; and forest-desert, Grand Canyon National Park, Saguaro National Monument. The sensitivity of ecotonal areas suggests that national parks and wilderness areas may be among the first and most severely affected by future climatic changes. Future vegetation changes will also undoubtedly affect the wildlife use and aesthetic value of these landscapes.

The general understanding of vegetation responses to climate must consider the time scales of climatic variations relative to the length of species life spans. Climate varies over different periods depending on the temporal characteristics of major controlling factors. Similarly, the mechanisms by which plants respond to climatic change vary depending on the length of their life spans relative to such variations. Many adjustments to changing conditions can be made only between generations. For example, genetic change most often occurs when offsprings are selected under conditions different from those encountered by their parents. Rates of change in species range limits also depend on inherent life spans, as well as reproduction, dispersal, and disturbance characteristics (Brubaker 1986, Davis 1986, Ritchie 1986).

This chapter discusses the implications of North American vegetation history for future vegetation change. These implications are discussed with respect to three time scales of variation: (1) *Long-term variations (10,000 to 100,000 years):* These variations represent changes between glacial and interglacial climates. For tree species, such variations may include as many as 500 generations. Vegetation responses over such long periods involve major displacements in species ranges and undoubtedly result in genetic adjustment through natural selection. (2) *Intermediate-term variations (2,000 to 5,000 years):* These variations, corresponding to five to twenty-five tree generations, represent major variations within glacial and interglacial periods. Species respond by range adjustments, although some evolutionary change is still possible. (3) *Short-term variations (up to 500 years):* Short-term variations occur within the life span of a single individual. Established plants make phenotypic adjustments by altering physiological or morphological characters. Reproduction and establishment rates may also be profoundly affected, sometimes resulting in compositional changes in the vegetation.

LONG-TERM VARIATIONS

Glaciers advanced and retreated over the North American continent many times during the last two million years. The best records of the magnitude and timing of glacial and interglacial episodes come from sediments of the deep oceans (Bradley 1985). These sediment records reveal variations in stable isotopes of oxygen and changes in composition of planktonic communities, which can be interpreted in terms of ocean temperatures and ice cap volumes.

According to the deep sea records (Figure 3-1, Davis 1986), glacial periods (50,000 to

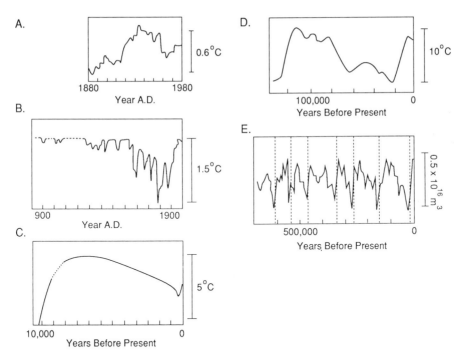

Figure 3-1. Temperature changes in the Northern Hemisphere for different time scales (after Davis 1986): (A) instrumental data for annual temperature, latitudes 23.6-90°N, (B) air temperature during the past 1,000 years reconstructed from accounts of sea ice, (C) annual temperature in northeastern United States over the past 10,000 inferred from fossil pollen data, (D) annual temperature over the past 100,000 years in Europe reconstructed from records of vegetation, sea level changes, and planktonic and geochemical changes in deep sea sediments, and (E) global ice volumes inferred from oxygen isotope variations in deep sea sediments.

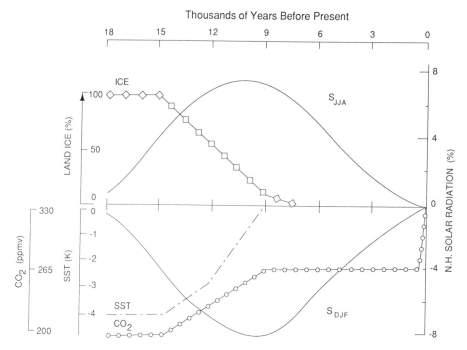

Figure 3-2. Major changes in external forcing factors and internal boundary conditions of the earth's climate since 18,000 years ago (after Kutzbach and Guetter 1986). S_{JJA}, S_{DJF}: Northern Hemispheric solar radiation in June-August and December-February, respectively, as percentage difference from the present; land ice as percentage of the present. SST: global mean sea surface temperature as departure from the present.

100,000 years) are generally much longer than interglacial periods (10,000 to 20,000 years) (Bradley 1985). The end of glacial episodes is often characterized by very cold conditions, and transitions from glacial to interglacial climates are typically abrupt. The current interglacial, called the Holocene, began about 10,000 years ago and is considered to be one of the warmest periods in the past two million years.

Shifts between glacial and interglacial conditions are controlled by changes in major boundary conditions of the earth's climate system (Figure 3-2, Kutzbach and Guetter 1986). The primary controls are changes in the earth's orbital parameters, which determine the intensity and latitudinal distribution of solar radiation reaching the earth's surface. The effects of radiation are modified by sea surface temperatures, continental and oceanic ice masses, and atmospheric aerosols. Current models of global circulation indicate the complexity of past climatic change (Kutzbach and Guetter 1986). Glacial and interglacial periods did not cause a simple north-south shift in climatic zones. Temperature and precipitation varied independently, and seasonal climates did not change in unison. As a result, many climates that occurred in the past do not exist today. Similarly, conditions that exist today may not have occurred in the past.

During the last ice age, glaciers covered most of Canada and northern portions of the United States (Figure 3-3, Nilsson 1983) (Porter 1983). The distribution and composition of North American vegetation showed little resemblance to modern conditions (Davis 1976, Delcourt and Delcourt 1984, Spaulding et al. 1983, Ager and Brubaker 1985). In eastern North America, a small band of tundra bordered the ice sheet (Figure 3-4, Delcourt

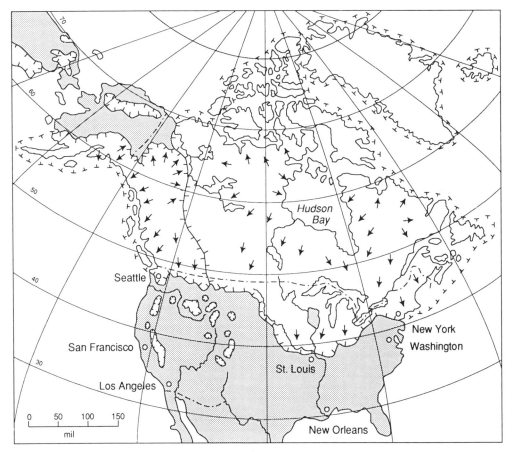

Figure 3-3. Extent of continental glaciers in North America during the last ice age (after Nilsson 1983). Arrows indicate direction of ice movement.

and Delcourt 1984) (Davis 1976, Delcourt and Delcourt 1984). To the south, a broad zone of conifer forest characterized by white spruce or jack pine covered most of the southeastern United States. Although boreal in character, the predominant species combinations in these forests differed from those of modern boreal forests. Farther to the south, this forest changed abruptly to oak, hickory, and southern pines. This steep vegetation gradient was presumably controlled by a persistent west-to-east airflow across the area during the full glacial. The modern gradient between boreal and deciduous forests is much more gradual and is associated with seasonal shifts in north-south airflows across the region. Another important contrast between modern and full-glacial times is that mesic deciduous forest species (e.g., beech, maple, basswood) common on the modern landscape were exceedingly rare during the full glacial (Delcourt and Delcourt 1984).

In western North America, woodlands of bristlecone pine, limber pine, and Engelmann spruce covered most of the area north of approximately 34°N latitude (Figure 3-5) (Spaulding et al. 1983). Shadscale, a species growing only below the tree line today, was also an important constituent of these woodland communities. Areas south of 34°N latitude were dominated by piñon pine and juniper woodlands. However, the

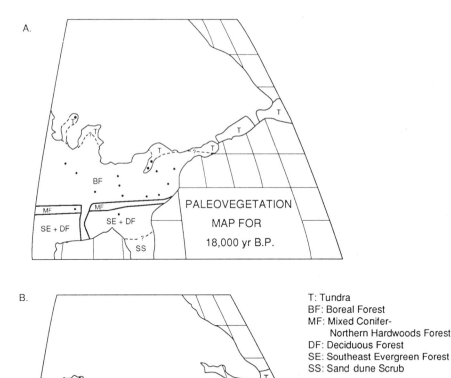

A.

PALEOVEGETATION
MAP FOR
18,000 yr B.P.

B.

T: Tundra
BF: Boreal Forest
MF: Mixed Conifer-
    Northern Hardwoods Forest
DF: Deciduous Forest
SE: Southeast Evergreen Forest
SS: Sand dune Scrub

PALEOVEGETATION
MAP FOR
14,000 yr B.P.

Figure 3-4. Major features of the vegetation in eastern North America during the last ice age based on fossil pollen percentages (after Delcourt and Delcourt 1984). Coastline represents sea level 100 meters lower than present. Dots indicate locations of pollen sites.

predominant juniper and piñon pine species of the ice-age communities are minor constituents of the modern piñon pine-juniper communities (Van Devender 1986). As in the eastern United States, most major forest types of the modern landscape were rare during the last ice age.

A general theme therefore arises from studies of full-glacial vegetation: species that dominate the modern landscape occurred in much smaller populations and in different species combinations during the full glacial. Paleoecologists discuss this as the "no analog problem," since there are generally no modern communities that serve as analogs (matches) for ancient communities (Birks and Birks 1980, Birks 1981). The lack of modern analogs makes it difficult to reconstruct glacial climates from biological evidence.

The disparity between modern and glacial vegetation suggests fundamental differen-

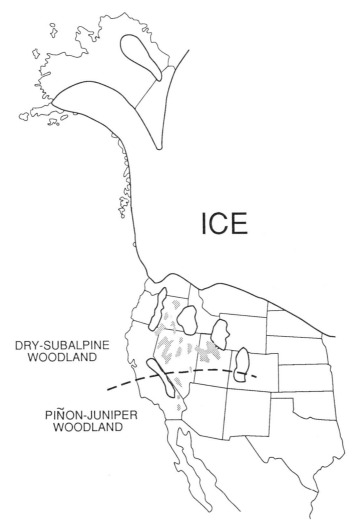

Figure 3-5. Major features of the vegetation in western North America during the last ice age based on plant fragments found in packrat middens.

ces between modern and glacial climates. Global climatic models, which are based on physical boundary conditions, also indicate very different conditions during the full glacial (Kutzbach and Guetter 1986). Plant and animal species, therefore, have not been able to escape climatic change by simply migrating within zones of stable climate that have been merely displaced geographically. One must assume that during the long ice ages, species experienced selection under climatic and competitive environments different from those of interglacials. The effect of glacial periods is evident in modern populations, since the genetic variation of many North American conifers is thought to reflect their glacial as well as modern environments (Critchfield 1978).

Continental ice sheets began to recede about 18,000 years ago, with the most rapid recession occurring over a period of about 3,000 years (Bradley 1985). The rapid disappearance of ice was apparently caused by a strong peak in summer insolation approximately 11,000 to 9,000 years ago. At this time populations of many trees increased

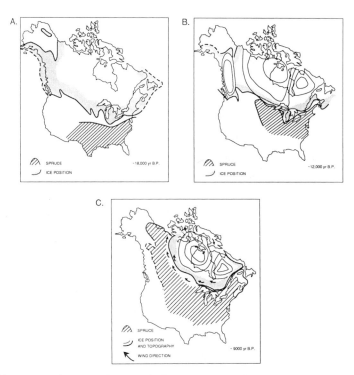

Figure 3-6. Changes in the range limits of white spruce in North America at 18,000, 12,000, and 9,000 years ago (after Ritchie and MacDonald 1986).

HOLOCENE VEGETATIONAL HISTORY OF THE EASTERN UNITED STATES

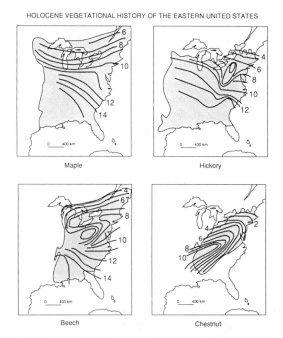

Figure 3-7. Changes in the range limits of four deciduous tree taxa during the late glacial and early Holocene. Isolines indicate range limits at different times in the past (1,000 year intervals) (after Davis 1981).

dramatically. Spruce forests moved northward and westward from the east-central United States into Canada and Alaska (Figure 3-6, Ritchie and MacDonald 1986). The estimated rates of spruce migration are remarkable (2 km/yr). Deciduous tree species also moved northward rapidly (300 to 800 m/yr), and many of the modern forest dominants became important on the landscape (Figure 3-7, Davis 1981). Similarly, vegetation was changing rapidly in western North America. Many of the dominant species of modern conifer forests (e.g., ponderosa pine) became common for the first time during this period (Spaulding et al. 1983).

In summary, the ice-age vegetation of North America was markedly different from the present-day vegetation. Most modern forest types did not exist in the past, and many of the most important forest species of today's forests were rare. Thus modern communities should not be thought of as highly coevolved complexes of species bound together by tightly linked and balanced interactions. Modern communities have not had long histories, and the species rather than the community should be the focus when considering the consequences of future environmental change. Historical records show that species can expand rapidly as climate becomes less limiting; they also suggest that species that are rare on the modern landscape have potential for becoming common under changed climates (and vice versa).

INTERMEDIATE-TERM VARIATIONS

Variations within glacial and interglacial periods, although less pronounced than those between glacial extremes (Figure 3-1), cause major changes in the composition of plant communities. Climatic variations over these time spans are also caused by changes in the same boundary conditions that control shifts between glacial and interglacial periods (Kutzbach and Guetter 1986). For example, high latitude areas of North America experienced warmer climate during the early to mid-Holocene because the extreme angle of tilt in the earth's axis caused a peak in summer insolation at northern latitudes.

Most of the information about vegetation during the present interglacial comes from pollen grains preserved in lake and bog sediments (Birks and Birks 1980, Faegri and Iversen 1975). In eastern North America (Davis 1981, Webb 1981) and northwestern Canada (Ritchie 1984) and Alaska (Anderson and Brubaker, in press) pollen data have been compiled in the form of maps showing temporal changes in the abundance and distribution of major plant taxa during the Holocene. Similar maps are available for Europe (Huntley and Birks 1983). All reveal the individualistic nature of species responses to Holocene climatic change. The major taxa of present-day forests in these regions generally became common during the early Holocene. However, most modern forest associations did not arise until the last half of the Holocene, when species reached their current range limits and populations (Figure 3-7, Davis 1981, Webb 1981). As an example, the northern hardwood forest of the Great Lakes region appeared approximately 5,000 years ago, when eastern hemlock and American beech first invaded forests dominated by eastern white pine and sugar maple (Davis et al. 1986). Available evidence therefore suggests that plants responded to Holocene climatic change according to their unique physiological, reproductive, and ecological characteristics. Thus, like the full-glacial record, the Holocene records shows little evidence that plant communities behave discretely in response to climatic changes.

A pollen diagram for Lake Washington (Figure 3-8) (Leopold et al. 1982) serves as an

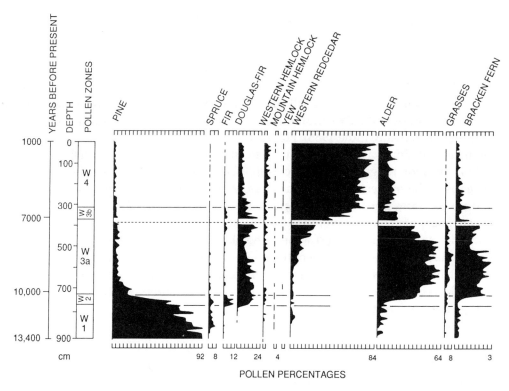

Figure 3-8. Pollen record in sediment core from Lake Washington, Washington State (after Leopold et al. 1982). Pollen percentages are plotted according to depth in sediment.

example for considering the implications of Holocene vegetation history. It is typical of most Holocene pollen sequences in North America, as it shows three major periods of differing vegetation composition. Terrestrial vegetation near Lake Washington began about 13,500 years ago. The new landscape supported an open vegetation of tundra and scattered trees or tree clumps. The most important tree species at that time were probably Engelmann spruce, lodgepole pine, mountain hemlock, and subalpine fir.

Vegetation of the Puget Sound basin changed abruptly about 10,000 years ago, when pollen of Douglas-fir, red alder, grasses, and spores of bracken fern became common. Concentrations of charcoal fragments in lake sediments of the region increased at that time, indicating an increase in fire frequency. The period is interpreted as warmer and drier than the present. The landscape may have been partly open because of frequent fires, and forested areas were presumably dominated by Douglas-fir in early stages of succession.

Modern forest communities of the Puget Sound basin became established 7,000 to 5,000 years ago, as evidenced by a dramatic increase in the pollen of western redcedar. Most pollen records in this area show decreases in Douglas-fir and increases in western hemlock pollen at that time. Charcoal concentrations in sediments also decreased, and presumably fires became less frequent. These changes mark the beginning of the western hemlock zone (Franklin and Dyrness 1973) in the Puget Sound area. Mature forests in this zone are characterized by scattered, large Douglas-fir dating from stand initiation, with abundant western hemlock in both the overstory and understory. Western redcedar is also common, especially on wetter sites. This was apparently a new assemblage in the Pacific Northwest 5,000 years ago, as there is no evidence of that community type existing in the region or elsewhere before then. The dominance of very old and large trees, which characterizes Pacific Northwest forests today (Waring and Franklin 1979), probably developed at that time.

Records of conifer needles in small lakes on the south flanks of Mount Rainier suggest that modern forests of the Cascade Range were established even more recently than those in the lowlands (Dunwiddie 1986). Figure 3-9 shows a record of conifer leaf accumulation in Jay Bath Pond, a small pond at 700 m on Mount Rainier. To the left is plotted the modern elevation ranges of each species shown in the sediment profile. If observations of species in the modern landscape accurately predict species behavior over time, one would expect trees to increase and decrease in the sediment record in the same order that they are encountered on an elevational transect in these mountains today. This is clearly not the case. Douglas-fir and western hemlock, which characterize lower elevation forests today, display very different histories. In contrast, Douglas-fir and Pacific silver fir, which have different site requirements in modern forests, show generally similar histories. The record of forests at this site, therefore, does not represent a simple displacement of modern forest zones.

The data from Mount Rainier indicate that field observations of plant-environment relationships may not always agree with data from the past, suggesting that modern studies provide incomplete knowledge of species behavior over time. Since major evolutionary change is unlikely during the Holocene, species in modern forests are probably capable of more interactions than we can measure in today's environment.

In summary, the dominant species of present-day North American forests became common during the early Holocene, but modern forest communities did not arise until the middle to late Holocene. Since the possibility of evolutionary change in relatively

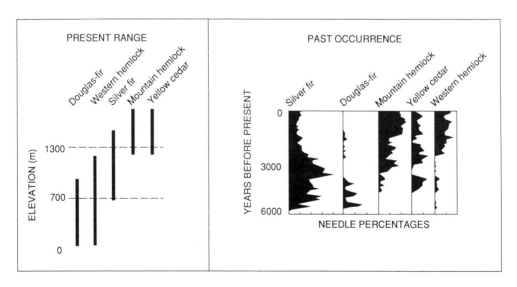

Figure 3-9. Elevation range of major conifer species in the western Cascade Mountains shown on the left. On the right, percentages of leaf fragments of the same conifer species plotted against depth in sediment core from Jay Bath Pond, Mount Rainier National Park (after Dunwiddie 1986).

long-lived tree species is minimal over the Holocene, one must conclude that the genetic makeup of species on the modern landscape reflects a wider range of selective environments than exists today. Thus modern species may be capable of more environmental relationships than can be deduced from observing the modern landscape, and observations of the modern landscape may be inadequate for predicting vegetation responses to future environmental change.

SHORT-TERM VARIATIONS

Climatic variations within the life spans of trees include seasonal, annual, decadal, and century-long periods. Adult trees must adjust to such variations phenotypically. The physiological and morphological plasticity of trees is well known, and the importance of such responses to survival is obvious when one considers the effect of the phenotypic response of deciduous tree species to shifts between summer and winter climates. Phenotypic adjustments to decadal and longer climatic variations are less obvious but have been documented in the literature, as described below. Such variations also alter reproductive and establishment rates. They are likely to cause greater mortality in the seedling stage than in adult stages.

Evidence of Short-term Climatic Variations

Short-term climatic variations are documented by historical records (Lamb 1972, Schneider and Londer 1984), instrumental climatic data (Jones et al. 1982), evidence of glacial activity (Porter 1983), variations in the growth rings of trees (Fritts 1976, Hughes et al. 1982), and a variety of ecological observations (Kullman 1981a, b, 1983, Payette and Gagnon 1979, Brink 1959, Agee and Smith 1984, Franklin et al. 1971). Historical records from Great Britain and the European continent document important short-term climatic variations over the past millennium (Figure 3-10) (Lamb 1972, Schneider and Londer 1984). Numerous accounts indicate warm conditions between approximately A.D. 1000 and 1200, a period commonly referred to as the Medieval Optimum. During this period, permanent settlements were established in Iceland, which were supported by local grain production and supplies from Europe. Viking explorers may have reached the North American continent, and vineyards were successful in England during this period.

Temperatures decreased during the thirteenth century, causing the Icelandic colonies to fail. Vineyards were no longer successful in England, and numerous accounts reported harsh winters on the European continent. This period of cold climate is called the Little Ice Age. Little Ice Age conditions ceased as temperatures began to rise during the nineteenth century. Instrumental weather records, which began in most areas at about that time, show an increase in average Northern Hemispheric annual temperatures between the nineteenth and twentieth centuries (Figure 3-1) (Wigley et al. 1985). But temperatures did not warm at the same time or by the same amount in all seasons or geographic regions (Figure 3-11).

The climatic trends revealed in historical documents and instrumental records in Europe are corroborated by records of mountain glacier fluctuations in the Alps and Scandinavia (Figure 3-12) (Porter 1986). Many glaciers in this region receded between about 1000 and 1300, advanced during the Little Ice Age, and receded again during the late nineteenth and twentieth centuries. Glacial records from North America are in general agreement with those from Europe.

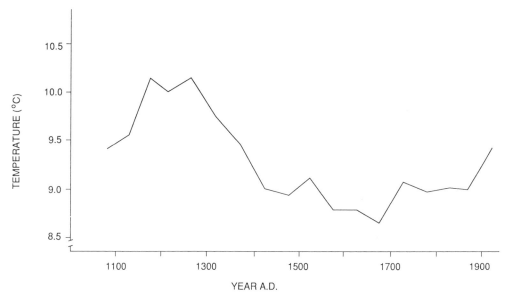

Figure 3-10. Estimated mean annual temperature in central England since A.D. 1100 (after Lamb 1972).

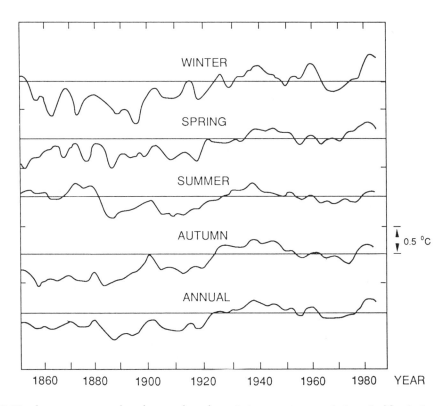

Figure 3-11. Average seasonal and annual surface air temperature variations in North America since 1860 (after Wigley et al. 1985).

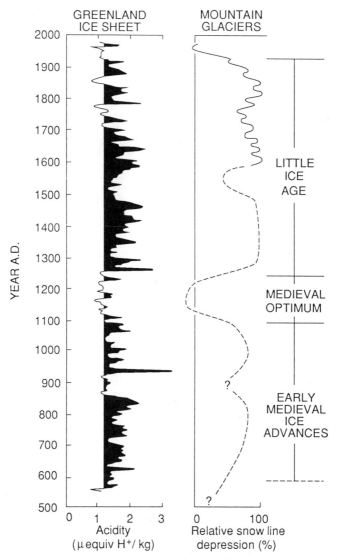

Figure 3-12. Inferred correlation of Greenland ice sheet acidity record with late Holocene mountain glacier variations in the Northern Hemisphere (after Porter 1986).

Causes of Short-term Climatic Variations

The causes of climatic shifts between the Medieval Optimum, Little Ice Age, and the twentieth century differ from those responsible for the long- and intermediate-term variations. Three external forcing factors are generally considered important for short periods (MacCracken and Luther 1985). First, variations in solar radiation, caused by variations in the sun's radius and sunspot activity, affect the amount of incoming radiation to the earth's atmosphere (Figure 3-13, Gilliland 1982). The fact that the coldest periods of the Little Ice Age correspond to intervals of exceptionally low sunspot numbers suggests the importance of solar radiation (Lamb 1972). Second, volcanic emissions, particularly sulfur-rich aerosols, are thought to reduce the earth's temperatures by increasing atmospheric reflectivity. Acidity measurements of annual laminae in the Green-

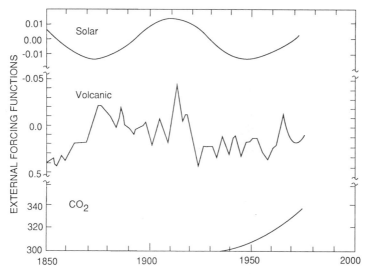

Figure 3-13. External forcing factors of short-term climatic variation (after Gilliland 1982).

land ice cap provide indirect records of volcanic activity (Figure 3-12) (Porter 1986). These records clearly indicate that the Medieval Optimum and twentieth century were periods of consistently low acidity, and thus presumably low volcanic activity. Finally, increased carbon dioxide and other trace gases affect the earth's climate by capturing longwave radiations that would otherwise escape from the earth's atmosphere (Figure 3-13). Atmospheric carbon dioxide concentrations have increased from approximately 280 ppm in the preindustrial period to approximately 350 ppm in 1985, and should exceed 400 ppm by 2050. The increase in atmospheric carbon dioxide over the past century coincides with temperature increases at the end of the Little Ice Age. It is not yet possible, however, to determine whether the temperature increase is due to natural or CO_2-related causes (Wigley et al. 1985).

Vegetation Responses to Short-term Variations

Two effects of short-term climatic variations are discussed in this section: (1) changes in range limits due to altered reproductive and establishment rates and (2) phenotypic adjustments of established trees.

Range Changes. The effects of short-term climatic variations on tree establishment have been documented at arctic, alpine, and prairie forest borders. For example, tree establishment has increased during the twentieth century at tree line in Alaska (Goldstein 1981) and northern Quebec (Payette and Filion 1985), in the Cascade Mountains of the Pacific Northwest (Franklin et al. 1971, Brink 1959, Agee and Smith 1984) and in the Scandes Mountains of Scandinavia (Kullman 1979, 1981a, b, 1983). The fate of young trees in most of these areas is unclear, because a return to cooler and snowier conditions in recent decades has prevented additional recruitment and slowed the growth of the newly established trees.

Some responses to short-term climatic variations are mediated by disturbance (White 1979, Payette 1980). For example, rates of range reductions may depend primarily on disturbance frequencies (Brubaker 1986). Although the onset of less favorable conditions may curtail reproduction or establishment, species range limits will not be affected until established trees die. Payette (1980) found that fire accelerated the recession of tree line in northern Quebec during periods of cold climate. Conversely, the expansion of late successional species may be accelerated in times of ample precipitation by the concomitant reduction of fires, which allows stands to reach late stages of development.

Responses to short-term climatic variations also depend on life history characteristics (Ritchie 1986, Brubaker 1986, Davis 1986). This is well documented in a study of Scots pine, Norway spruce, and tree birch growing close to tree line in the Handolan Valley, Sweden (Kullman 1979, 1981a, b, 1983). Each species responded differently to reduced snowpack and increased summer temperatures during the twentieth century (Figure 3-14). Scots pine showed no change in growth or recruitment during the twentieth century. The upper limit of spruce (defined by trees greater than 2 meters in height) has increased during the twentieth century because of a change in growth form. The leaders of krummholz trees were released during the mid-twentieth century, allowing these trees to grow vertically over the past several decades. This change in growth form has resulted in a 30 meter rise in the elevation of spruce tree line. In contrast, the upper limit of birch has increased by the recruitment of new individuals above tree line. The population response of birch compared with other species is expected. Birches typically produce large numbers of well-dispersed seeds each year and therefore should be able to take advantage of short-term climatic variation. In contrast, Scots pine and Norway spruce require longer periods of favorable climate to produce viable seeds and, even under the best conditions, produce smaller seed crops than birch.

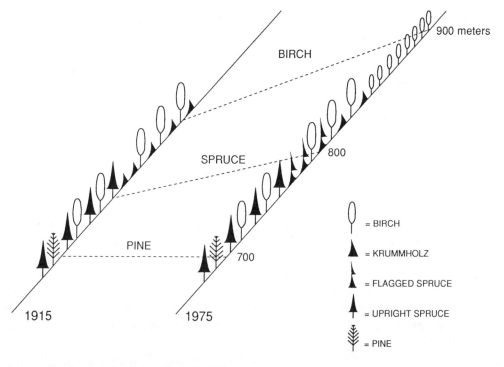

Figure 3-14. Comparison of 1915 and 1975 tree-line elevations of three species in the Handolan Valley, Sweden (after Kullman 1983).

The effect of short-term climatic change is less well documented in continuous forests than at forest borders. To a large extent this is because continuous forests are at temperate latitudes where landscapes have been severely disturbed by agriculture and logging. In such areas, it is extremely difficult to detect vegetation changes due to climate over those caused by human disturbance. Information on vegetation responses to climatic change must therefore come from paleoecological data for presettlement periods. Records of pollen in sediments of the Great Lakes region show range extensions of American beech and eastern hemlock at the beginning of the Little Ice Age (Woods and Davis 1982, Davis et al. 1986). There is also convincing evidence that the Big Woods forest type developed at this time (Grimm 1984).

The contrast in climate between the Little Ice Age and the twentieth century is of particular interest to managers of natural areas, because forest stands in such areas were typically initiated prior to the twentieth century. Current models of stand development emphasize the importance of initial conditions on the composition of forest stands (Oliver 1981). In closed-canopy forests, stand composition is determined primarily by species dominating a site at the time of canopy closure. The dense canopy of young stands prevents the establishment of trees for periods as long as one or two centuries in vegetation types with long-lived early successional species (e.g., Douglas-fir and tulip poplar) (Shugart 1984). Because seed germination and early tree survival is very sensitive to climate, conditions during stand initiation may affect forests for long periods. If climatic conditions change after stand establishment, one should not expect succession following a major disturbance to lead to comparable stands.

Adjustments of Established Trees. The importance of short-term climatic variations on tree growth has been documented in all major forest types studied in North America (Hughes et al. 1982). Growth records on stressful sites in most regions show strong annual variation in response to annual climatic variations. In some areas, growth records show longer term variations related to decadal and century-long climatic variations. For example, trees growing near latitudinal and altitudinal tree lines in western North America have often shown major increases in ring width in response to temperature increases during the twentieth century (Figure 3-15) (Jacoby 1982, Garfinkel and Brubaker 1980, Graumlich and Brubaker 1986). There is also evidence for significant increases in productivity in upper-elevation forests of the the Cascade Mountains of Washington during the twentieth century (Graumlich and Brubaker 1987). Conventional estimates of ecosystem productivity, based on five years of data, are certainly susceptible to variations related to climate.

Height growth may also be affected by climatic variations. In the boreal forest of eastern Canada, Payette and Filion (1985) compared height-age relationships between the Little Ice Age (sampled as dead stems) and the twentieth century (living trees). They found faster height growth during the twentieth century, again presumably due to more favorable climate. Thus site index, a major predictor of forest yield and an important criterion for commercial forest management, may be sensitive to climate; and site indexes estimated during the mid-twentieth century may not be representative of future centuries.

Implications of Short-term Climatic Variations
Annual climatic variations primarily affect radial and height growth rates. Decadal and

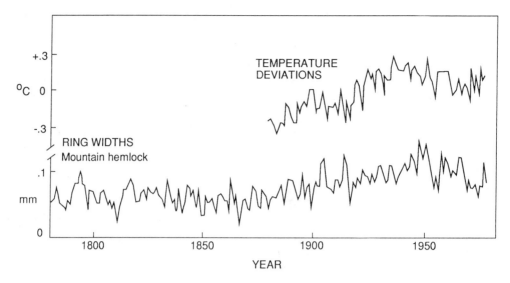

Figure 3-15. Ring-width variations of mountain hemlock at a site in the Cascade Mountains, Washington, compared to mean annual Northern Hemispheric temperatures since 1880 (expressed as deviations from mean value).

century-long climatic variations can affect both species ranges and growth rates. Measurements of site quality made at short intervals may not be representative of conditions over longer periods. Present-day forest stands may have established under different conditions than exist today and thus may not return to current composition following disturbance.

CONCLUSIONS

Climate varies on all temporal and spatial scales. Variations in climatic parameters (e.g., precipitation and temperature) follow unique paths, so a given set of conditions may not exist over long periods. Because tree species have been selected under constantly varying environments, they should be capable of coping with future change. However, since future conditions are likely to be different from twentieth-century conditions, it may be difficult to predict future responses solely from field observations in today's landscapes.

As a result, paleoecological records provide important information for anticipating the future. The simplest and most important implication of these records is that environments will change in the future by natural if not anthropogenic causes. Because species should respond individualistically, future vegetation change may not involve simple displacements of intact vegetation zones or habitat types. Considerations of the future conditions should, therefore, focus on the unique requirements of individual species. Furthermore, since modern environments may not span the full range of future environments, predictions should be based on experimental studies as well as on field observations in the modern landscape.

A recent assessment by Leverenz and Lev (in press) of the potential responses of western North American conifers to a CO_2-induced climatic change is an example of this approach. Their analysis was based on assumptions of the behavior of individual species deduced from the results of experimental studies and current field conditions. This study was based on temperature and site water balance conditions predicted for a doubling of atmospheric carbon dioxide. Major range adjustments were projected for some species (e.g., ponderosa pine, Douglas-fir), but not others (e.g., lodgepole pine, western hemlock). Their projections, however, were very sensitive to assumptions about future conditions (such as site water balance) and critical plant responses (such as chilling requirements). Because several scenarios of CO_2-induced climatic change are considered plausible (Jaeger 1988) and the climatic sensitivities of many species are not well known, current projections of vegetation changes are therefore largely speculative and should not yet be incorporated into management plans.

Even though no single scenario of future climate is widely accepted, land managers should be aware of the potential for future vegetation change. Paleoecological records, historical data, and climatic model predictions all suggest that future climate and vegetation will be different from today's. Because vegetation largely determines wildlife and aesthetic values of natural landscapes, the management of all aspects of natural areas must consider potential consequences of environmental change.

LITERATURE CITED

Agee, J. K., and L. Smith. 1984. Subalpine tree reestablishment after fire in the Olympic Mountains, Washington. Ecology 65:810-819.

Ager, T. A., and L. B. Brubaker. 1985. Quaternary palynology and vegetational history of Alaska. *In* V. M. Bryant, Jr., and R. G. Holloway (eds.) Pollen records of Late-Quaternary North American sediments, pp. 353-384. American Association of Stratigraphic Palynologists Foundation, Dallas, Texas.

Anderson, P. A., and L. B. Brubaker. Isopoll maps of Alaska: A preliminary vegetational history of northwestern North America. *In* H. E. Wright (ed.) Global climates for 6000 and 9000 years ago. University of Minnesota Press, Minneapolis. In press.

Birks, H. J. B. 1981. The use of pollen analysis in the reconstruction of past climates: A review. *In* T. M. L. Wigley, M. J. Ingram, and G. Farmer (eds.) Climate and history, pp. 111-128. Cambridge University Press, Cambridge.

Birks, H. J. B., and H. H. Birks. 1980. Quaternary palaeoecology. Edward Arnold Press, London.

Bradley, R. S. 1985. Quaternary paleoclimatology: Methods of paleoclimatic reconstruction. Allen and Unwin, Boston. 472 p.

Brink, V. C. 1959. A directional change in the subalpine forest-heath ecotone in Garibaldi Park, British Columbia. Ecology 40:10-16.

Brubaker, L. B. 1986. Tree population responses to climatic change. Vegetatio 67:119-130.

Bryant, V. M., Jr., and R. G. Holloway (eds.) 1985. Pollen record of Late-Quaternary North American sediments. Am. Assoc. Strat. Palyn. Found., Dallas.

Critchfield, W. B. 1978. Impact of the Pleistocene on the genetic structure of North American conifers. *In* R. M. Lanner (ed.) Proceedings of the Eighth North American Forest Biology Workshop, pp. 70-118. Utah State University, Logan.

Davis, M. B. 1976. Pleistocene biogeography of temperate deciduous forests. Geoscience and Man 13:13-26.

——. 1981. Quaternary history and the stability of forest communities. *In* D. C. West, H. H. Shugart, and D. B. Botkin (eds.) Forest succession: Concepts and application, pp. 132-153. Springer-Verlag, New York.

——. 1986. Climatic instability, time lags, and community disequilibrium. *In* J. Diamond and T. J. Case (eds.) Community ecology, pp. 269-284. Harper and Row, New York.

Davis, M. B., K. D. Woods, S. L. Webb, and R. P. Futyma. 1986. Dispersal versus climate: Expansion of *Fagus* and *Tsuga* into the Upper Great Lakes region. Vegetatio 67:93-104.

Delcourt, H. R., and P. A. Delcourt. 1984. Ice age haven for hardwoods. Natural History 9:22-28.

Dunwiddie, P. W. 1986. A 6000-year record of forest history on Mount Rainier, Washington. Ecology 67:58-68.

Faegri, K., and J. Iversen. 1975. Handbook of palynology. Hafner, New York.

Franklin, J. F., and T. Dyrness. 1973. Natural vegetation of Oregon and Washington. USDA For. Serv. Gen. Tech. Rep. PNW-8.

Franklin, J. F., W. H. Moir, G. W. Douglas, and C. Wiberg. 1971. Invasion of subalpine meadows by trees in the Cascade Range, Washington and Oregon. Arct. Alp. Res. 3:215-224.

Fritts, H. C. 1976. Tree rings and climate. Springer-Verlag, New York.

Garfinkel, H. L., and L. B. Brubaker. 1980. Modern climate-tree-ring relations and climatic reconstruction in sub-arctic Alaska. Nature 286:872-873.

Gilliland, R. L. 1982. Solar, volcanic and CO_2 forcing of recent climatic changes. Climatic Change 4:111-131.

Goldstein, G. H. 1981. Ecophysiological and demographic studies of white spruce (*Picea glauca* (Moench) Voss) at treeline in the Brooks Range of Alaska. Ph.D. diss., University of Washington, Seattle.

Graumlich, L. J., and L. B. Brubaker. 1986. Reconstruction of temperature (1590-1979) for Longmire, Washington, derived from tree rings. Quat. Res. 25:223-234.

———. 1987. Recent productivity changes in high elevation forests of the Cascade Mountains, Washington. *In* Proceedings of the ISEATRA Conference on Dendroecology, pp. 59-69. Lamont-Doherty, New York.

Grimm, E. C. 1984. Fire and other factors controlling the Big Woods vegetation of Minnesota in the mid-nineteenth century. Ecol. Monogr. 54:291-311.

Hughes, M. K., A. M. Kelly, J. R. Pilcher, and V. C. LaMarche, Jr. (eds.) 1982. Climate from tree rings. Cambridge University Press, London and New York. 223 p.

Huntley, B., and H. J. G. Birks. 1983. An atlas of past and present pollen maps for Europe: 0-13,000 years ago. Cambridge University Press, Cambridge.

Jacoby, G. C. 1982. The Arctic. *In* M. K. Hughes, A. M. Kelly, J. R. Pilcher, and V. C. LaMarche, Jr. (eds.) Climate from tree rings, pp. 107-114. Cambridge University Press, London and New York.

Jaeger, J. 1988. Developing policies for responding to future climatic change. World Climate Programme Impact Studies. WMO/TD-No. 225.

Jones, P. D., T. M. Wigley, and P. M. Kelly. 1982. Variations in surface air temperatures. Part I: Northern Hemisphere 1881-1980. Monthly Weather Review 110:59-70.

Kaup, P., and M. Posch. 1985. Sensitivity of boreal forests to possible climatic warming. Climatic Change 7:45-54.

Kullman, L. 1979. Change and stability in the altitude of the birch tree-limit in the southern Swedish Scandes 1915-1975. Acta Phytogeogr. Suec. 65. 121 p.

———. 1981a. Some aspect of the ecology of the Scandinavian subalpine birch forest belt. Wahlenbergia 7:99-112.

———. 1981b. Recent tree-limit dynamics of Scots pine (*Pinus sylvestris* L.) in the southern Swedish Scandes. Wahlenbergia 8. 67 p.

———. 1983. Past and present tree-lines in the Handolan Valley, central Sweden. *In* P. Morisset and S. Payette (eds.) Tree-line ecology, pp. 25-45. Centre d'études nordiques, Université Laval, Quebec.

Kutzbach, J. T., and T. J. Guetter. 1986. The influence of changing orbital parameters and surface boundary conditions on climatic simulations for the past 18,000 years. Journal of Atmospheric Sciences 43:1726-1759.

Lamb, H. H. 1972. Climate: Present, past and future. Vol. 1. Methuen, London. 613 p.

Leopold, E. B., R. Nickman, J. I. Hedges, and J. R. Ertel. 1982. Pollen and lignin records of late Quaternary vegetation, Lake Washington. Science 218:1305-1307.

Leverenz, J., and D. Lev. 1988. Effects of CO₂ induced climate changes on the natural ranges of six major commercial tree species in the western U.S. *In* W. F. Shands and J. S. Hoffman (eds.) The greenhouse effect, climate change and U.S. forests. Conservation Foundation, Washington, D.C.

MacCracken, M. L., and F. M. Luther (eds.) 1985. Detecting the climatic effects of increasing carbon dioxide. DOE/ER-0235. U.S. Department of Energy, Washington, D.C.

Nilsson, T. 1983. The Pleistocene: Geology and life in the Quaternary Ice Age. D. Reidel, Dordrecht, Holland.

Oliver, C. D. 1981. Forest development in North America following major disturbances. For. Ecol. Manage. 3:153-168.

Payette, S. 1980. Fire history at the tree-line in Northern Quebec: A paleoclimatic tool. *In* Proceedings of the Fire History Workshop, October 20-24, 1980, Tucson, Arizona, pp. 126-131. USDA For. Serv. Gen. Tech. Rep. RM-81. Rocky Mountain For. and Range Exp. Stn., Fort Collins, Colorado.

Payette, S., and L. Filion. 1985. White spruce expansion at treeline and recent climatic change. Can. J. For. Res. 15:241-251.

Payette, S., and R. Gagnon. 1979. Tree-line dynamics in Ungava peninsula, northern Quebec. Holarct. Ecol. 2:239-248.

Porter, S. C. (ed.) 1983. Late-Quaternary environments of the United States. Vol. 1: The Late Pleistocene. University of Minnesota Press, Minneapolis.

Porter, S. C. 1986. Pattern and forcing of Northern Hemispheric glacier variations during the last millennium. Quat. Res. 26:27-48.

Ritchie, J. C. 1984. Past and present vegetation of the far northwest of Canada. University of Toronto Press, Toronto. 246 p.

———. 1986. Climate change and vegetation response. Vegetatio 67:65-74.

Ritchie, J., and G. MacDonald. 1986. The patterns of post-glacial spread of white spruce. J. Biogeogr. 13:527-540.

Schneider, S. H., and R. Londer. 1984. The coevolution of climate and life. Sierra Club Books, San Francisco. 563 p.

Shugart, H. H. 1984. A theory of forest dynamics. Springer-Verlag, New York.

Spaulding, W. G., E. B. Leopold, and T. R. Van Devender. 1983. Late Wisconsin paleoecology of the American Southwest. *In* S. C. Porter (ed.) Late-Quaternary environments of the United States. Vol. 1: The Late Pleistocene, pp. 259-293. University of Minnesota Press, Minneapolis.

Van Devender, T. R. 1986. Climatic cadence and the composition of Chihuahuan desert communities: The late-Pleistocene packrat midden record. *In* J. Diamond and T. J. Case (eds.) Community ecology, pp. 284-299. Harper and Row, New York.

Waring, R. H., and J. F. Franklin. 1979. Evergreen coniferous forests of the Pacific Northwest. Science 204:1380-1386.

Webb T. III. 1981. The past 11,000 years of vegetational change in eastern North America. BioScience 310:501-506.

White, P. S. 1979. Pattern, process, and natural disturbance in vegetation. Bot. Rev. 45:229-299.

Wigley, T. M. L., J. K. Angell, and P. D. Jones. 1985. Analysis of the temperature record in detecting the climatic effects of increased CO₂. *In* M. L. MacCracken and F. M. Luther (eds.) Detecting the climatic effects of increasing carbon dioxide, pp. 177-186. DOE/ER-0235.

Woods, K. D., and M. B. Davis. 1982. Sensitivity of Michigan pollen diagrams to Little Ice Age climatic change, p. 181. Seventh Biennial Conference Abstracts, American Quaternary Association, Seattle.

Wright, H. E., Jr. 1983. Late-Quaternary environments of the United States. Vol. 2: The Holocene. University of Minnesota Press, Minneapolis.

4

Succession and Natural Disturbance: Paradigms, Problems, and Preservation of Natural Ecosystems

NORMAN L. CHRISTENSEN

ABSTRACT Managers of natural ecosystems are faced with four questions: (1) What should be preserved? (2) How much should be preserved? (3) In what state should preserves be maintained? (4) By what means should natural ecosystem preserves be maintained? The classical model of community succession as a directional, deterministic, and autogenic process of change converging toward a globally stable climax provided very clear and relatively simple answers to these questions. However, during the past two decades, virtually every assumption of that theory has been criticized. It is now recognized that a variety of natural disturbances play an integral role in the long-term maintenance of virtually all ecosystems. The consequences of natural disturbance and successional processes are discussed in relation to these four management questions.

In the broadest sense, preservation and management of natural ecosystems involves consideration of four general problems. (1) *What should be preserved?* This question must be answered in both philosophical and practical terms. We must first agree on the categories of items that will be the objects of preservation (i.e., genotypes, species, ecosystems, landscapes, etc.). Having made this decision, we must determine which items within a category are worthy of preservation. For the purposes of this paper, I shall assume that the items we are most interested in preserving are ecosystems. Given that resources for designation of preserves will always be limited relative to the need, how do we assign priorities to potential preserves? In many regions our ignorance of the nature of ecosystem variability prevents us from even making a "shopping list." (2) *How much should be preserved?* To answer this question we must not only consider practical constraints of management but also how much area is necessary to maintain ecosystem processes. (3) *In what state should preserves be maintained?* This question is especially important in situations where human interference has altered ecosystems from their primeval state. (4) *By what means should natural ecosystem preserves be maintained?* The Panglossian answer to this question is simply "let it be." However, a variety of constraints may prevent the natural processes that maintain such systems from operating as they did in the past.

I shall consider these questions from the standpoint of plant ecology and assume that the items we wish to preserve and manage are natural plant communities. I deliberately leave the terms "natural" and "community" undefined for the moment. I shall assert that answers to the four questions listed above were more apparent thirty years ago than they are today. Recent changes in our understanding of the nature and mechanisms of ecosystem change or succession following disturbance have greatly altered our understanding of ecosystem structure and function. Visions of deterministic and directional community development toward ecosystems structured by finely regulated autogenic feedback mechanisms have been blurred by the recognition that chance factors may play a considerable role in patterns of succession and that natural disturbances of various sorts play an integral role in the long-term maintenance of virtually all ecosystems.

In order to emphasize the impact of these changing ideas on preservation and management strategies, I shall review the classical paradigms and their implications for the management of natural communities. I shall then discuss the data that have led to the reassessment of these paradigms, placing special emphasis on the importance of natural disturbance.

SUCCESSION

The Classical Paradigm

Succession has been a central theme in North American plant ecology throughout this century. It formed the basis for the first (and perhaps the last) attempt to develop a comprehensive theory to explain the distribution and abundance of plants on the landscape (Clements 1916, 1928). Although components of this theory, such as the climatic climax and organismal concept of the community, received early criticism (e.g., Gleason 1917, 1927, Egler 1954), this view of community change was widely accepted up to the early 1970s and was the foundation for much of wilderness management policy during this era. Odum's (1969) "strategy of ecosystem development" presupposed many of Clements's theories, expanded them to ecosystem properties such as nutrient cycling and trophic dynamics, and explicitly applied them to problems of ecosystem management. The past fifteen years have witnessed an all-out attack on virtually every aspect of this paradigm. However, the demise of this theory, with its fifty years of accumulated baggage, has not followed the typical pattern of scientific revolutions (*sensu* Kuhn 1962): it has not been replaced by a more comprehensive or precise theory. Rather, it has led to uncertainty and even cynicism as to whether a comprehensive theory of community change is feasible. As Mark Twain said, about another subject: "The researches of many commentators have already shed considerable darkness on this subject and it is probable that, if they continue, we shall soon know nothing about it."

Clements (1916, 1928, and 1936) viewed succession as a stepwise, directional process driven by the effects of dominant plants on their environment. In his view, plant communities are highly coevolved and integrated systems that are structured largely by competition from dominant plants. Successional change occurs as a consequence of alteration of the environment by one community of plants such that some other community can compete at that site more efficiently. The ultimate endpoint of this process is the plant community that alters its environment in such a manner as to perpetuate itself (Figure 4-1).

Composition and structure of early successional communities was agreed to be largely determined by local site conditions such as moisture status and soil resources. Thus Clements imagined a diverse array of early successional seres reflecting the multitude of successional starting points. Alteration of the environment by plants in seral com-

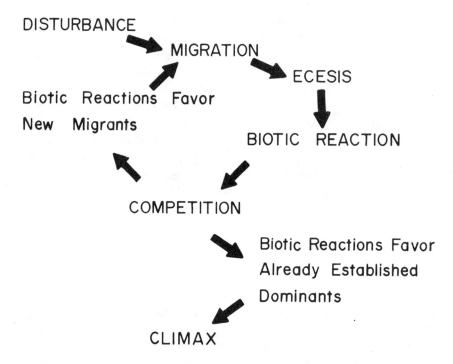

DISTURBANCE

MIGRATION

ECESIS

Biotic Reactions Favor
New Migrants

BIOTIC REACTION

COMPETITION

Biotic Reactions Favor
Already Established
Dominants

CLIMAX

Figure 4-1. Schematic representation of the classical model of successional change.

munities (biotic reaction) diminished such landscape variability (e.g., rock outcrops became more mesic, and lakes and bogs eventually filled and became more xeric) with the result that seres converged, regardless of starting point, on a single regional climax community. Note that this community convergence was caused by environmental (site) convergence, which Clements argued would result in a community of organisms determined largely by regional climate.

The notion of the climatic monoclimax received considerable criticism on the grounds that environmental amelioration on most landscapes never proceeds to complete monotony; certain site and soil differences will exist indefinitely, and these will result in differences among plant communities. Such criticisms led to the notion of polyclimax (Daubenmire 1952, Whittaker 1953, Oosting 1956), while Clements developed a complex classification set of terms to describe communities that did not fit his monoclimax scheme (e.g., disclimax, preclimax, postclimax, and subclimax; Clements 1936).

Several important points are explicit and implicit in this classical theory. (1) Plant communities are structured in a hierarchical fashion by competition and biotic reactions so that the distribution of subordinate species is determined largely by the distribution of dominants. The result is that communities are relatively homogeneous over their geographic range and separated from one another by comparatively abrupt ecotones that are sharpened by competition between dominants in adjacent communities. Similarly, seral communities were viewed as temporally homogeneous with relatively abrupt transitions from stage to stage. (2) Successional change is largely autogenic; that is, change occurs because communities alter their environment in ways that favor the invasion of other communities. (3) Assemblages of organisms comprising climax communities have coevolved over long periods. Thus, although a particular community type, say an oak-hickory forest, may never have inhabited a particular location, that community has existed at other locations. This formulation led to the notions of the abstract and concrete communities (Oosting 1956). (4) In the absence of disturbance, variations among communities on a landscape should diminish through time. (5) This process was viewed as directional in the sense that it leads to the most stable configuration of species possible in a particular region.

Clements focused primarily on changes in species composition; however, over the succeeding years, a variety of community properties were incorporated into the classical theory. These were enumerated in Odum's (1969) "trends to be expected during succession," and I shall mention only a few here.

The notion of stability is an integral part of Clements's theory: if stability is defined as resistance to change, the idea that stability increases during succession is a tautology (Peters 1976). The apparent importance of biotic interactions in structuring plant communities was a convincing argument for viewing such communities as cybernetic systems regulated by complex feedbacks among their various parts (e.g., Margalef 1963, 1968). Such systems were judged to be most stable when they were most diverse (Odum 1969). Ecologists were led to the conclusion that diversity increases with succession not because they found an abundance of empirical data but because they accepted the syllogism that greater diversity leads to greater stability, stability increases during succession, therefore diversity increases during succession. The use of information indices, such as the Brillouin and Shannon-Wiener indices, to measure species diversity further emphasized this relationship, since Margalef (1968), Odum (1969), and others argued that community information content (whatever that is in biological terms) increases during succession. In retrospect, the stability-diversity-information content debate appears to have been an intellectual cul-de-sac.

A number of generalizations regarding patterns of change in biomass and production were also incorporated into the classical theory. Odum (1969) proposed that aboveground phytomass (biomass) increased to maximum in climax communities. Net primary production was presumed to peak in midsuccession and then remain relatively constant, reflecting similar changes in leaf area. Consumption and respiration were assumed to increase and eventually come into equilibrium with primary production in climax communities, so that net ecosystem production would be zero (Odum 1969).

In general, it was presumed that nutrient cycles become more efficient and nutrient loss decreases from ecosystems with increasing successional age (Odum 1969). Certainly, the large nutrient losses from recently disturbed versus undisturbed watersheds (e.g., Likens et al. 1977) were consistent with this view. It also appeared that soil fertility increased with succession. Perhaps the most frequently cited evidence for this trend was the work of Crocker and Major (1955) on Glacier Bay, Alaska, and Olson's (1958) research on soil development in relation to succession on sand dunes near Lake Michigan. Data from secondary successional seres (e.g., Billings 1938 and Coile 1940) were certainly more equivocal on this point.

If we were to accept Clements's theory in its simplest form, the answers to the four management questions posed earlier would be relatively clear and this paper would be considerably shorter. (1) *What should be preserved?* Because successional convergence leads to specific climaxes in particular environments, an understanding of succession will lead to a natural classification of plant communities. In a sense, nature would designate the units of preservation. (2) *How much should be preserved?* Since community structure and function is determined by dominant plants, enough area should be preserved to maintain the populations of these dominants. (3) *In what state should preserves be maintained?* In a Clementsian world this is a moot question if stable climax communities are the management objective. Given sufficient time, all areas will converge to a stable climax community. (4) *By what means should natural ecosystem preserves be maintained?* Disturbance deflects successional trajectories. If we wish to maintain stable climax communities, we should attempt to prevent catastrophic natural disturbances, such as fire.

Many of these generalizations regarding successional change were criticized relatively early. However, criticism reached a shrill pitch following the publication of a challenge to Odum's (1969) "trends to be expected during succession" by Drury and Nisbet (1973). What became obvious was that many of the predictions of the classical theory were predicated on untested assumptions, uncertain logic, and inadequate data. During the past decade, the trends described above have been the focus of considerable research. Unfortunately, a new synthesis has not emerged. Indeed, we may now conclude that a grand unified theory of community succession such as that envisioned by Clements and Odum is not possible or even desirable. The bottom-line message to those who must manage natural ecosystems is that the world is considerably less tidy than we thought. Furthermore, this untidyness may be an integral part of maintenance of many ecosystems.

The Nature and Mechanisms of Succession

Gleason (1917, 1927) was among the first to challenge Clements's assertions that spatial and temporal community change was regulated by biotic reaction and dominance. He argued that organisms were distributed as a consequence of their ability to disperse and their individual potentials to establish and grow in relation to environmental variation. Given that environments varied in gradient fashion, vegetation should also vary continuously; communities and distinct seral stages are illusions. Many studies in a diverse array of ecosystems have largely substantiated Gleason's assertion (see Whittaker 1975), and it is generally agreed that systems of community classification, however useful, are arbitrary. A natural system of classification reflecting patterns of succession in the same sense that classification of species reflects evolutionary processes is not possible.

Drury and Nisbet (1971, 1973) suggested that successional sequences are stress gradients to which plants are adapted (i.e., succession is simply a gradient in time). Pickett (1976) argued that the replacement of species along this temporal gradient could be understood in terms of the interactions among species with different life histories and physiological tolerances; notions of deterministic progress toward climax are unnecessary. The identification of those features that characterize organism success at different portions of this temporal gradient has been an important focus of research in this area (e.g., the vital attributes approach of Noble and Slayter 1980).

Egler (1954, 1977) and Drury and Nisbet (1973) argued that succession in many areas was largely a matter of differential longevity. Most species that eventually will become dominants invade early when competitive pressures are low; climax species are simply those that survive longest. Evidence for differential longevity as an important mechanism of succession in forest ecosystems is based primarily on the presence of seedlings of climax species in early stages of a sere. Such seedlings are subject to high rates of mortality, and the actual individuals that form the climax community may not invade until much later (Peet and Christensen 1987). If this pattern of succession were important, failure of a species to establish early might greatly diminish its chances for subsequent dominance. Variations in initial site conditions, as well as year-to-year variations in climate and seed dispersal, could obviously play a significant and long-term role in determining community composition, and little, if any, successional convergence would be expected.

Connell and Slatyer (1977) proposed that three different mechanisms might account for these various patterns of change in species composition. The mechanism proposed by Clements wherein species modify their environment so as to pave the way for their successors they termed *facilitation*. They said that data to support such a mechanism as a widespread phenomenon were at best skimpy. Succession of species might also occur simply as a consequence of differences in dispersal and life history characteristics, and species interactions might play a minimal role in the exact sequence of invasion. They referred to this as the *tolerance* model. The differential longevity theory of Egler (1954) might fit under this rubric. This model certainly seems to apply to patterns of invasion early in many seres (e.g., Keever 1950). Connell and Slatyer suggested that successional change was most often a consequence of the preemption of space and resources by a species or group of species which prevented subsequent establishment. Only with the demise of these populations would subsequent replacement occur. They termed this the *inhibition* mechanism.

It is not expected that any one of these mechanisms is sufficient to explain all successional changes, or even change within a particular sere. Rather, mechanisms are expected to vary among species and successional stages. Furthermore, these mechanisms may not be easily distinguishable. For example, once established, pines generally inhibit the invasion of hardwoods (as a group) during old-field succession in the Southeast. However, the particular hardwood species that eventually replace the pines depend on demographic patterns in the pine population. If the pines die so as to create small gaps, shade-tolerant deciduous species replace them. However, patterns of mortality that result in large canopy openings favor establishment of somewhat more shade-intolerant species. Thus, at the species level, early invaders may facilitate the subsequent establishment of particular species by affecting competitive relations (Christensen and Peet 1981).

Predictability and Successional Convergence

The classical model of succession was, at the very least, deterministic. Indeed, Clements (1936) saw this process as predictable from beginning to end. Margalef (1968), on the other hand, suggested that predictability was itself a successional variable. Structure and function of early successional communities is determined largely by chance factors (meaning factors—such as history, dispersal, year-to-year climate—that are extrinsic to the community) and that the predictability of community characteristics increases as succession proceeds.

The questions of whether and in what manner communities converge during succession had not been explicitly addressed until the past few years (see Christensen and Peet 1981 for a discussion of the nature of data sets required to address this question). Convergence in the classical model would result in decreased variation among locations as succession proceeds. However, if success in early successional communities depends more on attributes such as dispersal and a wide range of tolerance, then recently disturbed locations might be inhabited by relatively similar communities of widely dispersed, comparatively ruderal species. Subsequent dispersal and intensified competiton might result in differentiation of communities in relation to local site conditions or successional divergence. (Whether this is convergence or divergence certainly depends on spatial scale [Allen and Starr 1982] and whether one's frame of reference is comparison of communities across a variable landscape or of communities on relatively similar sites.) Matthews (1979) observed that variability among locations actually increased during succession. Christensen and Peet (1984) observed a similar general trend in forest succession following old-field abandonment, but noted that this change was not monotonic. Indeed, changes in variability among stands were correlated with the successional stages of forest development described earlier. Compositional variability among stands was comparatively low in the establishment phase, reached a peak in the thinning phase (40- to 60-year-old pines), declined in the transition phase (mixed pine-hardwoods), and increased in the hardwood stands nearing the steady-state phase. The predictability of species-site relationships followed a similar pattern: they were highest in stands in the thinning and steady-state phases and lowest in establishment and transition phase stands. Species' habitat breadths (ecotopes)—that is, the range of conditions over which a particular species could be found—were high in establishment and transition phase stands and low in thinning and steady-state phase stands. Christensen and Peet (1984) argued that variability in composition among stands of similar age during succession is determined largely by the fidelity of species-site relationships. Species show the greatest site fidelity when competition is intense, and they are completely excluded at the extremes of their range of tolerance. They suggest that competitive relations may change in a variety of ways during succession and that no single pattern of convergence or divergence should be expected.

Diversity

Species diversity is a generic concept which has been used to describe several levels of ecological complexity. Whittaker (1965) classified diversity by geographic scales, distinguishing between alpha (within a community or stand), beta (among communities, or species change along environmental gradients), and gamma (landscape) diversity. Most assertions of classical succession theory regarding diversity deal at the alpha level. Alpha diversity is agreed to include measures of species richness (the number of species within an area), species evenness or equitability (the distribution of abundances among constituent species in a community), and species heterogeneity (synthetic measures sensitive to both richness and evenness) (Hurlbert 1971, Peet 1974). Christensen and Peet (1982) have reviewed the various approaches to measurement of these diversity components in the context of management goals.

The general prediction that late successional communities should be more species rich than very early successional communities is nearly a truism in primary successional seres. The number of species that can get to and survive at a newly created habitat is clearly limited relative to later successional stages. However, the exact trajectory of change in species richness along secondary successional chronosequences is quite variable. It may change very little along some seres (e.g., Christensen and Peet 1982); in others it may be highest in early successional compared to late successional stages (e.g., Specht et al. 1958, Parsons 1976, Walker and Peet 1983).

Many of these trends depend on the spatial scale one selects to observe them. For example, mean plant species richness per 0.1 ha in 75 loblolly pine stands on the North Carolina Piedmont was 51.0, and in 72 deciduous hardwood stands was 53.9. Thus, at the scale of 0.1 ha, we can conclude that there is no significant difference in species richness between successional pines and near-climax hardwoods. However, 347 species were encountered in all hardwood stands taken together, whereas only 260 were sampled in the pines. Whittaker (1965) might prefer to call these latter data measures of gamma diversity.

Why should we predict that climax communities ought to be the most species rich? Odum (1969) assumed that constituents of late succession communities are more highly coevolved and that their ecological niches are more precisely defined. As mentioned previously, higher species diversity was presumed to result in greater stability, the sine qua non of climax. In fact much of the discussion regarding successional change in species richness focused on its consequences rather than its causes. Considerable recent attention has been given to mechanisms that maintain species richness within communities and account for differences in richness among communities. I shall discuss five models here: (1) the species-abundance curve model, (2) the niche differentiation model, (3) the environmental heterogeneity model, (4) the reduction-mediated coexistence model, and (5) the island biogeographic model. These models are by no means mutually exclusive.

The species-abundance model might be thought of as something of a null model for variation in species diversity. All other things being equal, richness should increase as the amount of plant material sampled increases (Gleason 1922, Christensen and Peet 1982). As communities accumulate density and biomass, they are, in effect, sampling the surrounding landscape. Consequently, as total abundance per unit area increases, species richness should also increase; without invoking any biological interactions whatever, we predict that species richness should increase in succession so long as total abundance (e.g., biomass) also increases.

The niche differentiation model posits that communities vary in species richness because species divide up resources into relatively narrow niches (MacArthur 1965). Such differentiation is a consequence of long periods of coevolution with selection for specialization; and, as suggested previously, such differentiation is most expected in mature communities.

Proponents of the environmental heterogeneity model propose that species-rich communities are environmentally more variable and therefore offer more ways to make a living than species-poor communities (e.g., Bratton 1976, Ricklefs 1977). Tilman (1982) developed this model in a graphically elegant form, suggesting that the number of species that could be supported in a particular habitat was related to the number of potentially limiting resources and the variability in the supply rate of those resources. Grubb's (1977) "regeneration niche" hypothesis calls attention to the fact that much of the environmental heterogeneity "perceived" by plants is associated with small-scale disturbance and early establishment. Thus Grubb proposed that periodic disturbance at various scales increases diversity by increasing heterogeneity in establishment opportunities. Species "sort out" along these heterogeneity gradients (see Denslow 1985 for a review).

Both the niche differentiation and the environmental heterogeneity models assume that competition limits or restricts species to particular portions of their range of physiological tolerance: species diversity is greatest when competition is most intense, such as in late succession communities. The reduction-mediated model suggests the opposite, that when competition is reduced, especially when no species or small set of species is allowed to attain dominance, species diversity will increase. This is because competitive exclusion is prevented. This model is proposed to explain the high species richness of heavily grazed grasslands (e.g., Harper 1969) and of areas that are chronically disturbed (Connell 1978, Huston 1979, Pickett 1980, Walker and Peet 1983). Note that disturbance is proposed to increase diversity, not because it increases environmental variability but because it prevents competitive exclusion of many species.

The island biogeographic model of MacArthur and Wilson (1967) proposes that the species richness of a particular area is, quite simply, determined by the rate at which new species are able to invade an area (dispersal) versus the rate at which species go extinct in that area. They argued that, in the case of islands, dispersal and extinction were largely regulated by distance from the mainland and island size, respectively. Considerable debate has developed regarding the application of this model to the management of natural ecosystems on mainlands (e.g., Sullivan and Schaffer 1975, Diamond 1976, Simberloff and Abele 1976a, b), with much of the attention focusing on preserve size and distribution. However, the more significant notion implicit in this model is that species richness is a result of an equilibrium established between processes that favor species invasions as opposed to those that result in extinction. Clearly, these processes change in a complex fashion along different chronosequences and, at the scale of particular plant communities, will not be easily reduced to such simple parameters as size and distance from seed source. Nevertheless, this model provides a framework for empirical and experimental study of the mechanisms responsible for changes in diversity.

It is easy to imagine that each of these models is more or less appropriate at different times during succession and at different spatial scales. Given the multiplicity of factors involved, universal predictions for changes in species richness with succession may not be possible.

Changes in Biomass, Production, and Nutrient Cycles

Peet (1981) described four patterns of total live biomass change during succession. In the simplest, but apparently least common case, living biomass increases in a continuous logistic fashion toward an upper limit determined by site conditions. Documented examples include high elevation pine forests in the central Rockies (Forcella and Weaver 1977) and stands of jack pine in Canada (MacLean and Wein 1976). This is the pattern cited by Odum (1969) in his summary of successional trends. The second, and perhaps most widely documented, pattern fits well with the stages of forest succession described earlier; biomass increases to a peak at the close of the thinning stage, but then decreases during the transition stage. Biomass remains lower in the climax or steady-state stage than in the late thinning stage because of the importance of small-scale disturbance. This pattern is consistent with observations of Bormann and Likens (1979), Walker et al. (1981), and Peet and Christensen (1987). It is also predicted by computer simulation models of several forest types (e.g., Botkin et al. 1972, Shugart 1984). The third pattern is similar to the second, except that biomass recovers somewhat in climax communities, or may show damped oscillations. Such a pattern might arise as a consequence of different patterns of patch disturbance following the transition phase. In the fourth pattern, biomass steadily decreases after a peak early or midway in succession. This occurs as available nutrients are sequestered in biomass or as succession results in hydrologic changes that decrease site productivity (e.g., muskeg formation in boreal forest; see Van Cleve and Viereck 1981). This pattern occurs in a number of nonforested ecosystems, including grasslands (Kucera 1981) and a variety of shrublands (Specht et al. 1958, Gimmingham 1972, Christensen and Wilbur, in review).

A number of patterns of change in net primary production (NPP) have been documented (NPP = change in biomass plus loss to animal consumption and detritus amortized over a year). For example, following an initial increase, NPP remains relatively constant during succession in several forest types (see Peet 1981). Waring and Schlesinger (1985) argued that gross primary production (GPP) may increase to a maximum relatively early in succession and remain at that level as long as leaf area remains constant. The NPP will also increase to a maximum at the same time, but will subsequently decrease owing to respiration by the steadily increasing mass of nonphotosynthetic plant tissue (tree boles, roots, etc.). Although a decrease in NPP following a midsuccession maximum is a widely observed pattern, the rate of decrease is often greater than can be accounted for by increased respiration alone. Senescence, changes in stand structure, changes in species composition, and decreased nutrient availability may also account for this decline (Peet 1981).

Of considerable consequence to subsequent discussion is successional change in nonliving carbon pools, in particular soil organic matter, litter (forest floor), and coarse woody debris. In general, we expect these carbon pools to increase during succession to some steady-state level at which decomposition is equal to inputs into the pool. This is clearly the case with soil organic matter and litter; but the time required to reach such steady states and the pool sizes at steady state vary considerably as a consequence of regional climate, local microclimate, and physical and chemical characteristics of these pools (see Waring and Schlesinger 1985). However, woody debris may continue to accumulate over very long periods in many ecosystems, resulting in a general increase in the ratio of dead to living biomass as succession proceeds. This trend has been documented in xeric savannas (Parrott 1967), shrublands (Blaisdell 1953, Gimmingham et al. 1979, Christensen et al. 1981, Gray and Schlesinger 1981, and Specht 1981), and a variety of forests (see Harmon et al. 1986 for review). To the extent that such changes influence likelihood and behavior of fire, the stability (in the sense of their *resistance* to disturbance) of such ecosystems may decrease during succession. We shall return to this theme later.

Successional changes in patterns of nutrient cycling have proven to be far more complex than envisioned by Odum (1969) and others. For example, while soil fertility and nutrient availability generally increase along some chronosequences (particularly primary successions), the opposite is true along others. The notion that nutrient cycles become more complex and that ecosystems retain nutrients more efficiently during succession has not been borne out by observation (e.g., Vitousek and Reiners 1975).

So Where Does This Leave Us?

Perhaps the only generalization we can make regarding community change following disturbance is that it is *not* a monolithic process driven inexorably in some particular direction by a simple set of forces. While there can be no doubt that principles of thermodynamics and information apply to ecological systems, it is not at all clear how those principles apply to successional change or species diversity. Probably of greater consequence to ecosystem managers is the fact that successional change, by whatever mechanisms or pathways, does not necessarily lead to increasingly stable, self-reproducing climax communities (Connell and Slatyer 1977, Sousa 1984). Indeed, long-term climatic change may prevent succession to equilibrium communities such as envisioned by Clements (see Brubaker, this volume). Rather than culminating in stability, successional change often increases the likelihood of disturbances, which in turn alter the successional process.

NATURAL DISTURBANCE

Disturbance Regimes and Terminology

Clements and his disciples were certainly aware that natural disturbances such as fire often prevented many ecosystems from achieving true climax status. Such situations were termed "disclimaxes" and considered to be relatively unique. Watt (1947) recognized that disturbance of some sort was an inevitable part of even the most stable landscapes. He envisioned major disturbances as initiating widespread successional recovery, often resulting in a relatively even-aged community of plants. Death of individuals or groups of individuals creates a small-scale disturbance mosaic (i.e., the gap phase) in which miniature versions of the large-scale successional process occur. Whether or not such small-scale disturbances are sufficient to allow regeneration of all of the species on a landscape is an issue of central importance to ecologists and managers (Christensen and Franklin 1987).

With regard to patterns of forest succession, a general model of succession has emerged in a wide variety of forest types (see Oliver 1981 and Peet and Christensen 1987 for reviews). During the *establishment phase*, there is extensive seedling establishment and rapid growth. Competitive interactions are assumed to play a small role in community structure and composition. The closure of the tree canopy initiates a *thinning or stem exclusion phase* during which competition is intense and overtopped trees may die. Relatively little establishment occurs during this phase as tree density steadily decreases. A layer of shade-tolerant species may form beneath the canopy. Eventually tree density decreases to the stage where tree deaths create gaps which cannot be filled by the lateral growth of adjacent trees. Such gaps provide resources (light, nutrients) which allow recruitment of new seedlings. This initiates the *transition phase*. The final stage is the *steady-state phase* in which, as suggested by Watt (1947), the processes of establishment, thinning, and gap formation occur as a mosaic of patches.

We now recognize that one of the most important variables in this disturbance mosaic among and within ecosystems is patch size (Whittaker and Levin 1977). Whereas Watt viewed disturbance patch size as decreasing during succession, disturbances such as fire, blow downs, and pathogen attacks create patches that vary in size over several orders of magnitude.

Accepting the fact that natural disturbance has an important regulatory role in nearly all ecosystems, ecologists have sought to define a common set of parameters to describe such disturbances. White and Pickett (1985) have provided definitions for disturbance regime descriptors in general, and Romme (1980) summarized similar definitions with respect to fire. The number of disturbances per unit of time in a designated area is the *frequency*. Together with a measure of the average extent of disturbance, one can estimate the disturbance cycle or rotation as the time needed to disturb an area equal in size to the entire area of interest. Within a single rotation some locations may be disturbed several times and others not at all. *Return time* refers to the average time between successive disturbances at a particular site. On average, return time for a large area is a function of disturbance frequency and extent; however, mean return time at a particular location within that area may be unrelated to regional disturbance frequency. The *mag-*

nitude of disturbance can be expressed, independent of its specific effects on organisms, as *intensity*—the physical force of the event per unit of time. Thus fire intensity may be expressed as heat released per unit of area (or distance along the burning front) per unit of time. The impact of a disturbance on organisms per se is its severity; its units depend on the property of interest, but could be biomass consumed, number of stems killed, or change in the postdisturbance community. Note that a disturbance of particular intensity may have a different severity in different ecosystems. A disturbance parameter that has received considerably less attention is *predictability,* which can be defined as the inverse of the variability in each of the above measures.

In the discussion to follow I shall explore the consequences of temporal and spatial variation in ecosystems to the nature of fire regimes and then explore the consequences of fire regime variation on patterns of ecosystem change. I have chosen to dwell on fire in part because of personal bias, but mostly because management of fire regimes incorporates most of the dilemmas faced in the management of natural disturbance. Furthermore, human activities have probably altered fire regimes more than any other natural disturbance process.

Regulation of Fire Regimes

The fire regime for a particular ecosystem is a consequence of the interaction of (1) external influences (i.e., features unaffected by the structure and composition of the ecosystem), including sources and frequency of ignition, climate, topography, and the spatial relationship to other ecosystems, and (2) ecosystem properties, including fuel quantity, quality, and distribution. Reviews of the specific effects of these factors on fire regimes can be found in Byram (1959), Rothermel and Philpot (1973), Aston and Gill (1976), Agee et al. (1978), Chandler et al. (1983), Christensen (1985), and van Wagtendonk (1985).

The potential intensity of a fire is obviously limited by the amount of available fuel (living biomass and detritus), and return time may be limited by the rate of fuel accumulation (net ecosystem production) (see Olson 1981). However, taken by themselves, these factors account for relatively little of the variation in fire regimes that occurs either among ecosystems or within an ecosystem.

The extent to which available fuel is consumed by fire depends a great deal on the horizontal and vertical distribution of such fuels. Thus, despite heavy total fuel loads, ecosystems in which fuel distribution is vertically discontinuous (e.g., many western coniferous forests, savannas, etc.) experience comparatively light surface fires. Such fires, in turn, act to maintain fuel discontinuity (van Wagtendonk 1985, Christensen 1987). In the absence of fire, successional change often increases continuity, owing to invasion of shade-tolerant trees and accumulation of woody debris and so-called ladder fuels. The potential impact of such successional changes on subsequent fire behavior has been a matter of considerable concern to natural ecosystem managers.

Fuel moisture content influences both likelihood of ignition and subsequent fire behavior. Diurnal, seasonal, and year-to-year variations in rainfall and humidity clearly result in differences in fire regimes (including season of fire), both within and among ecosystems. Variations in topography and soil-water relations also influence changes in fuel moisture (e.g., Christensen 1981). All other things being equal, fuel moisture conditions can also be affected by successional change. For example, increased leaf area can result in increased evapotranspiration and more frequent water stress, whereas canopy closure may shade understory fuels, slowing the drying process. Changes in species composition may also affect fuel moisture conditions. For example, the litter layer of a pine-dominated mixed conifer forest remains loosely packed, owing to the geometry of the needles. It therefore dries out relatively quickly. Invasion of such stands by fir results in a more densely packed litter layer, which dries rather slowly. As a result, pine-dominated stands may burn in early spring, whereas stands with a heavy fir component may not carry a surface fire until the midsummer drought is well established.

The importance of the interaction between climatic conditions and fuel accumulation rates is obvious in a model developed by Martin (1982) for variations among ecosystems in western temperate North America. In very dry ecosystems, such as deserts and pine scrub, water stress may limit production and therefore rates of fuel accumulation. As moisture availability increases, fuel accumulation rates increase and fire return intervals decrease. This trend continues until fuel moisture begins to limit opportunities for successful ignition. Cooler and/or moister climates result in longer fire return intervals. Martin (1982) did not explore the consequences of this interaction on fire intensity; however, where return intervals are lengthened by factors other than available fuel, we might predict that fires would be more intense.

Variations in the ratio of dead to live fuel have a considerable impact on fire regimes. Factors affecting the accumulation of dead debris are reviewed by Rundel (1981) and Harmon et al. (1986). The rate of such accumulations is certainly affected by local climatic conditions and tends to increase at both the wet and dry ends of moisture gradients. Dead-to-live ratios tend to be highest in oligotrophic ecosystems, owing to slow rates of decomposition exacerbated by production of fuels high in lignin and low in nutrients (Aber and Melillo 1982, Vitousek 1982). Variations in this parameter often contribute to differences in fire regimes among ecosystems, such as between pine stands on the sterile soils of the southeastern Coastal Plain compared to pine stands on the more fertile, adjacent Piedmont (Christensen 1981, 1987). As discussed previously, the dead-to-live ratio also tends to increase during succession in many ecosystems, thus increasing the likelihood and potential intensity of fire as succession proceeds. However, successional change is not necessarily this simple. For example, replacement of pines by deciduous hardwoods on mesic sites in the southeastern Coastal Plain may result in decreased dead-to-live ratios and diminished fire probabilities (Christensen 1987).

Inorganic and organic chemical properties of fuel affect fuel flammability, and therefore fire regimes (Rundel 1981). Such factors include fuel mineral content and the concentration of flammable organic compounds. Mutch (1970) argued that natural selection has favored the evolution of chemical properties (and other characteristics) that increase flammability in species that dominate fire-prone ecosystems. Such adaptations might allow species to optimize fire regimes so as to maximize their reproductive success. This proposal has been criticized by Snyder (1984) and Christensen (1985). Regardless of their evolutionary origin, such features clearly influence fire regimes in different ecosystems and, as a consequence of changes in species composition, within particular ecosystems during succession.

The importance of overall landscape configuration to the fire regimes of component parts of that landscape has long been recognized (e.g., Harper 1911, Cooper 1922). Thus an isolated island of comparatively flammable vegetation in the midst of relatively non-flammable ecosystems is less likely to burn than its counterpart located near ecosystems with high fire frequencies. For example, fire return times in arctic heathlands are shortest near the transition to more easily ignited boreal forest (Rowe et al. 1974). The same pattern holds true for chaparral shrublands in southern California located near more flammable coastal sage scrub ecosystems (Radtke et al. 1982).

Human alteration of landscapes (in addition to direct human intervention in fire cycles such as accidental fires, prescribed fire, and fire suppression) has greatly altered fire regimes in some areas. In many cases, regional fire frequency has increased with increasing development, while fire size has decreased as a result of dissection of the landscape and fire suppression. As a consequence, mean fire return intervals and rotation periods have increased on many landscapes (Forman and Boerner 1981, Radtke et al. 1982, Minnich 1983, Peroni and Abrahamson 1986).

Given the nature of feedback, such as fuel accumulation and changes in dead-to-live ratios, which tend to maintain particular fire regimes, it is tempting to treat fire cycles as being precisely regulated in many fire-prone ecosystems. Managers of such ecosystems may thus wish to maintain the particular fire return intervals and intensities that characterize those ecosystems. However, while average fire return intervals have been calculated from fire chronologies in many ecosystems, the variances about those means are very large (e.g., Heinselman 1973, Kilgore and Taylor 1979, Arno 1980, Romme 1980, 1982, Martin 1982, Johnson et al. 1987). Furthermore, even when return intervals are regular, there is considerable variation in fire behavior among and within fires. I shall argue that such variability is an essential component of the maintenance of fire-prone ecosystems and must be a component of management programs in such ecosystems.

Fire Regimes and Successional Change

The extent to which a fire results in successional change is, almost by definition, determined by fire severity. For example, in the southeastern shrub-dominated wetland fires that burn quickly, killing only aboveground portions of shrubs, postfire succession is very rapid and a mature shrub community is regenerated within ten years. Severe burns in these ecosystems that consume organic soil and kill root systems initiate a prolonged successional sequence in which a mature shrub canopy may not be regenerated for several hundred years (Hamilton 1984, Christensen 1987). Similar patterns have been described for a variety of ecosystems (e.g., Heinselman 1981, Martin 1982, Myers 1985).

Such variation may be important within particular fires. For example, Christensen and Wilbur (in review) noted that small-scale (10 to 100 m) variation in fire behavior in shrub bog vegetation considerably affected postfire spatial heterogeneity, particularly with respect to the distribution of available phosphorus and water. Spatial patterns of postfire regrowth were clearly influenced by such heterogeneity. Where fire had been intense, reproduction from seed was important, whereas areas with light fire were revegetated by sprouts. Relative success among species was greatly affected by variability in the availability of phosphorus. Christensen and Wilbur propose that species richness in these shrublands is more dependent on the heterogeneity generated by fire than on changes in the average values for environmental factors.

The importance of chance variations in determining the structure, composition, and distribution of different ecosystems is clearly demonstrated in recent studies of sandhill pine forests and sand pine scrub in central Florida. Sandhill forests are dominated by a broken canopy of longleaf pine (*Pinus palustris*) with a flammable grassy understory, and typically experience short-return (three to eight years), low intensity fires. Sand pine scrub is dominated by scattered sand pine (*Pinus clausa*) with a dense shrubby understory. Intense crown-killing fires occur in these ecosystems at twenty to sixty year intervals. Until recently it was assumed that these differences in ecosystem structure were a consequence of subtle differences in soil characteristics (Laessle 1958, Christensen 1981), although evidence for such differences was weak. Kalisz and Stone (1984), using studies of soil phytoliths, showed that many sand pine scrub areas were previously inhabited by sandhill vegetation and vice versa. With Myers (1985), they suggested that these rather different ecosystems are the result of chance variations in fire regime. If an area of sandhill escapes fire for several years, sand scrub species may seed in and gradually displace the grasses. Flammability may actually decrease. In the absence of frequent surface fires, seedling establishment of longleaf pine is inhibited. When fire does occur, shrubs regenerate along with sand pines. Fire probabilities only gradually increase in the scrub, owing to slow fuel accumulation and comparatively low flammability. However, should such an area experience several fires at relatively short intervals, reestablishment of sandhill species is favored. Once reestablished, sandhill fuels increase the likelihood of short return, low intensity fires.

In many ecosystems fires are generally confined to a particular season, owing to the availability of ignition sources and fuel moisture. However, in some areas, such as the southeastern United States, fires may occur at any time of year, although the specifics of fire behavior may be season dependent. In such areas, the patterns of fire effects and postfire vegetation response vary depending on season of burn (Lewis and Harshbarger 1976, Gilliam and Christensen 1986, Snyder 1986).

In summary, not only can we characterize ecosystems and landscapes in terms of average fire regime properties such as fire return time or intensity, but we could conceivably describe them in terms of the variability in these properties. In fact, it may be more meaningful to do this. Much of the diversity of natural ecosystems depends on this variability. The problems inherent in including such variability in management schemes are discussed below.

ECOSYSTEM PRESERVATION

What Should Be Preserved?

Designation of areas for preservation as natural ecosystems has, until recently, been a rather haphazard process. More often than not, selection of sites for preservation was determined by political, economic, and aesthetic considerations more than ecological criteria. The result is that our current array of natural ecosystem preserves managed by both private and public agencies represents a rather biased sample of the landscape. This is not to suggest that the proper goal of a natural ecosystem preserve system should be balanced representation of ecosystem types, but rather that, in the absence of an organized agenda for designation of preserves based primarily on ecological criteria, we may overlook ecosystems in need of preservation or attempt to preserve particular units as natural ecosystems in locations where management options are especially constrained. This problem has become especially acute as landscape development and other human disturbance continue to reduce the spatial extent of natural ecosystems. Indeed, in many cases we may never know what we have lost. During the past two decades, groups such as the Forest Service, the National Park Service, the Nature Conservancy, and state natural heritage programs have recognized the need to develop natural ecosystem classifications, which serve as shopping lists for preserve designations and as natural area inventories of the specific areas suitable for preserve establishment.

Had the Clementsian model of succession proven to be the grand unifying theory of plant ecology, the task of determining what ecosystems to preserve would have been greatly simplified. Successional convergence would reduce the number of such types requiring preservation. Furthermore, managers could be less picky regarding site status with the knowledge that, without further molestation, sites would eventually converge to a particular natural ecosystem type. Most important, managers would have a naturally ordained classification system parallel to that for plant taxa. Although species designations are admittedly less tidy than once imagined, we still manage to identify various taxa for special attention (e.g., endangered species) in a nonarbitrary fashion. Alas, we have been forced to the realization that plant communities vary continuously in time and space, that patterns and mechanisms of successional development are very complex and not easily generalized, and that any classification of ecosystems involves arbitrary distinctions among categories rather than boundaries generated by natural processes. Despite this ugly fact, the development of a detailed classification of natural ecosystems should be a top priority. Furthermore, while admitting that a "natural system" of classification is not possible, this classification should reflect the processes that regulate natural ecosystems, as well as their structure and composition.

One of the great dead horses of plant ecology is the notion that classification and gradient analysis (ordination) are antithetical approaches to analysis of variation in plant communities (see McIntosh 1967). Without digressing into the virtues of specific ordination techniques, I wish to describe how gradient analytic techniques can be used to develop a community classification system that is not only sensitive to regulatory processes but also has predictive power.

Oosting (1942) recognized that deciduous forests in the Piedmont of the mid-Atlantic states could be classified as climax oak-hickory forests, occurring on mesic upland soils; "subclimax" blackjack oak-postoak forests, occurring on heavy clay soils; and postclimax beech-red maple forests, found on moist upland and alluvial soils. Considerable variation in species composition exists within these types; however, the complexity of these communities coupled with the absence of obvious environmental gradients made a more detailed classification difficult. Peet and Christensen (1980, 1987) sampled 105 deciduous forest stands in this same area, gathering data on species composition (herbs and trees), topographic position, soils, and disturbance history. Data on species abundances were compared among stands using detrended correspondence analysis (DCA), which identified major gradients (axes) of variation in this complex data set. These axes were then compared to data on environment using several different correlation techniques. In this manner, a detailed model of vegetation-environment relations was developed which revealed that much of the heretofore unexplained variation in vegetation was related to gradients in soil chemistry (and presumably nutrient availability) associated with the nature of the parent rock and patterns of weathering. Based on this model, Peet and Christensen (1980) identified eleven community types. They defined the boundaries between community types in a subjective fashion; however, numerical techniques are available for the designation of boundaries based on statistical criteria (Gauch 1982). Regardless of the approach, such classifications are arbitrary; nevertheless, they are often correlated with environmental variables that, in ways not yet understood, regulate community composition. Peet and Christensen were also able to identify that component of variation in plant community structure that was correlated with past disturbance. Such information can be used to identify stands of a particular community type that have been more or less disturbed.

Gradient models are also important predictive tools. For example, Christensen and Peet (1984) used this approach to identify successional trends in midsuccession pine stands and predict patterns of future change. In situations where development or disturbance has eliminated particular ecosystem types, this approach could be used to identify successional sites for preservation as means of eventually regenerating such lost ecosystems.

Although quantitative analytical techniques will be useful in developing operational classification systems, we should not attack the problem of developing such classification systems as if there were optimal solutions. Since our goal should be to preserve as much of the variation inherent in natural ecosystems as possible, our models of that variation should be as detailed as possible and flexible enough to accommodate more information as it becomes available.

How Much Should Be Preserved?

The simplest answer to this question might be "as much as possible." However, a variety of constraints will force us to identify some minimum amount of a natural ecosystem which must be preserved in order to achieve management goals.

As discussed previously, there has been considerable interest in the application of island biogeographic theory to the definition of preserve boundaries (e.g., Sullivan and Schaffer 1975, Simberloff and Abele 1976a, b). As preserve size decreases, extinction probabilities increase, in large part because smaller populations associated with decreased preserve size are more apt to be extinguished owing to chance events (MacArthur and Wilson 1967). Successful regeneration of many (perhaps most) plant populations is dependent on a wide variety of natural disturbances ranging in extent from gopher mounds and windthrows to landscape-scale catastrophes such as wildfire or pathogen outbreaks. Given that much of the diversity of natural ecosystems depends not only on the regular occurrence of disturbance but on the variance among occurrences, we might conclude that natural preserves must be sufficiently large to perpetuate the full range of natural disturbance for an ecosystem. I am not aware of any ecosystem where our understanding of natural disturbance is sufficient to prescribe a minimal area, and the limited data we do have suggest that preserves are usually too small to maintain the necessary variation.

In the case of fire, we must also consider the relationship of objects of preservation to other ecosystems. For example, fires that burn mixed conifer forests of the middle elevations of the Sierra Nevada are often initiated in downslope woodlands or chaparral. To maintain natural disturbance cycles in these forests, adjacent ecosystems must be considered in preserve design.

In What State Should Preserves Be Maintained?

Having designated an area for preservation as a natural ecosystem, in what state should it be preserved? In situations where the particular area is determined not to have changed significantly from its primeval state, the answer is obvious. However, there are several factors, including introduction of exotic organisms, loss of species, human disturbance, and interference with natural disturbance cycles, that have considerably altered the structure and composition of many ecosystems, and restoration of such ecosystems to some primeval state will be necessary. How do we determine what that state should be?

Management of the giant sequoia-mixed conifer forests provides an excellent case history study for this dilemma.

The Leopold Report (Leopold et al. 1963) asserted that the primary goal of the national parks in managing natural ecosystems should be preservation of a "vignette of primitive America." Although the main concern of that panel was wildlife management, they called special attention to the fact that long periods of fire exclusion from the mixed conifer forests of Lassen, Yosemite, Sequoia, and Kings Canyon national parks had resulted in marked changes in composition and structure compared with their presettlement condition. In particular, there had been invasion of saplings and pole-size individuals of shade-tolerant species such as white fir and incense-cedar, and increased accumulation of woody debris. The panel expressed concern that not only had the "vignette" been altered, but that these structural changes were apt to alter the pattern of future disturbance; future fires would be more intense and impacts on the communities would be more severe than those that would have occurred prior to fire suppression. In 1968 these concerns stimulated Yosemite, Sequoia, and Kings Canyon national parks to initiate prescribed fire management programs in the giant sequoia-mixed conifer forests in order to "maintain or restore natural fire regimes to the maximum extent possible" (Christensen et al. 1987). There is considerable debate regarding the exact structure of these forests prior to settlement and fire suppression and argument over the most appropriate methods to determine what that structure was.

Analysis of lake and bog sediment cores for changes in pollen or other fossil materials may provide us with measures of long-term vegetation change, but cannot provide the sort of resolution required to detect the changes in stand structure that have occurred as a consequence of fire suppression. Vankat and Major (1978) used historical records and photographs to examine changes in these stands. However, such records exist for relatively few sites and provide limited spatial information. In addition, they have a number of built-in biases. For example, photographers were often influenced by aesthetic concerns, therefore, dog-hair thickets of shade-tolerant saplings were rarely photographed. Bonnicksen and Stone (1982a, b, 1985) have advocated a site-intensive analysis in which characteristics of the existing vegetation and woody debris, coupled with conceptual and computer simulation models, are used to reconstruct past stand structure. Using such techniques, they suggest that past stand configuration can be determined. They expressed concern that prescribed burning may, by consuming woody debris and small trees, destroy data necessary for such reconstruction. Stephenson (1987) has criticized this approach from several standpoints, including uncertainty in the computer models and our understanding of the demographic processes, and the practicality of extrapolating from such site-intensive studies.

I would argue that, while a detailed picture of some particular community structure at some particular time in the past may be of interest in relation to a number of questions, restoration of communities to a specific primeval structure is neither practical nor desirable. For example, at any given time sequoia-mixed conifer forests displayed a wide range of structures, in part a consequence of chance variations in fire regimes. Based on a census of such forests over the landscape at some chosen time, one could conceivably construct frequency distributions such as the hypothetical distributions shown in Figure 4-2 for sequoia-mixed conifer forests. Chance variations in patterns of disturbance might result in more or less random fluctuations in the shape of this distribution over short periods (10 to 100 years), whereas climatic shifts and historical events such as the advent

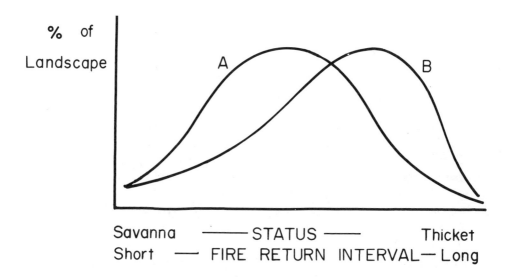

Figure 4-2. Hypothetical frequency distributions of landscape states in sequoia-mixed conifer forests during the Native American period (A) and after eighty years of fire suppression (B). Similar frequency distributions could be constructed for disturbance regimes on other landscapes; however, the precise shape of such distributions is expected to change through time owing to climatic change, chance factors, and changes in land use.

of Native Americans might result in directional and long-term shifts. In the case of many national park wilderness areas, it would appear that fire exclusion policies have resulted in a shift in such frequency distributions. I propose that no structure currently exists that has not occurred in the past, although particular structures are undoubtedly more common now. For example, parts of sequoia groves certainly escaped fire for many decades and must have been invaded by dog-hair thickets of white fir. Subsequent fires in those areas were undoubtedly severe. What has changed since the implementation of fire suppression policies is the frequency and spatial distribution of various forest structures, and consequently the potential for changes in spatial variability of fire intensity and severity.

Should the goal then be to restore a particular frequency distribution? Even if this were feasible, I do not think it would be desirable. As indicated above, such distributions were undoubtedly shifting over short and long time scales; the choice of a particular distribution would be arbitrary. Where human intervention has resulted in extreme shifts, it may be desirable to readjust the frequency of patch types such as has been done with prescribed burning programs (see Vale 1987 for a lucid discussion of this issue).

By What Means Should Natural Ecosystem Preserves Be Maintained?
In the best of all possible worlds, we would simply "let it be" and allow natural processes to regulate ecosystem structure and function. On landscapes where important natural disturbance cycles are unaffected by human activities or the size of the preserve, this strategy might indeed work. For example, such might be the case in the eastern deciduous forest with respect to windthrow and gap formation.

For a variety of reasons this approach will not be possible where fire regimes must be maintained. Natural ecosystem preserves are rarely sufficiently large that natural fire frequencies can be maintained by ignitions within the preserve boundaries. Fire suppression, or dissection and alteration of the landscape adjacent to a preserve, may greatly diminish the chance of fire within the preserve, or human activity may increase the likelihood of fire in some areas. The combination of increased ignition frequency owing to human activity and fire suppression has resulted in more frequent but smaller fires on many landscapes (e.g., Forman and Boerner 1981, Minnich 1983). Furthermore, in many preserves concerns for public safety and financial liability will not permit managers to allow fires to burn "at will" whenever they occur.

In situations where a passive management strategy will not maintain natural disturbance cycles, it will be necessary to artificially simulate those disturbances on the landscape; this has been the major thrust of prescribed fire management programs in many national parks (see NPS 1986, Christensen et al. 1987) and on Nature Conservancy preserves. Obviously, the specifics of such programs will vary from ecosystem to ecosystem; however, a few general points can be made.

Where human activities have altered fire regimes, especially where fire suppression has allowed accumulation of fuel, we cannot expect that fires will behave "naturally" (Bonnicksen and Stone 1985). This does not mean that fire cannot be used to restore natural fuel conditions; however, considerable prefire fuel manipulation or site preparation may be required to prevent excessively severe fire. Furthermore, a single fire in such situations often exacerbates fuel conditions owing to accumulation of partly burned debris. In these situations repeated prescribed burns may be required.

The goal of fire management programs (and I would maintain any program to maintain natural disturbance regimes) should not be the maintenance of average or "optimal" fire return intervals or intensities. In many ecosystems one of the most important consequences of fire (or natural disturbance in general) is to maintain landscape heterogeneity. The simulation and maintenance of that heterogeneity is one of the most significant challenges to natural landscape managers.

LITERATURE CITED

Aber, J. D., and J. M. Melillo. 1982. Nitrogen immobilization in decaying hardwood leaf litter as a function of initial nitrogen and lignin content. Can. J. Bot. 60:2263-2269.

Agee, J. K., R. H. Wakimoto, and H. H. Biswell. 1978. Fire and fuel dynamics of Sierra Nevada conifers. For. Ecol. Manage. 1: 255-265.

Allen, T. F. H., and T. B. Starr. 1982. Hierarchy: Perspectives for ecological complexity. University of Chicago Press, Chicago.

Arno, S. F. 1980. Forest fire history in the northern Rockies. J. For. 78:460-465.

Aston, A. R., and A. M. Gill. 1976. Coupled soil moisture, heat and water vapour transfers under simulated fire conditions. Aust. J. Soil Sci. 14:55-66.

Billings, W. D. 1938. The structure and development of old field shortleaf pine stands and certain associated properties of the soil. Ecol. Monogr. 8:437-499.

Blaisdell, J. P. 1953. Ecological effects of planned burning of sagebrush-grass range on the upper Snake River Plains. USDA Tech. Bull. 1075.

Bonnicksen, T. M., and E. C. Stone. 1982a. Managing vegetation within U.S. National Parks: A policy analysis. Environ. Manage. 6:101-102 and 109-122.

——. 1982b. Reconstruction of a presettlement giant sequoia-mixed conifer forest community using the aggregation approach. Ecology 63:1134-1148.

——. 1985. Restoring naturalness to national parks. Environ. Manage. 9:479-486.

Bormann, F. H., and G. E. Likens. 1979. Pattern and process in a forested ecosystem. Springer-Verlag, New York.

Botkin, D. B., J. F. Janak, and J. R. Wallis. 1972. Some ecological consequences of a computer model of forest growth. J. Ecol. 60:849-872.

Bratton, S. P. 1976. Resource division in an understory herb community: Responses to temporal and microtopographic gradients. Am. Nat. 110:679-693.

Byram, G. M. 1959. Combustion of forest fuels. In K. P. Davis (ed.) Forest fire: Control and use, pp. 61-89. McGraw-Hill, New York.

Chandler, C., P. Cheney, P. Thomas, L. Trabaud, and D. Williams. 1983. Fire in forestry. Vol. 1. John Wiley and Sons, New York.

Christensen, N. L. 1981. Fire regimes in southeastern ecosystems. In H. A. Mooney, T. M. Bonnicksen, N. L. Christensen, J. E. Lotan, and W. A. Reiners (eds.) Fire regimes and ecosystem properties, pp. 112-136. USDA For. Serv. Gen. Tech. Rep. WO-26.

———. 1985. Shrubland fire regimes and their evolutionary consequences. In S. T. A. Pickett and P. S. White (eds.) The ecology of natural disturbance and patch dynamics, pp. 85-100. Academic Press, New York.

———. 1987. The vegetation of the coastal plain of the southeastern United States. Chapter 11. In M. G. Barbour and W. D. Billings (eds.) North American terrestrial vegetation. Cambridge University Press, New York. In press.

Christensen, N. L., R. B. Burchell, A. Liggett, and E. L. Simms. 1981. The structure and development of pocosin vegetation. In C. J. Richardson (ed.) Pocosin wetlands, pp. 43-61. Dowden, Hutchinson and Ross, Stroudsberg, Pennsylvania.

Christensen, N. L., L. Cotten, H. T. Harvey, R. E. Martin, J. R. McBride, P. W. Rundel, and R. H. Wakimoto. 1987. Final report: Review of fire management programs for Yosemite, Sequoia and Kings Canyon National Parks. National Park Service. In press.

Christensen, N. L., and J. Franklin. 1987. Small-scale disturbance in forest ecosystems. Bull. Ecol. Soc. Am. 68:51-53.

Christensen, N. L., and R. K. Peet. 1981. Secondary forest succession on the North Carolina Piedmont. In D. C. West, H. H. Shugart, and D. B. Botkin (eds.) Forest succession: Concepts and application, pp. 230-245. Springer-Verlag, New York.

———. 1982. Measures of natural diversity. In J. L. Cooley and J. H. Cooley (eds.) Natural diversity in forest ecosystems: Proceedings of the workshop, pp. 43-58. Institute of Ecology, University of Georgia, Athens.

———. 1984. Convergence during secondary forest succession. J. Ecol. 72:25-36.

Christensen, N. L., and R. B. Wilbur. Fire effects in evergreen shrub bogs (pocosins) of the North Carolina coastal plain. I. Vegetation responses. J. Ecol. In review.

Clements, F. E. 1916. Plant succession: An analysis of the development of vegetation. Carnegie Institute Publication 242. Washington, D.C. 512 p.

———. 1928. Plant succession and indicators. Wilson, New York. 453 p.

———. 1936. Nature and structure of the climax. J. Ecol. 24:252-284.

Coile, T. S. 1940. Soil changes associated with loblolly pine succession on abandoned land of the Piedmont Plateau. Duke Univ. School For. Bull. 5:1-85.

Connell, J. H. 1978. Diversity in tropical rain forests and coral reefs. Science 199:1302-1310.

Connell, J. H., and R. O. Slatyer. 1977. Mechanisms of succession in natural communities and their role in community stability and organization. Am. Nat. 111:1119-1144.

Cooper, W. S. 1922. The broad-sclerophyll vegetation of California: An ecological study of chaparral and its related communities. Carnegie Institution of Washington Publication 319. 124 p.

Crocker, R. L., and J. Major. 1955. Soil development in relation to vegetation and surface age at Glacier Bay, Alaska. J. Ecol. 43:427-448.

Daubenmire, R. F. 1952. Forest vegetation of northern Idaho and adjacent Washington and its bearing on concepts of vegetation classification. Ecol. Monogr. 22:301-330.

Denslow, J. S. 1985. Disturbance-mediated coexistence of species. *In* S. T. A. Pickett and P. S. White (eds.) The ecology of natural disturbance and patch dynamics, pp. 307-324. Academic Press, New York.

Diamond, J. M. 1976. Island biogeography and conservation: Strategy and limitations: A reply. Science 193:1027-1029.

Drury, W. H., and I. C. T. Nisbet. 1971. Interrelations between developmental models in geomorphology, plant ecology and animal ecology. Gen. Syst. 16:57-68.

——. 1973. Succession. J. Arnold Arbor. 54:331-368.

Egler, F. E. 1954. Vegetation science concepts. I. Initial floristic composition—a factor in old-field vegetation development. Vegetatio 4:412-417.

——. 1977. The nature of vegetation. Connecticut Conserv. Assoc., Bridgewater.

Forcella, F., and T. Weaver. 1977. Biomass and productivity of the subalpine *Pinus albicaulis-Vaccinium scoparium* association in Montana. Vegetatio 35:95-105.

Forman, R. T. T., and R. E. Boerner. 1981. Fire frequency and the pine barrens of New Jersey. Bull. Torrey Bot. Club 108:34-50.

Gauch, H. G., Jr. 1982. Multivariate analysis in community ecology. Cambridge University Press, New York.

Gilliam, F. S., and N. L. Christensen. 1986. Herb-layer response to burning in pine flatwoods of the lower coastal plain of South Carolina. Bull. Torrey Bot. Club 113:42-45.

Gimmingham, C. H. 1972. Ecology of heathlands. Chapman and Hall, London.

Gimmingham, C. H., S. B. Chapman, and N. R. Webb. 1979. European heathlands. *In* R. L. Specht (ed.) Ecosystems of the world. Vol. 9A: Heathlands and related shrublands, pp. 365-413. Elsevier, Amsterdam.

Gleason, H. A. 1917. The structure and development of the plant association. Bull. Torrey Bot. Club 43:463-481.

——. 1922. On the relation between species and area. Ecology 3:158-162.

——. 1926. The individualistic concept of the plant association. Bull. Torrey Bot. Club 53:1-20.

——. 1927. Further views on the succession concept. Am. Midl. Nat. 21:92-110.

Gray, J. T., and W. H. Schlesinger. 1981. Nutrient cycling in Mediterranean type ecosystems. *In* P. C. Miller (ed.) Resource use by chaparral and matorral, pp. 259-285. Springer-Verlag, New York.

Grubb, P. J. 1977. The maintenance of species richness in plant communities: The importance of the regeneration niche. Biol. Rev. 52:107-145.

Hamilton, D. B. 1984. Plant succession and the influence of disturbance in the Okefenokee Swamp. *In* A. D. Cohen, D. J. Cassagrande, M. J. Andrejko, and G. R. Best (eds.) The Okefenokee Swamp, pp. 86-111. Wetland Surveys. Los Alamos, New Mexico.

Harmon, M. E., J. F. Franklin, F. J. Swanson, P. Sollins, S. V. Gregory, J. D. Lattin, N. H. Anderson, S. P. Cline, N. G. Aumen, J. R. Sedell, G. W. Lienkaemper, K. Cromack, Jr., and K.W. Cummins. 1986. Ecology of coarse woody debris in temperate ecosystems. Adv. Ecol. Res. 15:133-302.

Harper, J. L. 1969. The role of predation in vegetational diversity. Brookhaven Symp. Biol. 22:48-62.

Harper, R. M. 1911. The relation of climax vegetation to islands and peninsulas. Bull. Torrey Bot. Club 38:515-525.

Heinselman, M. L. 1973. Fire in the virgin forests of the Boundary Waters Canoe Area. Quat. Res. 3:329-382.

——. 1981. Fire intensity and frequency as factors in the distribution and structure of northern ecosystems. *In* H. A. Mooney, T. M. Bonnicksen, N. L. Christensen, J. E. Lotan, and W. A. Reiners (eds.) Fire regimes and ecosystem properties, pp. 7-57. USDA For. Serv. Gen. Tech. Rep. WO-26.

Hurlbert, S. H. 1971. The nonconcept of species diversity: A critique and alternative parameters. Ecology 52:577-586.

Huston, M. 1979. A general hypothesis of species diversity. Am. Nat. 113:81-101.

Johnson, E. A., D. Gregory, C. Larsen, and M. Pruden. 1987. Climatically-induced change in fire frequency 1586 to 1984 in southern Canadian Rockies. Bull. Ecol. Soc. Am. 68:332.

Kalisz, P. J., and E. L. Stone. 1984. The longleaf pine islands of Ocala National Forest, Florida: A soil study. Ecology 65:1743-1754.

Keever, C. 1950. Causes of succession on old fields of the Piedmont, North Carolina. Ecol. Monogr. 20:229-250.

Kilgore, B. M., and D. Taylor. 1979. Fire history of a sequoia-mixed conifer forest. Ecology 60:129-142.

Kucera, C. L. 1981. Grasslands and fire. In H. A. Mooney, T. M. Bonnicksen, N. L. Christensen, J. E. Lotan, and W. A. Reiners (eds.) Fire regimes and ecosystem properties, pp. 90-111. USDA For. Serv. Gen. Tech. Rep. WO-26.

Kuhn, T. S. 1962. The structure of scientific revolutions. University of Chicago Press, Chicago.

Laessle, A. M. 1958. The origin and successional relationship of sandhill vegetation and sand-pine scrub. Ecol. Monogr. 28:361-387.

Leopold, A. S., S. A. Cain, C. H. Cottam, I. N. Gabrielson, and T. L. Kimball. 1963. Wildlife management in the national parks. Am. For. 69(4):32-35,61-63.

Lewis, C. E., and T. J. Harshbarger. 1976. Shrub and herbaceous vegetation after 20 years of prescribed burning in the South Carolina coastal plain. J. Range Manage. 29:13-18.

Likens, G. E., F. H. Bormann, R. S. Pierce, J. S. Eaton, and N. M. Johnson. 1977. Biogeochemistry of a forested ecosystem. Springer-Verlag, New York.

MacArthur, R. H. 1965. Patterns of species diversity. Biol. Rev. 40:510-573.

MacArthur, R. H., and E. O. Wilson. 1967. An equilibrium theory of island biogeography. Princeton University Press, Princeton, New Jersey.

MacLean, D. A., and R. W. Wein. 1976. Biomass of jack pine and mixed hardwood stands in northeastern New Brunswick. Can. J. For. Res. 6:441-447.

Margalef, R. 1963. On certain unifying principles in ecology. Am. Nat. 97:357-374.

———. 1968. Perspectives in ecological theory. University of Chicago Press, Chicago. 111 p.

Martin, R. E. 1982. Fire history and its role in succession. In J. E. Means (ed.) Forest succession and stand development research in the Northwest, pp. 92-99. Forest Research Laboratory, Oregon State University, Corvallis.

Matthews, J. A. 1979. A study of the variability of some successional and climax plant assemblage-types using multiple discriminant analysis. J. Ecol. 67:255-271.

McIntosh, R. P. 1967. The continuum concept of vegetation. Bot. Rev. 33:130-187.

Minnich, R. A. 1983. Fire mosaics in southern California and northern Baja California. Science 219:1287-1294.

Mutch, R. W. 1970. Wildland fires and ecosystems—a hypothesis. Ecology 51:1046-1051.

Myers, R. L. 1985. Fire and the dynamic relationship between Florida sandhill and sand pine scrub vegetation. Bull. Torrey Bot. Club 112:241-252.

National Park Service. 1986. Fire management guidelines (NPS-18). U.S. Department of the Interior, Washington, D.C.

Noble, I. R., and R. O. Slatyer. 1980. The use of vital attributes to predict successional changes in plant communities subject to recurrent disturbances. Vegetatio 43:5-21.

Odum, E. P. 1969. The strategy of ecosystem development. Science 164:262-270.

Oliver, C. D. 1981. Forest development in North America following major disturbances. For. Ecol. Manage. 3:153-168.

Olson, J. S. 1958. Rates of succession and soil changes on southern Lake Michigan sand dunes. Bot. Gaz. 119:125-170.

———. 1981. Carbon balance in relation to fire regimes. In H. A. Mooney, T. M. Bonnicksen, N. L.

Christensen, J. E. Lotan, and W. A. Reiners (eds.) Fire regimes and ecosystem properties, pp. 327-378. USDA For. Serv. Gen. Tech. Rep. WO-26.

Oosting, H. J. 1942. An ecological analysis of the plant communities of Piedmont, North Carolina. Am. Midl. Nat. 28:1-126.

——. 1956. The study of plant communities. 2d ed. Freeman, San Francisco.

Parrott, R. T. 1967. A study of wiregrass with particular reference to fire. Master's thesis, Duke University, Durham, North Carolina. 130 p.

Parsons, D. J. 1976. The role of fire in natural communities: An example from the southern Sierra Nevada, California. Environ. Conserv. 3:91-99.

Peet, R. K. 1974. The measurement of species diversity. Ann. Rev. Ecol. Syst. 5:285-307.

——. 1981. Changes in biomass and production during secondary forest succession. In D. C. West, H. H. Shugart, and D. B. Botkin (eds.) Forest succession: Concepts and application, pp. 324-338. Springer-Verlag, New York.

Peet, R. K., and N. L. Christensen. 1980. Hardwood forest vegetation of the North Carolina Piedmont. Veröff. Geobot. Inst. Eidg. Hoch., Stif. Rübel (Zurich) 68:14-39.

——. 1987. Competition and tree death. BioScience 37:586-595.

Peroni, P. A., and W. G. Abrahamson. 1986. Succession in Florida sandridge vegetation: A retrospective study. Florida Sci. 49:176-192.

Peters, R. H. 1976. Tautology in evolution and ecology. Am. Nat. 110:1-12.

Pickett, S. T. A. 1976. Succession: An evolutionary interpretation. Am. Nat. 110:107-119.

——. 1980. Non-equilibrium coexistence of plants. Bull. Torrey Bot. Club 107:238-248.

Radtke, K. W., A. M. Arndt, and R. H. Wakimoto. 1982. Fire history of the Santa Monica Mountains. In C. E. Conrad and W. C. Oechel (eds.) Dynamics and management of Mediterranean-type ecosystems, pp. 438-443. USDA For. Serv. Gen. Tech. Rep. PSW-58.

Ricklefs, R. E. 1977. Environmental heterogeneity and plant species diversity: A hypothesis. Am. Nat. 111:376-381.

Romme, W. 1980. Fire history terminology: Report of the ad hoc committee. In M. A. Stokes and J. H. Dieterich (eds.) Proceedings of the fire history workshop, pp. 135-137. USDA For. Serv. Gen. Tech. Rep. RM-81.

——. 1982. Fire and landscape diversity in subalpine forests of Yellowstone National Park. Ecol. Monogr. 52:199-221.

Rothermel, R. C., and C. W. Philpot. 1973. Predicting changes in chaparral flammability. J. For. 71:640-643.

Rowe, J. S., J. L. Bersteinsson, G. A. Padbury, and G. A. Hermesh. 1974. Fire studies in the Mackenzie Valley. Can. Dep. Indian North. Aff. Pub. QS-1567-000-EE-Al.

Rundel, P. W. 1981. Structural and chemical components of flammability. In H. A. Mooney, T. M. Bonnicksen, N. L. Christensen, J. E. Lotan, and W. A. Reiners (eds.) Fire regimes and ecosystem properties, pp. 183-207. USDA For. Serv. Gen. Tech. Rep. WO-26.

Shugart, H. H. 1984. A theory of forest dynamics: The ecological implications of forest succession models. Springer-Verlag, New York.

Simberloff, D. S., and L. G. Abele. 1976a. Island biogeography theory and conservation practice. Science 191:285-286.

——. 1976b. Island biogeography and conservation: Strategy and limitations. Science 193:1032.

Snyder, J. R. 1984. The role of fire: Mutch ado about nothing. Oikos 43:404-405.

——. 1986. The impact of wet season and dry season prescribed fires on Miami Rock Ridge Pineland, Everglades National Park. South Florida Research Center Report SFRC-86/06. 106 p.

Sousa, W. P. 1984. The role of disturbance in natural communities. Ann. Rev. Ecol. Syst. 15:353-391.

Specht, R. L. 1981. Primary production in Mediterranean-climate ecosystems regenerating after fire. *In* F. di Castri, D. W. Goodall, and R. L. Specht (eds.) Mediterranean-type shrublands, pp. 257-267. Elsevier, Amsterdam.

Specht, R. L., P. Rayson, and M. E. Jackman. 1958. Dark Island Heath (Ninety-Mile Plain, South Australia). VI. Pyric succession: Changes in composition, coverage, dry weight, and mineral nutrient status. Aust. J. Bot. 6:59-88.

Stephenson, N. L. 1987. The use of tree aggregations in forest ecology and management. Environ. Manage. 11:1-5.

Sullivan, A. L., and M. L. Schaffer. 1975. Biogeography of the megazoo. Science 189:13-17.

Tilman, D. 1982. Resource competition and community structure. Princeton University Press, Princeton, New Jersey.

Vale, T. R. 1987. Vegetation change and park purposes in the high elevations of Yosemite National Park, California. Ann. Assoc. Am. Geogr. 77:1-18.

Van Cleve, K., and L. A. Viereck. 1981. Forest succession in relation to nutrient cycling in the boreal forest of Alaska. *In* D. C. West, H. H. Shugart, and D. B. Botkin (eds.) Forest succession: Concepts and application, pp. 185-211. Springer-Verlag, New York.

van Wagtendonk, J. W. 1985. Fire suppression effects on fuels and succession in short-fire-interval wilderness ecosystems. *In* J. E. Lotan, B. M. Kilgore, W. C. Fischer, and R. W. Mutch (eds.) Proceedings, Symposium and Workshop on Wilderness Fire, pp. 119-126. USDA For. Serv. Gen. Tech. Rep. INT-182.

Vankat, J. L., and J. Major. 1978. Vegetation changes in Sequoia National Park, California. J. Biogeogr. 5:377-402.

Vitousek, P. 1982. Nutrient cycling and nutrient use efficiency. Am. Nat. 119:553-572.

Vitousek, P. M., and W. A. Reiners. 1975. Ecosystem succession and nutrient retention: A hypothesis. BioScience 25:376-381.

Walker, J., C. H. Thompson, I. F. Fergers, B. R. Tunstall. 1981. Plant succession and soil development in coastal dunes of subtropical eastern Australia. *In* D. C. West, H. H. Shugart, and D. B. Botkin (eds.) Forest succession: Concepts and application, pp. 107-131. Springer-Verlag, New York.

Walker, J., and R. K. Peet. 1983. Composition and species diversity of pine-wiregrass savannas of the Green Swamp, North Carolina. Vegetatio 55:163-179.

Waring, R. H., and W. H. Schlesinger. 1985. Forest ecosystems: Concepts and management. Academic Press, New York.

Watt, A. S. 1947. Pattern and process in the plant community. J. Ecol. 35:1-22.

White, P. S., and S. T. A. Pickett. 1985. Natural disturbance and patch dynamics: An introduction. *In* S. T. A. Pickett and P. S. White (eds.) The ecology of natural disturbance and patch dynamics, pp. 3-13. Academic Press, New York.

Whittaker, R. H. 1953. A consideration of climax theory: The climax as a population and pattern. Ecol. Monogr. 23:41-78.

——. 1965. Dominance and diversity in land plant communities. Science 147:250-260.

——. 1975. Communities and ecosystems. 2d ed. Macmillan, New York.

Whittaker, R. H., and S. A. Levin. 1977. The role of mosaic phenomena in natural communities. Theor. Popul. Biol. 12:117-139.

5

Managing Ecosystems for Viable Populations of Vertebrates: A Focus for Biodiversity

HAL SALWASSER

ABSTRACT Different areas in large regional ecosystems must be managed under coordinated goals and strategies to sustain their biological diversity. One park, wilderness, forest, or refuge, unless it has millions of acres, cannot sustain a broad enough distribution of seasonal habitats to supply the needs of all species. This is especially true for animals with large home ranges (wolves, bears, eagles, large cats) or distant migrations (salmon, elk, and many birds). Population viability for such species depends on favorable conditions in many different places and freedom for individuals to move throughout a population of large size. This paper discusses the biology of population viability, the potential areas in the United States where coordinated management of large regional ecosystems can sustain viable populations of native species, and the use of an indicator species (the spotted owl) to delineate a coordinated ecosystem management system across geographic scales and land use classes and ownerships.

Aldo Leopold (1966) captured the essence of a goal for biological diversity when he said that the first step is to save all the parts: "To keep every cog and wheel is the first precaution of intelligent tinkering." Recovery of threatened or endangered species and maintenance of viable populations of all other species is thus the foundation for any policy. But the scope of biological diversity extends beyond the parts to include processes through which the parts interact: biological diversity is the variety and variability of life and its processes in an area (U.S. Congress 1987). This paper is about keeping the parts around, especially the species parts. We must assume that if all the parts are healthy, the processes are free to work.

The biological diversity of an ecosystem can easily encompass thousands of species. Many of these species are microscopic; some have not even been identified or classified. Biodiversity also includes assemblages of plants and animals that are recognized as distinct communities. And it includes countless processes and pathways through which species interact, such as mutualism, competition, predation, and parasitism. This richness of species and their interactions continually changes and is difficult to measure. Compounding this difficulty, scientists often debate the limits of acceptable variation within species—the points at which different species, subspecies, or races are recognized. This makes it difficult to know when one part is really two or two really one. The result is that biological diversity defies precise definition. It is a concept that must be translated into tangible, measurable aspects. Unless managers identify specific aspects of diversity to focus planning and management, it will never be clear when the goal is achieved.

Two kinds of indicators have been used to focus conservation plans: species and communities (Holbrook 1974, Siderits and Radtke 1977). This paper shows the use of species as management indicators and how planning for viable populations of vertebrates integrates actions across ownership boundaries and geographical scales. Using species as indicators is complementary to using biological communities. Since most species cannot persist without an array of communities, planning for species helps determine the kinds, amounts, and arrangements of communities needed in an area. If there are concerns for biological communities that are not well served by indicator species, those communities should also be used as management indicators.

Concerns about biological diversity often focus on viability of particular species populations. For example, recovery to self-sustaining condition of threatened or endangered species and protection of declining species are commonly identified as diversity issues. Current cases in the United States include grizzly bears (*Ursus arctos*) in the northern Rocky Mountains and spotted owls (*Strix occidentalis*) in old-growth forests of the Pacific Northwest (Heinrichs 1984, Simberloff 1987).

The key to sustaining the full variety of species in an area is to reduce, minimize, or mitigate threats to the continued existence of those species most in jeopardy. Many, perhaps most, species in large areas of wildlands are not vulnerable to extirpation. Prudence dictates that attention be directed to those that are. Several scientific theories and methods are useful in planning a management strategy. But none are complete or universally applicable; feasible strategies cannot be derived solely or conclusively through science and technology. Broadly coordinated, adaptive resource management that includes monitoring and research as active parts of the whole strategy is also needed (Holling 1978, Walters 1986).

To illustrate these points, the paper is divided into three parts: (1) brief discussion of the biology of population viability, (2) presentation of potential areas in the United States where coordinated management of large regional ecosystems can sustain viable populations of most, if not all, native species, and (3) the use of a management indicator species, the spotted owl, in coordinating ecosystem management across geographic scales and land use classes and ownerships.

THE BIOLOGY OF POPULATION VIABILITY

Viability for individual organisms is the ability to survive to reproductive age. For populations it is the ability to continue to exist through their own reproductive success: a self-sustaining population (Soulé 1980, Shaffer 1981, Salwasser et al. 1984, Samson et al. 1985, Soulé 1987a).

Shaffer (1981) proposed that a viable population would have a 95% likelihood of existing in 1,000 years. The implications are that (1) future existence cannot be guaranteed; a viable population has some chance of not surviving, and (2) viability is a long-term concept; centuries rather than years or decades are involved. Shaffer's parameters—likelihood of existence and time—are accepted by many scientists (see Soulé 1987b). But there is nothing sacrosanct about 95% and 1,000 years. Public policy or social preferences may legitimately argue for criteria of 75% for 100 years or 99% for 50 years. A major problem with any long-term standard is that existing models and theories do not provide for long-term predictions with much realism or precision. And what, for example, should managers do if it is not physically possible to provide for high likelihoods of survival for long periods? As Soulé (1987a) points out, the biological issue remains alive until the last individual is gone. In any case, policy and strategy for population viability are not purely biological issues, because solutions will be shaded by costs, trade-offs, balances of land uses, and the risk tolerance of the shapers of public policies. Rather than search for standard scientific criteria for viability, it is more useful to understand the factors that can jeopardize the existence of a species in an area and implement management plans to limit their potential effects.

Extirpation of Populations

The basic task in preventing loss of species from an area is to minimize or mitigate threats to their future existence. There are two kinds of threats: those that operate internal to populations and those that are external.

Internal Threats: The Importance of Numbers. Three factors that affect viability operate internal to populations: demographics, genetics, and behavior. And they interact. The demography of a population is its vital statistics: number, sex ratio, age structure, natality, survivorship, and recruitment rates. The demographics of a viable population provide resilience to the random variations in birth and death rates, migrations, colonizations, weather, and resources that occur in all populations (Soulé 1980). Over the long term, net recruitment (births plus immigration minus deaths plus emigration) must equal or exceed zero.

Population number is perhaps the most important demographic factor, because large numbers buffer the effects of extreme events, and small numbers make even minor fluctuations critical (Belovsky 1987, Goodman 1987). Population numbers that buffer effects of random variations in births and deaths depend on the life history of the species. Long-lived animals with low reproductive rates, such as large birds and mammals, may only need populations on the order of high tens to low hundreds for demographic resilience over the short term. Conversely, species like mice and songbirds may require populations on the order of thousands for similar resilience.

Genetic variation in a viable population provides for continual adaptation of the species. Environments are constantly changing and species must possess the ability to adjust to those changes and produce offspring that can persist in the face of new environments, new competitors, and new predators. Viewed over a sufficiently long period, this whole process is called evolution. On a human time scale the effects of change are less noticeable, though still important.

As with demographics, numbers that provide sufficient genetic variation vary according to life history. An additional concern is that not all members of a population make equal contributions to the genetic makeup of subsequent generations. Therefore, geneticists have developed the concept of an effective population number to describe the genetic characteristics of actual populations (Lande and Barrowclough 1987). If there are an equal number of adult males and females in a population, they all have an equal likelihood of reproducing with one another and contributing offspring to the next generation, and if total population number is constant, the genetically effective population number (N_e) is approximately equal to the total number of adults (N). This is rarely, if ever, the case with wild populations of vertebrates, and effective population numbers are often lower than census population sizes by a factor of 0.5 to 0.1 (Soulé 1980).

The importance of effective population number is due to the relation between effective number and loss of genetic variation over time in populations of various sizes and demographics. The smaller the population and the faster the turnover of generations, the quicker inbreeding may occur and genetic variation be lost. Scientists are currently debating the importance of genetic variation to viability and the ability to be precise in estimating effective population numbers and their meaning. In any case, effective numbers should be relatively high, ideally greater than high hundreds or low thousands, and it must be kept in mind that actual population size may need to be two to ten times larger than a desired effective size (Lande and Barrowclough 1987).

The third internal factor is behavior. Many vertebrates function through complex social systems, such as packs or matriarchies, and depend to some extent on transmission of learned behavior from one generation to the next. Reductions in density or total numbers, or even alterations in sex ratio or age structure, may disrupt behavior that is critical to survival or reproduction. A viable population would possess a wide range of behavior and the social structure needed for survival in an area.

External Threats: The Importance of Distribution. External threats include many things, and they can be either chronic or acute. For example, chronic factors could include invasion of an area by a superior competitor (often humans); gradual, unfavorable changes in climate, such as described in this volume by Brubaker; or systematic alteration of suitable habitat, as through agricultural development, atmospheric acidification (Grigal, this volume; Schofield, this volume), reservoir construction, or permanent deforestation. Acute external threats might include volcanoes, fires, violent storms, or epidemic disease.

Because external threats vary greatly over time and space, an essential attribute of a viable population is broad geographic distribution. Distribution is the location of individuals or groups of individuals within a population relative to the geographic range of the species. It must buffer the effects of unfavorable local events, and provide for the continued functioning of individuals as parts of a larger biological population. That is, distribution must minimize the likelihood for small, permanently isolated populations that would have low total numbers and low genetically effective numbers. Such populations would lack the ability to disperse throughout the species range to colonize new or vacated habitats and naturally restore individuals following local extirpations.

For population viability, distribution must allow for (1) survival and reproduction of a relatively large number of individuals in many different places, (2) periodic recolonization and genetic interchange throughout the population, and (3) occupancy of the array of environments to which the species is adapted. A general rule emerges with regard to numbers and distribution and their effects on viability (one might argue it is just common sense): more is better. Its corollary is: there is no magic number.

A General Model for Population Viability

Providing for demographics, genetics, behavior, and distribution that buffer internal and external threats to a population translates into high population numbers and, for many species, large geographic areas. High numbers provide protection from the negative effects of random changes in demographics and genetics and for high retention of learned behavior. Broad geographic distribution allows for resilience to change and for local catastrophic events to occur without significant threat to the total population.

A general model of these relationships is that viability is proportional to numbers and distribution (Figure 5-1). The quantitative relationships of such a model would vary according to species life histories in different environments. Species with high turnover rates, high reproductive potentials, and short life spans, such as mice and songbirds, would require higher numbers and more locations of occupancy for a given likelihood of continued existence than would a species with low turnover rates, low reproductive potentials, and long life spans, such as bears, eagles, and mountain sheep. The differences for a similar viability between mice and bears could easily be an order of magnitude or more.

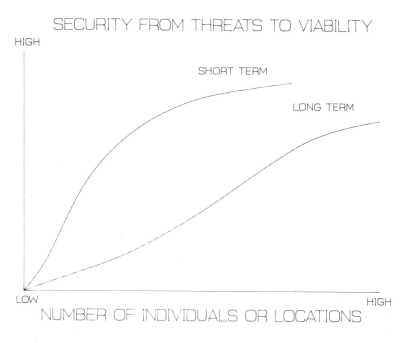

Figure 5-1. A general model of population viability. The likelihood of continued existence for a population increases in proportion to the number and geographic distribution of individuals. Below a lower threshold of numbers or distribution, changes do not significantly affect viability: the population is in great jeopardy of extirpation from demographic, genetic, or catastrophic threats. Above an upper threshold, changes in number or distribution do not measurably add to viability: a point of diminishing returns has been reached and there are few threats to viability. Exact, quantitative relationships between numbers and viability have not been determined for any species. This model is intended as a general guide, not a precise prediction tool.

The relationships between numbers and viability in the general model are hypothetical. It may be years or decades before the relationships for many species will be known precisely. But that does not weaken the utility of the model. Its purpose is to offer general guidance on adaptive management, not to predict with the illusion of science or precision. For example, if existing conditions or a proposed management strategy appear to result in unacceptable high risks to the viability of a species, cooperative agreements with other landowners or a different management strategy can be employed to yield higher total numbers or a broader distribution. If that is not possible, intensive management of habitats, populations, competitors, or predators; research; and monitoring might be employed as parts of a strategy to minimize a particular threat, say barriers to dispersal. If high value trade-offs are involved, such as recreation facilities, timber, minerals, or water development, the relative effects of altering population numbers and distributions can be assessed as part of determining mitigations or enhancements to offset the effects.

The viability model is intended to focus planning, management, research, and monitoring on the major factors that control viability, and allow comparison of the relative merits of alternative public policies. For population viability there are no scientifically correct or incorrect answers, just shades of better or worse. Only future conditions will tell if a particular strategy sustained viable populations as part of overall biological diversity.

COORDINATED MANAGEMENT OF LARGE REGIONAL ECOSYSTEMS

The general model shows that a public policy for biological diversity that includes viable populations of large or wide-ranging animals will require management of areas that can sustain thousands of individuals in many different locations if that is possible. This is supported by empirical evidence on carnivorous mammals (Schonewald-Cox 1983) and recent planning for the spotted owl (USDA Forest Service 1988). Areas exceeding millions of acres may be needed to support populations of large vertebrates with demographics, genetics, and distributions that would provide a high likelihood of continued existence well into the future. In the United States no such area exists as a distinct unit of any one management agency or owner. Nor is it politically or economically likely or feasible to combine enough area under one ownership. The only reasonable option is to manage different areas as if they were integral parts of a large ecosystem (Salwasser et al. 1987).

Can coordinated management of large ecosystems work? Only broad coordination has characterized interagency relationships to date. And it has been argued recently that individual units of protected lands, such as national parks in western North America, function as if they were land-bridge islands surrounded by an ocean of inhospitable habitat (Newmark 1986). If such is the case, the faunal richness of parks or wilderness areas would reflect size and time since isolation. It doesn't (Quinn et al., in preparation). National Park mammalian faunas are richer than would be predicted from island biogeography theory. Furthermore, mammalian richness of surrounding managed forests is as high or higher than that of the parks.

Managed wildlands that surround parks in western North America are not always, perhaps not often, inhospitable to wild vertebrates. This indicates that a network of different kinds of conservation areas, managed under similar policies and practices, can sustain biological diversity while producing natural resources. Such a network exists in national parks, national forests, and the matrix of other public and private lands surrounding them in the United States.

There are approximately 19.6 million acres (8 million ha) in the National Park System in the contiguous forty-eight states (all land area data from USDI 1985). These lands are managed primarily for recreation and protection of natural diversity. Wilderness areas in the National Forest System in the same states comprise 26.8 million acres (nearly 11 million ha). They are managed for minimal human impact and primitive recreation experiences. Together these constitute 2.3% of the area of the lower forty-eight states.

Approximately 176 million acres (71 million ha) of public lands in the forty-eight states are managed by the USDI Bureau of Land Management; 141 million acres (57 million ha) of lands not in the wilderness system are managed for other multiple uses by the USDA Forest Service (a total of 168 million acres including wilderness areas in the National Forest System in the forty-eight states); 9.4 million acres (3.8 million ha) of national wildlife refuges and about 28 million acres (11 million ha) of other federal lands, including military reservations, are protected in these states. Thus approximately 400 million acres (162 million ha) of public lands in the lower forty-eight states are managed for a variety of uses, including protection of natural resources. That is about 21% of the entire area of those states.

Many of these public lands occur as large areas of contiguous wildland (Figure 5-2). If one uses the criteria that (1) no significant barriers to free movement of ground-dwelling or flying animals exist, (2) large amounts and multiple locations of suitable habitat exist, and (3) human activities, as regulated by state and federal laws and rules, do not threaten the resilience or productivity of populations, the following areas of contiguous public and intermingled private lands could function as large regional ecosystems. They

Figure 5-2. Selected areas of the United States that contain contiguous public wildlands that are managed under policies to protect biological diversity (after Salwasser et al. 1987).

hold a high potential to sustain vertebrate diversity under existing land uses and designations (approximate area is principally the national park and national forest lands in each ecosystem aggregated from USDI and USDA data presented in National Geographic Society 1984):

Northern Cascades: 7.9 million acres (3.2 million ha); a large national park and several national forests that contain large wilderness areas

Southern Cascades and Klamath Mountains: 14.1 million acres (5.7 million ha); several small national parks, many national forests with large wilderness areas, and other public forest lands

Sierra: 11.1 million acres (4.5 million ha); several large national parks, many national forests with large wilderness areas, and adjoining public and private forest lands

Grand Canyon and Mogollon: 14 million acres (5.7 million ha); a large national park, many national forests with large wilderness areas, and adjoining public forest and rangelands

Central Rockies: 11.4 million acres (4.6 million ha); a large national park, many national forests with large wilderness areas, and large areas of other public lands

Greater Yellowstone: 16 million acres (6.5 million ha); a large national park, many national forests with large wilderness areas, and adjoining public and private wildlands

Northern Rockies: 32.4 million acres (13.1 million ha); several large national parks, many national forests with large wilderness areas, several large Indian reservations, and large areas of other public lands; contiguous with similar lands north into Canada

Southern Appalachian Highlands: 3.1 million acres (1.3 million ha); a large national park, and several national forests with small wilderness areas

These are only a few prominent examples. There may be other large ecosystems, and there are undoubtedly many effective smaller ones. These areas have the biological capability to sustain their full biological diversity, though protection of large predators may require special actions due to human intolerance. Each "regional ecosystem" is managed under policies to recover threatened or endangered species and maintain diversity. Additional policies and plans provide for many human uses of various plant, animal, geological, and scenic resources. These are multiple-use ecosystems at the regional scale with dominant uses at any point in time at local scales.

In addition to public wildlands there are approximately 817 million acres (330 million ha) of forests, parks, wetlands, and rangelands managed by states, counties, and private owners. These have a variety of purposes, but many of them are compatible with goals for biological diversity. This is about 42% of the area of the lower forty-eight states. If some or all of these lands make contributions to viability of different species populations while meeting people's other needs for resources, then up to 63% of the area of the lower forty-eight states could be considered as informal parts of a conservation network. These data are not presented to argue for new laws, regulations, land acquisitions, exchanges, or easements. They merely show the potential for different ownerships with different goals and management practices to contribute to overall biological diversity.

Improving coordination and cooperation between management agencies and private landowners in large regional ecosystems should prolong their effectiveness in conserving biological diversity while meeting people's many needs for wildland resources (Salwasser et al. 1987). Park and wilderness areas must be managed within that context—for their roles in contributing to the overall diversity and values of the ecosystem, not as if they were preserves that function as isolated islands with distinct biological boundaries.

Vertebrate populations are one of the influences that can bring management of disparate units of land into coordination. This is especially true for species that have large home ranges or that range widely in their annual movements. Goals for vertebrate population viability can shape management of a large, regional ecosystem in ways that also provide protection for smaller or less demanding species. The indicator species that will be used to illustrate this is the spotted owl, a medium-size bird that inhabits mature and old-growth forests of western North America. It is related in size, habits, and habitat affinities to the barred owl (*Strix varia*) of eastern North America and the tawny owl (*Strix aluco*) of Europe and Eurasia, though these two species appear to be more adaptable to open, wooded areas (Mikkola 1973).

Habitats suited for spotted owls are also used by dozens of other birds, mammals, amphibians, reptiles, and hundreds of invertebrates and plants. Since managers cannot plan for all of these species individually, they use the spotted owl, which appears to require the largest tracts of such habitat, to help determine the kinds, amounts, and distribution of habitats to provide in an area (the spotted owl is not the only indicator used to make these determinations).

Management of forest ecosystems to maintain viable populations of spotted owls is a major conservation issue. Its preferred habitats also have high value as a source of timber (Heinrichs 1984). It is not the purpose of this discussion to argue the merits or demerits of a specific course of management for spotted owls (see Dawson et al. 1986, Marcot and Holthausen 1987, Simberloff 1987, Salwasser 1987, USDA Forest Service 1988). The case is used to illustrate how a strategy for population viability of a rare but wide-ranging vertebrate can integrate policies and practices of ecosystem management across agency jurisdictions and at several geographic scales. The cases of grizzly bears or red-cockaded woodpeckers would provide similar examples of the use of vertebrates to integrate ecosystem management at the regional scale.

Species Range and Biology

In the United States, the spotted owl occurs throughout forests of the Pacific Rim states and across the southwestern states north into the central Rocky Mountains and south into northern Mexico (Figure 5-3). Forest types occupied vary as well as elevation zones. But preferred habitats have the common traits of containing large diameter trees, relatively closed canopies (often of several distinct vertical layers), and the presence of standing and fallen dead trees. These traits are believed to be critical to production of prey, arboreal rodents primarily, and thermal regulation for the owls (Carey 1985). Such habitats commonly occur in natural, old-growth stands, but have also been induced by historic selective logging in some areas. Young stages of forest development, such as occur following clearcutting and planting of closely spaced trees of a single age and species, are not suitable for the spotted owl.

Studies of spotted owls fitted with radio-transmitter devices show relatively large home ranges, varying from 1,250 to 10,450 acres (500 to 4,300 ha) (USDA Forest Service 1988). Amount of suitable habitat in these home ranges varies from 370 to 3,800 acres (150 to 1,500 ha). Juvenile owls have been observed to travel up to 62 miles (100 km) during dispersal from their fledging area, but only 20% of 58 juveniles studied traveled more than 20 miles (32 km) (USDA Forest Service 1988). Empirical data indicate that

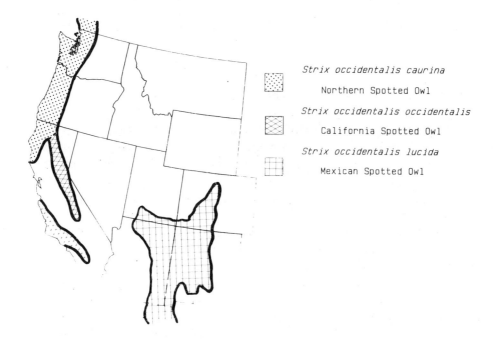

Figure 5-3. Geographic distribution of spotted owls in western North America.

home range sizes and amounts of suitable habitat within home ranges tend to increase from south to north in the species' range.

Current taxonomy recognizes three subspecies, but recent studies of morphology and field distribution (USDA Forest Service 1988) indicate that spotted owls are contiguous from the southern Sierra Nevada in California to Canada. They also show that (1) a small population may be isolated on the Olympic Peninsula of Washington State, (2) the Columbia River Gorge may present a partial barrier to free movement north and south, and (3) high fragmentation of forests characterizes several areas in Washington, Oregon, and California. Spotted owls in southern California and the southwestern United States are believed to be disjunct from northern populations.

Demographics, as with all wild populations, are only generally known (USDA Forest Service 1988). There are an estimated 2,700 pairs of owls from the southern Sierra Nevada in California north to Canada, and population trend is declining at approximately 1 to 2% per year in direct response to harvest of old-growth forest (USDA Forest Service 1988). Affinity for large areas of mature and old-growth forests coupled with declining population due to continued harvest and fragmentation of habitats led to concern for the long-term viability of the spotted owl in the Pacific Northwest. Projection of historic trends showed increased fragmentation and isolation of subpopulations in an overall population of smaller size. Spotted owls would thus be increasingly vulnerable to threats from random variations in births and deaths, inbreeding or loss of genetic variation, and local catastrophes.

Policy

The National Forest Management Act of 1976 (16 U.S.C. 1604) requires that national forest plans "provide for diversity of plant and animal communities in order to meet overall multiple-use objectives." Diversity is defined in regulations for implementing the act (Federal Register 1982) as "the distribution and abundance of plant and animal communities and species within the area covered by a land and resource management plan." The regulations further identify criteria for distribution and abundance of animal species as "[f]ish and wildlife habitat shall be managed to maintain viable populations of existing native and desired non-native vertebrate species in the planning area. For planning purposes, a viable population shall be regarded as one which has the estimated numbers and distribution of reproductive individuals to insure its continued existence is well-distributed in the planning area."

Current Status

Habitat inventory is available for only the states of Oregon and Washington. In 1988, there were approximately 6,100,000 acres (2.5 million ha) of spotted owl habitat in those states on all ownerships. Nearly 1,300,000 acres (500,000 ha), or 21%, occur in federal parks and wilderness areas. Approximately 4,145,000 acres (1.7 million ha) exist in the National Forest System, 68% of all spotted owl habitat in Washington and Oregon. National forest lands suitable for timber production hold about 2,560,000 acres (1 million ha), and lands not suited for timber production and outside of wilderness hold the remaining 820,000 acres (300,000 ha). Thus 2,120,000 acres (800,000 ha), or 34%, of all existing spotted owl habitat are in wilderness, national parks, or national forest areas unsuited for timber production. The USDI Bureau of Land Management manages about

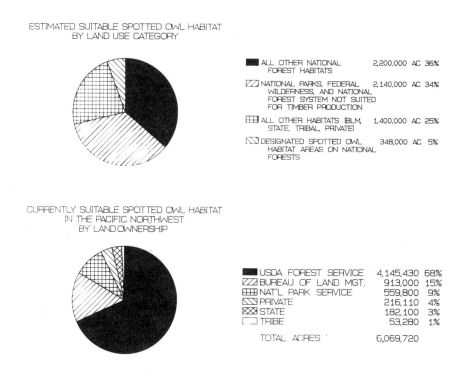

ESTIMATED SUITABLE SPOTTED OWL HABITAT
BY LAND USE CATEGORY

■ ALL OTHER NATIONAL FOREST HABITATS — 2,200,000 AC 36%

▨ NATIONAL PARKS, FEDERAL WILDERNESS, AND NATIONAL FOREST SYSTEM NOT SUITED FOR TIMBER PRODUCTION — 2,140,000 AC 34%

⊞ ALL OTHER HABITATS (BLM, STATE, TRIBAL, PRIVATE) — 1,400,000 AC 25%

⊠ DESIGNATED SPOTTED OWL HABITAT AREAS ON NATIONAL FORESTS — 348,000 AC 5%

CURRENTLY SUITABLE SPOTTED OWL HABITAT
IN THE PACIFIC NORTHWEST
BY LAND OWNERSHIP

■ USDA FOREST SERVICE	4,145,430	68%
▨ BUREAU OF LAND MGT.	913,000	15%
⊞ NAT'L PARK SERVICE	559,800	9%
⊠ PRIVATE	216,110	4%
⊠ STATE	182,100	3%
☐ TRIBE	53,280	1%
TOTAL ACRES	6,069,720	

Figure 5-4. *Top*: projected relative contribution of different land use classes and ownerships to population number of spotted owls in the Pacific Northwest during the next ten to fifteen years. *Bottom*: currently suitable habitat in the Pacific Northwest by landownership.

900,000 acres (370,000 ha), 15%, and all other state, tribal, and private lands hold about 450,000 acres (180,000 ha), or 8% of the total (Figure 5-4).

Many large reserve areas with numerous pairs of spotted owls are currently under management policies that will protect owls. Major concern is over what will happen to owl habitats and the population on the remaining 66% of the habitat that could be under timber production. Most pressing is how much change is likely to occur during the current planning period of the next ten to fifteen years. Without specific action to protect habitats outside of wilderness and national parks, spotted owls could eventually become restricted to those areas in small, isolated populations that would be highly vulnerable to extirpation threats.

A Strategy to Integrate Biological and Geographic Scales

Providing for the future of any wild population requires attention to different biological and geographic scales. In this case the biological scales are breeding pairs, local populations, and the regional or species population.

Breeding Pairs. Breeding pairs must have sufficient amounts and arrangements of suitable habitat to survive from year to year and periodically produce enough offspring to replace themselves. This occurs at the geographic scales of single forest stands and watersheds of approximately 5,000 to 10,000 acres (2,000 to 4,000 ha). It requires that plans specify conditions for suitable stands and how those stands should occur on the landscape of a watershed—that is, the biogeography of the watershed. For example, managers may establish standards, based on field studies, that suitable stands are greater than 60 acres (25 ha) in area and have large diameter trees with moderately dense canopy closure and standing dead trees. Each pair of owls in a particular area would be provided

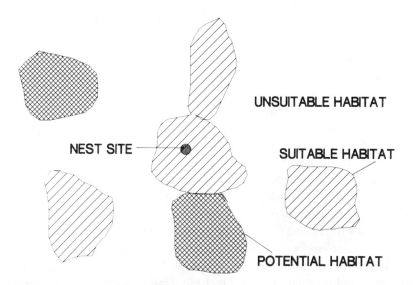

2.1 MILES FROM NEST SITE

UNSUITABLE HABITAT

NEST SITE

SUITABLE HABITAT

POTENTIAL HABITAT

Figure 5-5. Schematic representation of an area designated to provide habitat for a breeding pair of spotted owls.

with at least 2,200 acres (900 ha) of such habitat within 2.1 miles (3.4 km) of the nest site. And those stands should be contiguous or separated by open areas of not more that several hundred yards (meters) in width (Figure 5-5). These specifications are illustrative only, but are within the range of options considered for planning spotted owl habitat management by the Forest Service (USDA Forest Service 1988).

Local Populations. Local populations must have sufficient breeding pairs to provide for yearly replacement of individuals lost to mortality or emigration, and withstand normal, annual fluctuations in births and deaths (Soulé 1987a). If such populations are not significantly isolated from the rest of the species' population, they should behave as if they had the demographics and genetics of the larger population. This is ideal. However, if fragmentation or geographic barriers isolate local populations, threats to existence will increase and extra management attention will be needed. For example, it may be necessary to provide breeding pairs with larger amounts of suitable habitat to increase the likelihood of survival and reproductive success. And it may prove useful to provide for periodic genetic interchange by introducing individuals from larger populations.

Local populations should ideally have at least several hundred pairs of adults in a network of habitats that allows for adequate recruitment to offset mortality, dispersal of juveniles throughout the population, colonization of vacant habitats, and interchange of genetic materials. This calls for attention to hot spots, where reproduction is atypically high, and for connectedness of areas suitable for occupancy by pairs (Harris 1984). For example, plans may call for spacing of habitat areas for pairs of owls to be not more than 6 miles (10 km) apart for areas that can sustain fewer than three pairs, and not more than 12 miles (24 km) apart for areas that sustain three or more pairs. And special provisions for travel corridors, such as riparian forests or ridge tops, may be specified.

A pair of spotted owls can be protected in a single watershed completely under the jurisdiction of one owner or agency. But local populations of several hundred pairs will cross administrative and ownership boundaries. And it is highly unlikely that a single park or wilderness area could sustain even this size population. In the southern Cascades of Oregon, for example, a population of several hundred pairs of spotted owls would depend on the USDA Forest Service, USDI Bureau of Land Management, USDI Park Service, and state and private forest managers of more than twenty specific ownerships or administrative units working in coordination.

Regional Populations. At the scale of regional or whole species populations, total population number and connectedness are crucial. Barring total isolation of local populations, all individuals in a regional population can contribute to viability. Populations at the regional scale should have the characteristics described above for local populations, but ideally would also have population numbers in the thousands rather than hundreds of pairs. This, and the presence of the species at many more geographic locations, provides for long-term security from genetic erosion and large-scale catastrophes. Plans at the regional scale thus focus on sustaining relatively high total numbers and ensuring that those numbers do not occur in small, isolated, local populations. Special attention to areas of current or potential isolation and high fragmentation is important. For the spotted owl, regional population issues include dealing with possible isolation on the Olympic Peninsula, where large areas of private land separate public forests, and preventing further isolation in other parts of the species' range.

Sustaining spotted owls as part of the biological diversity of a park, wilderness, or single forest thus requires a regional ecosystem strategy. It calls for integration of actions at three geographic scales (Figure 5-6): stands and watersheds for individuals and breeding pairs, and larger areas for local and regional-species populations. It therefore requires coordination across agency and ownership boundaries. These are relatively new issues in natural resources planning and management. If spotted owl habitat was "free" (unencumbered by other uses or values), the planning and coordination task would be relatively easy: protect all the habitat that exists and grow more if necessary. This is rarely the case for rare or endangered species. It is certainly not the case for spotted owls.

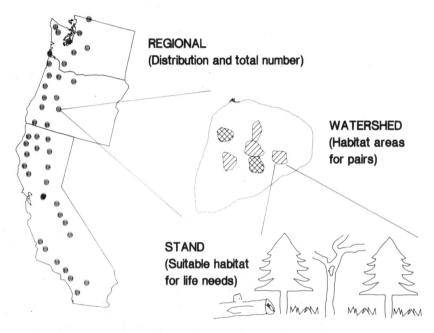

Figure 5-6. Principal geographic scales at which land and resource planning must address kinds, amounts, and distribution of habitat to sustain population viability of large or wide-ranging vertebrate species.

Integration of Land Use Classes

Protecting spotted owl habitats outside of national parks and federal wilderness areas will affect timber-based industries, jobs, and regional economies. An estimated 44 and 28% of the economies of Oregon and Washington, respectively, depend on timber supplies from national forests. Approximately 30% of those supplies come from stands that are also suitable spotted owl habitat (USDA Forest Service 1988). Thus protecting the biological diversity of parks and wilderness areas, which depends on ensuring regional viability of spotted owls, has significant economic overtones.

The task in such situations is to build upon the effectiveness of areas that already provide suitable future environments, such as the large reserve areas of parks and wilderness plus other lands that will be managed under compatible uses. The ways that people are dependent on the resources, and especially the significant negative effects on their livelihoods and life-styles, should be weighed against what is necessary to protect the species. Thus a critical planning issue is how to determine criteria for deciding when measures to conserve biological diversity must take precedence over the other needs of people from an area.

There are several approaches to this task, ranging from a kind of analytical imperative, or urgency, to various forms of adaptive planning and management. The former is warranted when uncertainties are few and conditions are at a crisis stage—that is, population numbers or distribution are known to be so low that immediate extirpation or extinction is likely. In such cases, scientific evidence or analysis would argue for immediate and drastic actions to protect the species regardless of costs to other uses of the land. If conditions are not at crisis proportions, say long-term trends are down but there is time to learn more and adjust management, the adaptive approach is prudent.

The adaptive approach is proposed for spotted owls, because 6,100,000 acres of habitat remain in Oregon and Washington alone, the entire population exceeds 2,700 pairs, including those in California, and trends are only minus 1 to 2% per year. The current planning period covers only the next ten to fifteen years, and a major research and development effort is under way.

The most important issue in current plans is the extent to which activities carried out or committed to under the plan would compromise long-term viability or cause irreversible processes of decline to begin. The important reference points are (1) now, (2) the end of the plan period, and (3) a future time when effects of actions taken during the plan period would have played themselves out. Since the spotted owl lives to age 15 to 20 years, lag effects might show up for several decades following the plan period.

Any plan to meet a future goal entails costs, risks, and uncertainty. In general, those increase as the goal becomes longer in time. When costs are high or uncertainty jeopardizes success of the plan, monitoring and research are warranted. In this case, there are potentially high costs in forgone timber revenues and loss of jobs. And there are risks to spotted owls due to small population dynamics and isolation. Therefore, a Research, Development, and Application Program of intensified inventory, monitoring, and research is part of the overall management strategy (USDA Forest Service 1988). This will allow revision of plans in five years if new information indicates the necessity.

The framework of a regional strategy for spotted owl population viability during the current plan period of the next ten to fifteen years is generally the following:

Use wilderness areas and national parks in Oregon and Washington as large reserve areas to contain an estimated 1,300,000 acres (526,000 ha) of suitable habitat with capability to support 270 pairs of owls.

Assume that lands outside of the national parks and National Forest System in Oregon and Washington will sustain not more than an estimated capability to support 70 pairs of owls throughout the period.

Use lands in the National Forest System that are technically not suited for timber production, yet outside of wilderness, to sustain an estimated 822,000 acres (333,000 ha) of suitable habitat.

Augment the above habitats with Spotted Owl Habitat Areas designated in lands suited for timber production on the national forests at approximately 6 to 12 mile intervals to prevent isolation and extreme fragmentation of habitats. The designated areas could contain up to 348,000 acres (140,000 ha) of habitat depending on forest-level decisions. Designated areas would support several hundred pairs, but their principal purpose would be to provide for interchange of individuals throughout the population and prevent isolation of owls in the large reserve areas.

Remaining lands in the National Forest System will be under a variety of uses. At the end of the plan period they will still contain at least 1,935,000 million acres (780,000 ha) of suitable habitat. In total, all National Forest System lands in Oregon and Washington will sustain capability for about 1,130 breeding pairs of spotted owls after fifteen years under the plan.

Other owl habitats, principally in California, will contain an estimated 1,050 pairs within the contiguous biological population, thus contributing to an overall population of 2,180 pairs. The genetically effective population number should be on the order of 1,000 pairs or more (Salwasser et al. 1984).

Projecting the strategy out to fifty years, which implies three successive decisions to continue following the same strategy or to increase or decrease habitat protection, would result in a population of 1,600 to 2,000 pairs depending on the decisions, and assuming no new information that spotted owls are more or less numerous and adaptable than now thought.

In addition to intensive inventory and monitoring of the above estimates, the Research, Development, and Application Program is carrying out detailed research on habitat affinities, population dynamics, genetic interchange, and potential for silvicultural enhancement of habitats. Analysis indicates that the strategy described for the next ten to fifteen years would not jeopardize the long-term continued existence of spotted owls in the Pacific Northwest. However, the strategy will not work without coordination across agency and ownership boundaries or provision of sufficient kinds, amounts, and distributions of habitats at all geographic scales (Figure 5-6). And major assumptions and unknowns, along with adherence to planning direction, must be evaluated frequently through a wide array of studies and reviews.

SUMMARY REMARKS

The purpose of this paper was to present a perspective on population viability as an aspect of biological diversity in wildland ecosystems. Population viability is certainly not all there is to diversity in wildlands. But the continued existence of large vertebrate species will always be one important indicator of the health of wild ecosystems. Therefore, it will guide much of the management of those systems.

The perspective included an overview of the population viability concept. It was a simple discussion without pretense of precision or sophistication. It employed general models and rules of thumb. That is sufficient for most people to understand that large ecosystem areas under coordinated management are necessary to sustain the biodiversity of specific places within those areas. Many areas of the United States still have the capability to function as ecosystems that are effective in sustaining regional biological diversity. Several prominent examples were illustrated. More detailed discussions of population viability appropriate for scientists and technicians can be found elsewhere, most notably in Soulé (1987b).

The paper concluded with a presentation of how population viability for one indicator of diversity is approached for a large region of North America. The purpose was not to argue that the specific strategy described is correct or better than another possible strategy. Only time and continued research and monitoring will show that. Rather, the paper was intended to accomplish three things. First, it was to show that managing park or wilderness ecosystems for biological diversity that includes vertebrates with large home ranges must entail coordinated management of the larger ecosystems in which those park or wilderness areas are embedded. Second, it was to offer a glimpse of the type of guidance that appears to be needed at different geographic scales—stands, watersheds, and regional distributions—to integrate ecosystem management from local to regional areas and across ownerships or administrative units. That guidance would be even more complicated if human activities had a significant direct bearing on the goal, as would be the case for grizzly bears and wolves. Third, it was to show that biologically and politically complex cases such as the spotted owl probably cannot be resolved by force, however sound the evidence and analysis; they need an iterative approach that employs planning, monitoring, and research as active parts of adaptive resource management. The spotted owl could be used as one indicator of how well a coordinated ecosystem management is working from the Sierra to the northern Cascades.

LITERATURE CITED

Belovsky, G. E. 1987. Extinction models and mammalian persistence. *In* M. E. Soulé (ed.) Viable populations for conservation, pp. 35-58. Cambridge University Press, New York.

Carey, A. B. 1985. A summary of the scientific basis for spotted owl management. *In* R. J. Guttierrez and A. B. Carey (eds.) Ecology and management of the spotted owl in the Pacific Northwest. USDA For. Serv. Tech. Rep. PNW-185. Pac. Northwest For. and Range Exp. Stn., Portland, Oregon.

Dawson, W. R., J. D. Ligon, J. R. Murphy, J. P. Myers, D. Simberloff, and J. Verner. 1986. Report of the Advisory Panel on the spotted owl. Audubon Conservation Report 7. National Audubon Society, New York.

Federal Register. 1982. Rules and regulations for National Forest System land and resource management planning. Federal Register 36 CFR Part 219. 47(190):43026-43052.

Goodman, D. 1987. The demography of chance extinction. *In* M. E. Soulé (ed.) Viable populations for conservation, pp. 11-34. Cambridge University Press, New York.

Harris, L. D. 1984. The fragmented forest: Island biogeographic theory and the preservation of biotic diversity. University of Chicago Press, Chicago.

Heinrichs, J. 1984. The winged snail darter. J. For. 81:212-262.

Holbrook, H. L. 1974. A system for wildlife habitat management on southern national forests. Wildl. Soc. Bull. 2:119-123.

Holling, C. S. (ed.) 1978. Adaptive environmental assessment and management. John Wiley and Sons, New York. 377 p.

Lande, R., and G. F. Barrowclough. 1987. Effective population size, genetic variation, and their use in population management. *In* M. E. Soulé (ed.) Viable populations for conservation, pp. 87-124. Cambridge University Press, New York.

Leopold, A. 1966 (1949). A Sand County almanac. Oxford University Press, New York.

Marcot, B. G., and R. S. Holthausen. 1987. Analyzing population viability of the spotted owl in the Pacific Northwest. Transactions, North American Wildlife and Natural Resources Conference 52:333-347.

Mikkola, H. 1973. Wood owls. *In* J. A. Burton (ed.) Owls of the world, their evolution, structure, and ecology, pp. 116-146. A & W Visual Library, Milan, Italy.

National Geographic Society. 1984. A guide to our federal lands. National Geographic Society, Washington, D.C.

Newmark, W. D. 1986. Mammalian richness, colonization, and extinction in western North American national parks. Ph.D diss., University of Michigan, Ann Arbor.

Quinn, J. F., C. van Riper III, and H. Salwasser. Mammalian extinction from national parks in the western United States. Ecology. In press.

Salwasser, H. 1987. Spotted owls: Turning a battleground into a blueprint. Ecology 68:776-779.

Salwasser, H., S. P. Mealey, and K. Johnson. 1984. Wildlife population viability: A question of risk. Transactions, North American Wildlife and Natural Resources Conference 49:421-439.

Salwasser, H., C. M. Schonewald-Cox, and R. Baker. 1987. The role of interagency cooperation in managing for viable populations. *In* M. E. Soulé (ed.) Viable populations for conservation, pp. 159-174. Cambridge University Press, New York.

Samson, F. B., F. Perez-Trejo, H. Salwasser, L. F. Ruggiero, and M. L. Shaffer. 1985. On determining and managing minimum population size. Wildl. Soc. Bull. 13:425-433.

Schonewald-Cox, C. M. 1983. Conclusions: Guidelines to management: A beginning attempt. *In* C. M. Schonewald-Cox, S. M. Chambers, B. MacBryde, and W. L. Thomas (eds.) Genetics and conservation, pp. 414-445. Benjamin/Cummings, Menlo Park, California.

Shaffer, M. L. 1981. Minimum population sizes for species conservation. BioScience 31:131-134.

Siderits, K., and R. E. Radtke. 1977. Enhancing forest wildlife habitat through diversity. Transactions, North American Wildlife and Natural Resources Conference 42:425-433.

Simberloff, D. 1987. The spotted owl fracas: Mixing academic, applied, and political ecology. Ecology 68:766-772.

Soulé, M. E. 1980. Thresholds for survival: Maintaining fitness and evolutionary potential. *In* M. E. Soulé and B. A. Wilcox (eds.) Conservation biology: An evolutionary-ecological perspective, pp. 151-170. Sinauer Associates, Sunderland, Massachusetts.

——. 1987a. Where do we go from here? *In* M. E. Soulé (ed.) Viable populations for conservation, pp. 175-184. Cambridge University Press, New York.

——. 1987b. Viable populations for conservation. Cambridge University Press, New York.

U.S. Congress. 1987. Technologies to maintain biological diversity. Office of Technology Assessment. U.S. Government Printing Office, Washington, D.C. GPO Stock No. 052-003-01058-5.

USDA Forest Service. 1988. Supplement to the Final Environmental Impact Statement for the Pacific Northwest Regional Guide. USDA Forest Service, Portland, Oregon.

USDI Bureau of Land Management. 1985. Public land statistics 1984. U.S. Government Printing Office. Washington, D.C.

Walters, C. 1986. Adaptive management of renewable resources. Macmillan, New York.

6

The Pit or the Pendulum:
Issues in Large Carnivore Management
in Natural Ecosystems

ROLF O. PETERSON

ABSTRACT Even though most North American ecosystems lack naturally regulated populations of large carnivores, these species continue to attract a disproportionate share of the attention of resource managers and the general public. This is consistent with the role of top carnivores in ecological systems and in our own culture. This role includes major impacts on density and demography of large herbivores via predation and of sympatric carnivores via interference competition. The adequate conservation of large carnivores is of practical significance in resource management because, as "umbrella species," they may enhance the maintenance of species diversity in both fauna and flora. Because of low reproductive rates, large carnivores must be managed to maintain appropriate levels of adult survival to achieve management goals. Where large carnivores are absent, human predation has largely substituted for predation by top carnivores. Where these predators still exist, a major management challenge will be to accommodate the needs and interests of these obligate meat eaters as well as humans.

In most ecosystems containing a natural fauna, large mammalian carnivores have typically captured a disproportionate share of public attention and professional management efforts, positive and negative. As the embodiment of wilderness values for a large segment of the populace, they serve as a barometer of our efforts at ecosystem stewardship. These rare, sometimes dangerous, species require huge expanses of land to provide a resource base and requisite protection from people, who constitute the major source of mortality for large carnivores throughout the world.

Among the large carnivores, the wolf (*Canis lupus*) brings to the forefront most of the classical problems arising when humans mix with carnivores. Colored by our cultural myths portraying wolves as evil personified, and complicated by the legitimate issue of competition between wolves and humans for prey, the wolf has probably been the most difficult species for humans to deal with throughout history. Originally the most widespread of all modern mammals (Nowak 1983), wolves have now been greatly reduced worldwide, yet in North America they will continue to be ecologically prominent over a substantial portion of the continent (Canada and Alaska).

The significance of large carnivores to our society and culture is matched by the major ecological role played by these species. What can we say today about this role? Do these rare carnivores really have an important ecosystem function? Are wolves and other large predators efficient regulators of prey populations, or does loss of prey to predators merely substitute for other forms of mortality (compensatory mortality)? These are old but important questions, which will be examined with the perspective provided by long-term continuing studies of wolves and their prey in Isle Royale National Park, Michigan. The wolf population of Isle Royale is a unique scientific resource that has been the subject of continuous study for the past twenty-nine years. The original objective of this research program remains unchanged today—to clarify wolf and moose (*Alces alces*) dynamics and population regulation in this isolated, two-species system (Mech 1966, Jordan et al. 1967, Wolfe and Allen 1973, Peterson 1977, Allen 1979, Peterson and Page 1988). Although the program was originally conceived by Durward Allen as a bold, ten-year study, it is clear today that even a study three times that long has just begun to reveal important characteristics of this predator-prey system.

As a brief review, events at Isle Royale can be usefully separated into the three decades spanned by the study. The 1960s saw impressive stability in the wolf population, numbering twenty to twenty-eight animals, while the moose population slowly increased (Figure 6-1). The "balance of nature" was real indeed, or so it seemed. Wolves were thought to be maintaining the moose population within the limits of its food supply (Mech 1966). The tumultuous 1970s brought a veritable explosion in wolves, as their numbers increased almost every year for a decade. In contrast, the moose population plummeted, following several years of marginal foraging exacerbated by a series of severe winters. Overuse of forage by moose had clearly not been avoided, even in the presence of a naturally regulated wolf population. Peterson (1977) proposed that the moose decline was a fundamental response to a declining resource base for moose, caused by a maturing forest in the massive 1936 burn, but later events disproved this hypothesis. By the early 1980s it was clear that the wolves faced a critical food shortage, and soon starvation and interpack warfare reduced wolves by over 70% in just two years. Moose then began an impressive resurgence in old mature forests with, the textbooks tell us, little potential as moose habitat. Today, moose density continues to be as high on Isle Royale as anywhere in the world.

It is clear that we still have much to learn. Why has understanding of large mammal predator-prey dynamics been so difficult to attain, and so often clouded by disagreement? Some obvious difficulties arise from the following realities:

1. Spatio-temporal differences in predation effects are real, and simplifying generalizations elusive. Wolf-moose dynamics, for example, can be expected to vary greatly in different areas, depending on predator and prey density and presence of buffer prey species. Bergerud (1980) proposed that where caribou coexisted with wolves, there was a so-called predator pit effect (low prey density perpetuated by predation pressure). Similarly, Messier and Crete (1985) and Bergerud et al. (1983) concluded that the moose populations they studied were maintained at low density by wolf predation. However, Isle Royale supports five times as many moose per unit area, even with the world's highest wolf density.

Buffer prey species may completely transform the nature of predation pressure. For example, wolf packs in Minnesota rarely exploit moose if white-tailed deer are present (Mech and Frenzel 1971, Mech 1977a), and wolves in Algonquin Provincial Park in Ontario did not prey on moose even after a serious deer decline (Kolenosky and Standfield 1975). There are most likely some long-standing traditions in these social carnivores that influence prey choice.

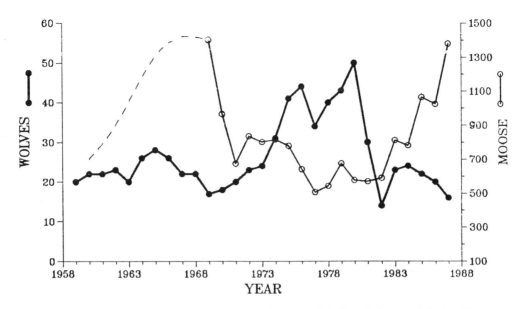

Figure 6-1. Fluctuations of wolf and moose populations at Isle Royale National Park, 1959-87.

Temporal changes in wolf-prey dynamics are very clear at Isle Royale. Wolf predation, the dominant mortality factor, consistently reduces the potential rate of increase of the moose population. However, the extent to which wolves have depressed moose numbers has varied widely over a span of three decades.

2. Large carnivores in forested regions are rare and elusive, and their prey are notoriously difficult to enumerate. There were few important predation studies of North American carnivores before the advent of radiotelemetry. Intensive use of this important study technique has taught us much about the behavior and population ecology of large carnivores (Hornocker 1970, Jonkel and Cowan 1971, Mech 1977b, Fritts and Mech 1981, Peterson et al. 1984a, Knight and Eberhardt 1985, Mech 1986). The task of counting forest ungulates, on the other hand, remains problematic, and no technological breakthroughs in this area appear imminent. As Pielou (1981) pointed out, this simple reality has often stymied attempts to test competing ecological hypotheses.

3. Most studies of large mammal dynamics have not been conducted over a long enough period. Fluctuating populations will tell us more about the ingredients of population change than stationary populations, but different species exhibit different time scales for population change, just as pendulums of different lengths swing back and forth at different rates. Calder (1983) and Peterson et al. (1984b) extended allometry into the realm of population cycles and suggested that the period required for regularly occurring population fluctuations depends on body size. Like time-based cellular and physiological functions (e.g., heart rate, respiratory rate), the time required, for example, for a population to double or to complete a population cycle is proportional to the quarter root of body mass for a given species. This arises fundamentally from the so-called Kleiber relationship between metabolic rate and body mass (Linstedt and Calder 1981, Calder 1984). Thus it has been predicted that if Isle Royale moose (and wolves) continue to exhibit regular population fluctuations, these "cycles" will have a period length of thirty to forty years (Peterson et al. 1984b). Most mammals larger than beavers would require

two decades or more to exhibit one entire population oscillation. Extending the argument to elephants, the largest terrestrial form, the time predicted for one complete fluctuation would be about seventy-five years. Obviously this is pertinent to our understanding of plant population changes that are induced by varying amounts of herbivore feeding pressure.

WHY ARE RARE CARNIVORES IMPORTANT?

The significance of large carnivores can be partitioned into both ecological and aesthetic contributions. Both areas should figure prominently in the rationale for carnivore conservation in any ecosystem, especially those including large parks and wilderness areas.

Ecological Roles for Predators

Herbivore Regulation. While generalizations are difficult, it is likely that in some cases large carnivores control prey density, and certainly they influence prey dynamics. Semantic difficulties abound here, since there are six commonly used definitions of the word "control" (Taylor 1984). The spatio-temporal variability already alluded to probably explains the divergent views of wolf predation offered by Mech (1966), Pimlott (1967), Pimlott et al. (1969), Mech and Frenzel (1971), Kolenosky (1972), Keith (1974, 1983), Mech and Karns (1977), Peterson (1977), Peterson et al. (1984a, 1984b), Bergerud (1980), Mech and Karns (1977), Bergerud et al. (1983), Gasaway et al. (1983), Carbyn (1983), and Mech et al. (1987).

Relatively few predator-prey systems contain only one large predator, especially when the effects of predation by humans are included. Further, it is quite likely that effects of different predators on prey are additive, not compensatory (cf. Gasaway et al. 1983). A conceptual model of multiple equilibria for prey of large carnivores (Messier and Crete 1985) offers some hope for reconciling the divergent conclusions referred to above (Figure 6-2). While there remain serious doubts about the validity of key assumptions that underlie this model, such as the nature of predator functional responses and prey recruitment curves (Van Ballenberghe 1980), it suggests the expected outcome of adding additional species of predators to a simple predator-prey system: it becomes increasingly difficult to maintain high densities of prey, and declines to lower prey equilibria may not occur in incremental fashion (in theory, equilibria do not exist at intermediate densities).

A common Holarctic prey for large carnivores, the moose supports several major predators: wolf, black bear (*Ursus americanus*), grizzly bear (*Ursus arctos*), and humans. However, high densities of moose ($>2/km^2$) seem to exist only in the presence of, at most, just one of these predator species. For example, abundant Scandinavian moose populations largely contend only with human predators, as do moose in Newfoundland (Bergerud et al. 1968, Markgren 1974). Isle Royale moose are preyed upon only by wolves. Moose in Gaspésie Provincial Park in Quebec are not hunted by humans or wolves, and the extent of predation by resident black bears is unknown (M. Crete, pers. comm.). Conclusions or tests of hypotheses in this controversial area must be refined by comparative analyses and experimental research. High density moose populations with two or more of these predator species are very rare, but in areas of exceptional habitat (synonymous with addition of food in Figure 6-2), moose may approach densities of 1 to

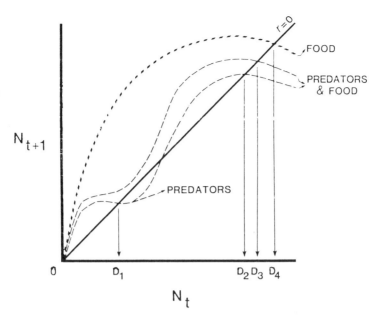

Figure 6-2. Conceptual model proposed by Messier and Crete (1985:510) for dynamics of predators, moose, and moose food supply. Dashed lines indicate moose recruitment at different predator densities and with enhanced food supply. Points D_1 through D_4 represent theoretically stable prey equilibria.

$2/km^2$ even with all three predator species, such as in a recent burn on Alaska's Kenai Peninsula (Bangs 1985). The multiple equilibrium hypothesis would permit such "escape" from predation if the herbivore food level was sufficiently high.

A recurring question that must be repeatedly addressed by wildlife managers in the contiguous United States involves regulation of ungulate numbers in the absence of large carnivores, a common condition in many so-called natural ecosystems. Throughout the contiguous forty-eight states, human predation has largely supplanted predation by large carnivores. Bubenik (1972) recommended that the health and welfare of prey could be best served by managing hunters to duplicate rather closely the age and sex selectivity of wolf predation, much as is done by moose hunters in Sweden (Lykke 1974, Markgren 1974), where annual hunter kill of moose exceeds that in all of North America. As a modern expedient, this may be the best we can do. Yet it is doubtful that selection by the gun, even in the hands of educated hunters, can match the subtleties of natural predation (Temple 1987).

A pertinent case to consider is the continued existence of the northern Yellowstone elk population in the absence of its pristine agent of natural selection, the wolf (Houston 1982). Studies in Canadian national parks demonstrate that where elk exist in multi-species prey systems, they constitute the major prey species for the wolf (Carbyn 1983). My own view is that if we could restore the wolf to the Yellowstone ecosystem as a naturally regulated ecological force (i.e., regulated by its own prey base), the dynamics of this elk population will be substantially changed. In the short term, the average rate of population increase will surely decline, and perhaps mean elk densities would be reduced. Given a very long-term perspective, whether or not there were changes in mean elk density, I would expect a reduction in the annual variance in elk density, causing secondary influences on virtually all scavenging species. In the Yellowstone ecosystem, Houston (1982:201) considered wolf absence as the greatest departure from the park's objective of maintaining natural ecosystems.

Interference Competition. Interspecific competition may be of two types: exploitative competition, in which common resources are used more successfully by one species than another; and interference competition, in which one species directly interferes with resource use or survival of another species (Schoener 1982). In the most extreme form, one species may kill a competing species. Although this phenomenon is poorly understood and not well documented, it is slowly becoming evident that large carnivores frequently determine the distribution and abundance of smaller carnivores, especially those with morphological and ecological similarities. In a spectacular natural experiment, wolves completely eliminated coyotes on Isle Royale (544 km^2) in about seven years (Mech 1966, Krefting 1969). Direct killing of smaller carnivores by large carnivores, while perhaps rare, seems to have led to strong avoidance behavior that produces a pattern of spatial or temporal nonoverlap between similar carnivore species (Harris 1981, Sargeant et al. 1987). This pattern seems best documented historically on a continental scale (Johnson and Sargeant 1977).

The significance of interference competition among carnivores may be completely masked by the substantial degree to which human-caused mortality determines carnivore abundance patterns (Figure 6-3). Large carnivores are most readily eliminated by

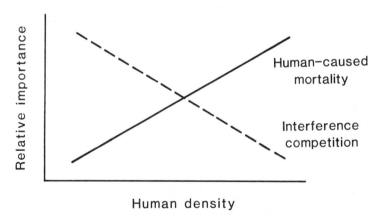

Figure 6-3. Postulated conceptual relationship between human-caused mortality and interspecific interference competition in population dynamics of wild canids.

humans, and thus people may inadvertently act as a keystone species, eliminating competitively superior carnivores and enhancing survival of smaller species in carnivore guilds at the expense of large species. The relative abundance of coyotes and red foxes in the Great Lakes area supports this contention (Figure 6-4). In the absence of wolves, coyotes appear dominant in forested regions, but as one moves out of the forest into more densely populated and cleared lands, foxes become numerically more significant.

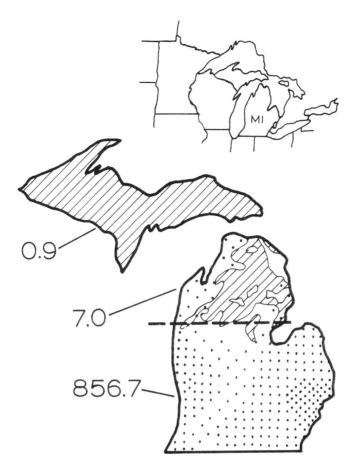

Figure 6-4. Ratios of red foxes to coyotes in Michigan, as reflected by state catch records (courtesy of J. Stuht, Michigan Department of Natural Resources), in relation to the approximate limit of continuous forest (hatched) and human density (dots).

Impacts on Vegetation and Ecosystem Processes. Large carnivore influence may extend into vegetation and nutrient dynamics, primarily via effects on dominant herbivores. At Isle Royale, tree density, species composition, age and height structure, and twig morphology are all influenced by levels of beaver and especially moose herbivory (Snyder and Janke 1976, Risenhoover and Maass 1986, Brandner 1986, Risenhoover, unpublished data), both of which are modified by wolf predation (Shelton and Peterson 1983, Peterson et al. 1984b). The extent to which these effects of herbivory alter nutrient flows, decomposition rates, and soil processes is currently under study (J. Pastor, pers. comm.).

Large species may also claim a disproportionately large share of the resources available within an ecological community (Brown and Maurer 1986). This concept, developed for specific groups of animals and plants in local communities, has yet to be extended to a larger scale including broader groups of animals. Yet there is the recurring suggestion that large carnivore significance is far greater than what one would project from their sparse densities.

Value to Human Society

Top carnivores can serve as integrators of lower trophic level dynamics, providing a means of discerning key ecological interactions. In the relatively simple three trophic-level system at Isle Royale (wolves, moose, vegetation), it now appears that life-long survival of annual cohorts of moose is determined by their nutritional level early in life (Peterson et al., in prep.), combined with intensive culling pressure from wolves. Moose cohort survival, then, is thought to be the driving force behind fluctuations of moose and wolves and, ultimately, the plethora of indirect influences mentioned above. A truly complete understanding of carnivore dynamics thus carries with it ecosystem-level understanding, provided that an initial "top-down" approach is followed by examination of key trophic interactions at all levels.

From a practical standpoint, large carnivores may provide an important focus for conservation efforts to establish adequate preserves for maintaining species diversity. The movements of these wide-ranging "umbrella species" will encompass vast areas containing hundreds or thousands of lesser known, or even unknown, species. Thus a newly established jaguar preserve in Belize will help maintain undiscovered species of insects. Wolf pack territories received important consideration when boundaries of an enlarged Denali National Park/ Preserve were drawn up in the 1970s. And the grizzly bear stands as the primary focus of interagency ecosystem management efforts in the Yellowstone region.

Large, slowly reproducing carnivores are especially susceptible to excessive human-caused mortality, as in the case of Yellowstone grizzlies (Knight and Eberhardt 1985), and thus serve as indicator species of wilderness. Populations of large carnivores that are truly naturally regulated obviously imply a high degree of effective protection from direct human impacts.

Finally, the symbolism of large carnivores in the public mind is an important element in our natural cultural heritage. The prominence of large carnivores in pre-Columbian lives and traditions of North American natives is obvious, and some of the same emphasis has been retained in the art and literature of the European colonizers that followed. It is clear that large carnivores such as the wolf, bear, and lion have the ability to spark the public imagination and sense of wilderness, serving as both an inspiration and a bioassay of our society's efforts at wildlife conservation. In the long run, this may be the most significant role for large carnivores in today's world, so dominated by our own species.

LARGE CARNIVORES IN A MANAGEMENT CONTEXT

Outside Alaska, almost all designated wilderness areas in the United States are deficient in large carnivores; most have none at all save the black bear and, to a lesser extent, the mountain lion (*Felis concolor*). All Long Term Ecological Research (LTER) sites and virtually all biosphere reserves outside Alaska lack the large, top carnivores. These areas have been set aside as natural benchmarks and genetic reservoirs; if these key research areas lack dominant carnivores, what are we missing? Is there any way to mitigate carnivore absence? Where large carnivores persist, how will we reconcile the interests of humans and these obligate meat eaters? These are the tough questions that managers must wrestle with and solve, hopefully with sufficient perspective to act in the long-term best interests of both the public and the wildlife resource.

Thus we return to a central question: what is "normal" or expected density for large herbivores in areas deficient in top carnivores? From a management standpoint, most wilderness ecosystems within the lower forty-eight states are so small that ungulate dynamics within can be dominated by substantial human predation (a dispersal sink) outside their boundaries. What about larger reserves, where this "edge effect" is reduced, or other areas that are literally fenced off by natural or human-made barriers? In the case of Isle Royale moose, it has generally been believed that high moose density resulted from a classical "fence effect" (Peterson et al., in prep.). Increased mammal density on islands or within fenced enclosures, attributable to restricted dispersal, is well known for certain small rodents (Krebs et al. 1969, Crowell 1981). Similar general arguments have been set forth for large ungulates (Owen-Smith 1983). However, the dynamics of small herbivores may have been uncritically extended to large forms (Caughley and Krebs 1983). As Crowell (1981) points out, density elevation can result as readily from fewer predators and competitors as from restricted dispersal. The extent to which dispersal actually regulates large herbivore populations needs further consideration, since the available evidence suggests that it is of little demographic significance (Gasaway et al. 1985, Clutton-Brock et al. 1985). This question is central for management actions designed to mitigate large carnivore absence, especially in areas where harvest by humans has been eliminated.

The larger the species, the slower it reproduces, so the population dynamics of large carnivores and other large mammals tend to be dominated by survival patterns. For example, when annual survival rates of Isle Royale wolves exceeded 80%, wolf numbers increased the next year; with 60 to 70% survival, numbers remained stable; and with survival at 50% or less, the wolf population declined (Peterson and Page 1988). The overriding significance of adult survival rates for large animals has been painfully learned in the case of the California condor and the Yellowstone grizzly. Large carnivores, especially, may require an extraordinarily high level of protection in order to maintain adequate numbers.

Another consequence of large size is long life span, which implies extended early development, a long period of parental care, and relatively "open" behavioral development that can accommodate substantial learning. Carnivores possess "culture" (i.e., transmit information nongenetically between generations) in much the same sense that humans do (Bonner 1980). This is quite relevant to the problem of carnivore behavior in the presence of humans. Wolf fear of humans and bear aggression toward humans are important aspects of their culture that land managers must appreciate and understand. Carnivore prey and food preferences are likewise modifiable by experience, especially early in life. The preference of wolves for certain prey species and the habitual garbage feeding by bears are examples of learned behavior that may not be readily changed during the lifetimes of individual carnivores. New behavior can be learned, of course, and it may be positive or negative. The substantial learning abilities of carnivores can be utilized to better manage potentially dangerous carnivores such as bears, as exemplified by the portable bearproof food containers required in backcountry areas and aversive conditioning now in use in Denali National Park (J. Dalle-Molle, pers. comm.). More research is needed on aversive conditioning of bears to develop alternatives to the heavy hunting pressure that has historically led to bear avoidance of humans. Restoration of such hunting would clearly be at odds with the management goals of most parks and wilderness areas.

Prior to the introduction of firearms, human ability to kill large carnivores was extremely limited. Grizzly bears and wolves were hardly a cowardly lot when Lewis and Clark traversed the continent. For reasons that are not understood, today wolves consistently show aversion to humans, grizzly bears may be aggressive, and black bears come in somewhere in the middle. While innovative management can probably solve most problems involving campground pests, it is doubtful that total aversion of humans by grizzly bears can be achieved. The potential for bear encounters is likely to remain a reality wherever management succeeds in retaining these great carnivores.

Cultural transmission of information may be vital for long-term survival of large carnivores, since their food resources are distributed sparsely and scattered in time and space. This must receive priority consideration when managers relocate individual carnivores—for example, to enhance genetic heterogeneity in isolated populations of the grizzly bear (Wilcox 1986). In such cases, serious thought should be given to artificial insemination or cross-fostering of young (involving nursing females and young of one species) to avoid undesirable mortality, which is likely when established individuals are relocated.

How should administrators and their research programs deal with the biological realities presented by large carnivores? Over the years these high profile species and their hoofed prey have received considerable attention, perhaps to the exclusion of other kinds of ecological studies (Stottlemyer 1987). Yet the types of long-term research commitments that are required for an adequate understanding of large mammal population dynamics have been almost nonexistent. Many national parks and forests, especially when adjacent units are considered together, contain relatively intact mammalian faunas (Salwasser, this volume). Their value as scientific resources should be reflected in administrative and funding priorities. It should be clear that we have much left to learn about the working of such ecosystems, and that in carefully selected cases it is efficient, cost effective, and most instructive to start at the top, with dominant carnivores.

LITERATURE CITED

Allen, D. L. 1979. Wolves of Minong. Houghton Mifflin, Boston. 499 p.

Bangs, E. E. 1985. Habitat differences and moose use of two large burns on the Kenai Peninsula, Alaska. Alces 21:17-35.

Bergerud, A. T. 1980. A review of the population dynamics of caribou and wild reindeer in North America. In E. Reimers, E. Gaare, and S. Skjenneberg (eds.) Proceedings, Second International Reindeer/Caribou Symposium, pp. 556-581. Direktoratet for vilt og ferskvannfisk, Trondheim, Norway.

Bergerud, A. T., F. Manuel, and H. Whalen. 1968. The harvest reduction of a moose population in Newfoundland. J. Wildl. Manage. 32:722-729.

Bergerud, A. T., W. Wyett, and B. Snider. 1983. The role of wolf predation in limiting a moose population. J. Wildl. Manage. 47:977-988.

Bonner, J. T. 1980. The evolution of culture in animals. Princeton University Press, Princeton, New Jersey. 216 p.

Brandner, T. A. 1986. The density-dependent effects of moose herbivory on balsam fir in Isle Royale National Park, Michigan. M.S. thesis, Michigan Technological University, Houghton. 29 p.

Brown, J. H., and B. A. Maurer. 1986. Body size, ecological dominance and Cope's rule. Nature 324:248-250.

Bubenik, A. B. 1972. North American moose management in light of European experiences. In

Proceedings, Eighth North American Moose Conference and Workshop, pp. 276-295. Ontario Ministry of Natural Resources.

Calder, W. A. III. 1983. An allometric approach to population cycles of mammals. J. Theor. Biol. 100:275-282.

———. 1984. Size, function, and life history. Harvard University Press, Cambridge, Massachusetts. 431 p.

Carbyn, L. 1983. Wolf predation on elk in Riding Mountain National Park, Manitoba. J. Wildl. Manage. 47:963-976.

Caughley, G., and C. J. Krebs. 1983. Are big mammals simply little mammals writ large? Oecologia 59:7-17.

Clutton-Brock, T. H., M. Major, and F. E. Guinness. 1985. Population regulation in male and female red deer. J. Anim. Ecol. 54:831-846.

Crowell, K. L. 1981. Islands—insight or artifact?: Population dynamics and habitat utilization in insular rodents. Oikos 41:442-454.

Fritts, S. H., and L. D. Mech. 1981. Dynamics, movements, and feeding ecology of a newly-protected wolf population in northwestern Minnesota. Wildl. Monogr. 80:1-79.

Gasaway, W. C., S. D. DuBois, D. J. Preston, and D. J. Reed. 1985. Home range formation and dispersal of subadult moose in interior Alaska. Fed. Aid Wildl. Res. Proj. Final Rep. W-22-2, Job 1.26R. 26 p.

Gasaway, W. C., R. O. Stephenson, J. L. Davis, P. E. K. Shepherd, and O. E. Burris. 1983. Interrelationships of wolves, prey, and man in interior Alaska. Wildl. Monogr. 84:1-50.

Harris, S. 1981. An estimation of the number of foxes in the city of Bristol, and some possible factors affecting their distribution. J. Appl. Ecol. 18:455-465.

Hornocker, M. G. 1970. An analysis of mountain lion predation upon mule deer and elk in the Idaho Primitive Area. Wildl. Monogr. 21:1-39.

Houston, D. B. 1982. The Northern Yellowstone Elk. Macmillan, New York. 474 p.

Johnson, D. H., and A. B. Sargeant. 1977. Impact of red fox predation on the sex ratio of prairie mallards. U.S. Fish and Wildl. Serv. Res. Rep. 6. 56 p.

Jonkel, C. J., and I. McT. Cowan. 1971. The black bear in the spruce-fir forest. Wildl. Monogr. 27:1-57.

Jordan, P. A., P. C. Shelton, and D. L. Allen. 1967. Numbers, turnover, and social structure of the Isle Royale wolf population. Am. Zool. 7:233-252.

Keith, L. B. 1974. Some features of population dynamics in mammals. Trans. Int. Congr. Game Biol. 11:17-58.

———. 1983. Population dynamics of wolves. In L. Carbyn (ed.) Wolves in Canada and Alaska: Their status, biology, and management, pp. 66-77. Canadian Wildlife Service Rep. Ser. 45. Ottawa.

Knight, R. R., and L. L. Eberhardt. 1985. Population dynamics of Yellowstone grizzly bears. Ecology 66:323-334.

Kolenosky, G. B. 1972. Wolf predation on wintering deer in east-central Ontario. J. Wildl. Manage. 36:357-369.

Kolenosky, G. B., and R. O. Standfield. 1975. Morphological and ecological variation among gray wolves of Ontario, Canada. In M.W. Fox (ed.) The wild canids, pp. 62-72. Van Nostrand Reinhold, New York.

Krebs, C. J., B. L. Keller, and R. H. Tamarin. 1969. Microtus population biology: Demographic changes in fluctuating populations of M. ochrogaster and M. pennsylvanicus in southern Indiana. Ecology 50:587-607.

Krefting, L. W. 1969. The rise and fall of the coyote on Isle Royale, Michigan. Naturalist 20:24-31.

Linstedt, S. L., and W. A. Calder III. 1981. Body size, physiological time, and longevity of homeothermic animals. Quart. Rev. Biol. 56:1-16.

Lykke, J. 1974. Moose management in Norway and Sweden. Naturaliste Can. 101:723-735.

Markgren, G. 1974. The question of polygamy at an unbalanced sex ratio in moose. *In* V. Geist and F. Walther (eds.) The behavior of ungulates and its relation to management, pp. 756-758. IUCN 2(24).

Mech, L. D. 1966. The wolves of Isle Royale. U.S. National Park Service Fauna Series 7. U.S. Government Printing Office, Washington, D.C. 210 p.

———. 1977a. Population trend and winter deer consumption in a Minnesota wolf pack. *In* R. L. Phillips and C. Jonkel (eds.) Proceedings, 1975 Predator Symposium, pp. 55-83. Montana Forest and Conservation Exp. Stn., University of Montana, Missoula.

———. 1977b. Productivity, mortality, and population trends of wolves in northeastern Minnesota. J. Mammal. 58:559-575.

———. 1986. Wolf population in the central Superior National Forest, 1967-1985. USDA For. Serv. Res. Pap. NC-270. North Central For. Exp. Stn., St. Paul, Minnesota. 6 p.

Mech, L. D., and L. D. Frenzel, Jr. 1971. Ecological studies of the timber wolf in northeastern Minnesota. North Central Forest Exp. Stn., St. Paul, Minnesota.

Mech, L. D., and P. D. Karns. 1977. Role of the wolf in a deer decline in Superior National Forest. USDA For. Serv. Res. Pap. NC-148. North Central Forest Exp. Stn., St. Paul, Minnesota. 23 p.

Mech, L. D., R. E. McRoberts, R. O. Peterson, and R. E. Page. 1987. Relationship of deer and moose populations to previous winters' snow. J. Anim. Ecol. 56(2):615-627.

Messier, F., and M. Crete. 1985. Moose-wolf dynamics and the natural regulation of moose populations. Oecologia 65:503-512.

Nowak, R. M. 1983. A perspective on the taxonomy of wolves in North America. *In* L. Carbyn (ed.) Wolves in Canada and Alaska: Their status, biology, and management, pp. 10-19. Canadian Wildlife Service Rep. Ser. 45. Ottawa.

Owen-Smith, R. N. 1983. Dispersal and the dynamics of large herbivores in enclosed areas: Implications for management. *In* Management of large mammals in African conservation areas, pp. 127-143. Haum Educational Publishers, Pretoria.

Peterson, R. O. 1977. Wolf ecology and prey relationships on Isle Royale. U.S. National Park Service Scientific Monogr. Ser. 11. U.S. Government Printing Office, Washington, D.C. 210 p.

Peterson, R. O., and R. E. Page. 1988. The rise and fall of Isle Royale wolves, 1975-1986. J. Mammal. In press.

Peterson, R. O., R. E. Page, and K. L. Risenhoover. Phenotypic variation in moose life-long survival. In preparation.

Peterson, R. O., J. D. Woolington, and T. N. Bailey. 1984a. Wolves of the Kenai Peninsula, Alaska. Wildl. Monogr. 88:1-52.

Peterson, R. O., R. E. Page, and K. M. Dodge. 1984b. Wolves, moose, and the allometry of population cycles. Science 224:1350-1352.

Pielou, E. C. 1981. The usefulness of ecological models: A stocktaking. Quart. Rev. Biol. 56:17-31.

Pimlott, D. H. 1967. Wolf predation and ungulate populations. Am. Zool. 7:267-278.

Pimlott, D. H., J. A. Shannon, and G. B. Kolenosky. 1969. Ecology of the timber wolf in Algonquin Provincial Park. Ontario Department of Lands and Forests Res. Rep. 87. 92 p.

Risenhoover, K. L., and S. A. Maass. 1987. The influence of moose on the composition and structure of Isle Royale forests. Can. J. For. Res. 17:357-364.

Sargeant, A. B. 1987. A case history of a dynamic resource: The red fox. *In* G. C. Sanderson (ed.) Midwest furbearer management, pp. 121-137. North Cent. Sect., Cent. Mountains and Plains Sect., and Kansas Chapter, The Wildlife Society.

Sargeant, A. B., S. H. Allen, and J. O. Hastings. 1987. Spatial relations between sympatric coyotes and red foxes in North Dakota. J. Wildl. Manage. In press.

Schoener, T. W. 1982. The controversy over interspecific competition. Am. Sci. 70:586-595.

Shelton, P. C., and R. O. Peterson. 1983. Beaver, wolf and moose interactions in Isle Royale National Park, USA. Acta Zool. Fennica 174:265-266.

Snyder, J. D., and R. A. Janke. 1976. Impact of moose browsing on boreal-type forests of Isle Royale National Park. Am. Midl. Nat. 95:79-92.

Stottlemyer, R. 1987. External threats to ecosystems of U.S. National Parks. Environ. Manage. 11:87-89.

Taylor, R. J. 1984. Predation. Chapman and Hall, Ltd., New York. 166 p.

Temple, S. A. 1987. Do predators always capture substandard individuals disproportionately from prey populations? Ecology 68:669-674.

Van Ballenberghe, V. 1980. Utility of multiple equilibrium concepts applied to population dynamics of moose. *In* Proceedings, Sixteenth North American Moose Conference and Workshop, pp. 571-586. Ontario Ministry of Natural Resources.

Wilcox, B. A. 1986. Extinction models and conservation. Trends in Ecology and Evolution 1:46-48.

Wolfe, M. L., and D. L. Allen. 1973. Continued studies of the status, socialization, and relationships of Isle Royale wolves, 1967-70. J. Mammal. 54:611-635.

7

Long-Range Impacts of Air Pollution on Terrestrial Resources

D. F. GRIGAL

ABSTRACT The major anthropogenic air pollutants include acidic deposition (occurring both as wetfall and dryfall and formed from sulfur dioxide and nitrogen oxides), gaseous sulfur dioxide, photochemical oxidants including ozone, and heavy metals. They can affect the soil portion of the terrestrial ecosystem or the vegetation—the latter either directly through toxicity or indirectly through changes in soil properties. In addition, aerosols of sulfate can impair visibility. Most of the pollutants have been hypothesized to affect forest health detrimentally, leading to significant tree mortality or forest decline. However, there are few forest systems for which damage due to air pollutants has been documented. Effects of pollutants on other kinds of natural plant communities have generally been ignored. Irreversible damage of the soil would constitute the major long-term impact of these pollutants. Vegetation or other organisms have the biotic potential to respond positively when a stress is removed; hence long-term negative impacts are less likely. Many natural processes also contribute to a high resilience or buffering of soil against changes in properties, and thus to an ability of the soil to recover or ameliorate after stress is removed. Natural ecosystems therefore have strong potential to recover from the adverse effects of air pollution if that pollution is reduced. The long-term national trend for most of these pollutants since the early to mid-1970s is level or downward, with some variation among regions. It is likely that the short-term effects of most pollutants in most locations will be small compared with other natural and anthropogenic agents of change to those systems. The long-term impacts of these pollutants in national parks and other wilderness areas depend on the reduction of pollution, on the rate of ecosystem recovery, and on management goals.

The issue of impacts of air pollution on terrestrial resources is important for any long-range planning. In at least some cases, rational discussion of those impacts has been obscured by drumbeating and misinformation in the popular press. Not all that has been published is true, nor is all of it false. The purpose of this paper is to clarify the issues and bring some of the relevant points to the attention of land managers. In doing so, broad coverage of a number of topics is necessary: definition of air pollutants, their impacts on terrestrial ecosystems, hypotheses to explain the mechanisms of those impacts, trends of pollutant loading, and, in view of all these data, long-range implications for management of parks and wilderness areas.

The term "air pollution" as used here will refer generically to acidic deposition, gaseous air pollutants, and other materials delivered to ecosystems via the atmosphere

(Abrahamsen and Tveite 1983). To place the discussion in perspective, I will briefly describe the nature of both acidic deposition and other air pollutants.

AIR POLLUTANTS

Acidic Deposition

Oxides of sulfur and nitrogen are among the gases that are released to the atmosphere as a result of human activity (i.e., are anthropogenically emitted), thus increasing their concentrations above natural background levels. The primary source of sulfur dioxide is combustion of sulfur-containing coal and oil in electrical generating plants; another major source is smelting of metal ores that contain sulfur compounds (Husar 1986). The primary source of nitrogen oxides is fuel combustion. These oxides arise from fixation of atmospheric nitrogen at high temperatures, hence are more dependent on the combustion process than on the properties of the fuel (Husar 1986). The transportation industry, with its close link to the internal combustion engine, is a major source of nitrogen oxides (Office of the Director 1985). Electric utilities and other industrial plants are lesser sources.

Through oxidation reactions in the atmosphere, often catalyzed by sunlight, the sulfur dioxide and nitrogen oxides react with other compounds to form aerosols, or fine liquid or solid particles. Some of these particles are acids (e.g., sulfuric acid and nitric acid) while others are salts (e.g., ammonium sulfate). Air masses can transport these compounds for long distances, in some cases thousands of kilometers (hence the term long-range transport) (National Research Council 1983).

Wetfall. Aerosols can directly combine with droplets of water as they condense during formation of precipitation ("scavenging") or they can be "washed out" of the atmosphere during a rain or snow event. Deposition of acidic aerosols in this manner is referred to as acid precipitation or acid rain.

Dryfall. Some of the acidic aerosols do not fall with precipitation, but come directly into contact with and remain on surfaces such as tree leaves. This process is continuous; deposition is not dependent on a precipitation event. Such deposition is referred to as dry deposition or dryfall. Depending on the nature of the atmosphere, of the collecting surface, and of climatic conditions, dryfall can account for as much or more of the acidic materials delivered to an ecosystem as does wetfall. For example, total wet and total dry deposition are thought to be of approximately equal magnitude over eastern North America (Stenslund et al. 1986). Since forest canopies, especially those of conifers, are very efficient at filtering these aerosols from the atmosphere, dry deposition is greater in forests than in more open vegetation types (Hultberg 1985). Some fraction of the nitric acid also remains in a gaseous form, and direct uptake of that gas by plants is an important mode of dry deposition for nitrogen (Lindberg et al. 1986).

The distinction between wetfall and dryfall is obscure in the case of fog. Radiation fog at low elevations and cloud-water fog at high elevations provide vehicles for delivery of acidic materials to terrestrial ecosystems. Both wind speed and water content affect the amount of materials deposited. The pH of cloud water can be quite low (e.g., mean annual pH of 3.5 and 3.9 in high elevations in New York State; RMCC Atmospheric Sciences Subgroup 1986).

Sulfur Dioxide

Either because of insufficient residence time in the atmosphere or insufficient quantities of reactants, not all of the sulfur dioxide emitted by a source forms salts or acids. Instead, the sulfur dioxide gas itself impinges upon ecosystems. Concentrations of sulfur dioxide are usually higher near point sources such as urban areas or electrical generating plants than in areas further removed from such sources (Hinrichsen 1986).

Photochemical Oxidants

The photochemical oxidants, another class of pollutants, are receiving increasing attention in terms of their impact on terrestrial ecosystems (Guderian 1985). Ozone is the member of this class mentioned most often, but peroxyacetal nitrate (PAN), hydrogen peroxide, and others have also been implicated in damage. The photochemical oxidants are similar to the acidic compounds mentioned above in that they are not directly emitted to the atmosphere, but form there by sunlight-catalyzed reactions of oxygen, nitrogen oxides, and volatile hydrocarbons.

The link between reactant and product for photochemical oxidants is more tenuous than the links between sulfur dioxide and sulfuric acid or between nitrogen oxides and nitric acid. The oxidants are not emitted directly from a single, identifiable source such as is the case with sulfur dioxide from a electrical generating plant. They form from an admixture of reactants from an admixture of sources. In urban areas they often build to high concentrations during the day under the influence of solar radiation; at night their concentrations drop through continuing reactions. These reactions occur because of the high concentrations of compounds that consume oxidants in urban air.

Photochemical oxidants were formerly presumed to be an urban problem—generated and destroyed in those areas. Studies have now shown that ozone is a regionally distributed pollutant, and that levels in rural areas can equal those in urban areas. Because of the low concentrations of reactants that consume oxidants in rural areas, the concentrations of oxidants do not drop at night but can remain elevated for longer periods. It is ironic that the current international concern about the reduction in the ozone layer is focusing on the stratosphere, while there appears to be a simultaneous increase in ozone in the troposphere or lower atmosphere (Becker et al. 1985:26). It is further ironic that ozone in the lower atmosphere can be harmful if it exceeds certain limits, while ozone in the stratosphere must exceed certain limits to protect life as we know it.

Heavy Metals

Heavy metals are released through anthropogenic processes and delivered to ecosystems via wetfall or dryfall. They include lead, zinc, and mercury. One source, especially in the past, was metal smelters. Anyone visiting Ducktown, Tennessee, or Sudbury, Ontario, could not help being impressed by the toxicity of high concentrations of heavy metals, albeit exacerbated by sulfur dioxide released during the smelting. Emissions from metal smelting have been reduced, so that source of metals is much less a problem than formerly.

Two heavy metals are of special recent interest. The first is lead derived from tetraethyl lead in gasoline. Although most emphasis on pollution from lead has centered on urban landscapes, atmospheric lead is also deposited on rural landscapes. For example, high levels of lead have been found in organic forest floors in the northeastern United States (Friedland et al. 1984). Another heavy metal receiving increased attention, especially in the aquatic environment, is mercury. This volatile metal occurs in some types of coal and is emitted to the atmosphere by coal burning, but other industrial processes also release it to the atmosphere. Because the loadings or amounts deposited on terrestrial systems are uncertain, discussion of the impacts is also speculative. Mercury's impact, or at least studies of its impact, are likely to become more prominent in the future.

Carbon Dioxide

Finally, the recently documented increase in carbon dioxide concentrations in the atmosphere is another kind of air pollution. This increase has been ascribed to increased burning of fossil fuel, clearing of tropical forests, plowing of the grasslands of the world, draining of wetlands, and a host of other anthropogenic activities. The effects are predicted to be increased temperature, changes in precipitation patterns, worldwide droughts or flooding, and a variety of other climatic shifts. Thus far the whole issue is extremely nebulous because the magnitude of sources and sinks remains undefined. There is no question that it is a relevant issue in long-range planning for wildlands. At present, the uncertainties so completely outweigh the certainties that further discussion is simply an exercise in science fiction.

IMPACTS ON TERRESTRIAL SYSTEMS

This paper primarily focuses on the potential impacts of air pollutants on terrestrial systems. There is a continuum of such impacts: the range is from increased productivity of biotic components of the system, to no change in any component, to subtle alteration of physiological functions and growth of organisms, to death.

Soil

The most important long-term impact of air pollution on terrestrial ecosystems is the potential of altering soil properties. This view may reflect my academic training as a soil scientist. Soils are the basic resource or substrate from which the terrestrial ecosystem derives its existence. Biotic components are transitory elements whose abundance can vary widely over the short term. The length of that short term depends in part on the life span of the organism. The maximum life span of a soil microorganism is considerably less than that of the giant sequoia. For most biotic components, however, periods of one or two centuries encompass the lives of nearly all individuals in the population. Biotic components can and do recover from catastrophic impacts that stop short of extinction. Witness the abundance of white-tailed deer in Iowa, the forests of the Northeast occupying what were once farm fields, or the current reforestation of the slopes of Mount St. Helens. In contrast, irreparable harm has befallen a terrestrial ecosystem where the soil resource has been irreversibly damaged, such as near Ducktown, Tennessee.

There are some facts that brighten this austere picture. First, soils are extremely resilient components of the ecosystem. Various natural processes tend both to buffer soil properties against change and to restore those properties to their initial state following disturbance. Accumulation of organic matter and weathering of minerals can rebuild an eroded soil. The amount of acids added annually by atmospheric deposition, even in the worst cases, is small compared with the total chemical buffering capacity of surface soils (McFee 1982).

Another perspective to consider when discussing impacts of air pollution on soil, or indeed on any component of the terrestrial ecosystem, is that impacts of many of the pollutants are simply the hastening of natural processes. For example, the process by which soils lose base cations and become increasingly acid begins immediately after a land surface is exposed to the biosphere. This process is continually occurring. One of the impacts of acidic deposition is an increase in the rate of that process.

Impacts of air pollution on soil cannot be considered in isolation. Soil is an integral part of the ecosystem, and changes in soil properties can affect other components. In fact, the greatest concern about the effects of air pollutants on terrestrial ecosystems most often centers on vegetation. It is in that context that the impacts of air pollutants on soil will be discussed, including additions and depletions of material and an increase in the concentration of toxic materials within the soil.

Additions and Depletions. One of the initial effects of acidic deposition on terrestrial ecosystems is often an increase in site productivity. The heathlands, or *Heide*, of Germany make up a unique plant community. These low-nutrient sites, with characteristic vegetation dependent on that status, are increasingly difficult to maintain because of the continual additions of nutrient elements such as nitrogen and calcium from anthropogenic sources (E. Matzner, pers. comm., 1985). Lack of response of Douglas-fir to nitrogen fertilization in the Pacific Northwest has been attributed to sulfur deficiency (Turner et al. 1977). Such a deficiency could easily be satisfied if levels of sulfur deposition in that region were similar to those that fall on the Adirondack Mountains of New York.

In fact, annual growth rings in increment cores from trees in areas that have had relatively high levels of acidic deposition often indicate accelerated growth. In Sweden, such cores showed growth rates for the period 1965-74 equal to or greater than those of the previous five decades (Swedish Ministry of Agriculture 1982). This increased growth was hypothesized to be due to fertilization from nutrient elements, especially nitrogen, deposited from the atmosphere. The response of many agronomists to the "threat" of acidic deposition is delight at an increased level of free fertilizer (Tabatabai et al. 1981). I do not necessarily advocate that perspective because of the uncontrolled nature of the treatment, but it is one that should be considered in the context of long-term management of resources.

Even as nutrients are added to the soil, some can also be lost. First, changes in soil solution, such as higher ionic concentrations than normal and the presence of mobile anions such as sulfate and nitrate, can occur as a result of acidic deposition. Because of these changes, hydrogen ions in solution exchange with the base cations calcium, magnesium, and potassium on soil colloids; these cations are subsequently leached from the soil (Fernandez 1985). The base cations are plant nutrients; where they are already in short supply, this accelerated leaching may affect plant nutrition. Base cations can also be added to soil colloids by weathering, or breakdown of soil minerals to soluble forms. The critical question for nutrient status of ecosystems is the balance between the rates of weathering and of cation leaching.

A second process of nutrient depletion from a soil is a consequence of base cations being leached from the soil, and the soil becoming more acidic. This has the potential of converting soil phosphorus to insoluble forms by chemical precipitation to aluminum and iron hydroxides, so that it is no longer available to plants (Persson and Broberg 1985). As might be expected, this is also more likely to affect plant nutrition in soils that are initially low in phosphorus.

Toxic Materials. All soils contain large quantities of aluminum, primarily as insoluble forms but with some as soluble organic complexes. As soils become more acidic, inorganic aluminum compounds become more soluble (Ulrich 1984). This is a fundamental chemical principle. Inorganic aluminum in solution is toxic to aquatic organisms; at fairly high concentrations, these ions are also toxic to tree roots (Cronan and Goldstein 1988). There are, however, relatively wide differences in tolerance among tree species. It also appears that the ratio of calcium to aluminum concentrations in solution affects toxicity (Cronan and Goldstein 1988).

Lower soil pH also interacts with anthropogenically derived heavy metals such as lead. Under the influence of low pH, these metals can also become more soluble. As a group, heavy metals are considered to be toxic to plants and microorganisms, in some cases in relatively low concentrations (Babich and Stotsky 1979, Rolfe and Bazzaz 1975, Wong 1982). Most of the work dealing with toxicity of heavy metals has been in relation to their depression of microorganism activity (Babich and Stotsky 1979). Such depression may lead to a slowdown of organic matter mineralization and hence of elemental cycling (Ruhling and Tyler 1973, Moloney et al. 1983). Despite these presumed effects, the overall impact of lead on either the flora or the fauna of terrestrial systems is uncertain.

Vegetation

Vegetation can be affected both directly by air pollution and indirectly by feedback from its substrate, the soil. It is clear both from observations and from experimental work that there is genotypic variation among trees and other plants in terms of response to air pollution. That is, not only do species vary in their response but individuals within a species also vary (Woodman and Cowling 1987). Some individuals are unaffected by the same insult that kills other individuals. The presence of a differential response has profound implications in considering long-range impacts of air pollution. For example, in the short term some individuals in a population may survive most insults and become the basis for a population with altered response. In this way, long-term evolutionary mechanisms may operate to protect a population against a specific insult. Some concern has been expressed, however, about loss of other traits during this adaptation.

My discussion of impacts of air pollution on vegetation will concentrate on the response of forest trees for two reasons: (1) more work has been done on them compared with work on other components of natural terrestrial ecosystems, and (2) their health often defines or is used as an index for the health of the entire forest ecosystem. Responses of agricultural crops to air pollutants have been studied extensively; responses of forest trees have been less studied. The situation is much more vague for natural plant communities other than forests. For example, very little research has been conducted on the impacts of air pollution on vegetation types such as subalpine meadows or alpine tundra, or even on the understory vegetation in forests. If concern increasingly includes the effects of air pollutants on *all* natural terrestrial ecosystems, then a gap clearly exists in both our knowledge and the research in progress.

In the view of some, it is obvious that air pollution poses a great threat to forests in the industrialized countries. This view is based on three interconnected lines of reasoning: air quality in industrialized countries differs from that in less industrially developed countries (i.e., the air is more polluted); laboratory, greenhouse, or chamber work has shown that various air pollutants can have detrimental effects on the health of individual plants; and forests, or at least groups of trees, are dying in industrialized countries. The observation concerning tree death has been prominent in national and international news. Such a condition is termed forest decline, or, in German, *Waldsterben* (Schutt and Cowling 1985). The reality of forest decline above normal levels of tree mortality has been questioned by some, and numerous research efforts are examining the question. Because the impacts of air pollution on terrestrial ecosystems are intertwined with forest decline, that condition will be the focus of the following remarks.

A number of hypotheses have been offered to explain the current observations of decline as reported from Western Europe and the eastern United States. These hypotheses can be grouped into those concerned with anthropogenic air pollution and those dealing with natural phenomena; the anthropogenic effects can be further separated into those involving an interaction of vegetation and soil and those involving direct impacts of air pollution on vegetation.

Anthropogenic Decline Hypotheses. The soil-related hypotheses of tree decline are based on either a deficiency of nutrients or a toxicity of aluminum or other elements. A deficiency affects the entire tree, while toxicity is presumed to affect primarily the roots. The nutrient-deficiency hypothesis embraces both a number of sources of deficiency and a number of interactions with other effects. First, there is a hypothesized deficiency of base cations. As mentioned above, if these nutrients are leached from soil by acid or salt solutions, this could further deplete already low levels in soil, leading to deficiency. The hypothesis of cation deficiency has primarily centered on magnesium, an important constituent of chloroplasts. Chlorotic needles, one of the symptoms of decline, are associated with magnesium deficiency. Direct leaching of magnesium from leaves could further exacerbate any soil-caused deficiency. The magnesium hypothesis has been advanced and advocated by Rehfuess of the University of Munich (Schutt and Cowling 1985).

Other nutrients have also been hypothesized to be involved in forest decline. A deficiency of phosphorus because of chemical interactions in acid soils has already been mentioned. Formerly available elements may also become unavailable because of an accumulation of organic materials through inhibition of microorganism activity as a result of increased soil acidity. Activity of mycorrhizae may also be inhibited under some polluted conditions. These symbiotic relationships between fungi and higher plants are usually considered to enhance the ability of the higher plant to obtain nutrients from its substrate. Limited greenhouse work indicates inhibition of mycorrhizae formation on pine seedlings in association with simulated acid rain of pH 3.2 to 4.0 (Shafer et al. 1985), but fieldwork must be done to substantiate the results. If inhibition occurs, availability of nutrients to higher plants would be reduced.

Aluminum toxicity has also been hypothesized to be a primary cause of forest decline in the Federal Republic of Germany (Ulrich 1983, 1984, Huttermann and Ulrich 1984). This toxicity is related to unusually warm summer weather that enhances natural production of nitric acid (nitrification), further reducing already very low soil pH. As a result of low pH (4.0), aluminum in solution reaches concentrations that are toxic to fine roots. Trees are assumed to have redundancy in their root system, and an ability to tolerate some fine-root mortality. Under the aluminum hypothesis, however, high rates of mortality of fine roots exceed the ability of the tree to recover, and mortality of trees then begins to occur.

Several hypotheses to explain forest decline are related to direct impacts of air pollution on trees, although many of these hypotheses also have strong links to effects on soils. These hypotheses include nutrient deficiency, direct gaseous damage, and excess fertilization.

Additions of acid solutions to leaves are hypothesized to leach essential plant nutrients (Tukey 1980). As discussed in relation to magnesium, such leaching would be most injurious if soil nutrient levels were low. Foliar damage caused by pollutant gases would also contribute to leaching (Winner and Atkinson 1986). This hypothesis thus combines both soil and air-related impacts. Experimental work with microcosms found increased leaching of elements from small trees under treatments with low pH precipitation, but no significant biological response to the leaching (Kelly and Strickland 1986). It should also be noted that acidic deposition has not been shown to cause visible foliar damage to tree species except where treatments were conducted at extremely low and unrealistic pHs (i.e., below 3.2; RMCC Terrestrial Effects Subgroup 1986).

Sulfur dioxide affects vegetation by entering leaves through the stomata and dissolving in mesophyll fluids (Winner and Atkinson 1986). Oxidation and hydrolysis of sulfur dioxide within the leaf can injure or kill cells (Kozlowski and Constantinidou 1986). Stomatal conductance, and thus water use efficiency of the plant, can also be affected. Both the biochemical changes and those associated with conductance act to reduce rates of photosynthesis (Winner and Atkinson 1986). Ozone also enters vegetation through stomata, but may also enter directly through the cuticle (Winner and Atkinson 1986). Many of the symptoms of foliar injury due to ozone are similar to those due to sulfur dioxide. Other effects of ozone include premature leaf senescence, affecting the duration of carbon fixation.

The effect of both gases mentioned above and other gaseous oxidants is to alter plant metabolism and carbon allocation. As a result, direct injury of leaf tissue by sulfur dioxide, ozone, or other gases has been hypothesized to lead to forest decline. The greatest uncertainty in this hypothesis has to do with the concentrations of pollutants to be found in natural systems, and their effect on large mature forest trees compared with documented effects on seedlings or other plants (Hinrichsen 1986).

Another hypothesis relates forest decline to overfertilization by nitrogen (Nihlgard 1985). If wetfall or dryfall deposition to foliage is high in nitrogen, then direct fertilization is a result. This kind of fertilization could produce many potential effects in a plant such as upsetting the essential balance between belowground and aboveground components, making the plant more susceptible to stresses such as drought; upsetting elemental ratios within the plant, leading to deficiency of other nutrients; suppressing mycorrhizae formation, also leading to deficiency of other nutrients; and delaying cold hardening in preparation for winter, leading to frost damage (Nihlgard 1985). Because of the variety of effects and hence symptoms, this hypothesis can be applied to many situations where decline has been observed. One caveat in the acceptance of this hypothesis is that rates of addition of nitrogen to ecosystems by air pollution are many times lower than rates of addition by commercial forest fertilization, yet no similar adverse effects of fertilization have been documented.

Natural Decline Hypotheses. Although it is not news to most forest scientists, the decline of forest trees is not a recent phenomenon. Cowling (1985) lists five instances of regional decline of tree species in Europe and an additional thirteen in North America during the twentieth century. Such decline has occurred in a variety of species, both broadleaf and conifer. Several hypotheses therefore exist that ascribe recent changes in forest growth and mortality to natural impacts or stresses, such as drought. If these natural stresses occur at a critical stage in the development of a particular age class of trees, "cohort senescence" may predispose that stand to natural pathogens and to observed decline (Mueller-Dombois et al. 1983). An additional factor that may be involved in some of the European declines is the long-term exploitation of those forests for various products, including fuel, timber, and animal bedding. Such long-term exploitation, and especially depletion of nutrients, may adversely affect the ability of the system to withstand other stress (RMCC Terrestrial Effects Subgroup 1986).

Multiple Interacting Stresses. After careful review of the literature and consideration of all the locations and manifestations of forest decline, it appears most likely that decline is caused by a combination of the phenomena described above. It is further likely that the specific combinations of contributing factors differ among regions and forests where declines have been observed. This is not a new idea. Manion (1981) organized the concepts of forest decline into a logical package, and he defined decline as those situations in which a deterioration and death of trees is caused by a combination of biological and nonbiological stress factors (Manion 1985). This definition is consistent with the hypothesis of multiple interacting stresses.

According to this hypothesis, trees at any site are subjected to a multidimensional environment of insults or stresses. The symptoms that are observed on trees therefore reveal a combination of interacting effects or stresses. Reaching that recognition is not as meaningless as it may first appear. It demands that evaluation of causes of decline or prediction of decline at any site must couple knowledge of site characteristics with knowledge of the responses of trees to stress. The complex and unique nature of the combination of stresses at any site demands generic knowledge of processes and mechanisms of plant response, not empirically derived site-specific data that cannot be extrapolated. Finally, knowledge of multiple stresses reduces the tendency to identify any one factor as the ultimate cause of forest decline.

We must also remember, however, that tree mortality is normal. The natural process of forest stand development involves the continuous decline in vigor and ultimately the death of many trees (Woodman and Cowling 1987). The causes of the decline of an individual tree are many, including suppression in the understory, injury by wind or animals, or infection by a pathogen. The question that should be addressed is the difference between natural and accelerated mortality, or the difference between mortality due to one set of causes versus that due to another. Do such changes in mortality have any long-range impacts on the forest?

The line of evidence that suggests that we may be dealing with an anthropogenically induced acceleration of natural mortality is the simultaneous and extensive nature of the declines reported in Western Europe and eastern North America. Random coincidence of declines is improbable in natural systems over such a wide geographic range. Among the multiple stresses causing such reported declines, then, are likely to be some anthropogenically related stresses.

Growth Reduction. Although most attention in the literature has focused on forest decline, there are also abundant reports concerning reduced growth of forest trees over the past decade or two compared with previous decades (Figure 7-1). Sufficient space is not available to review carefully all the relevant studies, but methodological problems,

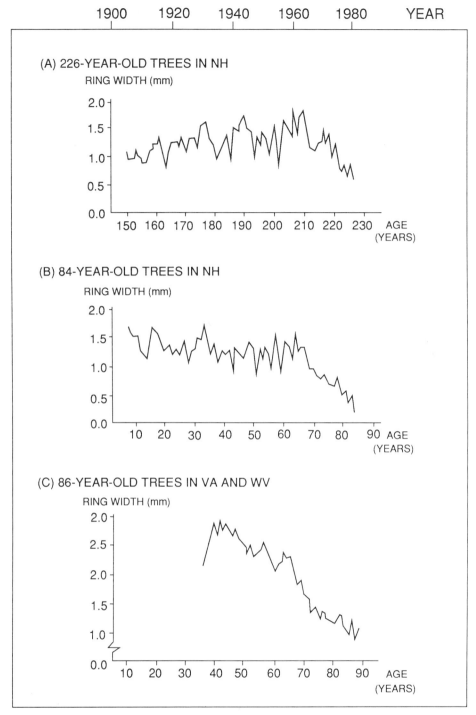

Figure 7-1. Ring-width sequences of red spruce from New Hampshire (A) and (B), and from Virginia and West Virginia (C). Sequences such as these have been used to suggest anthropogenically related growth decline (compiled by Zedaker et al. 1987).

particularly in the use of statistics, plagued some of the early work. Growth reduction has now apparently been documented both in stands that later succumbed to forest decline and in other stands that show no overt manifestations of decline. In North America, evidence of such growth reduction has been found in red spruce (*Picea rubens*) in the northern Appalachians (Johnson and McLaughlin 1986) and in commercially valuable "yellow" pines in the Piedmont and mountains of the southeastern United States (Sheffield and Cost 1987). In each case, the exact cause of the reductions has been open to debate.

The correlation between increased levels of various kinds of air pollutants and reduced tree growth has been used to imply a cause-effect relationship. Other potential causes of reduced growth include climatic trends, simple changes in stand dynamics (Zedaker et al. 1987), and depletion of nutrient reserves in the soil over a second rotation of forest crops. Inexplicable reduced productivity in the second compared with the first rotation has been noted for exotic conifers in the Southern Hemisphere (Keeves 1966, Whyte 1973). All of these causes are as likely as air pollution to be contributing to reduction in growth. As mentioned earlier, just as with other impacts, the reduction in growth has usually not occurred in all trees in a stand, implying genetic variability in response. Peterson et al. (1987), in the southern Sierra Nevada of California, have recently shown less growth in Jeffrey pine with foliar symptoms of ozone injury compared with those showing no injury. This circumstantial evidence for growth reduction due to air pollution is more definitive than is that for most observations of such reduction.

Atmosphere and Visibility

To this point my discussion has concentrated on the impact of air pollutants on terrestrial as opposed to aquatic systems. There is also a potential impact of pollutants on the atmosphere itself, and specifically on visibility. Although such a discussion may stray from the central topic of this presentation, it deserves some mention in this forum.

The same sulfate aerosols that combine with water and fall as acid rain, or impinge upon surfaces during rain-free periods, also scatter visible light (Trijonis 1986). About half of the reduction in visibility in the eastern United States is attributed to sulfate aerosols (Trijonis 1986). The fine particles of aerosols are hygroscopic, attracting water to further scatter light. A detailed study in the Shenandoah National Park determined that in summer, sulfate and associated water accounted for about 75% of the light extinction (Ferman et al. 1981).

The best visibility currently is found in the western and southwestern mountains and deserts, and the worst in the urbanized and industrialized areas east of the Mississippi River (Trijonis 1986). Trends in visibility indicate significant reductions during the period from 1950 to 1970, with no apparent trend since then (Trijonis 1986). This pattern and trend is consistent with anthropogenic sources of sulfate, hence reduction in visibility.

Before I leave this topic, however, I should point out that other factors also affect visibility, including dust and smoke, both of which may have both anthropogenic and natural sources. Based on the available data, it is likely than trends in visibility will follow trends in sulfur dioxide emissions (NAS 1986).

TRENDS OF POLLUTANTS

What are the trends of these air pollutants, and what are some likely future scenarios? I personally believe that the worst may be over in terms of air pollution. The national trends for both sulfur dioxide and nitrogen oxides, as indicated in the 1985 NAPAP (National Acidic Precipitation Assessment Program) Report (Office of the Director 1985), show declines (Figure 7-2). Sulfur dioxide, for example, showed a sharp decline starting

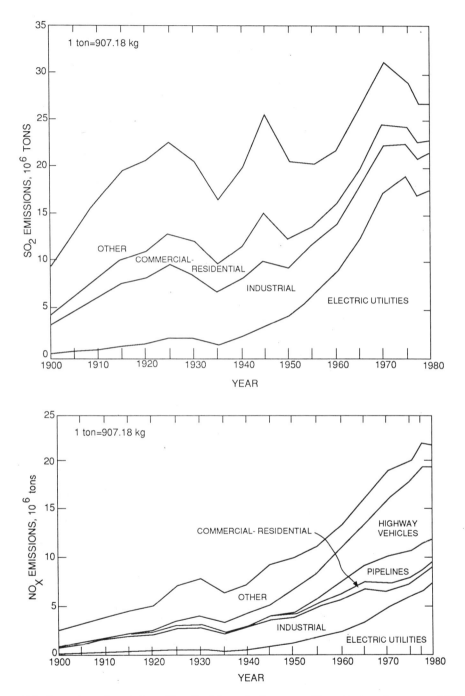

Figure 7-2. Long-term trends in sulfur dioxide and nitrogen oxide emissions by source (Office of the Director 1985).

about 1970. Some of this decline, of course, can be attributed to the economic downturn in the early 1970s. Similarly, nitrogen oxides show a decline starting about 1975 and a leveling off since then. Regional trends of these pollutants are more difficult to determine, but there is some indication of decreases in the northeastern United States and increases in the South and West (Husar 1986).

The trends for the photochemical oxidants such as ozone are more problematical. As mentioned earlier, the sources of these materials are not as obvious as the sources of oxides of sulfur and nitrogen. In a sense, the oxidants are products of general urban malaise. Work has indicated that reduction of reactive hydrocarbons is most promising for suppressing small-scale elevated ozone levels, but that for larger areas and time scales reduction of nitrogen oxides is probably more effective (Becker et al. 1985). It will require a high level of public awareness, probably expressed as legislation, to help hold oxidant levels either constant or declining.

The trend for heavy metals, and especially for lead, can be established. The phasing out of leaded gasoline has reduced lead emissions. Between 1975 and 1981, lead consumption in gasoline declined more than 50% (Ethyl Corporation 1982). Substantial decreases in lead concentration in precipitation have accompanied the decreases in emission (Eisenreich et al. 1986). This trend of decreased emissions and decreased deposition is likely to continue until leaded gasoline becomes a product of the past.

I interpret the general trend of all air pollutants to be downward. I foresee emissions to be increasingly regulated, leading to that declining trend. In addition, newer and cleaner technologies, introduced with new plants and automobiles, will lead to long-term reductions as older plants and automobiles are phased out. These newer technologies are often driven by legislation. The plain fact of the matter is that politicians have sniffed the wind, and have moved in for the kill. It may take them a while, but eventually the prey will be weakened and emissions will reach a lower level; as the trends that I have shown indicate, emissions are now lower than they have been in the recent past.

I do not mean to suggest that without political pressure this scenario would come about. The political animal responds only to continual stimulation. But as legal sanctions and obsolescence lead to phasing out of dirty operations, the trend of emissions will continue to be downward. Based on that premise, we have either seen the worst in terms of effects or the worst is not far away. Even with reduction in air pollutants, however, the possibility of problems continues to exist. Are there some damages that will be manifested only in the long term? Are the effects of some of the interacting anthropogenic stresses now accumulating on some terrestrial ecosystems so that a relatively minor natural stress such as a drought will kick the system into decline? That possibility cannot be ruled out.

LONG-RANGE IMPLICATIONS

What are the long-term consequences of the impacts of air pollutants that I have described? Just as the impacts can be separated into those that act upon soil and those that act upon vegetation, so too can speculation about long-term implications.

Over the long term, materials that have been added to the soil are likely to be leached away, and nutrient depletions can be restored by normal processes such as weathering and additions via dustfall. Of critical concern, however, is whether the ameliorating process will replace the lost nutrients within a reasonable period, from a human perspective, or will this effect be attained only over geologic time?

Even the most pessimistic among us will agree that the negative effects of air pollution have been produced in less than fifty years. Even if restoration takes twice that amount of time, that is still a short long-term process. Furthermore, just as some of the impacts of air pollution tend to be an acceleration of normal processes, that acceleration helps to move the system more quickly back to a normal condition. For example, weathering of minerals in soil appears to be accelerated by the effects of acidic deposition, hastening the potential rate of elemental replacement. This question about the time frame of restoration is so nebulous, however, that it cannot be reasonably answered by conventional formulation of our present knowledge. Mechanistic mathematical models, such as those developed to understand lake acidification (Goldstein et al. 1984), may help us extrapolate present knowledge into the future. Such models must simulate important processes such as the response of mineral weathering to changes in soil organic matter induced by acidic deposition, rates of recovery of soil colloidal systems from depletions, and other poorly understood processes.

The long-range implications of air pollution in regard to vegetation are no more easily discernible than those concerning soil. Any audience of wildland managers is clearly aware of the dynamic nature of vegetation: it is continuously changing, and even that which appears to be remaining constant is probably doing so by change. In many cases we have little or no control over either the rate or the direction of change.

Reduced growth of trees in a forest stand may be of little consequence to the manager of wilderness. Forests, or the trees within them, are not viewed as fiber factories by those managers. Whether or not a tree is growing slowly or quickly may have little impact on its aesthetic value. A reduction of growth, if not so severe that it leads to accelerated rates of mortality or visual symptoms of decline, may even retard rates of vegetation change—maintaining the status quo.

Differential mortality may or may not have adverse consequences in a forest community. If the stand is made up of a single species, the death of some individuals from anthropogenic causes may provide a thinning that would have occurred anyway under different circumstances. There is some limit, however, to the number of individuals that can die under the designation of normal thinning before that number becomes an epidemic. Mortality in mixed stands may have a different effect. If differential sensitivity to stress among species exists, some species are likely to be replaced by others in the stand. For example, in the San Bernardino Mountains of California, areas of the mixed conifer forest with severe ozone-induced injury of ponderosa pine are changing in composition. Projections indicate eventual shift in dominance of this forest from ponderosa pine to incense-cedar (*Calocedrus decurrens*) (McBride et al. 1985). This can be described as an anthropogenically induced succession. The consequences of such shifts to long-term management, including that of wilderness, depend on the direction that the shifts take, and on the presumed desirability of the replaced and replacing species.

Extensive work wherein forest vegetation was subjected to continuing severe stress over a long time has generally demonstrated a reversal of succession, with loss of trees occurring first, then shrubs; herbaceous species were the ultimate survivors. The best example of such stresses are high levels of experimentally induced gamma radiation (Odum 1971: 459). A similar sequence has occurred to plant communities near Ducktown, Tennessee, under the influence of severe heavy metal and sulfur dioxide pollution from a point source. Such a shift in community structure may (or may not) also be occurring at high altitudes in some parts of the Appalachians (Johnson and McLaughlin 1986).

These changes in plant communities that I have described or speculated about must be placed in perspective. As I mentioned earlier, natural vegetation is amazingly resilient. Consider the catastrophic decimation of vegetation associated with a dry-season forest fire in the Lake States. After ten years, only the snags remain to tell the tale. It is even difficult to find visual evidence, after a few decades, of genuine catastrophes such as the chestnut blight in the East. On the other hand, many areas near Ducktown or Sudbury, even after fifty or more years of healing, look like the dark side of hell. The lesson is clear. If we can avoid irreversible damage of the site, or better of the soil, and if effective regulatory mechanisms are imposed, then long-term consequences of air pollutants will be small. If the current trends of decreased emissions of anthropogenic pollutants in the air are not maintained, systems will continue to be degraded. We have a moral obligation to be good stewards of our resources.

LITERATURE CITED

Abrahamsen, G., and B. Tveite. 1983. Effects of air pollutants on forest and forest growth. *In* Ecological effects of acid deposition, pp. 189-219. Report PM 1636. National Swedish Environment Protection Board.

Babich, H., and G. Stotsky. 1979. Environmental factors that influence the toxicity of heavy metal and gaseous pollutants to microorganisms. Critical Reviews of Microbiology 8:99-145.

Becker, K. H., W. Fricke, J. Löbel, and U. Schurath. 1985. Formation, transport, and control of photochemical oxidants. *In* R. Guderian (ed.) Air pollution by photochemical oxidants, pp. 3-125. Ecological Studies 52. Springer-Verlag, Berlin and New York.

Cowling, E. B. 1985. Comparison of regional declines of forests in Europe and North America: The possible role of airborne chemicals. *In* Air pollutants effects on forest ecosystems, pp. 217-234. Symposium Proceedings, St. Paul, Minnesota, May 8-9, 1985. Acid Rain Foundation, St. Paul.

Cronan, C. S., and R. A. Goldstein. 1988. ALBIOS: A comparison of aluminum biogeochemistry in forested watersheds exposed to acidic deposition. *In* Case studies on acid precipitation. Vol. 5. Springer-Verlag, New York. In press.

Eisenreich, S. J., N. A. Metzer, N. R. Urban, and J. A. Robbins. 1986. Response of atmospheric lead to decreased use of lead in gasoline. Environ. Sci. Tech. 20:171-174.

Ethyl Corporation. 1982. Yearly report of gasoline sales by state. Ethyl Corporation, Houston, Texas.

Ferman, M. A., G. T. Wolff, and N. A. Kelly. 1981. The nature and source of haze in the Shenandoah Valley/Blue Ridge Mountain area. J. Air Poll. Cont. Assoc. 31:1074-1082.

Fernandez, I. J. 1985. Potential effects of atmospheric deposition on forest soils. *In* Air pollutants effects on forest ecosystems, pp. 237-250. Symposium Proceedings, St. Paul, Minnesota. Acid Rain Foundation, St. Paul.

Foy, C. D., R. L. Chaney, and M. C. White. 1978. The physiology of metal toxicity in plants. Ann. Rev. Plant Physiol. 29:511-566.

Friedland, A. J., A. H. Johnson, and T. G. Siccama. 1984. Trace metal content of the forest floor in the Green Mountains of Vermont: Spatial and temporal patterns. Water, Air and Soil Pollution 21:161-170.

Goldstein, R. A., S. A. Gherini, C. W. Chen, L. Mok, and R. J. M. Hudson. 1984. Integrated acidification study (ILWAS): A mechanistic ecosystem analysis. Phil. Trans. R. Soc. Lond. B 305:409-425.

Guderian, R. (ed.) 1985. Air pollution by photochemical oxidants. Ecological Studies 52. Springer-Verlag, Berlin and New York. 346 p.

Hinrichsen, D. 1986. Multiple pollutants and forest decline. Ambio 15:258-265.

Hultberg, H. 1985. Budgets of base cations, chloride, nitrogen and sulfur in the acid Lake Gardsjon catchment, SW Sweden. Ecol. Bull. 37:133-157.

Husar, R. B. 1986. Emissions of sulfur dioxide and nitrogen oxides and trends for eastern North America. *In* Acid deposition long-term trends, pp. 48-92. National Research Council, National Academy of Sciences. National Academy Press, Washington, D.C.

Huttermann, A., and B. Ulrich. 1984. Solid phase-solution-root interactions in soils subjected to acid deposition. Phil. Trans. R. Soc. Lond. B 305:353-368.

Johnson, A. H., and S. B. McLaughlin. 1986. The nature and timing of the deterioration of red spruce in the northern Appalachian Mountains. *In* Acid deposition long-term trends, pp. 200-230. National Academy Press, Washington, D.C.

Keeves, A. 1966. Some evidence of loss of productivity with successive rotations of *Pinus radiata* in the south-east of South Australia. Aust. For. 30:51-63.

Kelly, J. M., and R. C. Strickland. 1986. Throughfall and plant nutrient concentration response to simulated acid rain treatment. Water, Air and Soil Pollution 29:219-231.

Kozlowski, T. T., and H. A. Constantinidou. 1986. Responses of woody plants to environmental pollution. Forestry Abstracts 47(1):5-51.

Lindberg, S. E., G. M. Lovett, D. D. Richter, and D. W. Johnson. 1986. Atmospheric deposition and canopy interactions of major ions in a forest. Science 231:141-145.

Manion, P. D. 1981. Tree disease concepts. Prentice-Hall, Englewood Cliffs, New Jersey. 399 p.

——. 1985. Factors contributing to the decline of forests: A conceptual overview. *In* Air pollutants effects on forest ecosystems, pp. 63-73. Symposium Proceedings, St. Paul, Minnesota. Acid Rain Foundation, St. Paul.

McBride, J. R., P. R. Miller, and R. D. Laven. 1985. Effects of oxidant air pollutants on forest succession in the mixed conifer forest type of southern California. *In* Air pollutants effects on forest ecosystems, pp. 157-167. Symposium Proceedings, St. Paul, Minnesota. Acid Rain Foundation, St. Paul.

McFee, W. W. 1982. Sensitivity ratings of soils to acid deposition: A review. *In* Response of agricultural soils to acid deposition, pp. 2-1 to 2-12. Research Project 1904-1. Electric Power Research Institute, Palo Alto, California.

Moloney, K. A., L. J. Stratton, and R. M. Klein. 1983. Effects of simulated acidic, metal-containing precipitation on coniferous litter decomposition. Can. J. Bot. 61:3337-3342.

Mueller-Dombois, D., J. E. Canfield, R. A. Holt, and G. P. Buelow. 1983. Tree-group death in North American and Hawaiian forests: A pathological problem or a new problem for vegetation ecology? Phytocoenologia 11:117-137.

National Academy of Sciences. 1986. Acid deposition long-term trends. National Academy Press, Washington, D.C. 506 p.

National Research Council. 1983. Acid deposition: Atmospheric processes in eastern North America, a review of current scientific understanding. National Academy of Sciences. National Academy Press, Washington, D.C.

Nihlgard, B. 1985. The ammonium hypothesis: An additional explanation to the forest dieback in Europe. Ambio 14:1-8.

Odum, E. P. 1971. Fundamentals of ecology. 3d ed. W. B. Saunders, Philadelphia. 574 p.

Office of the Director. 1985. Annual report, 1985. National Acid Precipitation Assessment Program. Prepared for the Interagency Task Force on Acid Precipitation, Washington, D.C. 113 p.

Persson, G., and O. Broberg. 1985. Nutrient concentrations in the acidified Lake Gardsjon: The role of transport and retention of phosphorus, nitrogen and DOC in watershed and lake. Ecol. Bull. 37:158-175.

Peterson, D. L., M. J. Arbaugh, V. A. Wakefield, and P. R. Miller. 1987. Evidence of growth reduction in ozone-injured Jeffrey pine (*Pinus jeffreyi* Grev. and Balf.) in Sequoia and Kings Canyon National Parks. J. Air Poll. Cont. Assoc. 37:906-912.

Rolfe, G. L., and F. A. Bazzaz. 1975. Effect of lead contamination on transpiration and photosynthesis of loblolly pine and autumn olive. For Sci. 21:33-35.

RMCC Atmospheric Sciences Subgroup. 1986. Assessment of the state of knowledge on the long-range transport of air pollutants and acid deposition. Part 2: Atmospheric sciences. Federal/Provincial Research and Monitoring Coordinating Committee, Canada. 108 p.

RMCC Terrestrial Effects Subgroup. 1986. Assessment of the state of knowledge on the long-range transport of air pollutants and acid deposition. Part 4: Terrestrial effects. Federal/Provincial Research and Monitoring Coordinating Committee, Canada. 108 p.

Ruhling, A., and G. Tyler. 1973. Heavy metal pollution and decomposition of spruce needle litter. Oikos 24:402-416.

Schutt, P., and E. B. Cowling. 1985. Waldsterben, a general decline of forests in Central Europe: Symptoms, development, and possible causes. Plant Disease 69:548-558.

Shafer, S. R., L. F. Grand, R. I. Bruck, and A. S. Heagle. 1985. Formation of ectomycorrhizae on *Pinus taeda* seedlings exposed to simulated acidic rain. Can. J. For. Res. 15:66-71.

Sheffield, R. M., and N. D. Cost. 1987. Behind the decline. J. For. 85:29-33.

Stenslund, G. J., D. M. Whelpdale, and G. Oehlert. 1986. Precipitation chemistry. *In* Acid deposition long-term trends, pp. 128-199. National Academy Press, Washington, D.C.

Swedish Ministry of Agriculture. 1982. Acidification today and tomorrow. Swedish Ministry of Agriculture, Environment '82 Committee, Stockholm.

Tabatabai, M. A., R. E. Burwell, B. G. Ellis, D. R. Keeney, T. J. Logan, D. W. Nelson, R. A. Olson, G. W. Randall, D. R. Timmons, E. S. Verry, and E. M. White. 1981. Nutrient concentrations and accumulations in precipitation over the North Central Region. Res. Bull. 594. Iowa State University, Agriculture Experiment Station, Ames.

Trijonis, J. 1986. Patterns and trends in data for atmospheric sulfates and visibility. *In* Acid deposition long-term trends, pp. 109-127. National Academy Press, Washington, D.C.

Tukey, H. B., Jr. 1980. Some effects of rain and mist on plants, with implications for acid precipitation. *In* T. C. Hutchinson and M. Havas (eds.) Effects of acid precipitation on terrestrial ecosystems, pp. 141-150. Plenum Press, New York.

Turner, J., M. J. Lambert, and S. P. Gessel. 1977. Use of foliage sulphate concentrations to predict response to urea application by Douglas-fir. Can. J. For. Res. 7:476-480.

Ulrich, B. 1983. A concept of forest ecosystem stability and of acid deposition as driving force for destabilization. *In* B. Ulrich and J. Pankrath (eds.) Effects of accumulation of air pollutants in forest ecosystems, pp. 1-29. D. Reidel, Dordrecht, Holland.

———. 1984. Effects of air pollution on forest ecosystems and waters: The principles demonstrated at a case study in Central Europe. Atmospheric Environment 18:621-628.

Whyte, A. G. D. 1973. Productivity of first and second crops of *Pinus radiata* on the Moutere gravel soils of Nelson. N.Z. J. For. 18:87-103.

Winner, W. E., and C. J. Atkinson. 1986. Absorption of air pollution by plants, and consequences for growth. Trends in Ecology and Evolution 1:15-18.

Wong, M. H. 1982. Metal cotolerance to copper, lead, and zinc in *Festuca rubra*. Environ. Res. 29:42-47.

Woodman, J. N., and E. B. Cowling. 1987. Airborne chemicals and forest health. Environ. Sci. Tech. 21:120-126.

Zedaker, S. M., D. M. Hyink, and D. W. Smith. 1987. Growth declines in red spruce. J. For. 85:34-36.

8

Lake Acidification in Wilderness Areas: An Evaluation of Impacts and Options for Rehabilitation

CARL L. SCHOFIELD

ABSTRACT The process of atmospheric transport and deposition of pollutants in remote wilderness ecosystems poses a number of problems for management and protection of these sensitive resources. The problem of lake acidification in the Adirondack Mountains of New York is used to illustrate the nature of the problems associated with options for protection, management, and rehabilitation of these lake systems. More than 20% of the Adirondack Lake resource has been acidified by atmospheric deposition of strong acids. Loss of fish populations, reductions in genetic diversity of the remaining stocks, and adverse changes in fish community composition have occurred. Protection and restoration of water quality in these lake systems would require reductions in sulfate deposition of more than 50% of current levels, by control of primary emission sources. Mitigative strategies, such as lake neutralization by liming, do not constitute ecosystem rehabilitation. Furthermore, implementation of lake liming programs for protection and management of endangered fish stocks and restoration of fisheries is currently limited by regional policy restrictions on management activities in wilderness zones. Although both source control and mitigative lake neutralization may effectively improve water quality in acidified lakes, neither approach alone will result in complete rehabilitation of these ecosystems. The drastic changes that have occurred in the structure of the fish communities and their supporting invertebrate forage base as a result of acidification would also require biological restructuring of these communities for restoration to preacidification conditions.

A major pathway of pollutants to aquatic ecosystems in wilderness areas is atmospheric transport and deposition. Anthropogenic emissions to the atmosphere of a variety of pollutants—including toxic organics, heavy metals, and acids—are derived from an equally diverse array of industrial and agricultural activities. Because the sources of pollutants are usually considerable distances from these wilderness areas, identification of specific sources, establishment of cause and effect relationships, and development of control strategies are extremely difficult. The atmospheric deposition of acidifying substances, popularly referred to as acid precipitation, is currently a widespread, regional phenomenon in eastern North America, western Europe, and Scandinavia. The impacts on aquatic ecosystems in one such area, the Adirondack Mountains of New York State, and the problems associated with the management and rehabilitation of affected wilderness systems in this region, are specifically addressed in this paper.

Annual average pH levels of 4.0 to 4.2 (weighted for volume) have been reported for precipitation in the three regions of the world mentioned above (Linthurst et al. 1986). In the northeastern United States, about 60 to 80% of the acidity in precipitation is due to sulfuric acid, with nitric acid accounting for most of the remaining contribution. Anthropogenic emissions of SO_2 and NO_x are believed to be the major sources of strong acids found in precipitation within these areas. On a global scale, this kind of sulfur loading to the atmosphere amounts to 60 to 70 Tg/yr (Tg = teragrams, or millions of metric tons)—an amount that equals or slightly exceeds all known natural sources of sulfur emission (e.g., volcanoes, biological decomposition). Unfortunately, approximately 60% of the global anthropogenic sulfur emission occurs over less than 5% of the earth's surface, principally in western Europe and eastern North America. Fossil fuel combustion is the primary source of SO_2 emissions in these industrialized regions, and of the 25 to 30 Tg of SO_2 emitted annually in the United States over the past twenty years, about two-thirds originates from the electric utility industry (Placet and Streets 1987). Biological emissions of sulfur to the United States atmosphere are estimated to be only 2% of the annual anthropogenic emissions. National emissions of SO_2 increased from about 9 Tg in 1900 to a peak of about 27 Tg in 1970, and have since declined to about 25 Tg in 1984. Some 75 to 80% of these emissions occur east of the Mississippi River. The trend toward fewer but larger emission point sources, tending to be located more frequently in rural rather than urban areas, has resulted in the emitted sulfur being distributed over wider regions. Transformation of gaseous SO_2 emissions to acid sulfates results in the production of submicron particles, which have a long residence time in the atmosphere (three

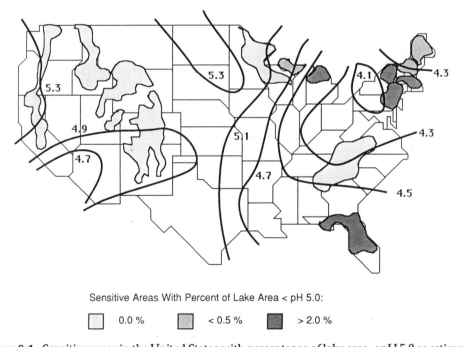

Sensitive Areas With Percent of Lake Area < pH 5.0:

☐ 0.0 %　　☐ < 0.5 %　　☐ > 2.0 %

Figure 8-1. Sensitive areas in the United States with percentages of lake area < pH 5.0 as estimated from statistical survey of subregions potentially sensitive to acidic deposition and 1985 isopleths of precipitation weighted average annual pH of wet deposition. Source: adapted from Linthurst et al. 1986.

to five days) and can extend the impact of sulfate pollutants over 1,000 km or more from the original SO_2 sources (Albritton et al. 1987). Precipitation scavenging and wash out are the primary means by which these acid pollutants are removed from the atmosphere, thus creating the phenomenon of acid precipitation, currently prevalent in the eastern United States and Canada.

Underlying this mantle of acid deposition in eastern North America are aquatic ecosystems that exhibit considerable sensitivity to acidification. On a broad, regional scale, sensitivity to acidification may be defined simply on the basis of prevailing bedrock geology (Norton 1980). Thus waters draining regions characterized by granitic or other hard, weathering resistant bedrock formations tend to have low acid neutralizing capacity. Numerically, the vast majority of salmonid producing waters in eastern Canada on the Precambrian Shield and the northeastern United States fall into this vulnerable category. Other potentially sensitive areas in the United States include the northern areas of Michigan, Wisconsin, and Minnesota and the mountainous regions of the Far West (Rocky, Sierra, and Cascade mountains). Currently, significant levels of surface water acidification have been detected only in sensitive regions of the eastern United States receiving precipitation more acidic than pH 4.6 to 4.7 (Figure 8-1).

THE ADIRONDACK PARK: A CASE STUDY OF IMPACTS AND MANAGEMENT PROBLEMS

The Adirondack Mountain region of New York State is the largest sensitive lake district in the eastern United States where extensive lake acidification has been documented (Schofield 1976). The New York State Forest Preserve, which includes the Adirondack Mountains, was set aside for protection in 1885. In 1895 it was afforded further protection by the New York State Constitution, which declared that the "Forest Preserve shall be forever kept as wild forest lands." Under this provision the Adirondack Mountains became the Adirondack Park, which is the largest defined park in the United States. This concept of wilderness has been nurtured for over a century through constitutional protection and more recently by a State Land Master Plan of use classification which specifically designated approximately half of the Adirondacks as a wilderness area, which is by definition essentially identical to the federal Wilderness Act of 1964 classification governing land use and management activities (APA 1985). It is thus somewhat ironic and problematic that this "forever wild" concept should now be so insidiously violated by the unforeseen consequences posed by the acid precipitation problem. The primary issues resulting from this dilemma are: (1) Can and should these sensitive aquatic resources be protected from remote sources of pollution? (2) Are mitigative strategies, such as lake liming, effective and appropriate for the protection and management of fisheries in wilderness areas? (3) What is the potential for restoration of these acidified ecosystems to "pristine" conditions?

There are about 2,800 lakes encompassing an area of some 114,000 hectares within the Adirondack Park (Figure 8-2). There are also more than 9,000 km of streams draining the four major watersheds of the region (Hudson, Champlain, St. Lawrence, and Black River basins). Recent water quality surveys conducted in the Adirondack Park (Pfeiffer and Festa 1980, Linthurst et al. 1986) indicate that more than 30% of the lakes exhibit pH levels below 5.5, a marginal level for the support of healthy fish populations. Nearly 70% of the lakes in the Adirondacks are small (< 10 ha), headwater lakes, and 40% of these waters currently exhibit pH values below 5.0—a level considered unsuitable for fish survival (Schofield et al. 1986). These acidified headwater lakes are numerically most prevalent in the western Adirondack watersheds (e.g., Black River drainage contains 1,050 lakes of which 60% are < pH 5), which, by virtue of their higher mean elevation, receive more precipitation and have thinner soils with low acid neutralizing capacity.

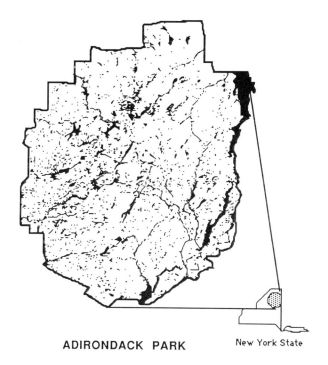

ADIRONDACK PARK   New York State

Figure 8-2. Distribution of lakes in the Adirondack Park, New York State.

Comparisons of historical records of water quality and fish population status (1920s-1930s) with recent surveys (1970s-1980s) indicate that significant surface water acidification and fish population losses have taken place over the intervening period (Schofield 1982). An estimated 40% of the small, western Adirondack headwater lakes are currently in a chronically acidified (pH < 5) condition. There are some twenty-two fish species native to the Adirondack region, many of which were historically present in these currently barren lakes (Pfeiffer and Festa 1980, Schofield 1976). Although there are no endangered species indigenous to the region, the loss of habitat resulting from extensive headwater acidification has resulted in an irreplaceable loss of genetic diversity due to extinction of fish populations uniquely adapted to these sensitive waters.

The apparent relationships between the presence or absence of fish species and changes in acidity over time, documented by the surveys noted above, constitute the primary evidence of acidification-induced impacts on fish populations in the Adirondack Park. The mechanisms responsible for fish population losses from acidified lakes are not precisely known and probably vary, depending on physiological sensitivity of the species originally present and their life history patterns (Haines 1981). Early life stages of many fish species tend to be particularly vulnerable to acid stress as a result of limited mobility and access to refugia from acidification events, such as acidic snow melt or storm runoff (Schofield 1976). Acidification induced changes in the quantity and quality of food available to fish can also result in reduced growth and reproductive potential (Mills and Schindler 1986). Recruitment failure and population extinction may result from either high mortality of early life stages or reduced reproductive success of adults.

The integrated effects of differential physiological tolerances to acidification and behavioral regulation (through emigration and immigration) of environmental quality were found to be of significance in determining distribution patterns of fish species in Adirondack drainage systems exhibiting marked spatial acidity gradients (Schofield and Driscoll 1987). Long-term records of fish species occurrence in one drainage system

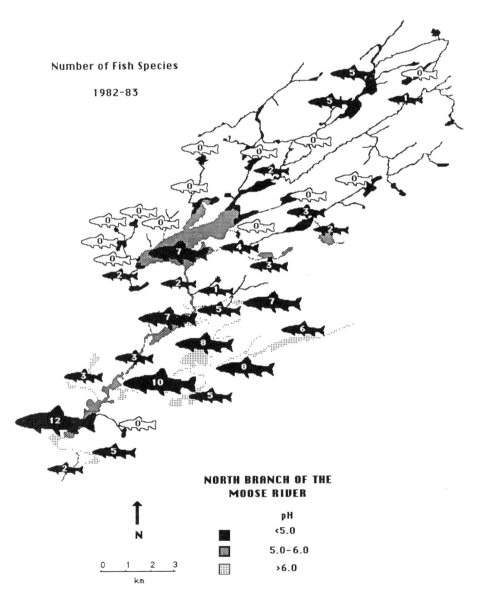

Figure 8-3. Number of fish species found in lakes and streams of the North Branch of the Moose River and average summer pH levels observed during surveys conducted in 1982-83.

(North Branch of the Moose River, western Adirondacks) were also utilized to reconstruct chronological changes in fish distribution, in relation to acidification and other ecosystem perturbations, such as the introduction of exotic and nonnative fish species. Dramatic changes in the fish communities inhabiting this drainage system first became apparent during the 1940s, following a long period of relative stability from 1882 to 1931. During the latter period, the native species complex—consisting primarily of lake trout, whitefish, suckers, and several species of cyprinids—remained essentially intact. The loss of whitefish and decline in abundance and distribution of the cyprinids during the 1940s was followed by a decline in growth and survival of lake trout, the top predator in the system. Paleolimnological evidence of the acidification of the Moose River system during this period when shifts in fish community structure were occurring strongly suggested acid stress as a primary cause of the population declines (Charles et al. 1987). A similar pattern of forage base collapse, followed by reduced growth and recruitment failure of a lake trout population, was documented during the experimental acidification of a lake in Ontario (Mills and Schindler 1986).

The hypothesis that current fish species distribution patterns across acidity gradients in the Moose River watershed reflect physiological tolerances of the species to acidification was also supported by the observed species distributions relative to acidity (Figure 8-3) and experimental determination of their tolerances to acidity by *in situ* transfers of the species across the acidity gradient in the watershed (Johnson et al. 1987, Schofield and Driscoll 1987). Native cyprinids and salmonids were found to be most sensitive to acidity in these experiments, and although isolated populations of these sensitive species still exist in limited, downstream areas of the drainage basin that have higher pH levels, the opportunity for recolonization of the main drainage system is seriously limited by acidity levels that exceed their physiological tolerances.

At the opposite end of the sensitivity spectrum, the most tolerant fish species found in the Moose River drainage system were represented primarily by exotics, such as the yellow perch and mud minnow. These exotic species either were inadvertently introduced to the system or immigrated from downstream areas, after initiation of acidification in the 1940s. These relatively acid tolerant species are now widely distributed throughout the Moose River (as they are also in other acidified Adirondack basins) and are currently dominant in acidic, upland reaches.

Lake Acidification Processes and the Potential for Recovery

Lake and stream water chemistry observations represent an integrated measure of ecosystem modifications of water inputs from atmospheric precipitation. When these observations are evaluated in concert with other watershed information on flow paths and chemical transformations affecting water transported through the drainage systems, a basis is provided for evaluating system responses to changes in atmospheric loading levels of strong acids. This was the approach taken in the Integrated Lake Watershed Acidification Study (ILWAS), which resulted in the development of a quantitative model of the acidification process (Gherini et al. 1985). Differences in acidity of two western Adirondack lakes (Woods, pH 5, and Panther, pH 7) receiving similar atmospheric acid deposition levels were found to result primarily from different base cation supply rates from the watersheds (Schofield et al. 1985). Dominant flow paths and the residence time of water in the soils were found to be primary determinants of the relative degree of acidification in the two basins. Thus, in circumneutral Panther Lake, deep glacial tills and high soil permeabilities in the basin led to a greater proportion of base rich groundwater discharge to the lake. In Woods Lake basin, shallower soils and till with lower permeability resulted in less groundwater discharge and a predominance of shallow, acidic surface flow to the lake.

Model simulations of the responses of these two lake-watershed systems to changes in atmospheric acid loading were equally divergent. Reductions in sulfate deposition levels of 50% or more resulted in significant increases in Woods Lake pH levels (from about pH 5 to 6), whereas little change was observed in Panther Lake, where sufficient neutralization of acid inputs already occurs through cation release from weathering and cation exchange processes in the soils (Gherini et al. 1985). The primary source of uncertainty in predicting the response of these ecosystems to changes in acid loading levels is the degree of compensation that occurs through sequestering of acid inputs by weathering and cation exchange. Rates and levels for these critical processes are likely to be highly variable between basins, as has already been shown in the ILWAS study involving only three lakes.

Time frames for system responses to changes in acid loading are also variable, depending not only on hydraulic residence times of water in the system but also on the time required for new equilibria to be reached between sulfate levels in the soils and the new input levels. Simulations for systems like Woods Lake, which is typical of the small, acidified lakes of the western Adirondacks, suggested that recovery times would be on the order of ten years following change in the sulfate loading levels. However, a much longer recovery period was predicted for the larger, Moose River drainage basin (Davis et al. 1987).

Mitigation of Lake Acidification Impacts

Currently, two options are available for control of lake acidification: (1) reduction of acid sulfate inputs via source emission control, and (2) mitigation of lake acidification by adding neutralizing materials (such as agricultural limestone) to the lakes and/or their watersheds. Lake neutralization does not constitute ecosystem rehabilitation, since the structural and functional components of the new systems created are quite different from pristine, neutral aquatic ecosystems that have not been affected by acid deposition (Fraser and Britt 1982). The implementation of lake liming programs can be justified only in relation to fisheries-related management goals, and the decision to neutralize acidified systems is entirely subject to regional policy constraints, particularly in wilderness areas.

The primary objective of lake neutralization, from a resource management perspective, is to maintain water quality suitable for the support of healthy fish populations. While healthy fish populations are certainly a desirable outcome of a management level liming program, in reality the objectives must be more specific and guided by both regional policy considerations and fisheries management goals. Indiscriminant liming programs could be counterproductive to established fisheries management objectives and policies. For example, the liming of acidified Adirondack waters currently dominated by exotic species (such as yellow perch) with no potential for development of recreational fisheries or reestablishment of native species, without extensive eradication of undesirable fish species, might not be desirable from a fisheries management point of view. The main target species for potential management involving lake neutralization in the Adirondack region are the brook trout, lake trout, and prey species associated with the lake trout. The appropriate strategies and utility of liming as a tool for maintaining these species have not been adequately addressed. While this can be attributed in part to a lack of policy consensus on the application of liming as a management tool, there are also significant gaps in our knowledge at the operational level that would prohibit implementation of effective management at the present time. Preliminary findings from research programs addressing these major management questions suggest that high flushing rates may obviate the effectiveness of liming in most of the small headwater lakes that are potential candidates for neutralization (Figure 8-4). Lakes with average annual flushing rates greater than two to three times per year were found to reacidify within a year after liming and were unable to sustain stocked trout populations (Schofield et al. 1986). These studies also suggest that predation-induced changes in the forage base of these previously fishless lakes lead to reductions in average prey size that may result in decreased fish growth and yield under programs of long-term maintenance liming.

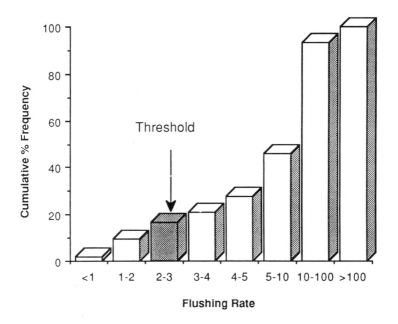

Figure 8-4. Cumulative frequency distribution (%) of annual flushing rates in Adirondack lakes with surface areas < 10 hectares. Lakes that flush more than two or three times per year (threshold) are unsuitable candidates for liming.

CONCLUSIONS

The documented impacts of acid deposition on aquatic ecosystems in the Adirondack region and other areas in the northeastern United States and Canada demonstrate the sensitivity and vulnerability of wilderness ecosystems to pollution via long-range atmospheric transport and deposition. Protection of threatened resources and possible restoration of impacted systems would require substantial levels of emission control to provide significant, maintained improvements in water quality. Reductions in sulfate deposition in the Adirondack region of at least 50% would be required to restore water quality in currently acidified systems.

Mitigative liming, as an alternative or even stopgap strategy for maintaining fish populations in acidified waters, suffers from a variety of legal, ethical, and logistical constraints. This is particularly true in remote wilderness areas—unfortunately the predominant resource type affected in the Adirondack region.

Finally, although it may be technologically feasible to restore water quality in these ecosystems, either through direct mitigative actions or by regulation of emissions at the sources, ecological rehabilitation would be difficult at best, given the drastic changes in community structure that have accompanied the acidification process.

LITERATURE CITED

Albritton, D. L., S. C. Lui, and F. C. Fehsenfeld. 1987. NAPAP Interim Assessment: The causes and effects of acidic deposition. Vol. 3: Atmospheric processes and deposition. Chapter 4. National Acid Precipitation Assessment Program, Washington, D.C.

Adirondack Park Agency. 1985. Adirondack Park State Land Master Plan. State of New York. 68 p.

Charles, D. F., D. R. Whitehead, G. Blake, D. Engstrom, B. Fry, R. Hites, S. Norton, J. Owen, L. Roll, S. Schindler, J. Smol, A. Uutala, J. White, and R. Wise. 1987. Paleolimnological evidence for recent acidification of Big Moose Lake, Adirondack Mountains (U.S.A.). Biogeochemistry 3:267-296.

Davis, G. F., J. J. Whipple, S. A. Gherini, C. W. Chen, R. A. Goldstein, A. H. Johannes, P. W. Chan, and R. K. Munson. 1987. Big Moose Basin: Simulation of response to acidic deposition. Biogeochemistry 3:141-161.

Fraser, J. E., and D. L. Britt. 1982. Liming of acidified waters: A review of methods and effects on aquatic ecosystems. U.S. Fish and Wildlife Serv., Air Pollution and Acid Rain Rep. 13. FWS/OBS-80/40.13. 189 p.

Gherini, S., C. Chen, L. Mok, R. Goldstein, R. Hudson, and G. Davis. 1985. The ILWAS model: Formulation and application. Water, Air and Soil Pollution 26:425-459.

Haines, T. A. 1981. Acidic precipitation and its consequences for aquatic ecosystems: A review. Transactions of the American Fisheries Society 110: 669-707.

Johnson, D. W., J. Colquhoun, F. Flack, and H. Simonin. 1987. *In situ* toxicity tests of fishes in acid waters. Biogeochemistry 3:181-208.

Linthurst, R. A., D. H. Landers, J. M. Eilers, D. F. Brakke, W. S. Overton, E. P. Meier, and R. E. Crowe. 1986. Characteristics of lakes in the eastern United States. Vol. 1: Population descriptions and physico-chemical relationships. EPA 600/4-86-007a. U.S. Environmental Protection Agency, Washington, D.C.

Mills, K. H., and D. W. Schindler. 1986. Biological indicators of lake acidification. Water, Air and Soil Pollution 30(3-4):779-789.

Norton, S. A. 1980. Geologic factors controlling the sensitivity of aquatic ecosystems to acidic precipitation. *In* D. Shriner (ed.) Atmospheric sulfur deposition, pp. 521-531. Ann Arbor Science Publishers, Ann Arbor, Michigan.

Pfeiffer, M., and P. Festa. 1980. Acidity status of lakes in the Adirondack region of New York in relation to fish resources. NYSDEC Pub. FW-p168(10/80).

Placet, M., and D. G. Streets. 1987. NAPAP Interim Assessment: The causes and effects of acidic deposition. Vol. 2: Emissions and controls. Chapter 1. National Acid Precipitation Assessment Program, Washington, D.C.

Schofield, C. L. 1976. Acid precipitation: Effects on fish. Ambio 5:228-230.

——. 1982. Historical fisheries changes as related to surface water pH changes in the United States. *In* R. E. Johnson (ed.) Acid Rain/Fisheries Symposium, pp. 57-68. American Fisheries Society, Bethesda, Maryland.

Schofield, C.L., and C.T. Driscoll. 1987. Fish species distribution in relation to water quality gradients in the North Branch of the Moose River Basin. Biogeochemistry 3:63-85.

Schofield, C. L., J. N. Galloway, and G. R. Hendry. 1985. Surface water chemistry in the ILWAS basins. Water, Air and Soil Pollution 26:403-423.

Schofield, C. L., S. P. Gloss, and D. Josephson. 1986. Extensive evaluation of lake liming, restocking strategies, and fish population response in acidic lakes following neutralization by liming. USFWS NEC-86/18. 117 p.

9

Human Ecology and Environmental Management

WILLIAM R. BURCH, JR.

ABSTRACT Human ecology is the study of the relations between human communities (groups or populations) and their respective environments. This approach employs a systems perspective of both society and nature; describes the interactions between social systems and ecosystems in terms of transfers of energy, materials, and information; and is concerned with networks, hierarchies, and the dynamics of change. Human ecology takes a comparative approach and assumes that universal principles can be developed that describe the regularities of forms of social organization, the ecosystem, and individual behavior. Four broad orientations for research and management of parks, historic sites, and recreation areas are suggested and a heuristic model of social ecological system processes and structures is presented. To realize the potential of applied human ecology will require an interdisciplinary, biologically informed effort. Such an effort will require considerable rethinking on the part of both scientists and managers. Yet we should expect no less if parks and wilderness areas are to remain sustainable in the challenge of coming decades.

Human ecology is a field of study that seems to be eternally searching for the center of its identity. Many disciplines, from anthropology to zoology, have fashioned a specialized definition of human ecology, and more than a few have treated the field as private property. Thus we have human ecologies as numerous as the academic departments growing in a multiversity.

The confused identity of academic human ecology seems to drop away, however, when we are confronted with the real problems presented by natural resource issues. At the level of resource assessment, planning, monitoring, action, and evaluation, human ecology is an essential framework holding together the many aspects of management. We will explore the relation between human ecology and environmental management by examining (1) the sources of definition and redefinition of the discipline, (2) some examples of disciplines incorporating human ecology without knowing it, and (3) some specific examples of the application of human ecology to parks and wildlands.

The academic origins of human ecology are usually to be found in early twentieth-century studies of urban succession in Chicago or in Howard Odum's regional geography studies. Although these are important intellectual sources, they are not a sufficient foundation on which to build a discipline of applied human ecology. The human ecologist looks to students such as Charles Darwin, Frederick Law Olmsted, and John Wesley Powell for guidance in theory, design, and planning approaches.

The young Darwin's *Voyage of the Beagle* is particularly inspiring. His observations of diverse and exotic plants, animals, and peoples as examples of adaptation to variation in environments led to the first consideration that human beings were not apart from the natural order. Indeed, Darwin established that the only proper study of the human species was as part of the same evolutionary pressures and processes that affected all life forms.

Olmsted, in the 1850s, was one of the first students of applied human ecology. Whether he was observing the political economy of the slave South, designing urban parks with a vision of combining present and future patterns of social behavior with biological potential, perceiving the role of wildland spaces such as Yosemite, or advocating the necessity for sustained yield forestry at the Biltmore estate, Olmsted was practicing the integration of human behavior and natural resources. Unlike Darwin, his approach was design rather than scientific theory, yet the results remain exciting, functioning examples of applied human ecology.

Powell, in the 1860s, clearly emphasized that all resource planning required attention to the interdependence of biophysical and sociocultural systems. His classic study on the western arid lands used patterns of adaption and property rights institutions developed by aboriginal and Mormon peoples as the model for "gentile" development in the arid West. He combined scientific observation of resource constraints with study of the normative patterns that emerge from attempts to adapt to such constraints. The accuracy of his observations can be judged from present and future battles over limited and declining water supplies in a growing Southwest.

The work of Darwin, Olmsted, and Powell exemplifies three essential dimensions of human ecology if it is to be effective in its application: (1) it must have a testable theory of stability and change; (2) it must have a design approach that orders patterns of behavior and resources at the same time that it permits flexibility and adjustment to inevitable changes in behavior and resources; and (3) planning must be based on empirical observations of resource opportunities and constraints and well-established normative adaptions. Each of these students of human ecology saw humanity as a natural part of nature, yet with the opportunity to intervene in natural processes to guide them systematically toward preferred outcomes. However, such preferences, like those of other life forms, were always subject to basic natural constraints.

FROM HUMAN ECOLOGY TO SOCIAL ECOLOGY

Most of the traditional approaches of human ecology have used biological concepts as metaphors for observed regularities in human behavior. This paper argues for a different approach. It asks two main questions about the reciprocal influences between nonhuman ecosystem structures and processes and human social system structures and processes: (1) Under what conditions do natural ecosystem variables serve as a prime, facilitating, or consequent factor in the observed social system variation? (2) Under what conditions do social system variables influence the natural ecosystem in such a manner that reciprocal feedback alters the basis of the social system?

For lack of a better term, I call this emerging biosocial perspective "social ecology," to distinguish it from the traditional social and geographic approach of human ecology. The distinction is not trivial. Biological processes are a fundamental part of explanations in social ecology. Consequently, social ecology joins its many insights and solid empirical studies to a larger life science.

Our definition of human ecology incorporates both the biological and the social science traditions. Thus human ecology is the study of the relations between human communities (groups or populations) and their respective environments, especially their physical environments. For the most part, sociological human ecology has emphasized synecology (relations between communities and their environments) rather than autecology (relations between individual organisms and their environment), which has been considered by psychologists such as Irwin Altman (1975) and Ken Craik (1968).

The common thread in all such studies is the measurement of the "causal" contributions natural environments make to observed social and behavioral patterns. In this discussion we give most attention to sociological or synecology studies. Rambo and Sajise's (1984:2) definition of human ecology seems closest to this attitude of the social ecologist. Their definition (1) employs a systems viewpoint on both human society and nature, (2) describes both the internal behavior of social systems and ecosystems and their interactions with each other in terms of transfers of energy, materials, and information, (3) is concerned with understanding the organization of systems into networks and hierarchies, and (4) includes the dynamics of system change.

There have been at least five cycles of vision and moral concern in human ecology from the late 1800s to the present. Each of these offers lessons for our times. The five cycles are: concern with food scarcity and rural productivity (1862-1920), concern with the "new" immigration and the urban melting pot (1915-35), concern with rationalizing levels of urban living (1930-55), concern with the social meaning of abundance and life-style variation (1950-65), and concern with resource scarcity and productivity (1960-present). All the cycles overlap and represent visions that are still actively pursued, in one form or another. Since I have discussed these cycles in detail elsewhere (Burch 1979), I will give attention here only to the last phase, which has most relevance to natural resource management issues.

The fifth vision of human ecology is still being written. For the most part, it is being written by biologists. They are the ones who have raised and often documented the issue of the finiteness of world resources. In response to this pessimism, social scientists—mainly—have sought glimmers of hope and, now and then, some indications that the biologists are wrong.

To be sure, some social scientists have picked up the lead from the biologists. Lionel Tiger and Robin Fox (1971) may be wrongheaded and "sexist," yet they seek to develop systematic cross-species comparisons. Sam Klausner (1971) and this author (Burch 1971) may be opaque and confused, but we have sought to incorporate the biological characteristics of humans into classic sociological theories. Roy Rappaport (1967) and Pete Vayda (1977) may have looked too deeply for functionalist explanations, yet their studies are the first systematic attempts at including human social systems within the ecosystem. Vayda's (Kartawinata and Vayda 1984) recent work contains little of a functionalist approach.

Wilson's *Sociobiology* (1975) remains the most influential work of this fifth phase. Although Wilson may have found explanations more to his satisfaction in genetics and too quickly dismissed sociology, his work is the first to offer a truly comparative human ecology. The social scientists now could speak of this specialization within a zoological frame of reference, rather than fumbling with the analogies of physics and other mechanical persuasions.

Of course, like all other species, ours is unique. Our primary mode of adaption may be through culture, which is symbolically communicated. Therefore, our social transcript has a potentially infinite persistence and is easier to track than the stories my biology colleagues tell me they read in the scats of their subject species. Still, this very important and unique adaptive strategy of symbolically transmitted information does not negate the many similarities we share with other social species.

Indeed I argue that all forms of science study, in some manner, the way the natural world is organized. Human ecologists study the ways in which humans organize themselves, and how these patterns affect our collective and individual behavior. Such a human ecology is interested in the basic regularities exhibited by all forms of social organization. It uses a comparative approach as the best way to check ignorance. It assumes that universal principles can be developed such that our predictions of the behavioral consequences of certain organizational patterns can include a troop of Japanese macaques, a tribe of Trobriand Islanders, and a claque of twentieth-century university professors.

Orientations

From this perspective, four broad orientations are necessary for research and management of parks, historic sites, and recreational areas. It is reasonably certain that we have not exhausted the range of possible issues.

First, social ecology will recognize intertrophic exchanges as being of equal importance to interest in how variations in intercultural, interinstitutional, and interpersonal exchanges affect levels of living, life-styles, and long-term survival opportunities. For example, studies of nomadic peoples (Burch and Cheek 1974) in North Africa illustrate how transhumance cycles affect cycles in organizational and symbolic structures. Thus small nuclear kin units are widely scattered during dry periods, while large, concentrated tribal units emerge during wet periods. One wonders what transhumance cycle affects the migratory and grouping patterns of the "airstream" nomads in the modern American Southwest. Or what are the world consequences as more persons consume grain in the form of beef?

The second orientation considers how variations in the forms and amounts of energy affect stability and change in social bonding, social integration, and social solidarity. An excellent example is Rappaport's (1967) study of the relation between ritual, bioenergetics, warfare, and the symbolic value of pigs in Maring society. Denton Morrison's (1976) study on the equity impacts of various energy supplies and systems is another. We have been exploring ways in which one can use time budget analyses over time (Burch and Burch-Minakan 1979) and between cultures to see if variations in per capita energy consumption have any significant influence on life-style.

A third orientation examines how stability and change in the shape, size, and scope of social hierarchies are affected by resource access, modification, and supply. A good example is Gross and Underwood's (1971) study of a new sisal factory in a developing country. They trace how the fairly equal caloric distributions among the population prior to the establishment of the new factory were soon converted into steadily increasing differences. This deficit began to form a biological basis for a new class structure. Since working men required more calories, their women and children received less. The nutritional loss for children at critical periods in their development contributed to severe mental and physical handicaps among the working class, thereby perpetuating class position from generation to generation.

The fourth orientation encourages attention to temporal regularities such as individual and group life cycles, diurnal rhythms, work-nonwork cycles, and so forth. Social scientists perhaps have a pathological fascination with work. They seem to ignore the fact that their "natives" spend more time at war, making love, picking lice off one another, gambling, and kicking a ball around a field than they devote to utilitarian pursuits. Cheek and Burch (1976) argue that research on work tells a good bit about how the division of labor contributes to social integration, but it does not help us understand the nature of the social bond or the linkages between the basic associations of kinship or friendship and the larger collective groups such as the ethnic community or nation-state. We argue that nonwork permits the conversion of certain biosocial propensities into symbolic structures which sustain social bonds and link smaller human associations to larger ones.

Conceptually, social ecology is interested in the nature of a population, its size, distribution, and demographic configuration as it combines with biophysical resource elements like soil, water, plants, and animals. These are the essential inputs into the system. The interaction of population characteristics and ecological characteristics influences the human social relationships (social bonds) that result. Social bonding mechanisms are structured by values associated with household, kinship, friendship, or other intimate human relationships to create and sustain loyalty toward those relationships. Such mechanisms also encourage performance of age, gender, and status roles which are the basic building blocks of larger, more general associations such as the institutions of a community. Social solidarity is structured by values that make individuals feel shame, guilt, or pride in their role performance.

Table 9-1 provides an idealized model of the variables we are considering. As in *all* ecological studies, we are operating at the level of whole systems, rather than reducing our analysis to the individual level. Like biological ecology, social ecology is a historic and synthetic discipline that deals with collectivities rather than individual organisms or their component parts.

Table 9-1. A heuristic model of social ecological system processes and structures.

HABITAT FLOWS	POPULATION FLOWS
Energy	Size
Nutrients	Differentiation (age, gender,
Information	ethnic background, etc.)
Materials	Distribution, in time and space
SOCIAL STRUCTURE	
Values (cultural prescriptions and proscriptions regarding use of time, space, and persons) Hierarchy Social norms and institutions	
AFFECTED SOCIAL UNITS	AFFECTED SOCIAL PROCESSES
Individual	Social bonding
Household	Social solidarity
Community	Social integration

The basic questions of human ecology, like biological ecology, revolve around (1) how unity is created out of diversity and (2) what the relations are between structures of order and processes of change. Much of our attention is directed to the forms of hierarchy that regulate patterns of dominance between species and individuals over access to particular niches. In short, hierarchy is universal and ubiquitous in all ecological systems.

Furthermore, humans, like all social species, share certain patterns of regularity and predictability. The following are examples of this regularity: (1) For social species the survival of individuals is dependent on the regular presence of members of the same species. (2) The exploitation of environment is mediated through organizational forms. (3) These forms tend to establish a hierarchy—individual dominance patterns or dominance by one social stratum over another. (4) These forms generate a high degree of predictability regarding the behavior of individual members. (5) These organizational forms are membranes that serve an intermediate function between individual organisms and the external environment they exploit and to which they adapt. (6) Social species vary on a continuum from where primary transfer of information is predominately genetic to where primary transfer of information is predominately symbolic.

In developing survival strategies to cope with the dynamics of ecological and social change, all social species create nongenetic means of information exchange. In human society, culture is the coin of that exchange. This is because genetic change is slow, particularly for those social species that follow a strategy where a lot of energy is devoted to the production of a phenotype that is capable of successfully competing for environmental resources. Thus large mammals, such as *Homo sapiens* or elephants, have a long developmental time and a very low offspring production (as contrasted to a strategy where a large number of seeds are produced). Humans are a unique species in that culture is their primary adaptive mechanism and communication is primarily symbolic. To ensure such communication, human societies develop social norms and institutions to socialize and to direct the behavior of individual members.

Our model notes that the habitat for human action—be it large city, small farm, or "crown jewel" park—has certain potential and actual processes of energy, nutrient, information, and material flows that shape opportunity and constraint. Human aggregates also exhibit certain demographic processes that alter demands on the habitat. That is, change in birth or mortality rates, sex ratios, or median age of population will greatly affect the nature of the demand upon wildlands. For example, in the 1960s, when all sorts of wilderness managers were predicting escalating demand for wilderness, I and a few others were pointing out that, like the youth culture, the demand for wilderness would soon stabilize (Burch 1974) as the "baby boomers" aged and began to form families. It did. These two sets of processes—energy and other resource flows and demographic change—are filtered through a human community's structure to ensure orderly transfer. This structure can be analyzed in terms of particular variations in values, hierarchy, and social norms and institutions. For example, in a wildland setting the values shaping behavior, the authority for ensuring behavioral compliance, and the means for distributing access to the "valued" resources will greatly differ from similar structures in a large city.

Social ecology's attention to temporal regularities such as individual and group life cycles, diurnal rhythms, work-nonwork cycles, and so forth, remains central to ecological analysis. For example, attention has been given to how different kinds of recreationists distribute themselves in space and time, how human-caused forest fires distribute themselves in space and time, and how boomtowns arise at certain times and places and decline with equal regularity. Studies have examined how religious and social cycles of celebration, holy days, fasting days, national holidays, and so forth, are as fixed and real as seasonal cycles. The behavioral regularities associated with sacred spaces such as wilderness areas seem to be not unlike those found in similar spaces elsewhere.

Social ecology documents how the regularities of human use of space and time map particular social relations, constraints, and opportunities as clearly as they map biophysical patterns. Intimate and distant social relations, high and low social classes, favored and despised ethnic, occupational, and caste groupings all have assigned and clearly regulated measures as to *when* and *where* those relations should and should not occur. Consequently, time and space are not simply physical parameters, but have a prescribed and predictable significance in cultural processes.

In sum, all human social systems have predictable, routine time-space patterns that overlay the biophysical ones. Social ecology asks how the human patterns overlay or conflict with those of ecosystems. Furthermore, in human systems, energy—its nature, types, and amounts—greatly affects patterns and processes of time and space. We can direct more energy in certain ways and gain more productivity in a smaller space and for a shorter time. We substitute human energy for fossil energy or for renewable energy (such as wind), and each change reflects changes in human organization. A city has a higher per capita fossil energy consumption than a rural village, and that is part of the attraction of the city, and part of the reason it has a different organizational form. Finally, human social systems have developed an abstraction to assign value to energy, time, and space and their products—money. Consequently, each person, household, or community has four regularized measures of their structure and functioning—space, time, energy, and material (money). Each can substitute for the other, and each can be incorporated into the other.

Metaphors for Understanding Wildlands and Parks

Parks and wildlands—whether a vest-pocket bit of greenery in Washington, D.C. or the Bob Marshall Wilderness—are essentially islands on the land. They are relatively small territories whose boundaries hold back all the seas of activity around them. Such islands are a refuge, a holding place of possibility. But they too erode, slowly or more speedily, in the currents of life.

The island metaphor permits us to examine wildlands both as semiclosed systems (composed of an assemblage of earth, plants, animals, and people) and as open systems in transaction with other systems (receiving and exchanging energy, nutrients, ideas, migrants, and so forth). Wildlands are separated from the larger social and ecological world by a thin membrane of institutional and normative patterns. This membrane operates much as the littoral shore does on islands: it buffers and serves as a transactive edge between island properties and processes, and those properties and processes of the surrounding environs. So the wildland as island gains a certain isolation and means to retain archaic patterns and processes. Yet it also incorporates and adapts to changing forces—political, social, economic, and ecologic. A Gatlinburg or West Yellowstone emerging on the edge of wildland parks is as natural a consequence as the emergence of phragmites when a marsh regime has its water quality and quantity altered.

Similarly, as Alston Chase (1986) has convincingly argued, parks and wildlands can serve as models, examples, guides, and inspiration to other ways of living for man and nature. Just as island biogeographic studies can give us clues to processes and consequences of certain evolutionary patterns, so can wildlands serve as tests of diverse social strategies for living and adapting. This is because neither wildlands nor islands are static, nor are their boundaries formed by an iron wall. They are naturally part of the realm in which they exist, and the boundary membrane simply filters the traffic of information, energy, materials, ideas, and persons between the different systems.

Another metaphor for analyzing wildlands is viewing them as a series of nested boxes—where each analytic element fits into the next. A wildland system of social roles—superintendent, rangers, seasonal workers, tourists, and so forth—can be examined as a separate social unit with serving and maintaining functions for the larger community. Yet, within this complex of habitat and population flows, structure and process, there are individual, household, and community-organizational patterns affecting the "successful" accomplishment or failure to accomplish aspects of the microsystem. Thus we can examine the dynamics of this semiclosed system as to inputs, outputs, and consequences.

We can also examine the wildland system as an exchange network that processes transactions with its immediate or potential social and biophysical environments. The establishment of a park, or other wildland reserve, can create demands that organizations external to the wildland emerge to serve—hence the emergence of the Gatlinburg and West Yellowstone urbanized opportunities, the rafting companies, and trail riding and other tourist serving enterprises. The transactions between these several organizational elements can be examined using the same model. In short, the establishment of an official park or wilderness area, an underwater trail, a phantom ranch, or a going-to-the-sun highway will generate highly predictable outcomes in the adjacent private sector.

Finally, an even higher level of analysis can consider the entire resource management agency as a cultural organization in competition with other cultural organizations over access to scarce resources, authority to control access to resources, alternative patterns of distribution, or wholesale changes in the culture's value hierarchy. Only in recent years have park and forest managers made attempts to coordinate and complement their efforts rather than compete. Notable examples are the Glacier, North Cascades, and Yellowstone regions.

In the following pages, we will look at two common problems of application—patterns of wildland demand and patterns of wildland capability. We will not make direct, specific application of the conceptual ideas presented above. Those ideas will serve as guides to the applied questions.

BIOSOCIAL APPROACHES TO RECREATIONAL MOTIVES AND RESOURCE CAPABILITY

There is a substantial amount of long-term social ecology theory, methods, and findings that can be applied to the understanding and management of wildland social systems. For several reasons, however, the necessary channels of information exchange have not been opened.

As Burch and DeLuca (1984) demonstrate in a detailed discussion, there are numerous middle-range social science "theories"—culture contact studies, adoption of innovations studies, time budget studies, life cycle studies—that were developed out of the need to resolve practical problems. Despite the available midrange theories, the analysis of outdoor recreational systems has developed almost entirely without the benefit of social theory.

Such research emerged when various public resource agencies were suddenly confronted with a postwar growth in noncommodity, recreation-directed client populations. The agency response was to throw into the breach any available professionals with a social science bent. Most often the primary training and orientation of these professionals was biological. However, by the early 1960s the purely empiricist approach was seen to be clearly limited. Professionals from outside the resource fields introduced behavioristic approaches. Extensive attitude surveys were made and correlated to certain demographic features. But the correlations usually explained only 30% or less of the observed variance between independent and dependent variables. There was considerable use of economic supply and demand models and a good deal of exploration along the lines of unpriced benefits. Therefore, surrogates for price—such as distance traveled, equipment purchased, willingness to pay a fee, and so forth—gained a research following. Still, in recreation, supply seemed to create demand and behavior strayed from the rationality of gravity flow models.

In the early 1960s, the measurement of individual attitudes and the rationalistic economic model were complemented by a social group approach. This approach suggested that it was not ecosystems, activities, or individuals that were the primary organizing units of recreation: it was small intimate groups such as friends and kinship associations.

Each of these four conceptual and methodological approaches—mensuration, attitude survey, economic surrogates, social groupings—emphasizes a particular dimension of outdoor recreation. There must be a place for the activity. There must be some individual preference and consideration of cost constraint. The social characteristics of the organizing group have a great deal to do with the nature, types, and "satisfactions" of the on-site behavior. Each approach has its specialized means of data collection. The mensurationists have automatic road and trail counters, permit lists, visitor registrations, and seasonal employees going about counting. The studies emphasizing individual psychological and economic "motives" use attitude survey techniques. The social group behaviorists use group interviews, key informants, and systematic observation.

Measuring and understanding the effects of park management, policy, and development activities on existing outdoor recreation systems can be enhanced by considering lessons from the approaches outlined thus far. The first lesson is that there are several midrange theories that may serve as models for specific cases. Second, we have a batch of data, ideas, and mistakes from over three decades of research on outdoor recreation that can guide our efforts. Third, an "outdoor recreation system" consists of a place or stage that is "fit" for certain individually preferred and affordable activities which vary behaviorally at the recreational site as the social nature of the recreating group varies. Fourth, what the outdoor recreation field lacks in theory it more than makes up for in extensive techniques of data collection and statistical manipulation. Like all lessons, these four oversimplify reality while giving an indication of trends in three decades of research literature on the social ecology of outdoor recreation.

Defining an Outdoor Recreation Activity System

An outdoor recreation opportunity is *not* a resource. It becomes such only through human definition. A huntable deer population nearby does not necessarily mean that a community will define it as a hunting resource. On the other hand, a segment of the community's population might never have considered, let alone "demanded," a "wilderness camping experience" until a public agency happened to develop a nearby facility. Then the "demand" for the service will fluctuate in a pattern remarkably similar to fluctuations in expansions and contractions of particular age cohorts and cycles of managing agency activities.

Any outdoor recreation system has both a recreation resource potential (what could be done) and an actual set of circumstances (what is being done) that can be referred to as behavioral clusters. Understanding the dynamics of the system, and understanding the possible resource-facility impact cycle, requires combining the four approaches (mensuration, attitude survey, economic surrogates, social groupings) developed over the past three decades of outdoor recreation research. Our examination will begin by considering the elements that affect the potential of a recreation resource.

Identifying a community or region's potential recreation resource returns us to the early decades of outdoor recreation research. We inventory the biophysical, cultural, and organizational opportunities and constraints (Table 9-2).

For the biophysical opportunities and constraints we need to know within a radius of two hours' travel time for a given "target" or "client" population the kinds of landforms, types of ecosystems, and climatic patterns. This information should provide estimates of (1) *capability* (the range of possible recreational uses), and (2) *capacity* (the range of ecosystem durability for various recreational uses). The information for making these estimates can be gained from U.S. Geological Survey maps, satellite photographs, agency reports, and state, regional, and municipal recreation plans. It is important to note that we are not considering a specific park or other recreational site, but the entire range of possibilities for serving certain activities.

The analyst may find considerable value in clustering activities. There seem to be certain universal groupings of nonwork activities among all peoples and for all times (see Cheek and Burch 1976). Benjamin Franklin and Marco Polo may have traveled by sailing vessel, carriage, horse, and ox cart, while Aunt Bea takes a Concorde to Paris and drives a Porsche to Rome. Still, the sense of movement, touring, and status accomplishment are not greatly different. Persons tend to cluster their preferred activities: hunters tend to fish and camp; backpackers tend to be bicyclists and joggers; snowmobilers tend to favor water skiing and dirt motorcycles.

The cultural inventory would identify the traditions, values, beliefs, and tastes of the community at large and significant segments within it. Here we are considering the constraints and prohibitions that would affect certain recreational practices and the traditions that would encourage others. The cultural inventory can be made using a variety of established techniques—social survey, content analysis of community documents, key informant interviews, and systematic observation. The intention is not to produce a formal social science study but to collect enough information to make a reasonable estimate as to what the community deems as likely and unlikely recreational pursuits.

The analyst should not expect absolutes. We are interested in the activities a community considers to be "musts," "must nots," and "maybes." For able-bodied males in a rural Maine community, hunting and snowmobiling are "must" activities, while weaving and knitting are "must not" activities, and dry-fly fishing or bait fishing are "maybes." A useful index of cultural tradition might be derived from a *preference* survey, an equipment survey, or an examination of retail sales.

Table 9-2. Inventory of information needed to define the opportunities and constraints of a recreation resource.

Category of Information	Principal Forms of Analysis
BIOPHYSICAL FEATURES	
1. Landform (mountains, plains, etc.)	Estimates of
2. Ecosystem (vegetation, soils, successional stage, etc.)	(1) capability (what can be done) (2) capacity (impacts of use)
3. Climate (seasonal variations, temperature ranges and mean, precipitation, etc.)	
CULTURAL FEATURES	
Values, traditions, beliefs, tastes affecting nonwork activities	Ranking of top preferences and dislikes
ORGANIZATIONAL FEATURES	
1. Ownership patterns and regulatory options and constraints affecting all lands 5 acres and larger	Regional or local per capita index of potential access opportunity by activity cluster
2. Proportion of agency (private, profit, nonprofit, local, state, federal) budget devoted to specific recreational investments	Per capita activity investment index by ownership acres
3. Characteristic work-nonwork cycles (e.g., proportion of region's labor force whose free time is highly seasonal, or whose work time takes nonstandard forms such as flextime, shift work, etc.; nature and distribution of school vacation and holiday cycles)	
4. Predominant allocational institutions affecting the recreation resource (e.g., property institutions, market institutions)	
ACTUAL BEHAVIOR (for at least the past decade)	
1. How many participate in particular activities and the proportion of various demographic characteristics they represent	
2. The characteristic size, age, and gender distribution of the organizing unit by activity, facility, and ownership acres	

The organizational inventory considers one other factor that structures a potential recreation resource. Here the analyst is interested in the number and types of private and public agencies that affect recreation. For example, the Bureau of Land Management, the Corps of Engineers, the Fish and Wildlife Service, the Forest Service, and the National Park Service all provide marginally differentiated camping opportunities—some less restrictive than others. State agencies, private corporations such as Georgia-Pacific or Scott Paper, and nonprofit organizations such as the Girl Scouts or the Nature Conservancy vary their provision of a recreation resource in fairly predictable ways.

There are also variations in the kinds of investments made in recreational activities. Fish and wildlife departments tend to concentrate on a few huntable species and ignore nongame species. These investment patterns are well documented and reasonably predictable.

Another organizational feature is the characteristic work-nonwork cycles of the "target" or "client" population. All rural areas tend to have their time budgets dominated by a particular industry—agriculture, mining, tourism, forestry—which regulates a community's flow of activities, daily and seasonally. These time cycles constrain and open certain opportunities for specific outdoor recreational activities.

A final organizational consideration is the institutional structure of a community—the regularized ways it has for allocating basic resources. Most American communities have several such mechanisms—the market allocating by price, the political system allocating by political pressure, tradition using the past as a guide for the present, and so forth (for discussion see Burch 1986). For example, it may be a local tradition that all residents have the right of trespass in the pursuit of game, while an outsider who becomes a landowner might insist on exclusive rights and so deny access, or only permit access for a price. Clearly, established social institutions affect the organization and delivery of recreation resources.

The behavioral inventory of recreation resource information asks what people actually do, how frequently they do it, where they do it, and with whom. Again, there are limits to the information that can be gained with the time and financial resources available. If the target population is a large one, it may be necessary to rely on national or local surveys, a public land agency's records, Department of Transportation travel studies, Fish and Game license sales, and so forth. Since the most frequent organizing unit for most outdoor recreation activities is a social group, it is important to know how group structure and composition match up with the activity and the space available for it.

A Synthesis for Public Resource Agency Analysis

It is obvious that our paradigm of information needed for a recreation resource definition simplifies a complex subject. Ironically, the analyst must make such leaps of faith if there is to remain a core of rationality in decision making (see Thompson and Warburton 1985). The emphasis in the paradigm is on identifying readily measured constraints and opportunities. Table 9-3 lists the elements that affect outdoor recreation and suggests some indicator measures. The analyst has a start at identifying limits to the impact of any given public resource agency policy, plan, or action; the effects that are likely to result; and the probable response of the existing and anticipated human ecosystem in the particular region.

The available inventory data on our recreation elements have been collected, analyzed, and used to set policy by a variety of organizations for a variety of reasons, usually in supreme ignorance of one another. Since these data sets are a mixed bag, we can convert them to a standard dimension—a map. The analyst will need to develop a series of map overlays using the best summary data that time, finances, and the problem permit. Table 9-3 suggests one way to develop overlays following our paradigm.

This series of overlays defines the existing outdoor recreation system: what could be done, what is done, how often, and with whom. The analyst is ready to forecast how a public resource management agency's policies and activities are likely to affect specific outdoor recreation clusters. There seem to be at least three likely outcomes of interest to managers: (1) certain activities increase with no impact; (2) future activities fit existing trends with no impact; and (3) projected increases in specific activities overextend the capacity, as defined by managerial standards of limits of acceptable change, and capability of the recreation resource.

Table 9-3. Application of the recreation resource definition paradigm in the form of map overlays.

Category of Information	Process
Biophysical features	On this base map, identify the potential recreational *capability* within the region of impact. This map should represent certain gross recreational compartments (in the style of a soil map, for example). Identify *capacity* in terms of fragility, uniqueness, and so forth.
	Overlay with:
Cultural features	A map that identifies and ranks the five to ten recreational activities most approved. This is simply an estimated preference display with one color for high preference and another for high dislike.
	Overlay:
Organizational features	1. Identify landowners by classes of openness or restrictiveness.
	2. Identify existing and planned facility investments.
	3. Estimate areas where use is likely to be positively and negatively influenced by regional work-nonwork cycles.
	Overlay:
Behaviorial features	1. Map the distribution and frequency of participation in specific activity clusters.
	2. Map the distribution and frequency of *types* of recreating groups by activity cluster.

In this discussion I have described a regional process. Obviously, one can simply cluster a grouping of areas administered by a public resource agency or a specific unit within that cluster to conduct the same sort of analysis. The point is that the natural resources student or manager has a means for identifying and combining trends in "demands," group factors organizing that demand, and the biophysical factors shaping and adapting to that demand. Within this framework, one can do analyses and predictions based on the available time, space, energy, and material budgets discussed earlier. What I am attempting in this section is to demonstrate that a marriage between perceived problems, available methods of measurement, techniques of analysis, and social ecology theory need not wait for heavenly intervention, but can begin whenever we find the will.

CONCLUSION

Our discussion suggests that a social ecological framework may not only prevent natural resource students and managers from engaging in the "right" political struggle with the wrong technical data; it may also help them to start collecting data that will give them real understanding of the system rather than confirming their heartfelt desires. There is a great need to interweave the biological and social ecological theory and methods in order to check and improve the reliability, validity, and genuine utility of the data and interpretations on wildland capacities.

This task of systematic integration is neither simple, quick, nor inexpensive. It is merely essential if we are to have a sound means for making crucial decisions in the coming decades, during which a relatively stable base of wildlands may need to adapt to rapidly changing demographic and perceptual patterns. The emergence of a tertiary political economy in the advanced industrial societies may be only a passing phase, but for the foreseeable decades it will be a dominant one. And unlike the secondary political economy of production, the third phase sees expectations shifting from a satisfactory standard of living to a satisfactory life-style. Thus parks, wildlands, historic sites, and landscapes will reflect the coming class struggle. Managers of natural resources will be well advised to fully understand the total systems they purport to regulate.

We have traveled some distance only to find more questions than we hoped for, and to find some of our most cherished solutions are wrong. We have seen that human ecology has a diverse parentage and a history of confronting rising social issues. We have sought new definitions and orientation for the field. To that end, we suggested some models, methods, approaches, and applications. The changes we have advocated mean considerable rethinking by social scientists, natural resources biologists, and managers. Yet the coming decades of challenge require no less if wildland resource systems are to remain sustainable means for improving the public life.

LITERATURE CITED

Altman, I. 1975. The environment and social behavior. Brook/Cole, Monterey, California.

Burch, W. R. 1971. Daydreams and nightmares. Harper and Row, New York.

——. 1974. Adapting forest resources management to its social environment: Some observations. For. Chron. 50:276-280.

——. 1979. Human ecology and environmental management. The Environmental Professional 1:285-292.

——. 1986. The rhetoric of wilderness. Habitat 3:36-41.

Burch, W. R., and L. Burch-Minakan. 1979. Time-budget studies and forecasting the social consequences of energy policies: A summary and selected annotations. Social Science Energy Review 21:1-62.

Burch, W. R., and N. H. Cheek. 1974. Social meanings of water: Patterns of variation. In D. R. Field et al. (eds.) Water and community development: Social and economic perspectives, pp. 41-58. Ann Arbor Science Publishers, Ann Arbor, Michigan.

Burch, W. R., and D. DeLuca. 1984. Measuring the social impact of natural resources policies. University of New Mexico Press, Albuquerque.

Chase, A. 1986. Playing God in Yellowstone. Atlantic Monthly Press, Boston.

Cheek, N. H., and W. R. Burch. 1976. The social organization of leisure in human society. Harper and Row, New York.

Craik, K. 1968. The comprehension of the everyday physical environment. J. Am. Inst. Planners 34:29-37.

Gross, D. R., and B. A. Underwood. 1971. Technological change and caloric costs: Sisal agriculture in northeastern Brazil. American Anthropologist 73:1-18.

Kartawinata, K., and A. P. Vayda. 1984. Forest conversion in East Kalimantan, Indonesia: The activities and impact of timber companies shifting cultivators, migrant pepper farmers and others. In F. di Castri et al. (eds.) Ecology in practice, pp. 98-126. Tycooly International Publishing, Dublin.

Klausner, S. Z. 1971. On man in his environment. Jossey-Bass, San Francisco.

Morrison, D. E. 1976. Growth, environment, equity and scarity. Social Science Quarterly 57:292-306.

Rambo, T., and P. E. Sajise. 1984. An introduction to human ecology research on agricultural systems in Southeast Asia. University of the Philippines at Los Baños, Laguna.

Rappaport, R. A. 1967. Pigs for ancestors. Yale University Press, New Haven.

Thompson, M., and M. Warburton. 1985. Knowing where to hit it: A conceptual framework for the sustainable development of the Himalaya. Mountain Research and Development 5:203-220.

Tiger, L., and R. Fox. 1971. The imperial animal. Holt, Rinehart and Winston, New York.

Vayda, A. P. 1977. An ecological approach in cultural anthropology. In W. R. Burch, Jr. (ed.) Energy and human society: Contemporary perspectives, pp. 3-8. Harper and Row, New York.

Wilson, E. O. 1975. Sociobiology. The Belnap Press, Cambridge, Massachusetts.

10

Things Wild and Free: Any Room for Economics in the Wilderness?

LLOYD C. IRLAND

ABSTRACT The choices in wildland ecosystem management are becoming more costly and controversial. Legal mandates, of which the Resources Planning Act (RPA) is the prime example, require the use of economic analysis in planning. Economics, though often subject to abuse, offers a tool kit of concepts for thinking about choices. There is nothing in benefit-cost analysis that requires analysts to quantify inappropriately or to ignore incidence and equity questions. Benefit-cost analysis, as a tool for displaying options, values, and costs in suitable accounting stances, should be a basic element in any systematic analysis of a practical problem. The most valuable use of economics is in framing a disciplined thinking process for the precise definition of objectives, decision criteria, options, costs, and accounting stances. Economic thinking is valuable as a solvent for specious arguments and as an aid in listening to the future.

Economists have had an ambiguous relationship with the enterprise of managing America's heritage of wilderness. Their claims to be able to measure the value of the wilderness resource, or of the wilderness experience, have met with skepticism on the part of many. Their capacity to demolish the economic rationale for various mining, hydropower, and logging road projects is prized by some and a source of frustration to others. There remains a lingering concern that disciplinary imperialism has crossed a sacred frontier—that the higher values of wilderness ought to be protected from crude attempts to quantify, value, and evaluate. Is there room for the perspective of the real estate appraiser in the wilderness? Is "that awesome space" (Hart 1981) of America's wilderness beyond the reach of systematic analysis?

But the nation's decision processes concerning wilderness and backcountry ecosystem management have demanded more and more quantification of economic and social values and impacts. The congressionally adopted legal frameworks used in drafting wilderness bills, the administrative procedures under the Resources Planning Act (RPA) for devising management plans, the clash of interest groups offering selectively edited and biased advocacy—all create a demand for quantitative analysis. Clearly, the RPA is an extreme instance of faith in complex, multidisciplinary analysis. Since it offers clear paradigms for analysis and for decision criteria, economics has come to the forefront. The tendency of economic tools to dominate others in policy analysis has been described as disciplinary imperialism. One economist even described economics as "the universal grammar of social science" (Hirshleifer 1985:53; see also Nelson 1977).

Some observers of our nation's wildland policy problems argue that more use of economics is necessary in resolving conflicts (Walker 1983). Others feel that commodity values are overweighted already (see, e.g., Sagoff 1982 for a stimulating critique). What can economics deliver to elected decision makers and senior administrators of our nation's heritage of wildlands? Have its capabilities been oversold? Should the invading economists be driven out of the wilderness, their confident notions replaced by some other decision-making paradigm, some other source of a universal grammar? This essay will consider these questions (for more complete treatments, see Krutilla and Fisher 1975, Peterson et al. 1987, Irland 1979).

Rather than take a disciplinary perspective, this paper assesses how economics, as a framework for quantitative analysis, can help us perform five distinct functions better: (1) understanding values and trade-offs, (2) evaluating programs for effectiveness, (3) analyzing market behavior, (4) scrutinizing specious argument, and (5) listening to the future. In disciplinary terms, I address valuation, local economic impact, benefit-cost analysis, program evaluation, incidence analysis, and assessing market responses to change. I do not cover the many issues raised by traditional investment analysis, the analysis of common pool resources, or complex forest planning optimization models. Within Johnson's (1986) fields of disciplinary, subject matter, and problem-solving knowledge, this essay is concerned with using economics in problem solving.

Economics is a tool kit for decision support. It is the saw for cutting the framing, not the pen for designing the house. I do not see economics as the ultimate decision paradigm for wilderness allocation and management decisions. Those who use quantitative analysis in that way have contributed to the disrepute of a perfectly good carpenter's tool.

MANAGEMENT AND ALLOCATION ISSUES

Wilderness and backcountry ecosystem managers face a new generation of issues, even while the issues of a decade ago continue to smolder on the political griddle. The crown jewels of the park system—the majestic sweeps of national forest mountain wilderness—spoke grandly for themselves. Conveniently, they rarely held major mineral or timber reserves, so appeals to their grandeur, plus a nudge from railroad promoters, ensured their conservation in parks and similar units. The more subtle beauties of Bureau of Land Management desert rangelands and riparian ecosystems, of less rugged national forest backcountry, are posing more difficult questions for analysts and politicians—particularly when they are underlain by coal or oil.

Besides having positive value, wilderness is also a favored preventive for projects some people don't like. A large wilderness promotion infrastructure has been built, and battles between interest groups over land allocation decisions will continue. But in the past two decades—on tens of millions of acres, notably in Alaska—the question of land allocation has been settled. Most of the existing wilderness and backcountry lands are not ecological units in themselves. The bears, ducks, elk, and fish migrate in and out of them. We are now concerned about the miners, drillers, subdividers, and recreationists over wide areas, not just in the dedicated wild areas (Sax and Keiter 1987).

Our attention has turned also to managing the areas we have, some of which are being loved to death. Preserving the Grand Canyon is not an issue—that has been decided. The issue is how many river runners can use it and whether they can use motors. The conflicts are among different user groups and between users and the administering agencies over the ground rules for use, and who should pay for what costs. We have learned that success in one conservation effort often breeds new problems. The fires we put out in the Rockies would have consumed fuels and perpetuated a vegetative mosaic. Under fire control, we now have vast areas of overmature, overstocked forest, with different wildlife habitat values and far more vulnerable to fire and insects than the forest of the past. Moreover, threats to the parks and wildernesses from upstream water pollution, visibility losses from distant power plants, and tourism-promoted development sprawl are escalating daily.

Much of the economic literature concerning wilderness was stimulated by the allocation controversies of the past. Should we dam Hells Canyon? Cut trees out in the White River National Forest? Dig coal next to Utah parks? That literature focused on a small set of problems: defining what the value of wilderness was to its users, critiquing the justification for development projects, and identifying impacts of allocation decisions on nearby communities.

We are moving up into steeper regions of marginal cost curves everywhere. We've done the low-cost energy conservation. We've installed secondary treatment most places; the next increments of improved water quality will cost far more than the ones already paid for. We've put most of the rocks and ice into wilderness. Now the decisions are creating large costs and benefits for different groups. The fact that the stakes are rising helps explain the increased demand for systematic analysis of decisions.

Today, conflicts between recreational user groups, debates over who should pay, and responses to complex ecological interactions over wide areas are moving up on our agenda. We now must write soundly based management plans to address these concerns. This decision agenda is bringing new areas of economics and social science, and new methodological problems, to the fore.

HORIZON ISSUES: LISTENING TO THE FUTURE

If economics can help to demystify many aspects of wildland management, perhaps its natural terminology for thinking about supply, demand, and substitutes would be handy in listening to the future. Here is a sampling of issues that lie on or beyond the horizon:

1. Management regulations for wilderness related to controlling fire, insects, and disease have yet to be tested in a really difficult situation. The current conflict over managing the southern pine beetle in and near national forest wilderness is an example. Some very tough situations are certain to arise, concerning risks to visitors, to private property, and major environmental values. Will our policy framework, our knowledge base, our management and logistical preparation, and our political and communication skills be adequate?

2. When will the West's water situation begin to drive wildland management as it has never done in the past? What balance will be struck between business-as-usual water use policies and respect for the value of water in rivers?

3. The increasing suburbanization, strip development, and subdivision of remote mountain areas offer the latest empirical proof of Irland's Iron Law of Real Estate Markets: "Nice places attract capital until they are no longer nice." Equilibrium ensues, capital flees to other sources of profit, and depreciation begins. Looking at the broader environment, perhaps an obsession with wilderness areas is just rearranging the deck chairs on the Titanic. The people who are subdividing and paving the valley-floor winter

range are demanding that the Forest Service and Park Service save the elk—for tourism's sake.

4. How will the trade-offs between energy, wood, water, and recreation look in 50 or 100 years? In 100 years North America will be a green island in a largely deforested world. The opposite may well be true for oil. It is also true that technological advances will continue to generate more efficient modes of use, more substitutes, and more opportunities. Where will a reasonable prudence draw the line when development versus preservation decisions must be made? Do we have opportunities to loosen some of the constraints those future decision makers will feel?

We live in a time of commodities glut: oil prices are down; copper prices are below profitable levels for most U.S. mines and smelters. Canadian forests now supply a third of U.S. softwood lumber consumption at prices that have our mills against the wall. Can it last a hundred more years? If not, what are the implications?

5. Enormous increases in park and backcountry use are predicted by some analysts. Are these predictions sufficiently well validated to serve as a basis for land allocation and development decisions? If they are, shouldn't we be scared out of our wits at what this means for the wildlands we love so well? But today we are dealing with just the first few buffalo. The rest of the herd is over the brow of the hill—headed this way.

UNDERSTANDING OPTIONS, VALUES, AND TRADE-OFFS

Economics, as a science of making allocative choices, a science of scarcity, is where people often turn for guidance in making choices. Economics has much to say about ways to value costs and benefits, about the appropriate form of decision criteria, about measuring economic changes, and about comparing time streams of benefits and costs.

Economics provides mathematical characterizations of behavior, and mathematical formulations of decision criteria that offer precise solutions. Applications of these theories generate numbers in profusion. High levels of empirical precision are not attained in applied social science research, whether in marketing toothpaste, valuing timber, or appraising the outlook for hiking demand. Realistically, most of our decisions do not demand levels of precision much closer than plus or minus 20% anyway. If they do, we have probably misformulated or oversimplified the problem.

Economists formulate objectives in fairly abstract ways. Most would say that the objective of land management is to maximize over time the present worth of social benefits that accrue from using the resource. But when the management or allocation problem is stated so generally, it becomes difficult to solve. Managers are much more interested in obtaining economic information to support decisions that are highly constrained by existing policy, budgets, and political factors. Near-term costs and benefits weigh heavily. For these reasons, the balance of this essay speaks of economics in terms of land management objectives rather than more general formulations of a maximization problem.

The economic approach to problem solving can be organized around a series of questions (Table 10-1) that most people might ask about a complex decision. First, the economic approach asks us to state precisely what commodity or service we are examining, and what its market is. Many wildland resources are used to produce commodities. Water, timber, ore, and grass are not commodities themselves, being too diverse and their values too dependent on costs determined by highly local factors. But they are used to manufacture commodities—alfalfa, studs, copper, and beef. In many cases, the resource is in demand by a number of distinctly different markets. A given stand of lodgepole pine might go to a distant stud mill, to a firewood dealer, to a pulp mill, or to the cabin log processor.

Table 10-1. Questions and some concepts useful in systematic analysis of ecosystem management questions.

Question	Concept
What is the product?	Market and market segments
	Consumer demand
	Substitution
	Price sensitivity
What is it worth?	Travel cost
(Valuation)	Contingent valuation
	Market value comparability
	Residual value appraisal
	Capitalization
	Policy decision
What will it cost?	Opportunity costs
(Cost analysis)	Alternative sources
	Commodity prices versus resource amenities
	Cost accounting (real costs)
Is it worth it?	National economic efficiency
(Benefit-cost analysis)	Overquantification
	Multiple accounting stances
	Discounting
	Tactical versus strategic decisions
	Display of options, costs, values
Who wins? Who loses?	Rent seeking
(Incidence)	Income groups
	Interest groups
	Equity and political power
What about us?	Regional science
(Local economic impact)	Double counting
	Community stability
	Multiplier effects
Is it working?	Resistance to evaluation
(Program evaluation)	Misapplied techniques
	Cost effectiveness
What next?	Pricing to ration access
(Prediction)	Market adjustment to supply
	Long-run opportunity

What Is the Product?

Recreational services of wilderness also serve different markets. At any given moment in the Mission Mountains there are people seeking many kinds of experiences. For each experience there may be quite different demographic submarkets or market segments, consisting of people who value the opportunity differently and face different substitutes.

The notion of substitution is fundamental to an economist's view of consumer demand. To an economist, potatoes and rice are just sources of carbohydrate. Consumers will substitute rice for potatoes if potatoes get too expensive. Substitution seems quite a foreign notion to apply to wilderness—for which we are commonly told there is no substitute. In fact, for the bulk of wilderness users, wilderness is a commodity just like lumber. It is a standardized product whose specific source is not important to the user and which is likely to be selected on the basis of price. This fits the majority of wilderness users—who are day users. These users face many alternatives (i.e., other wildernesses or national forestry backcountry) and are likely to be highly price sensitive. Their demand may not grow with income. Most of them do little, see little, learn little in their one-day wilderness visits. For other users, wilderness is a highly prized, highly differentiated product. These users may not be price sensitive at all, and their demand may well grow with income.

What Is It Worth? (Valuation)

Valuation is the process of estimating what a commodity or service is worth. Valuation is essential not only to allocation decisions but to ongoing management decisions. The demand to know "what it's worth" probably generated some of the earliest uses of economics in the wilderness setting. Economists are inclined to place the most reliance on values established by exchange between willing buyers and sellers, or on estimates of consumer willingness to pay. This perspective helps protect against "blue sky" claims. But when we cannot directly observe transactions, there are several ways to learn "what it's worth."

First are various econometric estimators for consumer willingness to pay. There have been serious debates over how we justify using consumer willingness to pay instead of other measures, or whether to include total consumer-producer surplus or only price times quantity; these are beyond the scope of this essay. Another method is to find "comparables" in which similar market transactions can be used to extrapolate values. For commodity resources, residual value appraisal is often used. Finally, it is possible to measure how environmental amenities are capitalized into property values.

One way to assess consumer willingness to pay is to use econometric analysis—formulating statistical models of user demand that enable analysts to calculate the in-place values in terms of user willingness to pay. In all areas of economics, econometrics has generated a vigorous flow of critical literature (Blaug 1980, McAleer et al. 1985, Leamer 1983, 1985, Dewald et al. 1986, and especially McCloskey's powerful 1985 essay).

Travel Cost and Contingent Valuations. Based on its simplicity and utility in dealing with survey data, the Hotelling-Clawson formulation of demand analysis for valuing recreation became widely used (Clawson and Knetsch 1966). This method relies on actual travel costs experienced by visitors to infer their demand curve for the experience. To attempt to read all this literature and synthesize and evaluate it would be a daunting task. Used with suitable care, it can provide rough initial estimates of consumer willingness to pay to use a given site (an excellent synthesis is Kneese 1984, with a good bibliography; a good recent application is Mendelsohn 1987).

The travel cost method has the virtue of relying on actual consumer behavior. But it does not help in valuing how people feel about resources they will never visit (many of those who contributed to refurbishing Miss Liberty will never visit her). A more recent line of work has attempted to use a "contingent valuation" technique to elicit measures of the value that consumers place on wildlife or other resources. A consensus seems to be emerging that contingent valuation is reliable when properly used. Perhaps it is too soon to declare victory for the econometricians over this particular valuation problem, but the effort bears watching (see, e.g., abstracts in Program Abstracts 1986 and an application by King et al. 1987).

How useful are these estimates? After a costly and methodologically careful study, Vaughan and Russell (1982) were discouraged to find that their high and low estimates of the fishery benefits of water quality improvement differed by an order of magnitude. They were pessimistic as to the likelihood of improving this performance very much, and looked to more direct contingent valuation and related methods as being more promising. Sorg and Loomis (1984), in a careful review, found that differences in techniques account for much of the difference in results across studies. They adjusted different studies for a variety of recreational activities and found that the adjusted values tended to cluster in reasonable ranges. Certainly their results lead to useful general statements concerning user willingness to pay for recreation experiences.

Market Value Comparability. For many forms of recreation, similar forms of activity are priced in private markets. One may argue whether these markets approximate conditions of perfect competition or not, but they often offer suggestive information. Individuals do pay for the right to fish for salmon—in the United Kingdom, for example. They pay to own large wilderness preserves for their own exclusive use. They rent duck blinds; they lease deer hunting rights; they pay outfitters to ride them off into the mountain sunset and cook their steaks. On the other hand, some individuals behave altruistically and donate to Ducks Unlimited to foster ducks they will never shoot or to the Nature Conservancy to save marshes they will never see.

The notion that wilderness and backcountry services cannot be and are not priced in markets is simply false. The real question is how good is our information on the transactions that we can identify, what can we infer from them, and in what way do we use the resulting data?

Residual Value Appraisal. Timber and minerals are generally valued by using a residual value approach. This approach begins with market sales prices for finished lumber, ore, or oil, and deducts all processing, transport, and extraction costs. In principle, this measures the in-place value of the resource. For oil and some minerals, statistical methods are used to allow for the risks of discovery. In addition to calculated residual values, analysts often rely on comparable sales from private transactions to assist in determining values.

Prices or in-place values of resources will be affected by the degree of competition for the right to use the product. While most resource products ultimately enter commodity markets with many buyers and sellers, the immediate resource deposit, timber stand, or pasture may be accessible to only one or a few bidders. In such cases, market outcomes are typically indeterminate in formal terms. Even then, however, economic analysis can assist in analyzing the efficiency and equity of the various bureaucratic procedures used to allocate access to publicly owned timber, grazing leases, or river running rights.

Is it easier to value commodities than "noncommodity" services of wildland? It turns out that it isn't. Bids for timber frequently vary widely from the appraisals; new geological knowledge and technology often create new mineral values. For example, the new technology of "heap leaching" is revolutionizing the gold mining industry and creating mineral value where none existed before. Look at the price of oil in recent years. What is the value of the right to explore for oil? How can we develop plausible planning assumptions about this when oil prices can move by 50% to 200% in a year?

As a practical example, work has been done on measuring the timber production opportunity costs of streamside protective corridors (Irland 1986). But there has been no fully convincing effort as yet, even to the point of measuring timber opportunity costs, much less integrating those into a full benefit-cost framework.

Capitalization into Property Values. Many amenities have been appraised by trying to sort out statistically what they contribute to the value of real estate, most often residential property. The concept is that certain features of property—a beautiful tree, proximity to a park, the availability of clean air—are noticed by buyers and sellers and thus are "capitalized" into asset values. Many criticisms might be leveled against this approach (e.g., it accounts only for the values of those with the down payment for a house in their wallets). But applications of this idea clearly show that amenities can affect property values (Proudel 1979). This method has potential for setting lower limits of a commonsense sort on amenity values. It has the merit of using real transaction data and of being relatively easy for people to understand (Kneese 1984:36 and chap. 7).

Policy Decision. A simple solution for the valuation problem is simply to set a policy saying that "a day of recreation is considered to be worth $1.50." This is the merit-weighted user day method. Considering the weaknesses of the other methods, and their costs, I consider merit-weighted user days a sensible approach for many problems—especially when we require, as we often do, only a very general level of accuracy in the estimate.

Existence versus Instrumental Values. Standard economic methods rely on an instrumental approach to valuation—the idea that an asset's value is based on its yield of services. To value a bond, we take the present value of its future interest payments. To value a wilderness, we sum its individual services and take the present value. All of these methods help us value the wilderness asset by valuing its services. None states a direct measure of the wild area's value as such. In many examples, only one or a few benefits are even addressed (but see Brown 1984). It is surprising, given the multiplicity of values of unmanaged wildlands, how few rigorous studies have attempted to address a reasonable sampling of wilderness benefits on a given area.

Beyond the instrumental approach to valuation is the idea of existence values. As far as I can tell, there is little or no economic literature that treats existence values as such (but see Kneese 1984:124ff., where he discusses "intrinsic" values). But existence values are really what most people have in mind when they think about wilderness.

To use unit values per recreation day, we must forecast the future volume of use or consumption. If hikers value backpacking at $13.00 per day, how many hikers will there be? Thus even with unit values, we are often at sea in forecasting total numbers of units. And we know that unit values depend on how many users there are. Willingness to pay to use a crowded wilderness will be less than for an uncrowded one. And the volume of use can be controlled to some extent by management.

This discussion gives only a hint at the conceptual and practical problems in applying economics to valuing wildlands and their flows of services. In summary, the need for precision to support planning decisions is usually not great, and within that range we can at least place limits on the value of many services of wildlands. Many of the methods are hard to validate and are subject to abuse, as is true of any other analytical tool. Since our economic tools value service flows rather than existence values, however, economic thinking is somewhat at odds with the way many people perceive nature—that is, in terms of existence values rather than instrumental values. Still, in careful hands, the methods available allow analysts to make order-of-magnitude statements about valuations that can help when used in a display of benefits and costs.

What Will it Cost? (Cost Analysis)

Valuing costs is rarely as clean and neat as it often appears. Even forecasting the construction cost of large hydro dams is fraught with room for error (Haveman 1972). The most important costs are often opportunity costs—the forgone benefits of another, mutually exclusive alternative. One cost of keeping a free-flowing river may be forgone electrical power. What is this worth? By our traditional methods, it depends basically on the outlook for the price of oil—a topic on which forecasting is especially hazardous.

In valuing opportunity costs, analysts often tend to use the past three years to forecast the next century. Hence we see it asserted that demand for timber on a given national forest is small because prices went down in the last three years and it's hard to sell the allowable cut; therefore this should be assumed as a basis for the next century's management policy.

Another argument commonly heard about the opportunity cost of commodity resources is that we don't "need" this or that mineral deposit or timber stand because we can get the commodity elsewhere. There is often no convincing basis for valuating such arguments, since they presuppose forecasts over long periods as to the supply and price of alternative sources and the potential for conservation in end-use markets. Often the case is made that alternative or foreign sources are cheaper, at least at the moment. But this argument is often close to a suggestion that we let the Canadians, the Arabs, or someone else absorb the social costs of producing the materials and energy we consume.

Thinking about long-term trends in demand for resource services and about future trends in the relative prices of resource commodities versus resource amenities occupies a substantial niche in the economics literature. Wars and oil crises seem to revive interest in these topics. One school of thought, entitled the New Economics of Conservation, is identified with the proposition that over time resource commodity services will decrease in value relative to resource amenities (Porter 1982, Krutilla and Fisher 1975, Smith 1978). One reason is that the income elasticity of demand for amenities is high: as incomes rise, demand for amenities will increase, even as their supply declines. The body of evidence supporting this idea is impressive.

Cost analysis has a role to play in many areas aside from estimating opportunity costs. It is essential to measure resource management program costs, especially when construction is involved, by using suitable accounting conventions to ensure that real social costs are being accounted for. Budget information does not do this, since among other things it typically ignores depreciation. Also, important items of joint cost and overhead are not readily allocated. When costs of providing outdoor recreation, for example, are correctly analyzed, they turn out to be surprisingly high on a per user basis (Reiling and Anderson 1983, Irland 1980, Guldin 1981).

In another instance, the extensive debate over below-cost timber sales illustrates the slipperiness of cost analysis for long-run decisions. There is no question that large volumes of public timber are sold in the United States and Canada which cannot pay their way out of the woods. There has been little analysis to determine if on some long-term accounting basis there may be real benefits to bringing marginal and submarginal timberlands under low intensity management (see, for an intriguing case, Krutilla et al. 1983). Many of these sales are explainable at the management level by tunnel vision commitments to timber management, and at the congressional level by simple pork barreling. There has been considerable congressional and staff debate over accounting systems and other minutiae related to this issue, but little thoughtful analysis probing its long-term implications (USDA Forest Service Timber Management Staff, n.d., Pearse and Williams 1986, LeMaster et al. 1986). In this problem, the more mathematical methods of investment analysis and optimization have a role to play. They allow us to study how resource values are affected by management costs and constraints and by changing assumptions concerning utilization and prices over time (Iverson and Alston 1986, Hyde 1980, Jackson 1980, Sedjo 1985).

Is It Worth It? (Benefit-Cost Analysis)

The study of proper decision criteria for ranking projects in order of desirability is the subject matter of benefit-cost analysis (also called cost-benefit analysis). This approach was developed in the 1930s to the 1950s principally for use in analyzing water projects. Buttressed by tools of operations analysis developed for military purposes and by modern computing power, it has been extended as an overarching metaphor for efficiency in government and for sound management in all areas of life (Eckstein 1958, Convery, n.d., Howe 1971, Lal 1974). Thus we have benefit-cost analyses of worker training programs. An immense literature treats the best ways (often disputed) of setting up the investment criterion and solving the discounting and valuation problems.

In its classic application, benefit-cost analysis attempts to identify the impact on national economic efficiency of a given investment. It employs careful measures of the allocative effect of a proposal, using suitable adjustments where needed to account for imperfections in markets for products, capital, labor, or foreign exchange. From the standpoint of national economic efficiency, many important effects (like tax revenue) wash out because they are merely transfers. Of course, interest groups who receive or pay those transfers see the matter differently, as we will explore below in the discussion of privacy.

Benefit-cost analysis has become to many the image of economics. It has been abused frequently, at times by its critics, who find it an easy straw man to knock down when it provides what they consider to be the wrong answers (for two useful critiques, see MacIntyre 1985 and Kelman 1985).

Benefit-cost analysis is a suitable procedure for ranking projects that are instrumental in nature—that is, serving a well-defined objective. It works best when projects are of a similar scale and duration, and when they are of a tactical, not a strategic, nature. You use benefit-cost analysis to decide which kind of turbine to use, or which of a list of dams is worth building on given assumptions about power values and interest rates. This is to say, benefit-cost analysis applies best to problems with relatively clearly defined and agreed upon objectives. It is not a tool for setting those objectives in the first place. To condemn it because it cannot solve the problems of ultimate ends and values is to ask the carpenter's saw to do the work of the architect's pen.

Many criticize benefit-cost analysis because it demands too much quantification. This is a misconception. There is much research on using it for multiple objective problems and when some of the variables are not readily quantified. If we see inappropriate or inaccurate quantification used, we should oppose it, but not reject the framework because of it. There are many ways to display incommensurable values in a useful way without collapsing them all into single financial measures. Benefit-cost analysis relies on bringing time streams of benefits and costs into a single accounting framework in the present (a mathematician would qualify this somewhat, but it does not matter for our purposes here). To bring benefits and costs into a single framework implies the value perspective of a single decision maker. But in few wildland decision situations do we have a single accounting stance. If we cut timber, perhaps we benefit sawmills, sawmill employees, lumber consumers, and sawmill-dependent communities. But if this reduces the elk population, by altering their behavior, by reducing cover and habitat, or by making them easier to kill, then the elk hunters will lose. Naturally each group feels that its commodity uses of nature deserve priority.

In its simplest form, benefit-cost analysis assumes away the problem of the incidence of costs and benefits. But this is usually the key problem of both valuation and political acceptability. It is possible to address this deficiency by using formats that include poorly quantified values and that employ multiple accounting stances. In essence, a separate analysis is performed from the loggers' accounting stance and another from the elk hunters'. In any analysis, then, at least two basic accounts are needed: a national economic efficiency account and a local impact account. Most analyses will also benefit from accounts representing the way other specific interest groups view the issue.

Bringing all costs and benefits into a single account is therefore misleading. Likewise, there are difficulties in bringing all time streams to a single equivalent at one particular time. Technically, this is called "discounting." The plausible notion that society values future payments at less than present ones is translated into arithmetic to calculate "present values" of time streams of benefits and costs. For many discrete, operational choices, this raises no problems. But what about ecosystem allocation choices involving time spans of decades or centuries, when technologies, values, demands, and prices are highly uncertain?

The arithmetic involves choosing a "discount rate"—the rate at which a payment declines in present value when pushed forward one year into the future. The trouble is that when a discount rate is used that relates at all to today's perceptions of the opportunity cost of money, it means that events more than fifteen to twenty years out really have no impact on a decision. Thus the computer often tells us to cut the entire forest and invest in junk bonds. At this extreme, we are dealing with intergenerational equity. There has been considerable learned discourse on this problem, but no theoretical consensus has been reached. The inability to find a reasoned way out of the problem is a major reason for confining benefit-cost analysis to the tactical levels of decisions.

As a practical matter, there are ways to address the problem. One is to display the full time stream of costs or benefits graphically over the planning horizon so that people can see their level and shape. This avoids condensing a lot of information into a single number. Another option is to do the arithmetic at different discount rates to show how sensitive the result is to the discount rate.

In the past decade, benefit-cost analysis has been somewhat demystified and the range of practitioners has increased. A larger number of people can now probingly dissect government agency economic analyses. All too often they find poorly supported assumptions, flaky forecasts, incomplete analysis, neglected values, and even inaccurate calculations. Therefore, using benefit-cost analysis to keep the agencies honest is an important function (Teeguarden 1987).

The critiques of benefit-cost analysis make many valid points, but the most valid criticisms alert us to abuses of the methods or to poor valuation techniques, which are conceptually separate from the benefit-cost analysis method itself. A decision represents the final solution of problems of valuing and discounting. To choose A over B is to decide that on balance and over time, A is a better course. Even when A and B involve strategic choices and high-order values, benefit-cost displays can help decision makers see the implications of choices. In the many critiques of benefit-cost analysis, one will search in vain for a convincing alternative.

Who Wins? Who Loses? (Incidence)

The question of "who wins and who loses" is often critical in land-use decision making. If a powerline corridor is authorized, power users in a distant city obtain reliable, perhaps cheaper power. Corridor neighbors obtain an imposition on their view of the wide open spaces, and possibly other inconveniences. The people benefiting are not the same as the people losing. Economists call this the problem of incidence.

Incidence questions are ubiquitous in wilderness and park management. Despite the difficulty of measuring the benefits and the costs, some systematic way of doing so is essential to informed decision making. Often, the vehicle for doing so is an environmental impact statement. Ultimately, however, a decision maker will have to adopt some view of what constitutes a "fair" or "equitable" outcome in view of the conflicting interests at stake.

One characteristic of most of the empirical research is an extremely shallow notion of what "equity" means. Equity refers to fairness, to reasonably accepted notions of entitlement, and to due process. Measuring these things by proportional allocation of benefits, costs, or net benefits across income classes or access states (as is often done in the literature) is only an initial and very crude way of looking at the subject.

Clearly, the resource economy is shot through with market imperfections and direct and indirect subsidies. A reasonable concern for equity might begin by identifying existing subsidies and existing allocations of costs and benefits to see if they can be justified by generally recognized notions of fairness or accepted policy goals. For example, one of the most heavily subsidized groups is the recreational users (Guldin 1981).

Political power, broader policy goals, established tradition, and agency commitments to client group attitudes are all heavily involved in incidence and equity questions. Recreationist groups that criticize below-cost timber sales are unsympathetic to arguments questioning below-cost recreation programs. Oil and mining groups that benefit from policies that fail to capture resource rents for the government invoke higher values, such as improved U.S. mineral supply and improved balance of payments. Each of these groups manipulates a historic myth structure in support of the political clout that it uses to maintain benefits for its members. This behavior, known as rent seeking, is ubiquitous in wildland management settings (Baden and Lueck 1984).

We do know that many inefficiencies and inequities exist in current wildland management arrangements, and we have ways to deal with many of them. The principal constraints to improving efficiency and equity are usually at the political level, not at the level of social science knowledge.

What About Us? (Local Economic Impact)

Since the 1950s, a huge literature has arisen dealing with local economic impact questions (Schuster 1976, Irland 1979, Murdock and Leistritz 1980, Obiya et al. 1986). This was stimulated by a line of research into regional economic growth emphasizing the export base concept, and similar historical studies on the "staple theory" of Canadian economic growth. The strong interest in regional growth policy of the 1960s, as reflected in the Appalachian Regional Commission and others, also contributed. There was a well-founded concern that federal water development agencies were overcounting local development benefits in their analyses. Later in the 1970s, social and economic impact analyses became fashionable as boomtown and ski resort problems were addressed for the first time using these forms of analysis. The declines in federal timber harvests due to new policies and planning systems, or due to wilderness allocations (Redwood National Park, Voyageurs National Park), led to interest in the ways that local economies dependent on timber might be sustained when cut levels fall. All of this has led to a very busy subdivision of economics, known as regional science.

Today, local economic impact assessments are a normal part of federal land management plans, often under the guise of a concern with "community stability." This leads to the question whether the methods and data are capable of supporting firm conclusions for long periods. And, setting other previous questions aside, how should such information be used in the decision process?

Local economic impact information is yet another apples-and-oranges problem. Analysts should avoid simply dumping local impact information into an overall benefit-cost assessment. Instead, a local impact account should be used in addition to the national economic efficiency account.

In the abundant literature on local impact analysis, there is very little validation of predictions (for an exception, see Connaughton et al. 1985). While science is supposed to grow and develop on the basis of replicating results and validating predictions, the bulk of the regional science literature focuses on isolated case studies or technical tweakings of existing models. Journal editors and the academic reward structure appear to discourage validation (see Dewald et al. 1986).

In sum, methods exist for assessing local impact. While they are poorly validated, they have their uses, provided data limitations are recognized. Strong conclusions or long-term predictions cannot be supported. Perhaps the most important use of this form of analysis is to critically examine the claims of developers, promoters, and others concerning the multiplier effects of a given project or sector. Another important use is in providing the basis for assessments of social impacts, since many social impacts are mediated by economic changes in employment levels, land markets, and such (Burch and DeLuca 1984). Local economic impact work is on its firmest ground when simply attempting to clarify the "economic importance" of different sectors (Polzin and Schweitzer 1975, Irland 1982).

The most serious question is what is to be done with the information. I sense a significant gap between the high level of effort devoted to local impact analysis and the minimal role such information plays in decisions. It is not easy to define precisely how local impacts should be balanced with other considerations in reaching decisions. In part, this is a question of policy and not of economic analysis. At the policy level, it may also be unclear just what degree of emphasis an agency is to place on "community stability" compared with other considerations (Schallau and Alston 1987).

Is It Working? (Program Evaluation)

A powerful use for economics in resource management is in program evaluation. Program evaluation is now a growing, diverse field of its own on the boundaries between economics, operations research, political science, and public administration (Nagel 1984, Finsterbusch and Motz 1980, Greer and Greer 1982, Nelson 1977, Rich 1979).

Program evaluation is underutilized in wildland management. Probably this comes from our confidence that we are doing the Lord's Work, and the fact that our principal client groups have usually been satisfied. But more client groups are joining us at the table, budget pressures are becoming painful, and our unexamined notions and rules of thumb may no longer be adequate.

Few line managers welcome the appearance of a young MBA on their doorstep, sent by headquarters to evaluate their program. They prefer to do their own evaluation, so the answers will be the right ones. The abuse of program evaluation, by both line managers and outside practitioners, has been incredible. One of our most important applied uses for economics is to enable managers to spot misapplied evaluation techniques, and to enable outside groups interested in agency performance to do the same.

Careful, probing program evaluation can, at a minimum, initiate a fresh look at basic questions concerning established programs: What are the criteria established to monitor progress and success? (Do they make sense?) What are the intended program results? Are there important effects that we are not measuring? What are the unit cost trends? (Unintended side effects?) Is the pricing policy, if any, sound? What are the alternative ways to achieve the stated program objective? Is this program a sensible use of money and management time, compared with other needs?

Program evaluation should raise questions that make people uncomfortable. That is its job. It can be applied to a wilderness campsite management program, to logging roads, and to any other management activity. Again, it does not depend for its success on inappropriate quantification or indefensible assumptions.

For many applied problems, program evaluation cannot supply a fixed, clean answer. What it can do is clarify important questions, estimate some of the important allocative and equity consequences of choices, and give managers a clearer basis for choice. Or, alternatively, an evaluation can indicate what further information is required to make an informed decision.

What Next? (Predicting Market Behavior)

Many wildland policy problems depend on predictions of how firms or consumers will react to future outside trends (Arab oil prices) or to management's choices (campsite fees). Economics attempts to predict how actors will respond to different changes in the world. Theory predicts, for example, that consumers will usually use less of a good when its price rises. Producers, on the other hand, will offer more for sale when prices rise.

When dealing with long-term forecasts to support management strategies, we must deal with Boulding's dictum that the only certainty about the future is that we'll be surprised. It is preferable to speak of developing plausible planning assumptions for the future, rather than accepting econometric projections for fifty years hence as a basis for planning. The broad uncertainty in future prices and demands for resource services means that ultimately management and political judgment must make planning assumptions.

At the individual management unit or project level, projections are not necessarily easier. The number of underutilized campsite developments testifies to that. Trying to refine those individual unit or project forecasts with econometric demand projections is not usually helpful. But existing knowledge should enable planners to extrapolate from available studies some rough ranges of possibilities for visitor responses to changes in fees or regulations, for example.

Another area in which economics can make some contribution is by studying the cross elasticities, income elasticities, and demographic factors affecting market growth for different forms of recreation. How do increased prices for rafting trips affect demand for canoeing? How do user preferences and activities change over time? Will new uses supplant previously popular activities? Economic analyses can support insightful market research into the outlook for different activities (Siehl 1986).

One of the wildland manager's key problems is visitor peaking—both in time and in space. Most of the visitor load of western national parks and national forest wilderness occurs on nine to twelve days per year. And the bulk of this use, even in backcountry zones, is concentrated on no more than 5% of the land area. River use is also subject to pronounced peaking. The potential for creative use of pricing and regulations to manage this peaking for everyone's benefit has barely been tapped. There have been few careful program evaluations of the many existing efforts in this area.

Compared with our schemes of administrative rationing, first-come first-served policies, and freezing of rights to historical patterns, pricing as a means of rationing access and managing peaks has a number of advantages. It is transparent, arguably fair to all concerned, far less intrusive, and may in many cases be cheaper to administer. As a side benefit, it can help pay the freight and reduce subsidies to a minority. Whatever one's view of these issues, economic methods can be used to roughly predict consumers' responses to various fee levels, just as they are applied to analyzing effects of price changes for any commodity or service. For an intriguing analogy in water supply see Smith (1984).

Economists—their values, their view of fairness, and even their terminology—are somewhat at odds with most people and many resource managers when it comes to pricing (Harris and Driver 1987, Binkley and Mendelsohn 1987). Recreationists argue that pricing debases the wilderness experience, that it is fundamentally unfair to users, and that it favors the rich. Few people share economists' sense of the advantages of using marketlike processes in environmental policy. It may be that the case for pricing has not been stated in a way that its advantages come through clearly. The limited practical experience of using pricing has also reduced our ability to sell the idea widely. Finally, subsidized minorities usually resist cost-based pricing that would reduce their subsidies (rent seeking again).

Other issues that might be approached using economic analysis include the analysis of the demand for public transportation in parks compared with automobiles, and the effects of regulations or easement purchase programs on the demand for and price of land. Many other markets are of concern to wilderness managers. At the national level, analysts and decision makers attempt to predict how the markets for wood products will respond to changes in wood supply. How will prices, consumption, import-export balances, and employment be affected? For these questions, existing tools of economic analysis can, despite their shortcomings, provide reasonable guidance.

ECONOMIC THINKING AS A SOLVENT FOR SPECIOUS ARGUMENT

Over the years, debates over wilderness preservation and management have generated an abundance of specious nonsense. Some of this nonsense finds its way into management plans, some into public policies, some into interest group challenges to agency actions, and some even into serious research publications.

Perhaps the most significant use of economics in wildland management is not in valuation, in demand assessment, in predicting consumer response to price changes, or in analyzing costs. It is simply in the use of disciplined thinking to help managers and the public separate specious from sound arguments.

A disciplined analytical process proceeds from asking the right questions, to appraising outcomes, to comparing options, to analyzing the overall situation. In Johnson's (1986) terms, this is the pursuit of problem-solving knowledge rather than disciplinary or subject matter knowledge. This process, or portions of it, might well be applied to several issues facing wilderness managers today. I suggest a few initial topics for applying some disciplined, critical thought to sifting out specious from sound arguments:

1. What is the justification for backcountry recreational users being subsidized by paying less than cost for the experience?

2. What is the justification for assuming that a computer econometric model, embodying parameter estimates based on the past thirty years, will reliably tell us what resource services will be needed and valued in fifty years? Also, what is the basis for assuming that such aggregate forecasts, if valid at all, should determine what our management policy should be on an individual land unit?

3. What is the basis for the commonly offered view that recreation and tourism are really more important to our mountain regions than more traditional resource development activity? What evidence as to relative social and environmental costs, relative economic stability, skill level of employment, and harmony with different land uses has been assembled to support or refute this notion (Polzin and Schweitzer 1975)?

4. What is the basis for the pervasive preference for bureaucratic allocation systems over marketlike processes for allocating rights to recreation and other wilderness services?

5. What is the basis for applying benefit-cost analysis to socially strategic, long-term decisions like acid rain control, park preservation, conservation of rare species, and long-run resource supply conservation?

6. How do we decide when we have reached the point that incremental budget dollars really ought to go into stewardship of the existing park and wilderness base, rather than into expanded landownership?

7. Multiple-use conflicts generate enormous confusion and rhetoric. Results of

economic analysis depend critically on just what land uses and services are assumed to be mutually exclusive or mutually supportive. Our ability to muster firm evidence in place of rhetoric on these questions has been limited. Some means need to be found to chart a reasonable course between competing multiple resource uses. Is there a middle ground between multiple-use management and wilderness? Do we want linear tree plantations up to the boundary of the backcountry, and nothing in between?

ECONOMICS IN A BROADER APPROACH

Economics has become our principal vocabulary for framing quantitative analysis of land allocation and management issues. I am arguing that we must recognize the limits of any efforts to quantify values accurately. But I also argue that economics can help us in thinking about opportunity costs, local economic impacts, and how markets respond to changing prices and policies.

This approach places the focus on the policy issues: What are the policy objectives in a given land unit? What are the options? What are the effects of each option? Within this framework, analysts are not pushed to condense all information into a single benefit-cost ratio, but to display various kinds of data in an orderly way. They are not pushed to maximize "net public benefit" but to admit that policy goals and public values are often conflicting. Sound economic thinking in carrying out analyses within this framework could contribute a good deal to more effective ecosystem management.

REFLECTIONS

We are moving up the marginal cost curve: decisions facing society concerning the allocation and management of wildland ecosystems are becoming more costly both politically and economically. Economics can bring to bear many useful tools to help make these allocation decisions. The tools have their weaknesses, but should not be blamed for the faults of their frequent abusers. The tools do some things well but not others. It is up to their users to know the difference. A number of the most careful recent studies, and several trenchant methods critiques, help us appreciate the limitations.

For clearly defined lists of similar alternatives, we have forms of analysis that lead to helpful rankings of alternatives. We can clarify many questions about consumer demand, market behavior, and resource valuation. But the more important role of economics is as an aid in disciplined thinking about choices and in listening to the future. Also, as Leman and Nelson (1981) note, people often need to be reminded that programs have costs.

Economists' ideas produce skepticism and unease among many concerned with conserving our nation's wilderness heritage (Nelson 1982). It rubs us wrong to hear the view over Nankoweap Mesa described as a commodity with costs, substitutes, willingness to pay, and a demand curve. A deep sense of the sacredness of nature, of its being bigger than we are, is offended by such cold thinking. The many past abuses, the examples of excessive quantification, inappropriate discounting of the future, and abuse of cost accounting sound a warning. Is the answer to be simply the assertion that allocation decisions are better made without systematic analysis? Is the all too common tunnel vision of economists (Hirshleifer 1985; see also Miller 1982a,b) good reason for rejecting systematic analysis?

Wilderness allocation and management decisions ultimately express the values of an entire society. Such values transcend financial calculation. They transcend demands, markets, and discount rates. The leap between defining financial optima (or project rankings) and the long-run social good is simply too long—especially for strategic long-run decisions involving resource stewardship, survival of species, and cultural values (Sagoff 1981, 1982). But those making the decisions, and those affected by them, want the help that a disciplined thought process can offer. The intelligent use of economics can supply such a process—not to make decisions, but to illuminate the choices, values, and possible risks.

Is there room for economics in the wilderness? In my wilderness there is. Perhaps managers, decision makers, and political leaders would make more room for economics if we could develop ways of integrating economic analysis into a broader approach—an approach that has room for the sound of mountain streams, the scented breeze off the mesa, and the mystic historic clockwork of the annual cycles of migrating geese.

LITERATURE CITED

Baden, J., and D. Lueck. 1984. A property rights approach to wilderness management. In G. M. Johnston and P. M. Emerson (eds.) Public lands and the U.S. economy, pp. 29-80. Westview Press, Boulder, Colorado.

Binkley, C. S., and R. O. Mendelsohn. 1987. Recreation user fees: How much are users willing to pay? J. For. 85(5):31-39.

Blaug, M. 1980. The methodology of economics, or how economists explain. Cambridge University Press, Cambridge. 231 p.

Brown, T. 1984. The concept of value in resource allocation. Land Economics 60(3):231-239.

Burch, W. R., and D. DeLuca. 1984. Measuring the social impact of natural resource policies. University of New Mexico Press, Albuquerque. 207 p.

Clawson, M., and J. Knetsch. 1966. The economics of outdoor recreation. Johns Hopkins University Press, Baltimore. 198 p.

Connaughton, K. P., P. E. Polzin, and C. Schallau. 1985. Tests of the economic base model of growth for a timber dependent region. For. Sci. 31(3):717-725.

Convery, F. J. n.d. [ca. 1980]. Applications of economics in national forest planning. Southern Region, USDA Forest Service, Atlanta. 121 p.

Dewald, W. G., J. G. Thursby, and R. G. Anderson. 1986. Replication in economics. Am. Econ. Rev. 76(4):587-603.

Eckstein, O. 1958. Water resource development: The economics of project evaluation. Harvard University Press, Cambridge. 189 p.

Finsterbusch, K., and A. B. Motz. 1980. Social research for policy decisions. Wadsworth Publishing Co., Belmont, California. 203 p.

Greer, T. V., and J. G. Greer. 1982. Problems in evaluating costs and benefits of social programs. Publ. Admin. Rev. 42(2):151-156.

Guldin, R. W. 1981. Wilderness costs in New England. J. For. 79:217.

Harris, C. C., and B. L. Driver. 1987. Recreation user fees. I. Pros and Cons. J. For. 95(5):25-30.

Hart, E. R. (ed.) 1981. That awesome space: Human interaction with the intermountain west. Westwater Press, Salt Lake City.

Haveman, R. H. 1972. The economic performance of public investments: An ex post evaluation of water resource investments. Johns Hopkins University Press, Baltimore. 126 p.

Hirshleifer, J. 1985. The expanding domain of economics. Am. Econ. Rev. 75(6):53-68.

Howe, C. W. 1971. Benefit-cost analysis for water system planning. Water Res. Monogr. 2. Am. Geophys. Union, Washington D.C.

Hyde, W. F. 1980. Timber supply, land allocation, and economic efficiency. Johns Hopkins University Press, Baltimore. 219 p.

Irland, L. C. 1979. Wilderness economics and policy. Heath-Lexington, Lexington. 225 p.

——. 1980. Costs of managing backcountry recreation in Maine. Tech. Report 5. Maine Department of Conservation, Bureau of Parks and Recreation, Augusta. 4 p.

——. 1982. Natural resources in Maine's economy. State Planning Office, Augusta. 72 p.

——. 1986. Streamside protective corridors: Techniques for weighing costs and benefits. Unpublished paper prepared for XVIII Congress, IUFRO, Ljubljana, Yugoslavia. 36 p.

Iverson, D. C., and R. M. Alston. 1986. The genesis of FORPLAN: A historical and analytical review of Forest Service planning methods. USDA For. Serv. Gen. Tech. Rep. INT-214. Intermountain For. and Range Exp. Stn., Ogden, Utah. 71 p.

Jackson, D. H. 1980. The microeconomics of the timber industry. Westview Press, Boulder, Colorado. 136 p.

Johnson, G. L. 1986. Research methodology for economists: Philosophy and practice. Macmillan, New York. 252 p.

Kelman, S. 1985. Cost-benefit analysis and environmental, safety, and health regulation: Ethical and philosophical considerations. In M. Wachs (ed.) Ethics in planning, pp. 91-104. Center for Urban Policy Research, Rutgers University, New Brunswick, New Jersey.

King, D. A., D. J. Bugarsky, and W. W. Shaw. 1987. Contingent valuation: An application to wildlife. Proceedings, Division 4, pp. 189-201. XVIII IUFRO Congress, Ljubljana, Yugoslavia. College of Forestry, Oregon State University, Corvallis.

Kneese, A. V. 1984. Measuring the benefits of environmental improvement. Johns Hopkins University Press, Baltimore. 135 p.

Krutilla, J., M. D. Bowes, and P. Sherman. 1983. Watershed management for joint production of water and timber: A provisional assessment. Water Res. Bull. 19(3):403-414.

Krutilla, J., and A. C. Fisher. 1975. The economics of natural environments. Johns Hopkins University Press, Baltimore. 201 p.

Lal, D. 1974. Methods of project analysis. Staff Occas. Pap. 16. World Bank, Washington, D.C. 89 p.

Leamer, E. E. 1983. Let's take the con out of econometrics. Am. Econ. Rev. 73(1):31-43.

——. 1985. Sensitivity analysis would help. Am. Econ. Rev. 75(3):308-313.

Leman, C. K., and R. H. Nelson. 1981. Ten commandments for policy economists. J. Pol. Anal. Manage. 1(1):97-117.

LeMaster, D. C., B. R. Flamm, and J. C. Hendee. 1986. Below-cost timber sales conference proceedings. The Wilderness Society, Washington, D.C. 266 p.

MacIntyre, A. 1985. Utilitarianism and the presuppositions of cost-benefit analysis. In M. Wachs (ed.) Ethics in planning, pp. 216-232. Center for Urban Policy Research, Rutgers University, New Brunswick, New Jersey.

McAleer, M., A. R. Pagan, and P. A. Volker. 1985. What will take the con out of econometrics? Am. Econ. Rev. 75(3):293-307.

McCloskey, D. N. 1985. The rhetoric of economics. University of Wisconsin Press, Madison. 176 p.

Mendelsohn, R. 1987. Measuring the value of recreation in the White Mountains. Appalachian N.S. 46:73-84.

Miller, A. 1982a. Environmental problem solving: Psychosocial factors. Environ. Manage. 6(6):535-541.

——. 1982b. Tunnel vision in environmental management. The Environmentalist 2:223-231.

Murdock, S. H., and F. L. Leistritz. 1980. Selecting socioeconomic models: A discussion of criteria and selected models. J. Environ. Manage. 10:241-252.

Nagel, S. 1984. Contemporary public policy analysis. University of Alabama Press, University.

Nelson, R. H. 1982. The public lands. In P. R. Portney (ed.) Current issues in natural resource policy, pp. 14-17. Johns Hopkins University Press, Baltimore.

Nelson, R. R. 1977. The moon and the ghetto: An essay on public policy analysis. W. W. Norton, New York. 138 p.

Obiya, A., D. G. Chappelle, and C. H. Schallau. 1986. Spatial and regional analysis methods in forestry economics: An annotated bibliography. USDA For. Serv. Gen. Tech. Rep. PNW-190. Pac. Northwest For. and Range Exp. Stn., Portland, Oregon. 32 p.

Pearse, P. H., and D. H. Williams. 1986. Economic implications of timber supply regulation. Unpublished paper prepared for XVIII IUFRO Congress, Ljubljana, Yugoslavia. 13 p.

Peterson, G. L., T. C. Brown, and D. H. Rosenthal. 1987. Toward an improved framework for estimating RPA values. USDA For. Serv. Gen. Tech. Rep. RM-138. Rocky Mountain For. and Range Exp. Stn., Fort Collins, Colorado. 13 p.

Polzin, P. E., and D. C. Schweitzer. 1975. Economic importance of tourism in Montana. USDA For. Serv. Res. Pap. INT-171. 19 p.

Porter, R. C. 1982. The new approach to wilderness preservation through benefit-cost analysis. J. Environ. Econ. Manage. 9:59-80.

Program Abstracts: First National Symposium on Social Science in Resource Management. 1986. CPSU/OSU 86-4. National Park Service, California Polytechnic State University, and Department of Resource Recreation, Oregon State University. 230 p.

Proudel, P. K. 1979. Capitalization of environmental benefits into property values: Literature review. USDA For. Serv. Gen. Tech. Rep. RM-69.

Reiling, S. D., and M. W. Anderson. 1983. Estimation of the cost of providing publicly-supported outdoor recreation facilities in Maine. Bull. 793. Maine Agric. Exp. Stn., Orono. 63 p.

Rich, R. F. 1979. Translating evaluation into policy. Sage Publications, Beverly Hills. 123 p.

Sagoff, M. 1981. At the shrine of Our Lady of Fatima *or* why political questions are not all economic. Arizona Law Review 23(4):1283-1298.

———. 1982. We have met the enemy and he is us *or* conflict and contradiction in environmental law. Environ. Law 12:283-315.

Sax, J., and R. Keiter. 1987. Glacier National Park and its neighbors: A case study of federal interagency relations. Ecology Law Quarterly 14:206-263.

Schallau, C. H., and R. M. Alston. 1987. The commitment to community stability: A policy or shibboleth? Environ. Law 17(3):429-481.

Schuster, E. G. 1976. Local economic impact: A decision variable in forest resource management. Montana Forest and Conservation Exp. Stn., Missoula. 131 p.

Sedjo, R. A. (ed.) 1985. Investments in forestry. Westview Press, Boulder. 245 p.

Siehl, G. H. 1986. Trends in outdoor recreation and related factors, 1960-1985. Unpublished staff report for presidents. Commission on Americans Outdoors, Washington, D.C.

Smith, R. T. 1984. Troubled waters: Financing water in the West. Council of State Planning Agencies, Washington, D.C. 194 p.

Smith, V. K. 1978. Scarcity and growth reconsidered. *In* E. N. Castle (ed.) Contemporary issues in natural resource economics, pp. 39-48. Resources for the Future, Washington, D.C.

Sorg, C. F., and J. B. Loomis. 1984. Empirical estimates of amenity forest values: A comparative review. USDA For. Serv. Gen. Tech. Rep. RM-107. 21 p.

Teeguarden, D. E. 1987. Benefit-cost analysis in National Forest System planning: Policy, uses, and limitations. Environ. Law 17(3):393-427.

USDA Forest Service. Timber Management Staff. n.d. [ca. 1986]. Analysis of costs and revenues in the timber program of four national forests. Washington, D.C.

Vaughan, W. J., and C. S. Russell. 1982. Freshwater recreational fishing: The national benefits of water pollution control. Resources for the Future, Washington, D.C. 205 p.

Walker, J. 1983. National forest planning: A critique. *In* R. A. Sedjo (ed.) Governmental interventions, social needs, and the management of U.S. forests, pp. 189-200. Resources for the Future, Washington, D.C.

11

Cooperation in Ecosystem Management

VERNON C. GILBERT

ABSTRACT A cooperative approach to the management of ecosystems and natural resources is proposed using the United States Man and the Biosphere (MAB) program, which is part of an international scientific program designed to deal with people-environment interactions. Since natural ecosystems require broad, cooperative, integrated approaches, many natural resource problems cannot be solved by individual agency efforts, or by single jurisdictions. A proposed cooperative program in the southern Appalachian region is described. The region has increasing problems of atmospheric pollution, decline in water quality, and degradation of natural habitat. Two examples of international projects associated with MAB are also described. One is in Rwanda, a small African country which has serious problems of deforestation, soil erosion, and loss of its natural resource base. The other example is the Ecosystem Conservation Group, which promotes cooperation among the major international organizations that deal with ecosystems conservation. The paper concludes that the need for such programs is urgent, because the stress on natural ecosystems and renewable resources is undermining the ability of the land in many areas to produce the goods and services necessary for human well-being. The United States, as the recognized world leader in ecosystem research and management, must help solve these problems.

THE CONCEPT AND THE CONCERN

In a democratic society where many sectors and jurisdictions are responsible for managing natural resources, cooperation among the responsible parties is essential, but few models exist to show how this can be done on a large scale. The basic concept is that managers must take into account the nature of ecosystems and natural resources and the jurisdictional settings in which they occur if they are to manage the resources successfully. This is not a new idea. Dr. Stanley Cain and others had this "vision" more than twenty years ago (UNESCO 1970). They realized it would be difficult to achieve, but probably could not foresee how difficult, for the Conference on the Use and Management of the Biosphere was held in 1968 during a period of optimism and progress. The International Biological Program (IBP), which was coming to an end at that time, had advanced understanding of large ecosystems and shown how the sciences involved in ecosystem research could contribute to resource management and conservation. Largely because of the IBP experience, it was realized that a new international program was needed, one which would enable governments to cooperate effectively in dealing with the growing problems arising from human-environmental interactions. The basic ideas for this program, later to be called Man and the Biosphere (MAB), were conceived at that 1968 Biosphere Conference, in which Dr. Cain and many other distinguished scientists participated. Plans were then developed, over the next few years, to establish MAB as the major intergovernmental scientific research and training program devoted to improving management of the natural ecosystems and resources of the biosphere (Gilbert and Gregg 1981).

The focus of the Ecosystem Management Workshop was to develop goals and principles of ecosystem management in national parks and wilderness areas in the United States, but there are important reasons to extend our consideration to ecosystems throughout the world. Many of these areas are being destroyed now, so we urgently need to apply existing knowledge and expertise to solving these problems. I was optimistic about the possibilities for solving them in the early years of the MAB program, when I had the opportunity to participate in the development of the MAB Project 8, Conservation of Natural Areas and of the Genetic Material They Contain—now called the Biosphere Reserve Project. I am not so optimistic now, for environmental problems throughout the biosphere have far outstripped the efforts to solve them. Today the need for the multidisciplinary, multiagency cooperative approach that Dr. Cain advocated is vastly more urgent than it was at the time he proposed it. Ecological problems in some parts of the world have so seriously stressed the life support systems that millions of people are suffering. If this destruction of natural ecosystems and depletion of resources continues, it will eventually affect the welfare of us all. The effects already are more threatening than most people realize.

Thus far, most economic reports have ignored ecological trends, probably because natural systems in many parts of the world, with improved agriculture, technology, and petroleum resources, are still providing an abundance of goods and services to nations and people who can afford them. In the developing countries, however, there is little cushion between the welfare of the majority of the population and the condition of their natural environment. *State of the World, 1986: A Worldwatch Institute Report on Progress Toward a Sustainable Society* concludes that decision makers have failed to adopt an integrated and multidisciplinary approach for analyzing the relationship between ourselves and our environmental support systems, and that we are failing to sustain these system (Brown et al. 1986). The *State of the World* report for 1987 (Brown et al. 1987) indicates: "Deforestation, soil erosion, acidification, and desertification are undermining progress in scores of countries. Efforts to devise sustainable development policies will be further complicated by the global warming induced by greenhouse gases, the depletion of the ozone layer, and the wholesale loss of biological diversity associated with tropical deforestation. These new threats to progress confront industrial and developing countries alike. Future improvements in living standards rest more heavily than ever on international cooperation. And time has suddenly become one of the scarcest of all resources." The report also states: "National leaders who fail to comprehend the fundamental alteration between the 5 billion of us who now inhabit the earth and the natural systems and resources on which we depend will find themselves plagued by intractable problems and locked into economic decline."

I have observed these problems developing, particularly in Africa. Since I first went to Africa in 1965 to teach at the College of African Wildlife Management in Tanzania, the population in eastern Africa has almost doubled, and many people have been forced into marginal areas where tree removal and soil erosion are occurring at alarming rates.

Forests, woodlands, rangelands, and coastal and marine resources have been seriously depleted. Numbers of certain species have drastically declined, and some have completely disappeared. This breakdown of ecosystems and depletion of natural resources not only makes life more difficult for those who depend directly on the resources, it also hinders economic development. The need to improve ecosystem management to help sustain the supply of goods and services for people in many countries, and ultimately for the welfare of all, is at its highest level ever.

We in the United States have the experience and expertise, especially in fields related to ecosystem research and management, to help do something about these international problems. This is why the Ecosystem Workshop must consider them along with our own domestic problems, for they are interrelated. One way that we can help is to develop models in this country that will demonstrate intelligent, cooperative management of ecosystems, and to use these models in international training efforts.

NEED FOR A DELIBERATE PROCESS

There can be no lasting solution to ecosystem and natural resource management problems in democratic societies except through a joint planning approach such as Dr. Cain advocated. The very nature of ecosystems dictates that broad, cooperative, and integrated approaches to ecosystem management have to be developed. If we agree to this, we recognize that many natural resource problems will not be solved by individual agency or institutional efforts, or by single political jurisdictions. When individual agencies analyze their roles and jurisdictions regarding particular natural resources, the need for developing deliberate systems of cooperation becomes obvious. Why then has this goal been so difficult to achieve? It is not that the concept is new, for during the 1970s the nature of our environmental problems was widely recognized. There was also great progress in the sciences related to ecosystem research, and in technologies that could contribute to management and sustained use of natural resources. But management has not kept pace with the sciences to bring this knowledge into practice. Perhaps the main problem is that administrators and managers of agencies with specific mandates to manage natural resources, though they may recognize cooperation as necessary for dealing with most contemporary resources issues, are reluctant to relinquish any control. Cooperative activities require special interpersonal and managerial skills, yet training in these areas is insufficient. Cooperative agreements on specific issues are common, but there is little incentive or budget for planning broad, cooperative programs. As a result, natural resources are often treated and managed as isolated entities. This problem has to be overcome, perhaps through national leadership and grass roots movements; therefore, environmental education will have to be an important component of all efforts to achieve this goal.

It will also be important for managers to become better informed about programs that are attempting to develop cooperative approaches to achieve the goals of ecosystem management, so that as models are developed, experiences can be shared and the systems improved. Three examples that I believe have merit are described below. Two of them focus on specific regions and on natural resource issues that seriously affect people and economic development—one in the southern Appalachians and the other in Africa. The third is an approach to cooperation by the major international organizations that deal with ecosystem conservation.

PROPOSED SOUTHERN APPALACHIAN PROJECT

A Model Biosphere Reserve Program

The 1974 Summit Agreement. The Great Smoky Mountains National Park, as a representative, protected example of the southern Appalachians, has been recognized for its potential research and educational value to the region and to the nation. Ecologists have referred to the area as having potential for ecological research which greatly transcends the usual national park needs for interpretive and management research. In 1974, when I worked with the UNESCO MAB program in Paris, I used the Great Smoky Mountains National Park and its potential for cooperation with neighboring communities, adjacent national forests, nearby Tennessee Valley Authority lands and waters, and the universities in the area, to illustrate the idea of a "biosphere reserve." This particular example was used to promote the MAB program, and also in a proposal to the Department of State that the United States and the Soviet Union designate biosphere reserves in each country, and carry out cooperative activities under the program. The proposal was accepted and the two countries agreed in a summit conference in Moscow, July 1974, to support the MAB program. The interest stimulated by this agreement, and Department of State cables to our embassies in other countries to encourage their support, resulted in the designation of the first biosphere reserves and helped get the project under way. Dr. Jerry Franklin chaired the U.S. Biosphere Reserve Committee, which developed the concept of multiple reserves whereby experimentally oriented tracts were matched with large preserves to provide a biosphere reserve "cluster" representing a particular biotic region. As a result of this, the Great Smoky Mountains National Park and the Coweeta Hydrologic Laboratory in North Carolina were paired, and several other areas, including the Oak Ridge National Environmental Research Park, have since agreed to join the cluster.

With the summit agreement and the worldwide attention it caused, it was anticipated that MAB and the Biosphere Reserve Project would be provided adequate support for an effective beginning. But this was not to be the case. Support from the Nixon administration, which agreed to the program, and from participating U.S. agencies was very modest. Thus the program was slow to develop. In spite of this, there have been persistent efforts to develop the biosphere reserve concept, especially in the southern Appalachians.

International Plan for Biosphere Reserves. On the basis of the First International Biosphere Reserve Congress held in the USSR in 1983, an International Action Plan was developed and adopted in 1984 by the International Coordinating Council of MAB. A priority objective of the Action Plan is to use biosphere reserves to promote cooperative regional planning, research, and development. This role was recognized in 1985 by the U.S. Interagency Task Force Report to Congress, *U.S. Strategy on the Conservation of Biological Diversity*. The report recommended that increased support be considered for biosphere reserves as centers for developing the information and skills needed for sustainable development of regional ecosystems, and for the continuing assessment and improvement of management through research (USAID 1985).

In a recent assessment of the 243 biosphere reserves in the world, the southern Appalachian cluster was recommended as one of twenty areas for development of model biosphere reserves. Another area identified as one of the twenty emerging models was the Virgin Islands Biosphere Reserve, where, during the past four years, the National Park Service has been developing a biosphere reserve program centered around the only U.S. national park area in a developing region. The U.S. Biosphere Reserve Directorate decided in December 1986 to support the development of a model biosphere reserve program in the southern Appalachians, as part of the U.S. strategy to implement the International Action Plan.

Cooperative System Planning.   Another initiative now combined with the MAB project in the southern Appalachians is in cooperative system planning. Leaders of agencies with major responsibilities in natural resource management and environmental protection in the southeastern United States have held several natural resource management seminars to discuss how the agencies can bring together their technical capabilities to work with other public and private interests to manage natural resources on a sustained basis. National Park Service Southeast Regional Director Robert Baker, who initiated these seminars, has proposed that pilot projects in cooperative system planning be developed in several areas, including the southern Appalachians. In a memorandum of August 15, 1986, to the superintendents of the lead parks—Blue Ridge Parkway and Great Smoky Mountains National Park—he referred to the critical problems facing the region, such as increasing urbanization, pollution, competition for consumptive resources, and the shrinking of personnel and fiscal resources. He stressed the need to begin a process of identifying regional issues and developing objectives and strategies to address them on a scale reaching beyond park boundaries. He indicated that these efforts should draw their strength from interagency cooperation aimed at achieving common planning goals—an "ecosystem approach" which should be discussed with leaders in the area. The lead superintendents agreed that the MAB program would be the most appropriate vehicle for implementing a cooperative program in the region. It was recognized that individual agency outreach programs, as valuable as they are, could not be the principal means to achieve the desired goal of an integrated regional program. This broad objective might be achieved, however, by using MAB as a vehicle to bring together all of the concerned agencies and institutions in a program in which they could participate equally.

A proposal developed in 1985 (An Approach to Improving Natural Resource Management in the Southern Appalachian Region) is to be used as a basis for initiating this project (Gilbert 1986). The proposal suggests that the southern Appalachians can be characterized as a biogeographical region because of the ecosystem types, flora, fauna, climate, geology, and related human cultures that have developed to some extent because of these characteristics. This region is the highland unit consisting of portions of northern Georgia, western South Carolina, eastern Tennessee, western North Carolina, and southern Virginia. This large area is an appropriate "common ground" for cooperative management of many of the region's natural resources, because entire ecosystems can be treated, and more complete ranges of species can be included. Another advantage is that many people in the area feel the region is their "home," so they have a growing concern about what is happening to it. In my travels in the area to discuss natural resource issues of concern, I found that there was a great deal of interest in developing a cooperative project. The proposal was prepared and distributed by the National Park Service to key individuals and agency representatives in the region; responses were very positive and included many good suggestions. All of the key federal agencies and the major universities responded favorably. The proposal recognized that although the southern Appalachians would be an appropriate arena for cooperation, many of the natural resource problems originate outside of, or extend beyond, this large area; thus the scale of cooperation would depend on the issue (e.g., conservation of migratory breeding birds would involve even international cooperation). This would be one of the advantages of the MAB program, for it would provide us with another means to cooperate with those in the countries that share these resources.

Natural Resource Issues in the Southern Appalachians

The southern Appalachian region is a scenic and biologically diverse area. It has experienced rapid growth of communities and development of industry in some sections. The complex attendant problems of atmospheric pollution and acidic deposition, changes in water quality, deforestation, impacts of mining, and depletion of natural resources have caused growing concern about the potential of the area to meet the needs of people in the future. Some of the natural resource issues that require cooperative solutions are discussed below.

Land Use and Development. Poorly planned land development and lack of consideration for the environmental consequences are general problems in the region. Major efforts to establish land use planning and zoning structures have failed because of public opposition and the efforts of special interest groups. There is now, however, a growing awareness of the need for better management of land resources, and it can be encouraged through environmental education and programs to inform the public of land use trends. With the wealth of experience in the agencies and major institutions in the region, a significant program in cooperative system planning could be developed. The Tennessee Valley Authority (TVA), for example, has experience in assisting communities in development planning. The TVA has also begun a new international training program in integrated regional resource management which would assist in achieving this goal. The National Park Service has a history of working with local communities, especially in the development of environmental education programs. The challenge will be to put together and fund a program to make the best use of the significant expertise that exists, for there are many communities that need the assistance.

Water and Air Quality. The southern Appalachian highlands is a vital source of water, not only for the people in the region but for many towns, farms, fisheries, and industries supplied by the streams that flow from the mountains to the Gulf of Mexico and to the Atlantic Ocean. The Great Smoky Mountains National Park, for example, includes twenty-eight major drainage systems, three of which serve as official municipal watersheds. Serious problems have developed with the rapid growth in many communities because of inadequate waste treatment plants, increasing contamination of water supplies from sewage, and toxic pollutants entering surface and ground waters.

The effects of air pollutants on various plant species, aquatic communities, and even human health are also seriously threatening. This issue is being addressed through existing cooperative programs. For example, TVA has provided an annual forum on acid rain research which has encouraged coordination of research activities in that field. The U.S. Forest Service has funded a major program of research through the Southern Appalachian Research/Resource Management Consortium (SARRMC) to determine and assess the causes of the decline of the spruce-fir forests. SARRMC is a consortium of four federal agencies and six universities: the National Park Service, the U.S. Forest Service, the Tennessee Valley Authority, the U.S. Fish and Wildlife Service, Clemson University, North Carolina State University, the University of Georgia, the University of Tennessee, Virginia Polytechnic Institute and State University, and Western Carolina University. The consortium has been involved in many significant activities during the last decade, including analyses of southern Appalachian resource management problems and sponsorship of workshops to determine priorities for natural resources research in the region. These activities have been carried out by way of contributed services from the member institutions and small grants from member agencies.

Conservation of Biological Diversity. The importance of the diversity of plant species in the southern Appalachians is indicated in a recent ethnobotanical survey of the Great Smoky Mountains Biosphere Reserve and surrounding area, supported by U.S. MAB. Of the 1,500 or so plant species found in the area, there were recorded past or present uses for approximately half of the species (U.S. MAB 1985). Since many of these species range outside protected areas and through different political jurisdictions, the only practical way to conserve some species is through systematic regional cooperation strategies. This would be an effort in which many individuals and private landowners could participate, especially in maintaining appropriate habitats for certain rare or endangered species.

In regard to endangered species, the Fish and Wildlife Service indicates that this is a significant issue in the region. An estimated five mammals, five birds, eight fish, nineteen mollusks, one arthropod, and eight plants found in four of the seven states (North Carolina, South Carolina, Tennessee, and Kentucky) are listed as endangered species at the national level. Although the black bear is not yet an endangered species, it is a significant and limited resource that is under pressure from reduction of its habitat and illegal hunting. This is a case where there is a clear need for integrated management by the concerned federal, state, and local authorities, as well as a continuing need for environmental education to help people understand the requirements for conservation of the bear populations.

Control of Exotic Species. A number of troublesome exotic species must be treated in an integrated regional approach in order to understand and mitigate their effects. Among the most troublesome species are the nonnative wild hogs, which are causing extensive damage to native plants and animals in the Great Smoky Mountains. Both Tennessee and North Carolina regard the hogs as protected big game animals, so they are trapped from the national park and released some distance away for future hunting purposes. An independent assessment of their value for this purpose versus the damage they are causing is needed, so that information can be provided to the public and to decision makers regarding integrated management and control of the hogs. This assessment and information function could be carried out by MAB.

Actions Planned and Proposed

Based on a MAB feasibility report for the proposed southern Appalachian project, the U.S. National Committee for MAB has given high priority to building a model biosphere program in the region. Along with this development, the lead national park—Blue Ridge

Parkway—for the Cooperative System Planning Project has requested the National Committee to arrange an interagency meeting to explore possibilities to initiate cooperation on the resource issues described above. I have been asked to present the proposal for a demonstration program. The following actions will probably be necessary to initiate and carry out effective cooperative activities.

1. A process to identify the specific issues for cooperation must be established. This could be done under a policy-level regional steering committee, established to guide the project. The committee would consist of representatives of the major agencies, institutions, and sectors responsible for resource management in the region. The committee would decide the major issues to be considered and the roles of participating organizations based on studies of interdisciplinary groups of scientists set up for specific resource issues. The MAB program serves well as a means to carry out such a process because of its national and international experience in organizing expert panels and working groups for the development of specific MAB project areas. U.S. MAB, with contributions from member federal agencies, should provide the initial financial and staff support to organize the expert panels and work groups needed to identify and develop specific projects for cooperative activities.

There also are regional commissions, groups, and activities that will contribute greatly to the proposed project (e.g., SARRMC, which will assist in organization and coordination of research activities). In November 1987 SARRMC held a conference whose principal objective was to identify the key issues crucial to the effective management of the natural and human resources of the region during the next decade. Participants received a preconference publication, *A Profile of the Southern Appalachians*, summarizing the resource characteristics of the region. It includes items such as land tenure descriptions, land cover and land use patterns, census and demographic characteristics, transportation networks, and regional income and economic summaries.

2. To undertake a pilot project of this magnitude, a MAB regional secretariat must be established under the regional committee to handle the logistics and to coordinate the activities. This could be done along the same lines as the U.S. and international MAB secretariats, with both financial and staff support provided by the participating organizations. The success of the project will be largely dependent on this secretariat.

3. Although specific activities will be decided by the participating organizations through their regional committee, it will be essential to include a strong environmental education component in order to generate public awareness, understanding, and support. There should also be a strong international component to the project, based on the biosphere reserve program, and existing activities such as TVA's Integrated Regional Resources Management Training Program. Already in existence is a West German, Canadian, and U.S. MAB agreement to develop atmospheric pollution educational materials, which can contribute to both the domestic and international programs. The new Smithsonian/MAB Project on Biological Diversity has developed a protocol for a high resolution data-base management system to provide biological inventories in selected species-rich sites such as biosphere reserves, national parks, and other protected areas in developing countries. The protocol includes the recording of microdistribution and co-occurrence of species in time and space in permanent plots. This will allow long-term monitoring of selected species within those plots. The system also will incorporate data from past records, from museum specimens, and from inventory efforts or other data-base centers. Southern Appalachians biosphere reserves have been proposed as

areas where this program should be tested. Development and use of this program in the region would contribute to both federal and state agency objectives in conservation of biological resources and provide an excellent area for training professionals from other countries. Considering the current rapid loss and deterioration of biological resources in developing countries, and the urgent need to train personnel to deal with these problems, this could be one of the most important components of the proposed MAB program.[1]

INTERNATIONAL EXAMPLES

Eastern Africa Project

An important effort is under way in Rwanda, in eastern Africa, to establish an integrated regional approach to ecosystem conservation and development in a developing country. Rwanda is among the smallest and most densely populated countries in Africa and one with serious problems of deforestation, soil erosion, and loss of its natural resource base. The project is in the Ruhengeri region of northwestern Rwanda, which includes Rwanda's share of the Virunga Volcanoes—Africa's first national park, now an international biosphere reserve. It is the habitat of the mountain gorilla (*Gorilla gorilla beringei*), plus a great variety of other species. This mountainous region is also the country's most important watershed. Other parts of the Virunga ecosystem fall within Zaire and Uganda, a prime example of an ecosystem transcending national boundaries and one which definitely requires international cooperation if the total ecosystem is to remain viable in the long run. It is obvious that long-term conservation cannot succeed in this heavily populated region unless strategies are developed to meet the basic needs of the many people who live in the area, such as the improvement of agriculture and better management and use of the great variety of forest resources, because people depend on these resources for their very existence. To address these serious problems, a proposal was submitted to USAID and the Rwanda government, by the Environmental Management and Training Project in Africa (ETMA) in 1983, that an integrated regional project should be started in the Ruhengeri region, based on the MAB biosphere reserve concept. (I was the ETMA representative for eastern and southern Africa at that time.) This project was begun in 1984 with USAID and Rwanda government support. It is now entitled the Ruhengeri Resource Analysis and Management (RRAM) Project, designed to "help sustain the regional resource base and to minimize environmental problems associated with development in the Ruhengeri Prefecture." The project is intended to work closely with a Farm Systems Improvement Project and to assist the Rwandan government in developing an integrated data base for various renewable sectors—including forest, soil, water, wildlife, and human. Based on this approach, environmental trends are being assessed and priority problems identified. Of course, an important goal is to improve Rwandan institutional capacities to deal with these problems. This entails development of mechanisms for interministerial communication and cooperation, and integration of environmental factors into regional development planning (Weber 1985).

The Rwanda project could be a very important model for Africa if, under the difficult circumstances existing in Ruhengeri, it can demonstrate the potential for conservation and development by improving land use without further destruction of the resources. The area chosen for the project illustrates environmental problems typical of many other areas in Africa, but it also has some outstanding unique attributes, such as the mountain gorillas, which are valued internationally and have attracted important tourist revenue.

It is hoped that lessons from this project can be applied elsewhere, especially to comparable montane areas of eastern and central Africa. Whether it will be successful depends largely on the keynote—deliberate cooperation, not only among countries sharing this ecosystem but from countries that can provide the technical and financial assistance needed to build an example of sound environmental management.

Ecosystem Conservation Group

Since our domestic natural resource problems may not stop at national boundaries, and because degradation of the environment in other parts of the world will affect our vital interests, we need to make better use of mechanisms that promote cooperation in ecosystem conservation internationally. Therefore, my final example is about a little known mechanism to promote cooperation among the key international organizations that receive United States support and deal with ecosystem conservation: the United Nations Environment Program (UNEP), the United Nations Educational, Scientific and Cultural Organization (UNESCO), the Food and Agriculture Organization of the United Nations (FAO), and the International Union for the Conservation of Nature and Natural Resources (IUCN). The mechanism is called the Ecosystem Conservation Group (ECG), established in 1975 with the agreement that it would meet on a regular basis to discuss and plan the coordination of ecosystem conservation activities of its member organizations. By this means plans for international programs, such as MAB, can be integrated more effectively with programs of other major international organizations, such as the Tropical Forestry Action Plan of the FAO, and the Bali Action Plan of the IUCN.

Recently the ECG has provided a good example of cooperation by defining the common needs and objectives of its member organizations regarding *in situ* conservation of plant genetic resources. The International Board on Plant Genetic Resources (IBPGR) has also joined in these efforts. A Working Group has been established to (1) review ongoing and planned activities in *in situ* conservation (especially in relation to recommendations of the FAO Commission on Plant Genetic Resources, the Action Plan for Biosphere Reserves, the Tropical Forestry Action Plan, and the Bali Action Plan), and (2) identify ways and means to strengthen action and cooperation in response to these recommendations, with particular reference to improving information flow and promoting pilot demonstration areas.

The Working Group has, during its two sessions, recognized six major goals for coordinated action: (1) raise awareness of the importance of *in situ* conservation, (2) promote research (including inventories) on wild plants and their *in situ* conservation, (3) organize and provide an information service, (4) provide training in *in situ* conservation, (5) promote international cooperation, and (6) promote the application of methods of *in situ* conservation of plant genetic resources (FAO 1986).

I do not suggest that the work of the ECG is adequate, or that it always goes smoothly, for there have been times that the member organizations have gone their separate ways without the additional complications often associated with cooperative planning. However, there is a great deal of value in the regular communication of these organizations, because some duplication of efforts related to ecosystem conservation is avoided, and quite often good cooperation is generated. If the member nations that support these organizations were fully aware of the possibilities of the ECG, its role would be greatly strengthened. The United States has an important stake in this, since we have provided financial support and technical assistance to all of the member organizations.

The role of the ECG in promoting pilot demonstration projects could be very important to ecosystem management and conservation in the different biogeographical regions of the world. A proposal has recently been approved by U.S. MAB to recommend that the ECG be used to develop plans for pilot projects to assist developing countries to conserve important endangered ecosystems, especially where they are now being destroyed to satisfy basic human subsistence needs (Gilbert 1986b). Opportunities exist, as is being demonstrated in the Rwanda project, to develop better land use practices and management of areas so that a variety of goods and services can be produced without destruction of the natural resource base. There are numerous development aid and technical assistance programs that could contribute to such pilot projects, once sound plans have been developed. This project could be a way to bring together the usually well-funded development programs and the poorly funded conservation programs to demonstrate that conservation of ecosystems is important to development. The ECG is the logical group to work with the host countries to develop plans for these pilot projects.[2]

CONCLUSION

For many years the need for broad cooperative efforts in ecosystem management has been recognized, but they rarely get the support they need to be effective. In 1980, for example, a proposal for "cooperative regional demonstration projects" in the Lake Champlain basin, the Colorado Rockies, the Lower Colorado River basin, and the southern Appalachians was part of a national plan for the MAB program requested by the Executive Office of the President—Office of Science and Technology Policy (OSTP) and Office of Management and Budget (OMB). This plan called for MAB to bring together various agencies and institutions to develop pilot demonstration projects in regional resources management. The TVA, with its broad mandate to "plan for the proper use, conservation, and development of the natural resources of the Tennessee River drainage basin and its adjoining territory for the general, social and economic welfare of the Nation," provided key assistance in developing a plan for the project in the southern Appalachians. The national plan was then transmitted to OMB and OSTP, signed by assistant secretaries in the Departments of Interior, State, and Agriculture, who stated in the transmittal memorandum: "With the modest but necessary financial support recommended, U.S. MAB will have the base to institutionalize its unique capabilities. Since MAB has anticipated by nearly ten years the research, practical, and institutional problems described in the Global 2000 Report, and since it has developed a proven and flexible mechanism to bring together the otherwise fragmented elements needed to address them, we strongly support the enclosed program and recommendations" (U.S. MAB 1980).

The Office of Management and Budget did not even provide a response to the plan, for it did not fit the priorities of the new Reagan administration. An OMB official told me informally that the agencies could, if the MAB program was as important as they stated, include it in their individual budget priorities, but that they should not request funds as a separate program. Thus the plan died, because of lack of national direction from OMB and OSTP and a reluctance by the agencies to take the leadership to give MAB priority in their individual programs. Now that agency fiscal resources are shrinking, it may be even more difficult to get the support necessary to develop these new cooperative programs. However, such support is more important than ever, and it is the responsibility of resource management agencies to establish deliberate systems for cooperation, since there is no reasonable alternative to achieve their common goals in ecosystem management.

The need for such programs worldwide is urgent. The stress on natural ecosystems and renewable resources is undermining the ability of the land in many areas to produce the goods and services necessary for human well-being. National priorities have to be changed if efforts are to be mounted to reverse present trends of resource depletion. Scarcity of financial resources is often our excuse for limited activity in natural resources management and conservation. For example, at current levels of funding and scientific effort, fewer than 1% of the world's species are being investigated (Brown et al. 1987). Forests—especially tropical forests—are ecosystems with a great variety of species and genetic resources which will benefit us all if they are sustained, but development assistance to forestry and related fields is very small. The World Bank and the Inter-American, Asian, and African development banks allocate less than 1% of their annual financing to forestry (World Resources Institute 1985).

The real problem is not scarcity of financial resources but how the resources are allocated. Each year the world spends several times as much on research to increase the destructiveness of weapons as on all the efforts to improve agriculture and farm practices. This is a matter of priorities and choices that we have allowed our leaders to decide. If we realize that degradation of ecosystems and depletion of natural resources in many parts of the world are causing suffering and instability now, and that this will result in serious threats to our own security, surely we will change these priorities. Thus environmental education is an extremely important issue, for more people must be aware of the threat if the necessary changes are to be made.

A statement made in 1969, by former Secretary of State William P. Rogers, is quite relevant. As the negotiations between the United States and the Soviet Union on limiting nuclear arsenals and new defensive systems began, he said: "Strategic weapons cannot solve the problems of how we live at home or how we live in the world in the last third of the 20th century. Who knows the rewards if we succeed in diverting the energy, time, and attention—the manpower and the brainpower—to other more worthwhile purposes?" (U.S. Department of State 1969).

In the management of parks and wilderness areas the United States is generally recognized as the world leader. Therefore, we must devote our thoughts and efforts to programs of broad cooperation in ecosystem management, extending to the biosphere—our largest ecosystem. The MAB program is an appropriate vehicle for this cooperation, for it has the maturity resulting from the cumulative efforts of thousands of scientists, government officials, and resource managers from countries throughout the world, and from seventeen years of experience. We should make better use of it, for with our active participation and support, MAB could become a much needed constructive force in the world.

NOTES

1. An interagency, cooperative agreement for the establishment and operation of the Southern Appalachian Man and the Biosphere Cooperative was signed by key federal agencies August 10, 1988, in Asheville, North Carolina.

2. The Ecosystem Conservation Group will consider the proposal and discuss the means to develop a strategy for managing selected endangered ecosystems in September 1988.

LITERATURE CITED

Brown, L. R., W. U. Chandler, C. Flavin, J. C. Pollock, S. Postel, L. Starks, and E. C. Wolf. 1986. State of the world, 1986: A Worldwatch Institute report on progress toward a sustainable society. W. W. Norton, New York and London. 263 p.

Brown, L. R., W. U. Chandler, C. Flavin, J. Jacobson, C. Pollock, S. Postel, L. Stark, and E. C. Wolf. 1987. State of the world, 1987: A Worldwatch Institute report on progress toward a sustainable society. W. W. Norton, New York and London. 268 p.

Food and Agriculture Organization. 1986. Reports of the Ecosystem Conservation Group, Working Group on Plant Genetic Resources. FAO, Rome.

Gilbert, V. C. 1986a. An approach to improving natural resource management in the southern Appalachian region: A draft proposal presented to U.S. MAB by V. C. Gilbert, Gatlinburg, Tennessee. 19 p.

——. 1986b. A proposal to the Ecosystem Conservation Group through U.S. MAB, December 1986. Washington, D.C.

Gilbert, V. C., and W. P. Gregg. 1981. Development of the Biosphere Reserve Network. Paper presented at the Thirty-second Annual Meeting of the American Institute of Biological Sciences. Indiana University, Bloomington.

McGean, B. A. 1986. Beyond borders: A look at bioregionalism. Nexus 8(4):1-12. Atlantic Center for Environment, Ipswich, Maine.

UNESCO. 1970. Use and conservation of the biosphere: Proceedings of the Intergovernmental Conference of Experts on the Scientific Basis for Rational Use and Conservation of the Resources of the Biosphere, September 1968. UNESCO, Paris. 272 p.

——. 1984. Action plan for biosphere reserves. Nature and Resources 20(4):1-12.

USAID. 1985. U.S. strategy on the conservation of biological diversity: An interagency task force report to Congress. USAID, Washington, D.C. 54 p.

U.S. Department of State. 1969. Bulletin: U.S. Department of State, December 1, 1969. Washington, D.C.

U.S. MAB. 1980. The United States Man and the Biosphere Program National Plan. U.S. Department of the Interior, Office of the Secretary, Memorandum to OMB and OSTP, November 13, 1980. Washington, D.C.

——. 1985. Ethnobotanical study of the Great Smoky Mountains Biosphere Reserve. Unpublished study, National Park Service, Washington, D.C.

——. 1986. Report of the U.S. MAB Project Directorate on Biosphere Reserves, Meeting of December 18-19, 1986. U.S. MAB, Department of State, Washington, D.C.

Weber, W. 1985. Le Parc National des Volcans Biosphere Reserve: Cooperation between conservation and development. Parks 10(3):19-21.

World Resources Institute. 1985. Tropical forests: A call for action. Part 1: The plan. World Resources Institute, Washington, D.C. 49 p.

12

U.S. Forest Service Wilderness Management: Challenge and Opportunity

STEPHEN P. MEALEY

ABSTRACT The National Wilderness Preservation System has evolved from the first wilderness preserve in 1919 to nearly 89 million acres in 1985. The Forest Service administers 83% of the wilderness system in the conterminous forty-eight states, where most future use is expected. The Wilderness Act of 1964 specifies that wilderness areas are to be administered for the use and enjoyment of the American people, and managed to protect and preserve wilderness qualities. Establishing acceptable levels of wilderness area naturalness and associated levels of human impact is a fundamental management problem. A user preference concept is proposed to assist in decision making. A working philosophy for implementing Forest Plans to preserve wilderness qualities while allowing human use incorporates the user preference concept. The Greater Yellowstone Area presents a unique challenge in administering the wilderness resource because some of its parts are in different jurisdictions. More than 60% of the Greater Yellowstone Area is designated or proposed as wilderness, and primary dependents are wildlife and recreationists. Management of the area to optimize conditions for human uses while preserving unique wilderness ecosystem resources is progressing through increasing interagency cooperation.

"A wilderness, in contrast with those areas where man and his own works dominate the landscape, is hereby recognized as an area where the earth and its community of life are untrammeled by man, where man himself is a visitor who does not remain" (Wilderness Act of 1964). In 1964 the U.S. Congress, through Public Law 88-577, established a National Wilderness Preservation System (NWPS) composed of federal lands. The purpose of the system was to ensure "that an increasing population, accompanied by expanding settlement and growing mechanization, does not occupy and modify all areas within the United States and its possessions, leaving no lands designated for preservation and protection in their natural condition." Congress's intent was that wilderness areas "shall be administered for the use and enjoyment of the American people in such manner as will leave them unimpaired for future use and enjoyment as wilderness."

By December 1985 there were nearly 89 million acres in the NWPS, 63% in Alaska and 42% administered by the National Park Service (Table 12-1). More than 32 million acres of wilderness are administered by the Forest Service, equaling nearly 18% of all national forest lands. Most future use of the NWPS is expected in the conterminous forty-eight states, where the Forest Service administers 83% of the wilderness. It is likely, therefore, that the major wilderness management challenges and opportunities will occur in those forty-eight states.

Table 12-1. Number of units and acreage, by federal administrative agency, within the National Wilderness Preservation System as of December 1985.

Administrative Agency*	Units	Acres**	Percentage of Total Acreage
Forest Service, USDA	329	32,238,056	36
National Park Service, USDI	37	36,754,980	42
Fish and Wildlife Service, USDI	70	19,332,891	22
Bureau of Land Management, USDI	20	368,739	
Grand total	456	88,694,666	100
LOWER FORTY-EIGHT STATES AND HAWAII			
Forest Service, USDA	315	26,784,690	83
National Park Service, USDI	29	4,399,980	14
Fish and Wildlife Service, USDI	49	656,571	2
Bureau of Land Management, USDI	20	368,739	1
Total	413	32,209,980	100
ALASKA			
Forest Service, USDA	14	5,453,366	10
National Park Service, USDI	8	32,355,000	57
Fish and Wildlife Service, USDI	21	18,676,320	33
Total	43	56,484,686	100

*Each unit of wilderness is counted under the agency administering the largest land area within that wilderness. Each agency's acreage is listed under the agency. Detailed breakdowns by wilderness within each state and agency jurisdiction can be found in the Annual Wilderness Report to Congress.

**Some acreage is estimated pending final map compilation.

Note: The national forest acreage added to NWPS since 1964 totals 23,275,240 acres (some acreage estimated pending final map compilation). This includes 275 new units, 69 additions, and 6 deletions to existing wilderness units.

This paper has three major objectives: (1) to sketch the history and management philosophy of the National Wilderness Preservation System, (2) to discuss the challenge of establishing acceptable levels of wilderness area naturalness and associated levels of human impacts, and opportunities to address that challenge through a working philosophy for implementing national forest plans, and (3) to discuss the challenge of maintaining resources and human uses that depend on wilderness having different jurisdictions, and opportunities to address that challenge through improved interagency cooperation.

The dictionary defines "wilderness" as a place or region that exists in a state of nature, uncultivated and undisturbed by human activity. Although it was home to the American Indians, virtually all of what is now the conterminous forty-eight states was wilderness when European explorers arrived in the sixteenth century. The wilderness was viewed as an impediment and threat by settlers who sought to develop the American hinterlands during the sixteenth, seventeenth, and eighteenth centuries. Between 1850 and 1880, settlement of most of the West was completed and wilderness and associated wildlife such as bison, elk, grizzly bears, and wolves were rapidly disappearing.

The middle to late nineteenth century saw the best expression of American Romanticism in literature and the arts. A new "cult of nature" arose; authors including Whitman, Emerson, and Thoreau and artists such as Bierstadt and Catlin celebrated the simplicity and beauty of unspoiled nature and the moral purity of those who chose to be close to it. Catlin and Thoreau decried the loss of buffalo and the primitive landscape and called for national preserves where both man and animals could share the "wild and freshness of nature's beauty" (Nash 1973).

Forest Service employees Arthur Carhart and Aldo Leopold were probably expressing the influence of these Romanticists when they, respectively, in 1919 and 1921, recommended that Trappers Lake in the White River National Forest, Colorado, be left undeveloped and that 574,000 acres of the Gila National Forest, New Mexico, be set aside as a reserve for wilderness recreation. Approval of these recommendations also probably reflected the growing influence of the Romantic "nature ethic" idea in the Forest Service as the country continued to grow and develop and wilderness continued to shrink. Certainly a broadening of management emphasis during the first three Forest Service administrations of Gifford Pinchot, Henry Graves, and William Greeley is apparent (Hendee et al. 1978). While Pinchot headed the Forest Service, technically from 1905 to 1910, the principal emphasis was on management of forests for their wood products. Between 1910 and 1920, Chief Graves placed increasing emphasis on the value of the national forests for recreation. Greeley, who became chief in 1920, increased the emphasis on national forest recreation. He was enthusiastic about wilderness reserves and in 1926 formulated a wilderness policy that included protection for campsites, meadows for pack-stock forage, and special scenic areas.

In 1929, the Forest Service L-20 Regulation established the first official system of wilderness reservations, called "primitive areas." The few areas that had been set aside earlier as "wilderness areas," such as the Gila in 1924, were renamed primitive areas. Between 1929 and 1939, the period the L-20 Regulation was in effect, the wilderness reserve system expanded to include 14.2 million acres in 75 areas. The L-20 Regulation required management plans, including lists of prohibited and permitted activities for designated areas. Virtually all the traditional commercial uses were still permissible, although L. F. Kneipp, Greeley's associate chief, stated in a letter to forest supervisors in 1930 that the concept of "primitive simplicity" should be used as a criterion for development decisions and that "primitive areas are for the class who seek almost absolute detachment from evidences of civilization" (Gilligan 1953, cited in Hendee et al. 1978).

The Forest Service U-Regulation replaced the L-20 Regulation in 1939. These more stringent rules tightened protection for the more than 14 million acres that existed in wilderness reservations by 1939 and remained in effect until passage of the Wilderness Act of 1964. The new rules did not allow roads, motorized transportation, lumbering, dwellings, or permanent camps. They also provided for the reclassification of primitive areas: areas exceeding 100,000 acres into wilderness; areas between 5,000 and 10,000 acres into wild areas; and natural areas, primarily managed for recreation without roads, into roadless areas.

The L-20 Regulation and U-Regulation were administrative directives and were implemented at the discretion of the secretary of agriculture or the Forest Service chief. In 1962 the Wildland Research Center, in a report to the Outdoor Recreation Resources Review Commission, recommended enactment of legislation creating a wilderness preservation system protected by law (Hendee et al. 1978). The recommendation was based on the belief that the existing system was vulnerable to erosion resulting from increasing competition for public land resources. This viewpoint was shared by Howard Zahniser, executive director of the Wilderness Society, who sought a "persisting program" of wilderness preservation, "a cohesive program that would eliminate the need for continual, fragmented holding actions against various threats" (Hendee et al. 1978).

After many years of deliberation, Congress enacted the Wilderness Act in 1964. The act established a National Wilderness Policy and a definition of wilderness; it described the extent of the system and discussed appropriate use of wilderness, including prohibited uses and special provisions. The act established an "instant" wilderness system by including all those lands administered by the Forest Service as wilderness, wild, roadless, or canoe areas prior to 1964. This amounted to 9.1 million acres in fifty-four areas. No Department of Interior lands were initially included. The act also directed the secretaries of agriculture and interior to review certain lands within their respective jurisdictions and to make recommendations to the President, within ten years of the passage of the act, regarding the suitability of considered lands as wilderness. Lands specifically targeted for review by the Forest Service were the 5.4 million acres in the thirty-four remaining "primitive areas." Although not specifically directed to do so by the act, the Forest Service also included in its review for wilderness suitability the roadless and undeveloped areas lacking explicit classification. Lands targeted for review in the Department of Interior were all roadless areas in the National Park System and the national wildlife refuges and game ranges in excess of 5,000 acres as well as roadless islands.

The Wilderness Act did not provide the quantity and quality of wilderness many expected in the eastern United States (east of the 100th meridian). Few areas in the East appeared to qualify under the 1964 act. Consequently in 1975, Congress passed the Eastern Wilderness Act, which provided more lenient admission criteria. This act designated sixteen areas containing 207,000 acres of national forest land as wilderness. Seventeen areas totaling 125,000 acres were designated for review. As of December 1985, more than 23 million acres of national forest land had been added to the NWPS since 1964, representing an increase of more than 2.5 times the original contribution (Table 12-1).

A WORKING PHILOSOPHY FOR IMPLEMENTING NATIONAL FOREST PLANS

In their purest senses, the concepts of wilderness and management conflict. Wilderness implies the absence of human control, while management implies its presence. Section 2(a) of the Wilderness Act of 1964 states: "wilderness areas . . . shall be administered for the use and enjoyment of the American people in such manner as will leave them unimpaired for future use and enjoyment as wilderness, and so as to provide for the protection of these areas, the preservation of their wilderness character, and for the gathering and dissemination of information regarding their use and enjoyment as wilderness. . . ." Section 2(c) defines wilderness: "A wilderness, in contrast with those areas where man and his own works dominate the landscape, is hereby recognized as an area where the earth and its community of life are untrammeled by man, where man himself is a visitor who does not remain. An area of wilderness is further defined to mean . . . an area of undeveloped Federal land retaining its primeval character and influence, without permanent improvements or human habitation, which is protected and managed so as to preserve its natural conditions and which (1) generally appears to have been affected primarily by the forces of nature, with the imprint of man's work substantially unnoticeable; (2) has outstanding opportunities for solitude or a primitive and unconfined type of recreation. . . ."

In Figure 12-1, wilderness is characterized by its two major prescribed impacts: human use and enjoyment, and administration, protection, and management. Both impacts have the capacity to destroy wilderness: it can be "loved to death" by the former and "regulated to death" by the latter. The unstated congressional challenge to federal managers appears to be: provide the highest possible wilderness quality with the least possible human interference or restraint. This has been a difficult challenge, with critics arguing managers are either "too lenient or permissive" or "too pure" in meeting Congress's intent. The clear management challenge is to determine and then provide, for each particular wilderness area, levels of naturalness and human use and enjoyment which maintain the highest wilderness quality possible with the least possible human interference. Acceptable solutions will represent optimal levels for both naturalness and human use rather than maximums for either.

WILDERNESS:
TO BE ADMINISTERED,
PROTECTED,
AND MANAGED

WILDERNESS:
TO BE USED AND ENJOYED
BY HUMANS

REQUIRED RESULTS

1. Untrammeled by man
2. Retains primeval character
3. No permanent improvements or human habitation
4. Protected and managed so as to preserve its natural condition

5. Imprint of man's work substantially unnoticeable
6. Outstanding opportunities for solitude or a primitive and unconfined type of recreation

Figure 12-1. The Wilderness Act provides for public use and enjoyment within the constraint of the preservation of the areas as wilderness. Administration and management must ensure that use and enjoyment are consistent with preservation; however, management should not be inconsistent with solitude and an unconfined type of recreation.

National Direction

The general Forest Service approach to the challenge of acceptable naturalness and use was publicized in "A Colloquy between Congressman Weaver and Assistant Secretary Cutler," which appeared in the *Journal of Forestry* (Cutler and Weaver 1977). Cutler summarized the Department of Agriculture's major wilderness management objectives: "(1) Maintain an enduring system of high-quality wilderness. (2) Perpetuate the wilderness resources. (3) Consistent with these first two, provide opportunities for public use, enjoyment, and understanding of wildernesses and the unique experiences dependent upon a wilderness setting. (4) Maintain plants and animals indigenous to the area. (5) Accommodate and administer those 'nonconforming, but excepted' [accepted] uses provided in the act in a way to minimize their impacts. (6) Maintain stable watersheds. (7) Consider protection needs for endangered species and their habitats."

Cutler also stated that Forest Service wilderness management actions are guided by the basic principles embraced by the following questions: "(1) Is it necessary to protect the resource and manage the use? (2) Is it the minimum action or facility required to accomplish the objective? (3) Does it protect the wilderness values? (4) Does it pass a test of reason and common sense?"

Forest Service Chief R. Max Peterson, in remarks commemorating the twentieth anniversary of the Wilderness Act (Peterson 1985), elaborated five Forest Service wilderness management principles: "(1) Allow natural processes to operate freely. (2) Maintain outstanding opportunities for solitude. (3) Do necessary management work without motorized or mechanized equipment whenever possible. (4) Gather scientific information without the intrusion of permanent improvements or motorized use. (5) Manage special exceptions provided in wilderness bills for individual areas, while protecting wilderness values."

Official Forest Service wilderness management objectives and policy are listed in the *Forest Service Manual* (FSM) (USDA Forest Service 1986a). Essentially, they restate principles and objectives presented by Cutler and Peterson. Appeal decisions in 1986 by Chief Peterson related to outfitter camps in the Frank Church-River of No Return Wilderness, and Associate Deputy Chief Henson related to competitive events in the Granite Chief Wilderness, give further definition of the Forest Service approach to wilderness management. Other relatively recent decisions, related to motorized equipment in Alaska, EPA's request to use helicopters to routinely take lake samples, and installation of new weather stations, provide additional insight. The general approach in all the decisions was a rigorous application of the four questions stated by Cutler concerning necessity, minimum action, protection, and common sense. Most aspects of the proposals, generally made by single-interest proponents, failed to meet the tests and were rejected. Cost, convenience, and commercial values were not considerations in the decisions.

A wilderness management model (Figure 12-2) illustrates the basis for Forest Service wilderness management direction: "Manage wilderness toward attaining the highest level of purity in wilderness within legal constraints." The legal constraints refer to providing for human use and enjoyment, including opportunities for solitude or a primitive and unconfined type of recreation. The definition of wilderness in the act and the conditions defined by the appeal decisions help describe the lower boundary of "legal wilderness" (USDA Forest Service 1986a).

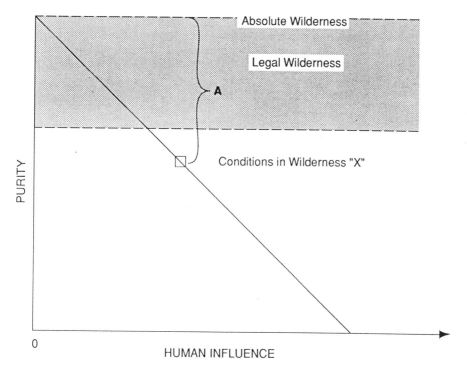

Figure 12-2. The Forest Service wilderness management model shows the relation between the natural, undisturbed purity of a wilderness area and human influence. The more human influence, the lower the purity of wilderness. The number and intensity of human influences cause a gap between the attainable legislative wilderness and the conditions that exist on a wilderness ("X"). The goal of wilderness management is to identify these influences, define their causes, remedy them, and close the gap ("A") between the attainable level of purity and the level that exists on each wilderness ("X") (USDA Forest Service 1986a).

The Purity Issue

In 1977, Senator Frank Church of Idaho, Senate floor manager of the Wilderness Act of 1964 and former chairman of the Senate Public Lands Subcommittee that had the oversight responsibility for wilderness, expressed his concern on the purity question (Church 1977):

> Time after time, when we discuss wilderness, questions are raised about how developed an area can be and still qualify as wilderness, or what kind of activities within a wilderness area are consistent with the purposes of the Wilderness Act. I believe, and many citizens agree with me, that the agencies are applying provisions of the Wilderness Act too strictly, and thus misconstruing the intent of Congress as to how these areas should be managed. It was *not* the intent of Congress that wilderness be administered in so pure a fashion as to needlessly restrict their customary public use and enjoyment. Quite to the contrary, Congress fully intended that wilderness should be managed to allow its use by a wide spectrum of Americans.

> There is a need for a rule of reason in interpreting the Act, of course, because wilderness values are to be protected. As I stated in 1972, while chairing an oversight hearing of the Subcommittee on Public Lands: ". . . The Wilderness Act was not deliberately contrived to hamstring reasonable and necessary management activities. We intend to permit the managing agencies

... latitude ... where the purpose is to protect the wilderness, its resources and the public visitors within the area.... [including, for example] minimum sanitation facilities ... fire protection necessities ... [and] the development of potable water supplies.... The issue is not whether necessary management facilities are prohibited; they are not. The test is whether they are necessary."

Thus, the wilderness management framework intended by Congress was for the agencies to do only what is *necessary*. The facilities just mentioned may be required—and restrictions on use may sometimes be needed to protect especially fragile locations. But in adopting regulations, common sense is required.

In summary, if purity is to be an issue in the management of wilderness, let it focus on preserving the natural integrity of the wilderness environment—and not needless restriction of facilities necessary to protect the area while providing for human use and enjoyment.

In essence, Senator Church affirmed the use of the four-question test of necessity, minimum action, protection, and common sense. He emphasized, however, the importance of human use and enjoyment in determining necessity as related to proposed facilities. Church saw the necessity question as: Is the facility necessary to protect the area while providing for human use and enjoyment? Clearly the necessity question cannot be answered without well-defined thresholds or minimum standards related at least to Peterson's five principles listed above, to be maintained for wilderness resources and, within those, well-defined levels for human use and enjoyment.

Forest Plans

The development of minimum standards for acceptable naturalness and use to protect and manage the wilderness resource is a part of the forest planning process. The National Forest Management Act of 1976 (Public Law 94-588) requires that each national forest develop, adopt, and revise land and resource management plans that guide all natural resource management activities, including those affecting the wilderness resource. Plans determine resource management practices, levels of production and management, and the availability and suitability of lands for resource management. Forest planning direction for wilderness management is stated in the Code of Federal Regulations at 36 CFR 219.18. Plans must provide direction for the management of wilderness—in particular for limiting and distributing visitor use in accordance with periodic estimates of social and physical carrying capacity—and evaluate the extent to which wildfire, and insect and disease control, may be desirable for protection of wilderness and adjacent areas. In addition, plans must ensure that natural ecological succession will be allowed to operate freely to the extent feasible (36 CFR 293.2); they must also recognize that the national forests are ecosystems and their management for goods and services requires an awareness and consideration of the interrelationships among plants, animals, soil, water, air, and other factors in the ecosystem (36 CFR 219.1(b)(3)).

The Shoshone Forest Plan (USDA Forest Service 1986b,c) contains wilderness management requirements in general forest direction which set baseline conditions that must be provided while meeting the intent of all management prescriptions. For example, a strong emphasis is placed on the free operation of natural ecological succession where plant and animal communities change over time without human interference unless legally mandated. The natural role of wildfire is recognized, and most natural fires are allowed to burn to predetermined natural barriers. A requirement for domestic livestock grazing is that riparian areas lacking firm, dry surfaces must be protected from livestock use. These management requirements can be understood as thresholds or minimum standards which describe the lower boundary of "legal wilderness" (Figure 12-2).

In addition to the minimum standards, there are three general management prescriptions for the approximate 1.4 million acres of wilderness. Prescriptions provide for pristine, primitive, and semiprimitive wilderness opportunities. An example: for semiprimitive wilderness, the intent of dispersed recreation management is to allow moderate to high contact among or between groups and individuals during summer. The maximum use and capacity level allows no more than nine trail and camp encounters per day with other parties during peak use days. These prescriptions specify conditions at different points within legal wilderness (Figure 12-2).

Forest Plan Implementation

Management prescriptions include statements of intent and lists of proposed and probable practices scheduled for implementation. Before any practices are applied, the following site-specific environmental analyses must be carried out: (1) internal and external identification of issues and concerns; (2) comparison of these issues and concerns with those already addressed in the Forest Plan and the environmental impact statement (EIS); (3) new environmental analyses for issues and concerns not dealt with in the Forest Plan and the EIS; (4) evaluation of the adequacy of existing analyses and disclosures for issues and concerns dealt with in the Forest Plan and the EIS; (5) disclo-sure in a Categorical Exclusion, Environmental Assessment, or EIS of site-specific and cumulative effects determined through new analyses; and (6) revision or amendment of the Forest Plan if decisions resulting from site-specific analyses differ from plan direction.

Thus management intent must be validated site specifically before any practices are applied. This includes validating minimum standards of wilderness quality for naturalness of biophysical components (soil, water, air, vegetation, and nonhuman animals), ecological succession, social considerations (opportunities for solitude and unconfined recreation), and other legal considerations. Other important wilderness planning decisions that require validation are shown in Figure 12-3. They include whether to (1) reduce human impacts to allow area naturalness to increase to at least legal limits, (2) decrease human impacts to allow area naturalness to exceed minimum standards, or (3) increase human impacts to levels causing area naturalness to decrease to minimum standards.

Once the relevance of minimum standards to a particular area has been determined, validation for biophysical components is, in general, a straightforward process relying on laws, regulations, and accepted professional methods. Reduction of human impact levels to allow the restoration of biophysical components to minimum conditions is also fairly straightforward. Nonlegal biophysical conditions can be monitored and the progress of component recovery to legal limits documented. However, the questions of improving area naturalness above minimum standards and of allowing naturalness to degrade to minimum standards are not as simple. Neither are questions involving validation of minimum standards for opportunities for solitude and alternative opportunities for solitude and unconfined recreation.

One way to approach these more difficult tasks is to examine some theoretical relationships between area naturalness, management control, and human enjoyment. The relationship between area naturalness and human enjoyment is direct (Figure 12-3).

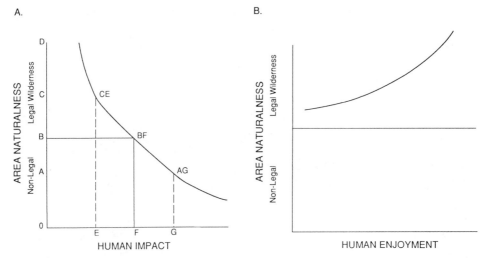

Figure 12-3. *Left* (A): The general relationship between wilderness area naturalness and human impacts is assumed to be inverse; naturalness decreases as human impacts increase. Legal wilderness exists only above line B-BF. Four primary tasks in wilderness management are (1) describing and validating minimum standards of wilderness quality (B-BF); (2) reducing human impacts from G to at least F; (3) deciding whether to move human impacts from F toward 0; and (4) deciding whether to move human impacts E toward F. *Right* (B): The general relationship between area naturalness and human enjoyment is assumed to be direct. Human enjoyment increases as an area's naturalness increases.

Human enjoyment increases as an area's naturalness increases. Management control is assumed to increase the physical naturalness of an area (Figure 12-4). But human enjoyment decreases as management control increases. Naturalness and enjoyment are both legal mandates, and any level of naturalness within legal wilderness is, by definition, acceptable, notwithstanding the nondegradation concept (Hendee et al. 1978). Within legal wilderness, alternative levels of naturalness, and control to achieve them, are functions of the different user perceived benefits and costs, in terms of enjoyment gained or lost, attributable to increased naturalness and control (Figure 12-5). Such benefits and costs are most likely to be accurately determined by managers through surveys of user preferences.

Since naturalness and enjoyment are mandated in wilderness, and any level of them within legal wilderness is acceptable, appropriate levels should reflect collective user preferences based on trade-offs between desire for naturalness and dislike of control. Because naturalness is gained through management control, decisions reflect comparisons between the amount of enjoyment gained as naturalness increases and the amount of enjoyment lost as control increases. In deciding to decrease human impacts to levels permitting area naturalness to exceed minimum standards, the critical question of users is: How much management control (confined type of recreation) are you willing to tolerate for a given increase in naturalness? In deciding to allow human impacts to increase to levels causing naturalness to decrease to minimum standards, the question is: How much naturalness are you willing to give up for a given decrease in control? In all cases, the deciding information should be the individual and collective preferences of users. Final-

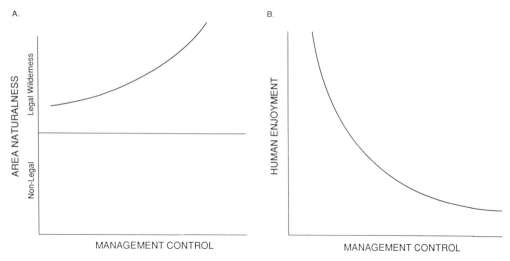

Figure 12-4. *Left* (A): The general relationship between area naturalness and management control is assumed to be direct. Management control increases the physical naturalness of an area. *Right* (B): The general relationship between human enjoyment and management control is assumed to be inverse. As management control of an area increases, human enjoyment, at least the part resulting from an unconfined type of recreation, decreases. The graph does not go to zero for human enjoyment because opportunities for solitude and naturalness, also components of enjoyment, exist.

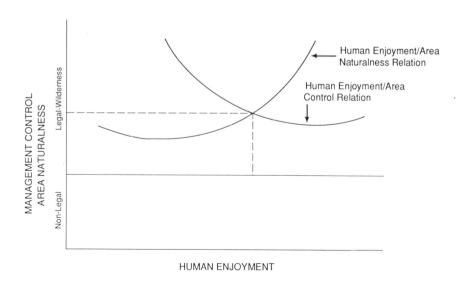

Figure 12-5. Human enjoyment increases as area naturalness increases, and decreases as management control increases. As seen in Figure 12-4, naturalness increases as control increases. Naturalness and enjoyment are both legal mandates. But any level of naturalness within legal wilderness is, by definition, acceptable. The level of naturalness and the degree of control to achieve it are therefore functions of the benefit (amount of enjoyment gained) from increased naturalness and cost (amount of enjoyment lost) attributable to increased control. Appropriate levels are optimums rather than maximums and are likely to be accurately determined only through user preference surveys.

ly, collective user preference is fundamental to defining minimum standards for opportunities of solitude, qualified by tolerance limits of biophysical components.

Applying the perspective of management decisions based on user preference to the necessity question discussed above in relation to the "purity issue" permits some refinements in the management process which could avoid "overpure" management decisions without compromising "legal" wilderness. As indicated, Senator Church saw the necessity question as: Is the facility necessary to protect the area while providing for use and enjoyment? That question can be refined: Is the facility or tool necessary to protect the area's naturalness at the minimum standards level while providing for human use and enjoyment as defined by user preference? Such an approach could increase options for management responses to predictable increases in use demands without compromising fundamental wilderness values. It should also provide the highest possible wilderness quality with the least possible amount of human restraint.

This discussion can be summarized as a working philosophy for implementing a Forest Plan, with philosophy defined as a system of rules for dealing with practical affairs. The following simple working rules for plan implementation can assist in establishing acceptable levels of naturalness and human impacts: (1) The Forest Plan intent is implemented through site-specific environmental analyses. (2) Analyses must validate minimum management standards for biophysical components, and social and legal considerations. (3) All human impacts must conform at least to validated minimum management standards. Alternative, acceptable impact levels are defined by collective user preference. (4) User preference is determined during the public involvement phase of environmental analysis.

If the theoretical analysis of human enjoyment benefits and costs related to naturalness, and management control, is valid, it is apparent that user preference information is absolutely vital to effective wilderness management. Perhaps effective public involvement, including user preference determination, is more important to quality wilderness management than to any other aspect of multiple-use management.

INTERAGENCY COOPERATION

Ecologically, the Shoshone National Forest is part of, and dependent on, the much larger Greater Yellowstone Area (GYA) (Figure 12-6) which covers an area of approximately 10 million acres centered around Yellowstone National Park in northwestern Wyoming and adjacent parts of Idaho and Montana. The maintenance of acceptable levels of Shoshone wilderness area naturalness and associated human impacts, especially the maintenance of the free operation of natural ecological succession in Shoshone wildernesses, depends on the ecological condition of adjacent lands. This is especially true since grizzly bears (*Ursus arctos*) and elk (*Cervus elaphus*), dominant Shoshone wilderness wildlife species, require much of the GYA as habitat (Figures 12-7 and 12-8).

The GYA lacks precise boundaries for policy, administrative, or management purposes; rather it is loosely defined by the area's biogeographic components. National forest land makes up about 80% of the area, with national park land the balance. Ten administrative units share principal land management responsibilities. These include: Beaverhead, Bridger-Teton, Custer, Gallatin, Shoshone, and Targhee national forests, Grand Teton and Yellowstone national parks, the National Elk Refuge, and Red Rocks

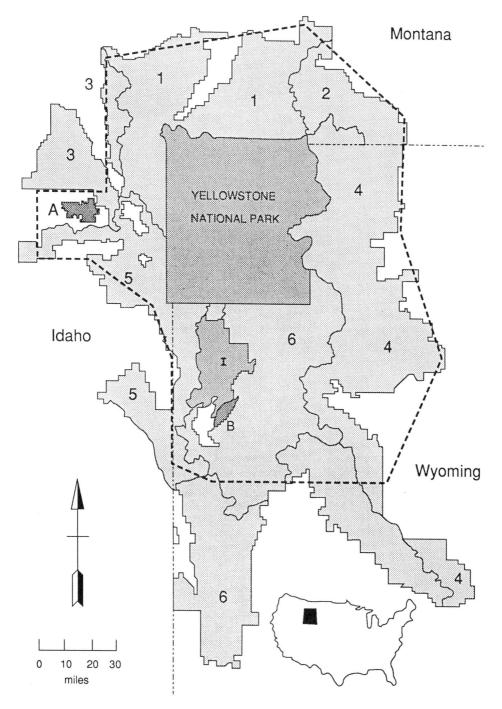

Figure 12-6. Administrative units in the Greater Yellowstone Area. National park: I = Grand Teton. National forests: 1 = Gallatin, 2 = Custer, 3 = Beaverhead, 4 = Shoshone, 5 = Targhee, 6 = Bridger-Teton. National wildlife refuges: A = Red Rocks Lake, B = Elk.

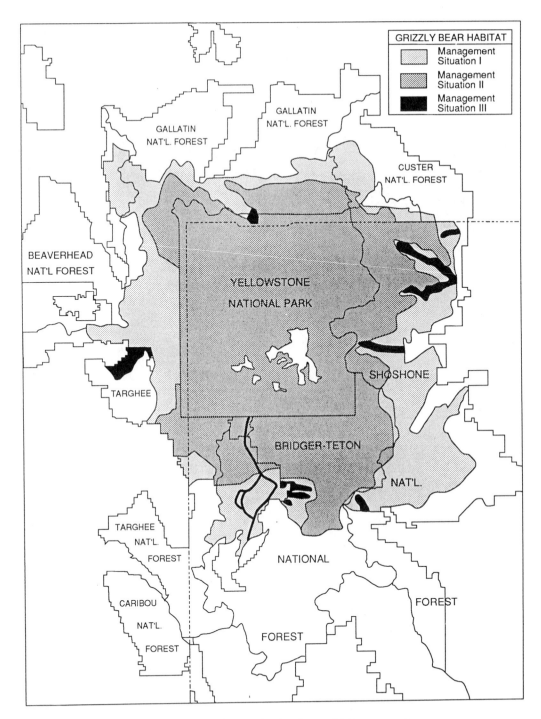

Figure 12-7. Grizzly bear habitat stratification in the Greater Yellowstone Area.

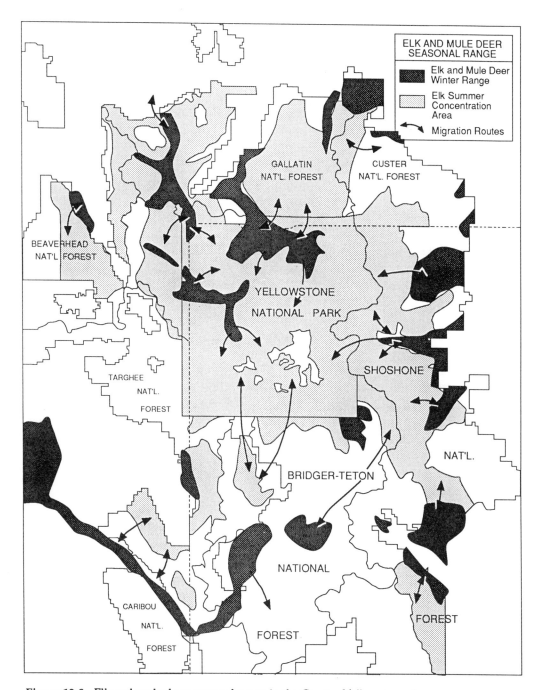

ELK AND MULE DEER SEASONAL RANGE

- Elk and Mule Deer Winter Range
- Elk Summer Concentration Area
- Migration Routes

GALLATIN NAT'L. FOREST

CUSTER NAT'L. FOREST

BEAVERHEAD NAT'L FOREST

YELLOWSTONE NATIONAL PARK

TARGHEE NAT'L. FOREST

SHOSHONE

NAT'L.

BRIDGER-TETON

CARIBOU NAT'L. FOREST

NATIONAL

FOREST

FOREST

Figure 12-8. Elk and mule deer seasonal range in the Greater Yellowstone Area.

Lakes Wildlife Refuge. Maintenance of wilderness-dependent resources and human uses in this ecological "commons" depends on successful interagency cooperation.

Background

The area known generically as Yellowstone was the birthplace for both the national parks and national forests and was the wellspring of the American conservation movement. William Henry Jackson, Thomas Moran, Arnold Hague, Theodore Roosevelt, George Bird Grinnell, Bernhard Fernow, and Gifford Pinchot were some of the visionaries of the American conservation movement who were inspired by the special values of the area and whose arguments shaped early conservation thought. That thought led to the establishment of Yellowstone National Park in 1872, the Yellowstone Park Timberland Reserve in 1891, and other forest reserves.

Since their inception, national forests and national parks have been managed differently, as specified in the original congressional mandates. National parks were founded on the principles of preservation, public enjoyment, and noninterference with natural processes. Therefore, logging, mining, hunting, livestock grazing, wildlife habitat improvement, fire control, and other development activities are limited or banned. Some exceptions exist, such as hunting in portions of Grand Teton National Park. While national parks were founded on preservation principles, national forests were established on conservation principles—the wise use of natural resources. Congress has mandated that the forests be managed for multiple uses of recreation, wildlife, grazing, mining, watershed, timber, and wilderness.

The different missions specified by Congress are reflected in how parks and forests within the GYA have historically been managed and how they are planned for future management. Timber harvest, livestock grazing, mining, mineral leasing, watershed improvement, and wildlife habitat improvement are standard activities in national forests. A large acreage of congressionally designated wilderness within the national forests is managed in accordance with the Wilderness Act. National parks, on the other hand, are withdrawn from mineral development, timber harvest is not permitted, and watershed and wildlife habitat modification projects are generally not undertaken. Some livestock grazing and hunting is allowed in Grand Teton National Park, but these activities are strictly limited in scope and location. National parks are also subject to the provisions of the Wilderness Act, and although no congressionally designated wilderness exists in Yellowstone or Grand Teton National Park, large areas are recommended. Fishing, hiking, camping, and motorized use occur in both parks and forests. These uses are generally more restricted in parks.

Table 12-2 summarizes the status of wilderness, recommended wilderness or wilderness study, and undeveloped areas in the GYA. Of the total area, 36% is currently designated wilderness and an additional 25% is proposed for wilderness or wilderness study; so 61% is being managed either as wilderness or to preserve wilderness characteristics. Land status and agency boundary relationships are shown in Figure 12-9.

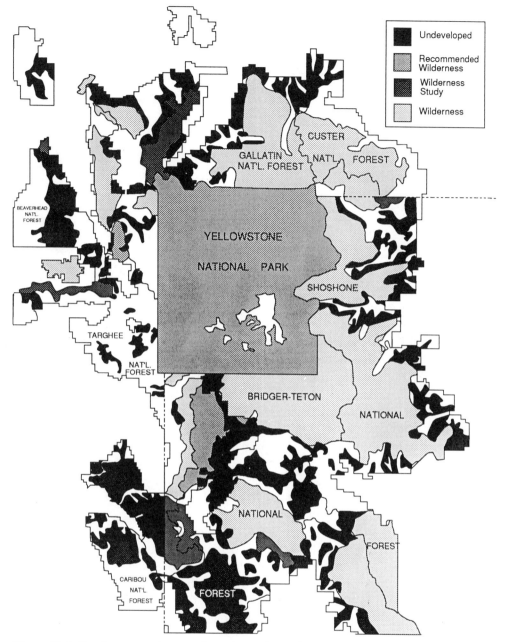

Figure 12-9. Land status and agency boundary relationships showing wilderness, recommended wilderness, wilderness study, and undeveloped areas in the Greater Yellowstone Area.

Table 12-2. Wilderness, recommended wilderness or wilderness study, and undeveloped areas in the Greater Yellowstone Area in 1987 (thousands of acres).

Unit	Wilderness	Proposed Wilderness or Wilderness Study	Undeveloped Areas
Beaverhead NF	101.4	4.5	211.6
Bridger-Teton NF	1,019.2	165.8	1,004.5
Custer NF	339.8	5.0	
Gallatin NF	716.0	126.9	379.0
Shoshone NF	1,277.1	43.5	432.5
Targhee NF	132.0	114.8	474.1
Grand Teton NP		156.0	114.3
Yellowstone NP		1,963.0	
National Elk Refuge			24.3
Red Rock Lakes Wildlife Refuge	32.4		7.8
Total	3,617.9	2,579.5	2,648.1

Wilderness Dependency

With more than 60% of the GYA designated as wilderness or proposed for wilderness, the obvious dependents are wildlife and recreationists. Table 12-3 shows total visitor use of Yellowstone Park for 1984, 1985, and 1986. The magnitude of visitor use is great. The importance of the interdependence of different jurisdictional areas within the GYA is emphasized by the fact that it is virtually impossible to enter Yellowstone Park without traveling through or adjacent to a national forest.

Dispersed recreation wilderness users are only a small fraction of total GYA visitors. But the interrelations among different areas are no less important, since many wilderness visitors follow routes through more than one national forest and national park. These interrelations are particularly important to the outfitting industry. The "dude ranch" industry had its beginning in the GYA, and the area remains a stronghold of the industry. Modern summer pack trips and fall big-game hunting trips typically include visits to more than one national forest and national park. Virtually all trips occur in designated wilderness or areas managed to preserve wilderness qualities.

Figure 12-7 and Table 12-4 show the habitat of the grizzly bear and bald eagle (*Haliaeetus leucocephalus*) respectively, two federally listed threatened and endangered species protected by the Endangered Species Act (Public Law 93-205). The important habitat for these species is distributed throughout the GYA. More than 40% of the GYA is needed for the survival and recovery of grizzly bears and is delineated and managed

Table 12-3. Yellowstone National Park recreation visitors for 1984, 1985, and 1986.

	1984 Visitors	1985 Visitors	Percent Change	1986 Visitors	Percent Change
May	127,555	159,597	25.1	147,767	−7.4
June	585,998	643,879	9.9	671,973	4.4
July	667,307	648,994	−2.7	663,295	2.2
August	586,631	572,352	−2.4	614,295	7.3
September	287,141	261,850	−8.8	295,089	12.7
Total	2,254,632	2,286,672	1.4	2,392,419	4.6

Table 12-4. Bald eagle nesting and winter habitat in the Greater Yellowstone Area 1987.

Unit	Occupied Nests	Acres (1,000) Nesting Habitat	Acres (1,000) Winter Habitat
Beaverhead NF	3	2.0	0.2
Bridger-Teton NF	3	1.0	1.0
Custer NF			
Gallatin NF	3	1.0	0.3
Shoshone NF			0.4
Targhee NF	8	3.3	1.1
Grand Teton NP	6	2.0	2.7
Yellowstone NP	15	15.4	5.0
National Elk Refuge			2.4
Red Rock Lakes Wildlife Refuge		0.6	0.1
Total	38	25.3	13.2

Table 12-5. Grizzly bear habitat delineations* in the Greater Yellowstone Area in 1987 (thousands of acres).

Unit	Situation I	Situation II	Situation III
Beaverhead NF			
Bridger-Teton NF	665.5	61.5	7.1
Custer NF	5.5	105.0	
Gallatin NF	450.2	386.0	1.1
Shoshone NF	412.0	819.6	17.4
Targhee NF	180.5	266.5	54.0
Grand Teton NP	118.4	212.7	2.6
Yellowstone NP	2,219.4	2.3	0.1
National Elk Refuge			
Red Rock Lakes Wildlife Refuge			
Total	4,051.5	1,853.6	82.3

*The grizzly bear is listed as a threatened species under the Endangered Species Act. Grizzly bear habitat is stratified into different "management situations." Habitat components, bear use, and presence of other uses or activities are the factors that determine the particular management situation for grizzly bear habitat. *Management Situation I:* These areas contain grizzly population centers and habitat components needed for survival and recovery of the species. Grizzly habitat and improvement receive the highest management priority. *Management Situation II:* Current information indicates that areas lack distinct grizzly population centers, and highly suitable habitat does not generally occur. However, some grizzly habitat components exist and grizzlies may occasionally be present. Habitat is either unnecessary for grizzly survival or recovery or the need has not yet been determined, but habitat may be necessary. The status of such areas is subject to review and change according to demonstrated grizzly population and habitat needs. *Management Situation III:* Grizzly presence is possible but infrequent. Developments such as campgrounds, resorts, or other areas for human use result in conditions that make grizzly presence untenable for humans and/or grizzlies.

to give the grizzly highest use priority (Table 12-5). Elk and mule deer (*Odocoileus hemionus*) also have large space requirements to accommodate their summer and winter needs; they use much of the area as shown in Figure 12-8.

Past Coordination

In view of the different missions of the Forest Service and National Park Service and the complex dependencies of recreationists and wildlife on areas delineated or proposed as wilderness in the GYA, it is not surprising that managing the contiguous areas in forests and parks has required extra coordination effort. In the early 1960s the forest and park managers recognized the need and organized the Greater Yellowstone Coordinating Committee (GYCC). The GYCC consisted of the regional directors of the Intermountain, Northern, and Rocky Mountain regions of the Forest Service; the regional director of the Rocky Mountain Region of the National Park Service; the forest supervisors of the Beaverhead, Custer, Gallatin, Shoshone, Targhee, and Bridger-Teton national forests; and superintendents of the Grand Teton and Yellowstone national parks. These managers met twice each year to discuss coordination needs and to agree on actions and activities to improve coordination. The original purpose of the GYCC was to identify and resolve priority coordination needs.

One of the most pressing early needs related to outfitter use. A coordinated policy was needed to provide consistent expectations among managers and consistent performance among outfitters. The result was the Greater Yellowstone Area Outfitter Policy (USDI and USDA 1985). The current revision, implemented June 1985, developed in consultation with the outfitting industry, states policy for application and award of use permits, permit preparation, conditions of use, permit administration, special operating procedures (emphasizing wilderness practices), special requirements for individual national forests and parks and other special provisions such as standards for handling, storage, and disposal of grizzly bear attractants in grizzly bear habitat.

Another relatively early need was to provide uniform policy and procedures for managing grizzly bears and their habitat. With the classification of the species as threatened in 1975 came the responsibility of federal agencies to conserve the species and its critical habitat. This was by necessity a shared responsibility since the species requires, as has been seen, much of the GYA as habitat. In 1978, interagency grizzly management guidelines for the GYA were approved by GYA managers. The guidelines provided uniform policies and procedures for all management activities affecting grizzlies. The guidelines (Interagency Grizzly Bear Committee 1986) were revised and reissued in 1986. Principal coordination responsibility for grizzly bear management shifted from the GYCC when the Interagency Grizzly Bear Committee Committee (IGBC), a broader based, more highly focused coordinating group, was formed in 1984. Other cooperative efforts, coordinated through the GYCC, were the Greater Yellowstone Elk Working Group, the Jackson Hole Elk Studies Group, and the Greater Yellowstone Eagle Working Group. The Yellowstone Ecosystem Grizzly Bear Subcommittee (YEGBSC), a subcommittee of the IGBC, has coordinated the preparation of a cumulative effects model for the grizzly bear in the GYA. The model permits the assessment of overall effects on the Yellowstone grizzly population of activities occurring throughout the GYA.

Most cooperative GYCC efforts involving wildlife have been formalized through a Memorandum of Understanding (MOU) or a Cooperative Agreement including all parties, most particularly state wildlife management agencies. In general, GYCC efforts appear successful. Since 1974, the Northern Yellowstone Elk Herd has quadrupled, the Yellowstone cutthroat trout population has increased an order of magnitude, the GYA bald eagle population has doubled, and the Yellowstone grizzly population appears to be approaching biological carrying capacity (Mealey and Varley, in prep.).

Present Coordination

In 1985, GYCC members recognized that past efforts had been primarily reactive; that is, no action had been taken before a coordination problem had emerged. The result had been a preoccupation with a few major issues such as outfitter policy, grizzly bear recovery, and elk management. GYCC members were concerned that continued reactive coordination could neglect other potential problems which could risk important GYA values.

To stimulate a new approach to coordination, the GYCC aggregated the management plans for the national forests and parks in the GYA to illustrate the degree of commonality and interrelationship of national forest and national park management (Greater Yellowstone Coordinating Committee 1987). The aggregation displays the condition and extent of resources and management activities within the GYA and illustrates the likely future condition of GYA resources as management plans are applied through the year 2000. Major purposes are to facilitate public understanding and to develop a comprehensive tool to aid in coordinated resource management problem identification and resolution. The principal method of disclosure is map displays (Table 12-6).

The importance of the aggregation effort for wilderness management in the GYA cannot be overstated. Since over 60% of the area is virtually wilderness, the aggregation amounts to a major, although low resolution, inventory of wilderness resources. The effort represents a significant opportunity to identify vital ecological relationships, challenges to maintaining such relationships, and opportunities to meet challenges through improved interagency cooperation.

A second initiative taken by the GYCC to improve its coordination efforts was the signing in 1986 of an MOU for coordination of management in the GYA. The MOU between the Rocky Mountain Region of the National Park Service and the Northern, Rocky Mountain, and Intermountain regions of the Forest Service formalizes the mutual commitment to cooperate and coordinate in all aspects of management where resources and management effects are shared.

Future Coordination

As with most scarce, high quality entities, the GYA with its vast, unique wilderness is likely to become more valuable with time. The sensitive, fragile qualities of wilderness components, primarily wildlife, fish, and geophysical features, will, at the same time, probably become more vulnerable to negative influences. Those influences are more and more likely to become international and global, and include world population pressure and consequences of disrupted global chemical cycles. As Worldwatch Institute President Lester R. Brown and researcher Sandra Postel write: "our relationship with the earth and its natural systems is changing, often in ways we do not understand. The scale of human activities threatens the habitability of the earth itself. A sustainable society satisfies its needs without diminishing the prospects of the next generation. But by many measures, contemporary society fails to meet this criterion" (Brown et al. 1987).

In order to leave GYA wilderness "unimpaired for future use and enjoyment as wilderness," in light of potential new and unexpected threats, coordinated and cooperative management must become thoroughly committed to establishing baseline data that describe critical wilderness components accurately. Commitment should also be made to monitoring critical resource conditions, particularly air and water quality, and broadening cooperative management compacts to include entities that can enhance or

Table 12-6. List of maps for the aggregation of national forest and park plans displaying condition and extent of resources and activities and future condition of resources in the Greater Yellowstone Area through the year 2000.

Number	Title
1	Land Ownership
2	Geology
3	Areas with High Potential for Mass Movement and Highly Erodible Soils
4	Groundwater Aquifer Recharge Areas
5	Riparian Areas
6	Seismic Activity, 1975-1985
7	Vegetation Classification
8	Mountain Pine Beetle Infestation—Present
9	Mountain Pine Beetle Infestation—Future
10	Geologic Potential for Minerals
11	Claims, Mines, and Mineral Rights
12	Noxious Weeds
13	Elk and Mule Deer Seasonal Range
14	Condition and Trend of Elk and Mule Deer Range
15	White-Tailed Deer Seasonal Range
16	Condition and Trend of White-Tailed Deer, Mountain Goat, Big Horn Sheep, and Antelope Range
17	Mountain Goat Seasonal Range
18	Big Horn Sheep Seasonal Range
19	Antelope Seasonal Range
20	Moose Seasonal Range
21	Condition and Trend of Moose Range
22	Bison Seasonal Range
23	Grizzly Bear Habitat
24	Trumpeter Swan Habitat
25	Osprey Habitat
26	Stream Classification (for Trout)
27	Management Areas/Zones
28	Unique Geologic Features
29	Air Resource Management
30	Fire Suppression Strategies
31	Potential Timber Harvest Lands
32	Areas Modified by Timber Harvest—1975-1985
33	Areas Modified by Timber Harvest—At the End of the Planning Period
34	Mineral Leases and Lease Applications
35	Mineral Leasing Opportunity
36	Livestock Grazing—Existing and Planned
37	Uses Authorized by Permit
38	Visual Resource Management
39	Land Adjustment
40	Transportation System—Existing and Planned
41	Administrative and Transportation Facilities
42	Trails
43	Developed Recreation Sites
44	Motorized Vehicle Use—Existing
45	Motorized Vehicle Use—Planned
46	Wilderness, Recommended Wilderness, Wilderness Study, and Undeveloped Areas—Existing
47	Wilderness, Recommended Wilderness, Wilderness Study, and Undeveloped Areas—Planned
48	Distribution of Native and Exotic Fish
49	Mature and Old Growth Habitat—Existing
50	Mature and Old Growth Habitat—Planned

degrade the very special wilderness values in the GYA. Special efforts should be made to minimize external threats that place GYA wilderness values at risk.

CONCLUSION

The wilderness resource, perhaps more than any other in the spectrum of the multiple uses, is a function of the human mind or mental perception (Nash 1973). Perception is a function of culture, and the constant in culture is change. Beyond minimum acceptable limits of wilderness quality based on ecosystem principles, there are many options for wilderness use and management. The "correct" option is the one consistent with perceptions of current wilderness users.

Two great challenges in Forest Service wilderness management remain: the first is for managers to develop compacts that minimize the effects of external activities that jeopardize wilderness values. The second is for managers to remain sensitive to ever-changing American culture, and provide opportunities for wilderness experiences consistent with the current American mind.

LITERATURE CITED

Brown, L. R., W. U. Chandler, C. Flavin, J. Jacobson, C. Pollock, S. Postel, L. Stark, and E. C. Wolf. 1987. State of the world, 1987: A Worldwatch Institute report of progress toward a sustainable society. W. W. Norton, New York and London. 268 p.

Church, F. 1977. The coming of a new deal? J. For. 75(7):388-389.

Cutler, M. R., and J. Weaver. 1977. A colloquy between Congressman Weaver and Assistant Secretary Cutler. J. For. 75(7):392-394.

Greater Yellowstone Coordinating Committee. 1987. The Greater Yellowstone Area: An aggregation of National Park and National Forest management plans. Shoshone National Forest, Cody, Wyoming.

Hendee, J. C., G. H. Stankey, and R. C. Lucas. 1978. Wilderness management. USDA For. Serv. Misc. Pub. 1365. 381 p.

Interagency Grizzly Bear Committee. 1986. S. P. Mealey (ed.) Interagency grizzly bear guidelines. Shoshone National Forest, Cody, Wyoming.

Mealey, S. P., and J. Varley. Wildlife and fish in the Greater Yellowstone: An assessment of the past and present. Shoshone National Forest, Cody, Wyoming. In preparation.

Nash, R. 1973. Wilderness and the American mind. Yale University Press, New Haven. 300 p.

Peterson, R. M. 1985. Wilderness research: An important link to wilderness management. Comments as delivered by R. Feuchter for R. M. Peterson, Chief, USDA Forest Service, at the National Wilderness Research Conference, Fort Collins, Colorado, July 23, 1985.

USDA Forest Service. 1986a. Forest Service manual title 2300: Recreation, wilderness, and related resource management. U.S. Department of Agriculture, Washington, D.C.

———. 1986b. Shoshone National Forest Plan. Shoshone National Forest, Cody, Wyoming.

———. 1986c. Shoshone National Forest Plan environmental impact statement. Shoshone National Forest, Cody, Wyoming.

USDI National Park Service and USDA Forest Service. 1985. Outfitter policy: Greater Yellowstone Area. Shoshone National Forest, Cody, Wyoming.

13

Managing Yellowstone National Park into the Twenty-first Century: The Park as an Aquarium

JOHN D. VARLEY

ABSTRACT Civilization continues to encroach on the borders of Yellowstone National Park. The ecological well-being of Yellowstone in the twenty-first century will depend on public policy decisions made today. Critical observers generally agree that the overall health of the park is inextricably linked with environmental conditions in the region, a vast area now being termed the Greater Yellowstone Ecosystem. Conservationists have presented numerous proposals to correct perceived problems in the agencies' approach to integrated resource management within the ecosystem. This perception generally dwells on the fundamental absence of commonly held goals, plus the lack of effective communication and data management systems within the managing entities. Despite the agencies' optimistic view of current and projected future conditions within the ecosystem, the widely held public view is that unless deficiencies improve, the future of Yellowstone National Park, and its broader ecosystem, will remain in doubt.

A disturbing question is being asked by a growing number of people, and the answer is as elusive as it is complicated. The question, indeed the issue, in Yellowstone National Park—and the National Park Service in general—is whether Americans are truly committed to the preservation of their parks in the face of rising economic costs and allied social tensions. The value of the national park idea seems widely accepted and supported by the American public. Certainly, the love affair shared by 250 million persons who visit parks annually and the fact that Congress, with some regularity, continues to create more parks (much to the delight of most citizens) attest to this. Nevertheless, even large, wild areas like Yellowstone National Park are confronted with ever-increasing threats to their integrity and health. One wonders if the parks in the twenty-first century will be left as a select congressional committee envisioned them in 1885: "The park should so far as possible be spared the vandalism of improvement. Its great and only charms are in the display of wonderful forces of nature, the ever varying beauty of the rugged landscape, and the sublimity of the scenery. Art cannot embellish them" (Hampton 1965:132).

Both the public and government must be committed to the protection of these parks so that they might be left, as Interior Secretary Franklin K. Lane stated early in the century, "unimpaired for future generations" (Lane 1918). The condition of Yellowstone National Park in the twenty-first century will depend largely on decisions made today, and there is little agreement among the decision makers about how that should be done.

Most early parks were set aside by Congress for their scenery and curiosities, and they reflected the public's fascination with monumentalism as well as their ignorance or naïveté when it comes to biology (Sax 1980). Laws creating parks were passed because individuals or special interest groups perceived threats to an area recognized to be of an unusual or superlative nature. Therefore, parks were set aside through a political process and are thus the children of politics.

Because of political compromises, park boundaries usually failed to encompass complete ecological units. This is a fundamental flaw for most parks. Many of the great natural area parks, to some extent or another, are in danger of becoming static islands, frozen in space, as mounting internal and external threats foster increasing isolation within fixed boundaries. The monumentalism ideal of the eighteenth century may become a self-fulfilling prophecy.

National parks were founded on the principle of preservation and public enjoyment. Sentiments expressed as early as 1885 (as noted in the congressional report cited) established the principle of "driving forces," later understood to be natural processes, and the importance of minimizing human interference. In the administration of these natural areas, management's primary purpose is to maintain the area's pristine condition to the fullest extent possible (National Park Service 1968). This includes the perpetuation of natural processes in the absence of human interference—processes essential to the existence of a healthy ecosystem. This means that ecological processes, including plant succession, lightning-caused fires, and the natural regulation of animal populations, should be permitted to proceed as they did under pristine conditions, and that human uses must generally be restricted to nonconsumptive ones (Houston 1971).

The implementation of this principle has been hindered because few of our parks are completely self-contained units, and problems are rampant. Lemons (1986) summarized the problem facing contemporary park managers: "The *State of the Parks* report (National Park Service 1980) was the first and most comprehensive attempt by the NPS to systematically identify threats to parks. The report identified 73 different kinds of threats in the following categories: aesthetic, air pollution, physical removal of resources, encroachment by exotic species, visitor physical impacts, water quality pollution and water quantity changes, and park operations and planning of facilities. A total of 1,954 internal threats and 2,391 external threats in these categories were reported. . . ." The overall summary of the report stated, "The results of this study indicate that no parks of the system are immune to external and internal threats and that these threats are causing significant and demonstrable damage. . . . In many cases this degradation or loss of resources is irreversible. It represents a sacrifice by a public that, for the most part, is unaware that such a price is being paid."

Although parts of it were challenged, the report was significant because it introduced to the American public the idea that not all is idyllic in their national parks. Applying comprehensive management to a park within the context of its ecosystem requires a consistent policy base, adequate administrative arrangements, and diverse technical capabilities—some of which have been developed, while others have not. Yellowstone National Park provides an excellent example of the difficulties encountered by modern park managers.

THE AQUARIUM ILLUSION

At first glance, an aquarium appears to offer the perfect, intact ecosystem. But on closer inspection, it is apparent that an aquarium represents an eclectic, incomplete collection of aquatic life preserved only through the labor of its keeper. Artificially extracted from most natural processes, the aquarium's uniform walls seem to emphasize the degree to which it has been made nearly sterile by isolation, and therefore totally dependent on continuous external input. An aquarium is dependent on its four fragile walls; they are all that stand between it and virtual nonexistence. Yellowstone Park, on the other hand, is hampered by what many perceive to be its aquariumlike walls—its boundaries. The park also suffers from the public's tendency to ignore and neglect the "fish" until it is time to peer at the life behind the "walls." An aquarium's walls allow all manner of diverse, unrelated activities to go on around it without imposing deleterious effects on the aquarium's inhabitants. This is not the case with Yellowstone, and this is the aquarium paradox.

Most of the renewable and nonrenewable resource problems that Yellowstone National Park faces today trace back to its creation over a hundred years ago and to the establishment of its boundaries. When the area was set aside in 1872, protection of geologic wonders was paramount. Wildlands and wildlife, two of the most important aspects of the park today, were recognized by Congress in a somewhat indirect, offhand fashion. The boundaries they set failed to encompass a complete ecological unit. When the park was designated a biosphere reserve a century later, it was again set aside within the existing park boundaries, denying recognition of the remainder of the ecosystem—thus repeating and reaffirming the earlier congressional oversight. While the congressional designation did not account for the ecological integrity of the area, the second failed to consider or recognize that the greater Yellowstone area is one of the largest, essentially intact, wild ecosystems remaining in the earth's temperate zone.

Because of their mobility, wildlife are one of the special resources that suffer from a lack of ecosystem integrity. In the future, both quality and quantity of Yellowstone's wildlife populations could be severely compromised as a result of the boundary designations, despite the existence of the greatest and most popular display of wildlife in the contiguous forty-eight states. Congress at one point extended and modified the boundaries of Yellowstone Park, created additional park lands, and established national forests. In many respects it was too little, too late. The tremendous growth and development of the Intermountain West has severed key connections between the greater Yellowstone ecosystem and the remaining Rocky Mountains. The greater Yellowstone region has become an ecological island, potentially an aquarium in the making, requiring more and more external lifelines to the outside world. Development encroaches on those misplaced boundaries with steady and cumulative results.

INTERAGENCY COOPERATION

A brief summary here of the various entities responsible for land management in the Greater Yellowstone Ecosystem will help define the size and complexity of the management problem. Located in an area of northwestern Wyoming, southwestern Montana, and eastern Idaho, the Greater Yellowstone Ecosystem includes two national parks; a national parkway; seven national forests answering to three U.S. Forest Service regions;

three wildlife refuges; numerous parcels of state, corporate, and private lands; and multiple town, city, and county jurisdictions. With the great number of parties involved—Yellowstone Park personnel meet with twenty-two governmental entities on an annual or more frequent basis—resource decision making throughout the ecosystem ranges from excellent to disjointed and inconsistent. There are superlative examples of cooperation (e.g., the Interagency Grizzly Bear Committee, Greater Yellowstone Bald Eagle Working Group), and examples of essentially no cooperation (e.g., hydrology and geology related topics, osprey and other sensitive species management).

The official stance of the federal agencies of the Greater Yellowstone Ecosystem toward ecosystem management is that it is achievable without altered administrative boundaries or legislatively induced change. The agencies are quick to point out that the concept of ecosystem management is very young and that critics have not given the agencies time to put the necessary processes in place. They point to the successes of the formally chartered groups, like the Interagency Grizzly Bear Committee, and informal ad hoc groups, like the Bald Eagle Working Group, as examples of the kind of integrated resource management that can be achieved, if given time.

Critics of the official stance argue that all parties involved do not necessarily look first to the care and maintenance of the ecosystem, which is experiencing serious, cumulative threats to its integrity. They point to a recent publication produced by a group that supports the idea of treating the greater Yellowstone area as an ecosystem (Greater Yellowstone Coalition 1984). Threats listed were varied and covered numerous topics: oil, gas, and geothermal development; proposed wilderness areas and wilderness study areas; numerous proposed timber sales; utility corridors; air and water pollution; proposed recreational developments (e.g., Ski Yellowstone, Squirrel Meadows); existing recreational developments (e.g., Fishing Bridge, Alpine Village); proposed hydroelectric plants and instream flow problems; old and proposed new mining districts; wildlife management (e.g., bears, elk, bison, wolves, swans); and trail and road management (e.g., snowmobile trails, highway truck traffic).

Reese (1984), McNamee (1987), and others present persuasive arguments that the federal agencies lack common policy, administration, and resource management vision and that the most significant barrier to meaningful management progress in the Greater Yellowstone Ecosystem is the illogical administrative boundaries that bear no relation to the biological world. Others claim that if the federal agencies can be accused of lacking cooperative vision, then the integration of state agencies, municipalities, and private landowners into areawide management can be said to be blind.

If Yellowstone Park is to survive as the healthy core of the Greater Yellowstone Ecosystem, its neighbors must treat it less like an aquarium and more like a park. The park is more dynamic and interactive than an aquarium. Every component of the park's environment—animals, vegetation, geologic features—change and interact; and this interaction extends beyond the artificial, politically created boundaries of the park. An aquarium is more static. While its components may interact with each other, they interact infrequently and in a limited fashion with entities beyond the aquarium's transparent, but nonporous, walls. A ripple in the aquarium stops at its walls. An "ecological ripple" generated from within or originating outside the park passes directly through the park boundary without hesitation.

Some citizens would like to think of Yellowstone as an aquarium; they believe that civilization can be brought to the very boundary of the park without producing harmful effects. Yellowstone Park cannot be thought of as functioning like an aquarium, and it cannot be managed like one. To be perpetuated, an aquarium requires much external manipulation and input. The ecosystem existed before modern man arrived on the scene and requires the least amount of management effort when undisturbed by the presence or encroachment of man.

The goal of the park's management program is to maintain the natural processes that support the special features, native biota, and landscape dynamics. Park management is based on the total array of components of the ecosystem within the park. It is most often passive management that allows natural processes to govern ecosystem behavior. Management actions are initiated primarily in ecological situations where human disturbances force the ecosystem outside of its normal pattern of fluctuation. But if the natural, relatively pristine condition of Yellowstone Park is to survive, an innovative strategy for management must be devised. This strategy must include the idea of total ecosystem management. The perception of the park's glass pane boundaries must be shattered, and management thought must assume a grander scale.

IMPEDIMENTS AND CHALLENGES

From an ecosystem management standpoint, the relative lack of ecosystem thinking within the National Park Service and among our neighbors is the fundamental problem, but there are other thorny difficulties as well, some independent of the ecosystem concept and some inextricably entwined.

1. The lack of commonly held policy and management goals among the agencies is the single greatest impediment to sound ecosystem coordination. The integrated management of the Greater Yellowstone Ecosystem is hindered for lack of an agreed-upon public policy. Many people and interest groups see the highest social value of the ecosystem to be the continuation of existing multiple-use policies. These proponents see the ecosystem's worth in terms of a balanced mix of commodity extraction, recreation, and preservation. Others (Reese 1984, McNamee 1987) see the preservation of the wildlands and all life in them as the desired primary goal. Clark (1987) proposed that management of the Greater Yellowstone Ecosystem should be the "management of natural resources using systems-wide concepts to ensure that all plants and animals in the ecosystem are maintained at viable levels in native habitats and that basic ecosystem processes (e.g., nutrient cycling) are perpetuated indefinitely." Theoretically, agencies could achieve that stated goal and carry out recreation and resource extraction activities at the same time. In practical terms, the agencies have difficulty proving (or convincing the public) that extraction projects are harmless (or may even be helpful) and that all types of recreation are compatible. Proponents of ecosystem preservation have an equally difficult time convincing bureaucrats that the agencies do not have a compatible management vision for the area.

2. The crushing complexity of coordinating management activities between scores of separate political and administrative entities looms as the second most important challenge. The agencies believe it can be done, but the fact is there are few examples of it ever having been accomplished successfully and efficiently. The venerable Adirondack State Park system in New York and the more recent New Jersey Pine Barrens project have been cited as successful examples in the East, but the West lacks analogous role models. Many observers believe different cultural values exist in the West and the fact that the federal

government has the lead responsibility in the Greater Yellowstone Ecosystem reduces the value, and example, of the successful eastern models.

The agencies may not be adequately prepared for such substantial coordination responsibilities. For instance, it appears that none of the administrative units involved in the Greater Yellowstone Ecosystem have staff people whose primary responsibilities include coordination activities with other agencies.

There is even some question that first-rate cooperation is attainable. One possible scenario, diagramed in Figure 13-1, predicts that maximum coordination efficiency is attained only when relatively few institutions are involved. Optimal conditions are created by enhancing the competitive spirit between agencies, reducing tunnel vision in any one agency through information sharing, and adopting the "small is beautiful" concept. According to this hypothesis, increasing institutional involvement beyond that optimum point incrementally decreases efficiency through lack of consensus, diluted leadership, and lack of accountability, leading to stagnating bureaucracy. Whatever the future may bring in this regard, improved coordination would be virtually automatic with any added measure of simplification.

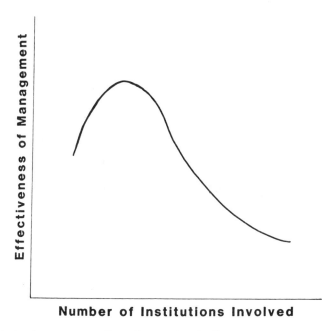

Number of Institutions Involved

Figure 13-1. Relation between coordinated operational efficiency of management and the number of institutions involved.

3. The chronic problems that fall under the umbrella term "internal threats" range from residues of leaded gas, to alien and exotic species, to heavy visitor use. High on that list is the difficulty of managing common property resources like park and national forest lands, which are free and open-access resources with unlimited entry (Hardin and Baden 1977). Despite repeated evidence that tighter controls are needed in order to ensure a quality park experience and protect resources, it is clear that the public resists any efforts by agencies to put capacity limits on parks.

4. External threats are in many ways more difficult to deal with than internal threats. Dealing with problems outside one's jurisdiction increases their magnitude of difficulty. This is a common impediment between agencies, but is most pronounced when dealing with privately owned lands. No one, it seems, wants to tackle the issue of threats to the park (or ecosystem) that arise on private lands.

5. The technical capabilities for dealing with specific problems lag behind problem identification. Since the National Park Service has a slender science budget, some decisions must necessarily be made on the basis of conventional wisdom, without benefit of scientific documentation.

OPTIONS AND SOLUTIONS

Innovative proposals have been presented that would solve, according to their proponents, the majority of the perceived problems in both the park and the ecosystem.

1. *Improved coordination through existing organizational structure.* The stance of federal agencies is largely based on continuing improvements of on-the-ground coordination within the greater Yellowstone area. They have chosen a stepwise procedure to achieve this goal beginning with an "overview" of the ecosystem. Each national forest and park has completed or is completing its land management plan. The information in these plans, along with planning documents from other federal and state agencies, will be combined to show current or planned direction for the ecosystem. The overview presents a picture of Yellowstone's ecological, economic, and social conditions and provides a blueprint of what these conditions might be like in ten to fifteen years (Tixier 1986, Greater Yellowstone Coordinating Committee 1987). The second phase, not yet begun, is to initiate dialogue between agencies to determine if a joint policy and management vision is possible to develop within the constraints of each agency's legislative mandate.

2. *Consolidation of all federal lands within the ecosystem under one management agency with a single management plan.* Perhaps because of the political difficulties involved, this is the proposal offered least often. A suggestion has been made to enlarge Yellowstone National-al Park (*Salt Lake Tribune* editorial, October 26, 1985), but most often the proponents of this idea do not directly address which agency would be the surviving (or ascending) entity. Instead, they argue the wisdom of having a single "Director of the Greater Yellowstone Ecosystem" (Clark 1987). Perhaps the most radical proposal suggests the establishment of a nonprofit, public corporation, governed by a board of trustees (Baden 1986). According to this view, the corporation would protect the resources of the region, manage them efficiently, and insulate the decision makers from political pressures.

3. *Retention of the existing administrative configuration but with new, commonly held guiding principles.* There are many variations to this basic proposal, including the establishment of a National Recreation Area (Reese 1984); the expansion of Yellowstone Park's current international biosphere reserve designation (Barbee and Varley 1985, Pritchard 1986) under the new concept of "ideal" or "model" biosphere reserves (Gregg and McGean 1985); the creation of a new national biosphere reserve program (McNamee 1987); the establishment of "common ecosystem management units" (Baucus 1986); and congressionally mandated principles, with built-in accountability, directing agencies to maintain the ecosystem's health "forever" (Anderson 1986). These ideas probably have the greatest chance to be implemented, simply because they are politically less volatile than most of the others.

4. *Retention of the existing administrative configuration but with an umbrella federal land use control system.* This concept encompasses several ideas that include phrases like "land use control systems" or "federal zoning." Considering the public attitudes in the western United States toward the principle of zoning, these concepts are bound to generate controversy. The conceptual basis for most of the variations proposed is rooted in the approximately fifteen-year-old "forever wild" clause in the New York State Constitution creating the Adirondack State Park. More recently Baden (1985) suggested that the concepts and language found in the Coastal Barriers Resources Act of 1982 could be used in solving the problems of the Greater Yellowstone Ecosystem. Others (Duerksen 1986) have proposed that public-private partnerships involving land trusts are the most sensible route to pursue within the ecosystem.

5. *Simplification of the existing interagency structure.* Based on the thesis that improved coordination would be virtually automatic with any measure of simplification, adherents to these proposals seek to redraw certain boundaries without tampering with overall agency proportions. Because of the complexity of the federal configuration (e.g., seven national forests reporting to three regional offices), proposals (Eno and Evans 1986, Congressional Research Service 1986, Clark 1987) generally involve consolidation within existing agencies. Suggestions for consolidation are generally directed toward Forest Service administrative structure, but closer scrutiny reveals it could be extended to all federal functions and perhaps some state functions as well.

None of the alternative proposals mentioned above appear to have enough adherents and public support to rally a sufficiently large constituency to force change. As the machinery of the ecosystem management debate continues to ease forward, so does the encroachment of human development. In time, the debate could very well be settled for us. In the event that Yellowstone comes to more closely resemble an isolated aquarium and much of the dynamic, interactive nature and the integrity of the Greater Yellowstone Ecosystem are lost, we could learn just how much effort is required to operate that type of aquarium. In a different context, Yellowstone has always been a "goldfish bowl" on public display. Given the national visibility of Yellowstone Park and the Greater Yellowstone Ecosystem issue, the ultimate resolution of this question may affect the way all natural area parks are managed in the next century. The common thread that unites virtually all of these proposals is the need for the agencies to establish common goals, data management systems, and an effective apparatus for communication. Unless this can be done, using any one of the suggested alternative structures or a combination of several, the future of Yellowstone Park and its broader ecosystem will continue to be in doubt.

ACKNOWLEDGMENTS

The author thanks his National Park Service and U.S. Forest Service colleagues for sharing their ideas about ecosystem management in the preparation of this paper. James K. Agee and two anonymous reviewers aided in a significant way during preparation of the final draft. The author is particularly indebted to Susan M. Mills for her many suggestions on the paper's content, as well as its construction.

LITERATURE CITED

Anderson, R. 1986. Testimony on behalf of the Greater Yellowstone Coalition. *In* U.S. Congress. House Committee on Interior and Insular Affairs. Oversight hearing on the Greater Yellowstone Ecosystem. October 24, 1985. 99th Cong. U.S. Government Printing Office, Washington, D.C. Ser. 99-18. 697 p.

Baden, J. A. 1985. Federal programs called Yellowstone area peril. Salt Lake Tribune, September 29, 1985.

——. 1986. Get the national parks out of Washington's hands. Houston Chronicle, July 8, 1986.

Barbee, R. D., and J. D. Varley. 1985. The paradox of repeating error: Yellowstone National Park from 1872 to biosphere reserve and beyond. *In* J. D. Peine (ed.) Proceedings of the Conference on the Management of Biosphere Reserves, pp. 125-130. Great Smoky Mountains National Park, Gatlinburg, Tennessee.

Baucus, M. 1986. National parks interagency management and coordination act of 1986. 99th Cong., 2d sess., discussion draft, May 12, 1986.

Clark, T. W. 1987. The Greater Yellowstone Ecosystem: The evolving ecosystem concept in policy, administration and management. Unpublished manuscript. Northern Rockies Conservation Cooperative, Jackson, Wyoming. 18 p.

Congressional Research Service. 1986. Greater Yellowstone Ecosystem. U.S. Congress. House Committee on Interior and Insular Affairs. 99th Cong. Committee print 6. U.S. Government Printing Office, Washington, D.C. 210 p.

Duerksen, C. J. 1986. Testimony on behalf of the Conservation Foundation. *In* U.S. Congress. House Committee on Interior and Insular Affairs. Oversight hearing on the Greater Yellowstone Ecosystem. October 24, 1985. 99th Cong. U.S. Government Printing Office, Washington, D.C. Ser. 99-18. 697 p.

Eno, A. S., and B. Evans. 1986. Testimony on behalf of the National Audubon Society. *In* U.S. Congress. House Committee on Interior and Insular Affairs. Oversight hearing on the Greater Yellowstone Ecosystem. October 24, 1985. 99th Cong. U.S. Government Printing Office, Washington, D.C. Ser. 99-18. 697 p.

Greater Yellowstone Coalition. 1984. Threats to the greater Yellowstone. Bozeman, Montana. 94 p.

Greater Yellowstone Coordinating Committee. 1987. The Greater Yellowstone Area: An aggregation of National Park and National Forest management plans. Shoshone National Forest, Cody, Wyoming.

Gregg, W. P., and B. A. McGean. 1985. Biosphere reserves: Their history and their promise. Orion Nature Quarterly 4(3):40-51.

Hampton, H. D. 1965. Conservation and cavalry: A study of the role of the U.S. Army in the development of a national park system, 1886-1917. Ph.D. diss., University of Colorado.

Hardin, G., and J. Baden (eds.) 1977. Managing the commons. W. H. Freeman Co., San Francisco. 278 p.

Houston, D. L. 1971. Ecosystems of national parks. Science 172:648-651.

Lane, F. K. 1918. Letter from Franklin K. Lane, secretary of the interior, to Stephen T. Mather, director of the National Park Service. 4 p. NPS Archives, Washington, D.C.

Lemons, J. 1986. National parks research. The Environmental Professional 8(2):128-131.

McNamee, T. 1987. Nature first: Keeping our wild places and wild creatures wild. Roberts Rinehart, Inc., Boulder, Colorado. 54 p.

Pritchard, P. C. 1986. Testimony on behalf of the National Parks and Conservation Association. *In* U.S. Congress. House Committee on Interior and Insular Affairs. Oversight hearing on the Greater Yellowstone Ecosystem. October 24, 1985. 99th Cong. U.S. Government Printing Office, Washington, D.C. Ser. 99-18. 697 p.

Reese, R. 1984. Greater Yellowstone: The national park and adjacent wildlands. Montana Geographic Series 6, Montana Magazine, Inc., Helena, Montana. 104 p.

Sax, J. L. 1980. Mountain without handrails: Reflections on the national parks. University of Michigan Press, Ann Arbor. 152 p.

Tixier, J. S. 1986. The greater Yellowstone: An introduction to an area and its issues. Western Wildlands 13(3)3:2-6.

USDI National Park Service. 1968. Administrative policies for natural areas of the National Park System. Government Printing Office, Washington, D.C. 144 p.

——. 1980. State of the parks: A report to Congress. U.S. Department of the Interior, Washington, D.C. 52 p.

14

A Direction for Ecosystem Management

JAMES K. AGEE and DARRYLL R. JOHNSON

Aldo Leopold, in his classic *A Sand County Almanac*, includes a chapter entitled "Thinking Like a Mountain." Successful management for the future of parks and wildernesses will necessitate "Thinking Like an Ecosystem," recognizing that the ecosystem concept includes social as well as natural components. Ecosystem management, however, is not yet a clearly defined or widely accepted concept. In this concluding chapter synthesizing workshop discussions, some principles of ecosystem management are outlined, approaches to ecosystem management are discussed, and critical current issues are prioritized. Although this is a concluding chapter, it charts a beginning rather than describing a course already traveled.

PRINCIPLES OF ECOSYSTEM MANAGEMENT

For park and wilderness areas, ecosystem management is a way to produce desired conditions and preserve future options. Several principles or characteristics of ecosystem management emerged from workshop discussions:

1. Cooperation and open negotiation are important to success. Given that park and wilderness ecosystems are bounded politically, and that things important to people move across those boundaries, cooperation, honesty, and openness are essential.

2. Different agencies and neighbors have different mandates, objectives, and constituencies, to which the interested parties must be sensitive.

3. Success should be measured by results—progress toward goals of component condition and ecosystem maintenance—not by amount or quality of coordination.

4. Threshold management goals are established by the park and wilderness legislation. Setting further goals will be a site-specific process taking account of the context of the park or wilderness within its regional and national social matrix.

5. Clearly defined problems have a greater chance of being resolved.

6. Over the long term, ecosystem management must accommodate multiple uses at a regional scale and dominant or restricted use at the unit or site scale.

7. High quality information is necessary to identify trends and respond to them intelligently and deliberately.

8. Social, political, and environmental issues must be viewed in a system context, not as individual issues. Individual components may be the focus within that context.

9. All management is a long-term experiment, and decisions are always made with less than complete information.

APPROACHES TO COORDINATED ECOSYSTEM MANAGEMENT

The ecosystem concept as applied to park and wilderness management often incorporates a geopolitical emphasis. Not all ecosystem management for various multiple uses necessarily involves big areas and multiple ownerships and agencies. But such coordination can be an effective way to achieve ecosystem management goals, particularly when boundary issues are significant.

Structured and Unstructured Approaches

Most coordinated ecosystem management initiatives have been the result of reaction to crises (Walters 1986). In park and wilderness ecosystems, such reactions have largely reflected concerns about endangered species. But there have been other cooperative management approaches between park or wilderness areas and adjacent lands. Once communication barriers are overcome, the chances improve of moving from crisis management to a more forward-looking, cooperative approach. All crises are not averted, but a greater proportion can be headed off before they become crises. Better data bases generated through interagency cooperation improve the outlook for accurate forecasting on a less insular and more integrated basis.

Both structured (formal) and unstructured (informal) approaches to ecosystem management are being used. Structured approaches, often mandated by legislation, are usually formal agreements of several parties to cooperate on a wide range of issues. Unstructured or informal approaches generally involve cooperation on an issue-by-issue basis. Whether the approach is highly structured or not, both the Forest Service and the National Park Service are moving toward more regional, integrative planning and management approaches as an effective way to achieve their land management goals. Ecosystem management is mandated in certain areas, such as Alaska's parks by the 1980 Alaska National Interest Lands Conservation Act (ANILCA). Although existing law does not mandate such approaches elsewhere, it does not preclude them (Coggins 1987; Keiter, this volume). Ecosystem management has been adopted as a firm policy by interagency agreements in the Greater Yellowstone Area (Mealey, this volume; Varley, this volume). In other areas, such as the North Cascades, a more informal, unstructured approach has been taken, with cooperation defined on an issue-by-issue basis. Opportunities may arise at different times for different areas to become involved in ecosystem management.

The biosphere reserve concept represents one well-known formal approach to ecosystem management. The original concept was to blend areas managed for natural values with those managed for a variety of uses such that all parties benefited from the cooperation. The concept sought to integrate conservation, experimental, and demonstration-application areas. But in the United States some of the biosphere reserves have been established coincident with national park boundaries, creating a perception that all other surrounding areas would be treated as a buffer to the core area. Such was not the intention of the biosphere reserve concept, particularly as it has been applied overseas. Indeed, recent progress in the southern Appalachian region (Gilbert, this volume) suggests that the biosphere reserve concept is one way to implement ecosystem management successfully. But neither this concept nor any other single concept, short of national legislation, will provide a way to implement ecosystem management in parks and wilderness areas nationwide.

Benefits and Costs of Structured and Unstructured Approaches

If ecosystem management is adopted as a process to meet objectives, both structured (formal) and unstructured (informal) approaches have unique advantages and disadvantages. Advantages of a structured approach, through law or policy, include a continuity of process independent of the personalities representing the various agencies. The extent of long-term cooperation will be greater if a cooperative program is written and publicized. A structured, formal approach is also most likely to encourage the definition of common goals from which individual units can make definitive plans. Such holistic management should improve interagency data bases and encourage a trend toward forecasting and avoiding crises. A structured approach may also respond well to constituencies that are concerned about specific management issues, whether or not they are primarily park and wilderness issues.

Highly structured approaches are not without disadvantages. Forcing compromise among conflicting points of view can be costly, in terms of both dollars and future willingness to cooperate. Too many participants engaged in an overly structured approach may result in inefficient management. A highly structured approach, by its nature, might also produce a psychological "fence" or unnecessary filter which may exclude minor participants on various issues.

On the other hand, informal approaches have the advantage of flexibility. A different mix of interests can be assembled for different problems. Various areas and units can proceed at their own pace rather than in lockstep with other agencies. An informal approach may be less threatening to interest groups that may have competing objectives. But the less structured approach also has some disadvantages. Cooperation can fall apart quickly with a change in park superintendent or forest supervisor, or among the technical staff. Potential for holistic approaches is lower with a less structured approach, because management efforts may be made primarily on an issue-by-issue basis, with data base planning focused on a single issue. The informal approach generally relies on crisis management; progressive "avoidance" or "risk" management is less likely to develop. Thorny issues may not be dealt with in an informal approach.

Although the two approaches are discussed as an either-or choice, some of the advantages and disadvantages may apply to both approaches in certain situations. A likely scenario is for cooperation to begin without a great deal of structure and evolve to a more structured form. For example, a park superintendent or forest supervisor might wish to begin such coordination informally, perhaps focusing on a current issue of concern, and use that cooperation to build a more formal approach with other neighbors as issues become more complex, the information base about those issues expands, and communication between the parties becomes easier.

Nevertheless, these approaches are not without limitations and costs. More staff time will be devoted to meeting with representatives of other institutions and constituencies. Greater coordination of activities within parks and wilderness with other activities inside and around those areas will be needed. The process of adopting more precise management goals at the unit level will continue to become more complex, and decisions may be more difficult in the short run. Cooperation among land management organizations is most likely if all parties recognize that the process will contribute to the ability of each agency to attain its own goals and objectives (Salwasser et al. 1987).

Workshop participants divided into four groups near the end of the week to discuss priority research and management issues. The four questions posed to individual groups were: (1) What are the important research needs associated with ecosystem management in parks and wilderness? (2) What are the important general management, planning, and communication issues associated with ecosystem management in parks and wilderness? (3) What are the important challenges to ecosystem management in parks and wilderness in the areas of conflict resolution and cooperation? (4) What are the important limits and constraints to ecosystem management in parks and wildernesses?

The process used to prioritize the issues within each of these subjects was a modified nominal group technique (Delbecq et al. 1975). Each person was allowed to contribute one issue to a list that grew as the group facilitator moved around the table. Once every person in the group had a chance to add an issue, the process was repeated until each person had an opportunity to add five issues or until the list was exhausted. Then each issue was discussed, any duplicate issues were combined, and the resulting list was ranked. Each person ranked his or her top five issues, and the facilitator tallied the votes to define the critical issues. The top priority issues for each question are presented in Table 14-1.

Several common themes emerged from the top priority issues. There is a need to define precisely the management objectives for park and wilderness areas and to integrate them with management policies governing the surrounding lands. The need for national as well as site-specific policy guidance was recognized. More information about physical, biological, and social components of park and wilderness ecosystems is needed. If benefits and costs to neighbors from various alternatives are to be accurately assessed, this information must be collected on both sides of political boundaries. Identification of key indicators of system condition must be made. These measures will clearly have to be done at the unit level. Finally, methods for evaluating management effectiveness need to be developed. All of these common themes point to a need for more precise direction in terms of management goal setting and more accurate assessment of progress toward goals.

CONCLUSIONS

Ecosystem management goals for specific parks and wildernesses may be somewhat different; in fact, each area's legislative mandate may point management in a slightly different direction. Natural process management will be an important but not exclusive goal in parks or wilderness areas. Therefore, ecosystem management in parks and wilderness should explicitly reflect multiple, measurable goals defining both natural environmental conditions and socioeconomic concerns. These goals should acknowledge the fact that social values, political pressures, and biological knowledge may be different ten to twenty years from now, and that park and wilderness management should be responsive to such changes within defined legal limits. No set of goals should be so firmly adopted that institutional adaptability is lost.

Agency transition to ecosystem management for achieving park and wilderness goals will require education of both the public and the agency personnel. Interagency training is proposed at three levels: (1) regional directors, regional foresters, Washington office,

Table 14-1. Top priority issues in ecosystem management.

Group 1. WHAT ARE THE IMPORTANT RESEARCH NEEDS ASSOCIATED WITH ECOSYSTEM MANAGEMENT?
- A conceptual model—area specific (including humans)—of ecological elements, interactions, and boundaries.
- Long-term studies of ecosystem processes.
- Identification of monitoring targets based on analysis of sensitive indicators.
- Definition of thresholds for changes in key elements and their relation to management strategies.
- Design of techniques for baseline inventory and monitoring.

Group 2. WHAT ARE THE IMPORTANT GENERAL MANAGEMENT, PLANNING, AND COMMUNICATION ISSUES ASSOCIATED WITH ECOSYSTEM MANAGEMENT?
- Consensus among affected parties on the specific indicators of desired conditions, benefits, minimum acceptable standards, or constraints to activities. Limit to ten or less indicators.
- Clarity of goals regarding optimum mix for increased production of certain benefits, goods, and services on a sustainable basis.
- Monitoring of both people and indicators relative to goals, costs, risks, and values.
- Quantification of indicators in units measurable over space and time.
- Need for regional focus in ecosystem management.
- A systematic process to assess effectiveness of management plans after implementation.
- Criteria for management planning success that reflect an agreed upon balance of outcome measures such as efficiency, equity, accountability, effectiveness, sustainability, and adaptability.
- Analysis of trends, risks, and potentials for each indicator.

Group 3. WHAT ARE THE IMPORTANT CHALLENGES TO ECOSYSTEM MANAGEMENT IN THE AREAS OF CONFLICT RESOLUTION AND COOPERATION?
- Finding common ground between agencies, their employees, and the public to establish unambiguous common goals.
- Establishing a good foundation of baseline information on resources and people involved.
- Overcoming lack of understanding by each of significant publics (external and internal) of values and purposes of ecosystem management.
- Organization moving toward network structure that emphasizes variety of means of effectively addressing challenges.
- Need for agency enthusiasm, commitment, rewards, and incentives.
- Consideration of responsibility for natural resources beyond the particular ecosystem jurisdiction and national boundaries.
- Need for expertise in conflict resolution.

Group 4. WHAT ARE THE IMPORTANT LIMITS AND CONSTRAINTS TO ECOSYSTEM MANAGEMENT?
- Boundary mentality (interagency mistrust, turf-power consciousness, insular management, different philosophies).
- Lack of a commonly understood concept of ecosystem management.
- Lack of leadership, vision, and followers (power base)—not on political agenda, no priority for funding.
- Multiple and conflicting values and objectives (different management philosophies, no systematic way of defining common goals).
- Lack of integration of human element into ecosystem management.
- Inherent limitation in developing inventory and research data.
- Disciplinary myopia (science unwilling to generalize).

(2) regional staff, and (3) unit and interunit representatives. Concepts discussed in this report should be a major focus of the training sessions, with examples drawn from the regional or subregional areas where the training is being conducted.

Educational institutions will be a valuable link in any training effort. They offer "neutral" sites for interagency meetings, can supply natural and social scientists who have the appropriate expertise, and can coordinate the input of field personnel in terms of case studies. Universities can also serve as forums for broadly oriented symposia that might appeal to the various publics interested in ecosystem management, and they can offer midcareer short courses to update managers. An initial symposium might focus on the planning framework envisioned in this chapter, with more detailed discussion of the rationale for a new approach and the costs and benefits of alternative approaches to ecosystem management. Other natural area management institutions in addition to the Forest Service and National Park Service, including those managing Research Natural Areas, Natural Heritage Program sites (such as Washington's Department of Natural Resources), and the Nature Conservancy, might appropriately contribute to and learn from such a symposium.

A benefit for educational institutions will be closer interaction with management. This interaction may then be reflected in curricula, producing graduates with better skills to deal with ecosystem management issues. Graduate training in ecosystem management is also needed. The new master's program in natural area management at the College of Forest Resources, University of Washington, is an example of a graduate university program that can offer conceptual and specific training in this area.

There are many potential benefits associated with the adoption of an ecosystem management approach in park and wilderness areas. First, the focus on interrelations of system components should be helpful in avoiding negative and unintended consequences of management actions. Second, if parks and wilderness areas are treated as "open systems," rather than "islands," the influences of these areas on external systems (and vice versa) should be more apparent. Third, a systems approach will help focus attention on important, long-term issues and avoid a continual "brushfire" approach to decision making. With the characteristic high turnover rate for managers in these areas, this benefit will encourage continuity and persistence in management efforts. A systems approach will also identify social systems as critical components of these ecosystems, helping to legitimitize the role of culture and values in problem identification and solution.

The benefits to ecosystem management must be tempered with several notes of caution. While a systems approach encourages more complex reasoning about interconnections in the world, this complexity can be overwhelming and paralyze the decision-making process. Just as there are problems in oversimplifying reality with simple models, there are also problems in overcomplicating and intellectualizing trivial issues. The coordination of multiple agency programs to achieve socially responsible system objectives may result in a lack of consensus in the short run. Managers waiting for consensus may find progress delayed by the impotence of political posturing.

In 1988, the National Parks and Conservation Association, with funding from the Andrew Mellon Foundation, established a seventeen-member Commission on Research and Resource Management Policy in the National Park System, chaired by Dr. John C. Gordon of Yale University. This commission will begin to develop a "holistic approach to park management," which should also be valuable for wilderness management. In the NPCA letter announcing establishment of the commission, the National Park Service recognized the need for such a commission as a logical, evolutionary outgrowth of the 1963 Leopold Report: "In the 23 years since that report was issued, knowledge about the complex systems that influence parks has grown, and it is increasingly obvious that neither all influences on parks, nor all resources to be managed, are confined within park boundaries." The same could be said for wilderness areas. With an eye on the twenty-first century, this commission will be providing a foundation for ecosystem management for natural areas.

The transition to ecosystem management in parks and wilderness will involve a gradual shift in management thinking and behavior. In some cases, complex interagency coordination may require more of a social consensus than exists at present. However, the shift is already under way in many park and wilderness areas. Ultimately, this shift should result in long-term effective strategies to protect park and wilderness ecosystems for the benefit of present and future generations.

LITERATURE CITED

Coggins, G. C. 1987. Protecting the wildlife values of national parks from external threats. Land and Water Law Review 22:1-27.

Delbecq, A., H. Van de Ven, and D. H. Gustafson. 1975. Group techniques for program planning: A guide to nominal group and Delphi processes. Scott, Foresman, and Company, Glenview, Illinois.

Leopold, A. 1966 (1949). A Sand County almanac. Oxford University Press, New York.

Salwasser, H., C. M. Schonewald-Cox, and R. Baker. 1987. The role of interagency cooperation in managing for viable populations. In M. E. Soulé (ed.) Viable populations for conservation, pp. 159-173. Cambridge University Press, New York.

Walters, C. 1986. Adaptive management of renewable resources. Macmillan, New York.

Glossary

Alpha diversity. The variety and relative abundance of biotic elements within a distinct habitat or stand of vegetation.

Beta diversity. Changes in species and community variety and abundance that occur along an environmental gradient.

Biocentric. A view of issues focused on biological components and largely ignoring social components.

Boundary. Arbitrary line where a system ends and its environment begins.

Concept. Abstract category of thought that allows perception of order and simplifies logical thought processes.

Conceptual model. A series of related concepts that form the building blocks of a unique perspective under study.

Ecosystem. Any part of the universe chosen as an area of interest, with the line around that area being the ecosystem boundary and anything crossing the boundary being input or output.

Ecosystem condition. The state of various elements or components of an ecosystem. For an ecosystem component such as a wildlife population, condition might be measured in terms of numbers or population structure; for vegetation, it might be measured in terms of species composition, cover, or growth; or for visitors, it might be measured in terms of preference or satisfaction.

Ecosystem management. Regulating internal ecosystem structure and function, plus inputs and outputs, to achieve socially desirable conditions.

Equilibrium. A short to long time within which the state of the system (its various components) is relatively stable.

Function. How various ecological or social processes are accomplished and at what rate they occur (e.g., production and cycling of organic matter, how recreational settings are used by visitors, etc.).

Gamma diversity. Total area diversity over a region: the sum of within-stand (alpha) diversity plus between-stand (beta) diversity.

Intrinsic value. Nonuse (nonmarket) values that accrue to a public good by virtue of consumer willingness to pay to preserve future options for use of the good, to bequeath use of the good for future generations, or simply to have knowledge that the good exists in relatively unused condition.

Key indicators. Important and measurable ways to assess the state or flux of various ecosystem elements or components.

Landscape ecology. Principles and theories for understanding the structure, functioning, and change of landscapes.

Model. A representation of a set of variables that shows the effects of those factors important for a given purpose.

Structure. Spatial arrangements of various components of the ecosystem: political linkages, architecture of the plant communities (both horizontal and vertical), and so forth.

Suggestions for Further Reading

These publications supplement the literature cited in the book. They address current issues in park and wilderness management.

Bonnicksen, T., and E. C. Stone. 1982. Managing vegetation within U.S. national parks: A policy analysis. Environ. Manage. 6:101-102 and 109-122.

Chase, A. 1986. Playing God in Yellowstone. Atlantic Monthly Press, New York.

Despain, D., D. Houston, M. Meagher, and P. Schullery. 1986. Wildlife in transition: Man and nature on Yellowstone's northern range. Roberts Rinehart, Inc., Boulder, Colorado.

Frome, M. (ed.) 1985. Issues in wilderness management. Westview Press, Boulder, Colorado.

Irland, L. C. 1979. Wilderness economics and policy. Lexington Books, Lexington, Massachusetts.

———. 1986. Strategic thinking: A critical gap in American forestry planning and management. Renewable Resour. J. 4:14-18.

Ittner, R., D. R. Potter, J. K. Agee, and S. Anschell. 1978. Recreational impact on wildlands: Conference proceedings. USDA For. Serv. Pub. R-6-001-1979. Seattle, Washington.

Lotan, J. E., B. M. Kilgore, W. C. Fischer, and R. W. Mutch. 1985. Proceedings, Symposium and Workshop on Wilderness Fire. USDA For. Serv. Gen. Tech. Rep. INT-182.

Lucas, R. C. (comp.) 1986. Proceedings, National Wilderness Research Conference: Current research. USDA For. Serv. Gen. Tech. Rep. INT-212.

———. 1987. Proceedings, National Wilderness Research Conference: Issues, state-of-knowledge, future directions. USDA For. Serv. Gen. Tech. Rep. INT-220.

Machlis, G. E., and D. L. Tichnell. 1985. The state of the world's parks: An international assessment for resources management, policy, and research. Westview Press, Boulder, Colorado.

President's Commission on Americans Outdoors. 1987. Report of the President's Commission on Americans Outdoors. Island Press, Covelo, California.

Schonewald-Cox, C. M., S. M. Chambers, B. MacBryde, and W. L. Thomas. 1983. Genetics and conservation: A reference for managing wild animal and plant populations. Benjamin/Cummings, Menlo Park, California.

Sinclair, A. R. E., and M. Norton-Griffiths. 1979. Serengeti: Dynamics of an ecosystem. University of Chicago Press, Chicago.

Soulé, M. 1987. Viable populations for conservation. Cambridge University Press, New York.

List of Participants

Dr. James K. Agee
NPS Cooperative Park Studies Unit
College of Forest Resources
(AR-10)
University of Washington
Seattle, Washington 98195

Dr. Robert Bilby
Weyerhaeuser Company
Western Forestry Research Center
Centralia, Washington 98531

Dr. Richard Briceland
Science and Technology Advisor
National Park Service
Rm 3410, Interior Building
P.O. Box 37127
Washington, D.C. 20013-7127

Professor Linda B. Brubaker
College of Forest Resources
(AR-10)
University of Washington
Seattle, Washington 98195

Professor William R. Burch
School of Forestry
and Environmental Studies
Yale University
New Haven, Connecticut 06511

Professor Norman L. Christensen
Department of Botany
Duke University
Durham, North Carolina 27706

Dr. Roger Clark
USDA Forest Service
Pacific Northwest Research Station
4043 Roosevelt Way
Seattle, Washington 98105

Associate Dean Dale Cole
College of Forest Resources
(AR-10)
University of Washington
Seattle, Washington 98195

Professor Robert Edmonds
College of Forest Resources
(AR-10)
University of Washington
Seattle, Washington 98195

Mr. Boyd Evison
Regional Director, Alaska Region
National Park Service
2525 Gambell Street
Anchorage, Alaska 99503

Dr. Donald Field
NPS Cooperative Park Studies Unit
College of Forestry
Oregon State University
Corvallis, Oregon 97331

Professor Jerry Franklin
College of Forest Resources
(AR-10)
University of Washington
Seattle, Washington 98195

Mr. Vernon C. Gilbert
Route 3, Buckhorn Road
P.O. Box 415
Gatlinburg, Tennessee 37738

Professor David F. Grigal
Department of Soil Science
University of Minnesota
St. Paul, Minnesota 55108

Dr. Douglas Houston
Research Biologist
Olympic National Park
600 E. Park Avenue
Port Angeles, Washington 98362

Dr. Lloyd C. Irland
The Irland Group
7 North Chestnut Street
Augusta, Maine 04330

Mr. Darryll R. Johnson
NPS Cooperative Park Studies Unit
College of Forest Resources
(AR-10)
University of Washington
Seattle, Washington 98195

Professor Robert B. Keiter
College of Law
University of Wyoming
Box 3035, University Station
Laramie, Wyoming 82071

Professor Robert G. Lee
College of Forest Resources
(AR-10)
University of Washington
Seattle, Washington 98195

Professor Christopher Leman
Graduate School of Public Affairs
(DP-30)
University of Washington
Seattle, Washington 98195

Mr. Doug MacWilliams
Supervisor, Mount Baker-Snoqualmie
National Forest
1022 1st Avenue
Seattle, Washington 98104

Mr. Cliff Martinka
Supervisory Research Scientist
Glacier National Park
West Glacier, Montana 59936

Mr. Stephen P. Mealey
Supervisor, Shoshone National Forest
225 W. Yellowstone, Box 2140
Cody, Wyoming 82414

Dr. David Parsons
Research Scientist
Sequoia and Kings Canyon National
Parks
Three Rivers, California 93271

Mr. Gerald Patten
Manager, Denver Service Center
National Park Service
P.O. Box 25287
Denver, Colorado 80225

Professor Rolf O. Peterson
Department of Forestry
and Wood Products
Michigan Technological University
Houghton, Michigan 49931

Superintendent John Reynolds
North Cascades National Park
Service Complex
2105 Highway 20
Sedro Woolley, Washington 98284

Dr. Hal Salwasser
Deputy Director, Fish and Wildlife
USDA Forest Service
P.O. Box 2417
Washington, D.C. 20013

Professor Carl Schofield
Department of Natural Resources
Fernow Hall, Cornell University
Ithaca, New York 14830

Dean David B. Thorud
College of Forest Resources
(AR-10)
University of Washington
Seattle, Washington 98195

Mr. John Varley
Chief of Research
Yellowstone National Park
P.O. Box 168
Yellowstone National Park,
Wyoming 82190

Mr. Walt Weaver
Mount Baker-Snoqualmie National
Forest
1022 1st Avenue
Seattle, Washington 98104

Professor Stephen West
College of Forest Resources
(AR-10)
University of Washington
Seattle, Washington 98195

DATE DUE